Introduction to

Barcelona

It's tempting to say that there's nowhere like Barcelona – there's certainly not another city in Spain to touch it for sheer style, looks or energy. The glossy mags and travel press dwell enthusiastically on its outrageous architecture, designer shopping, hip bars and vibrant cultural scene, but Barcelona is more than just this year's fad. It's a confident, progressive city, one that is tirelessly self-renewing while preserving all that's best about its past. As neighbourhoods are rebuilt with panache, and locals and visitors alike pursue the latest, most fashionable sensation, there's also an enduring embrace of the things that make life worth living – the daily market visit, strolling down the famous Ramblas, a lazy harbourside lunch, frenetic festival nights, a Sunday by the beach or a ticket for FC Barcelona's next big game.

It's no accident that Barcelona is the least Spanish city in Spain. With the return to democracy following the death of Franco, the various regions were allowed to consolidate their cultural identities through varying degrees of political autonomy. **Catalunya** (Catalonia in English), of which Barcelona is the capital, has a historical identity going back as far as

Talking the talk

Catalan (Català) is a Romance language, stemming directly from Latin, and closely resembling Occitan. It's spoken by over ten million people in total, in Barcelona and Catalunya, part of Aragón, much of Valencia, the Balearic islands, Andorra, and parts of the French Pyrenees – and is thus much more widely spoken than Danish, Finnish and Norwegian. Other Spaniards tend to belittle it by saying that to get a Catalan word you just cut a Castilian one in half but, in fact, the grammar is more complicated and it has eight vowel sounds compared to Castilian's five. During Franco's time in power, Catalan was banned from the radio, TV, daily press and schools, which is why many older people cannot read or write Catalan (even if they speak it all the time) – the region's best-selling Catalan-language newspaper sells far fewer copies than the most popular Castilian-language daily paper. Virtually every Catalan is bilingual, but most regard Catalan as their mother tongue and it's estimated that Catalan is the dominant language in over half of Catalunya's households – a figure that's likely to grow given the amazing revival of the language in recent times.

the ninth century, when the first independent County of Barcelona was established, and through the long period of domination by Castile, and even during the Franco dictatorship when a policy of cultural suppression was pursued, it proved impossible to stifle Catalan identity. Barcelona itself has long had the reputation of being at the forefront of Spanish political activism, and of radical design and architecture, but these cultural distinctions are rapidly becoming secondary to the city's position as one of the most dynamic commercial centres in the country.

The economic and physical transformation of Barcelona in recent years is an extraordinary phenomenon. Entire districts have been given root-and-branch makeovers, from the harbour to the suburbs, with some remarkable new buildings sharing the limelight with renovated historic quarters, revamped museums and a sparkling city beachfront. Gaining the **1992 Olympics** was an important initial boost. Along with a construction programme that touched every corner of the city went the indis-

putable knowledge that these had been Barcelona's Games, and not Spain's – an important distinction to the Catalan people. Since then the developments have continued unabated, with 2004's Universal Forum of Cultures only the latest significant event to go hand in hand with the dramatic remodelling of yet another once-neglected part of the city.

If there's a pattern emerging in how Barcelona presents itself to the outside world, it's the emphasis on a remarkable fusion of economic energy and cultural expression. This is seen most perfectly in the glorious **modernista** (Art Nouveau) buildings that stud the city's streets and avenues. Antoni Gaudí is the most famous of those who have left their mark on Barcelona in this way: his Sagrada Família church is rightly revered, but just as fascinating are the (literally) fantastic

> **Much of what you'll want to see in the city centre – Gothic cathedral, Picasso museum, markets, Gaudí buildings, history museums and art galleries – can be reached on foot in under twenty minutes from the central Plaça de Catalunya.**

houses, apartment buildings and parks that he and his contemporaries designed. The city also boasts a stupendous **artistic legacy**, from national (ie Catalan) collections of Romanesque, Gothic and contemporary art to major galleries containing the life's work of the Catalan artists Joan Miró and Antoni Tàpies (not to mention a celebrated showcase of the work of Pablo Picasso). Add a medieval old town – full of pivotal buildings from an earlier age of

v

expansion – a welter of churches and markets, and an encircling belt of parks and green spaces, and Barcelona demands as much time as you can spare.

For all its go-ahead feel, though, Barcelona does have its problems, not least a high petty crime rate. However, there's no need to be unduly paranoid and it would be a shame to stick solely to the main tourist sights, since you'll miss so much. Tapas bars hidden down alleys little changed for a century or two, designer boutiques in gentrified old town quarters, street opera singers belting out an aria, bargain lunches in workers' taverns, neighbourhood funicular rides, unmarked gourmet restaurants, craft outlets and workshops, *fin-de-siècle* cafés, restored medieval palaces, suburban walks and specialist galleries – all are just as much Barcelona as the Ramblas or Gaudí's Sagrada Família.

What to see

Barcelona is a surprisingly easy place to find your way around, despite a population of around three million people. Most things of historic interest are in the old town, with the modern city beyond a late nineteenth century addition, part of a vast project conceived to link the small core of the old town with the villages around it. The greater city remains, in effect, a series of self-contained neighbourhoods stretching out from the harbour, flanked by a brace of parks and girdled by the wooded

Collserola mountains. Much of what you'll want to see in the city centre – Gothic cathedral, Picasso museum, markets, Gaudí buildings, history museums and art galleries – can be reached on foot in under twenty minutes from the central Plaça de Catalunya, while a fast metro system takes you directly to the more peripheral attractions and suburbs.

The **Ramblas** – a kilometre-long tree-lined avenue mostly given over to pedestrians, pavement cafés and performance artists – splits the **old town** (Chapter 1) in two. On the eastern side of the avenue is the **Barri Gòtic** (Gothic Quarter), the medieval nucleus of the city – around 500 square metres of twisting streets and historic buildings, including La Seu (the cathedral) and the palaces and museums around Plaça del Rei. Further east lies the equally venerable *barri* of **Sant Pere** and the fashionable boutique-and-bar neighbourhood of **La Ribera**, home to the Picasso museum; while over on the western side of the Ramblas is the edgier, artier neighbourhood of **El Raval**, containing both the flagship museum of contemporary art and the pick of the latest designer shops, bars and restaurants.

At the bottom of the Ramblas is **the waterfront** (Chapter 2), whose spruced-up harbour area is known as **Port Vell** (Old Port). Walking east from here takes you past the marina, through the old fishing and restaurant quarter of **Barceloneta**, past the **Parc de la Ciutadella** and out along the promenade to the cafés and restaurants of the **Port Olímpic**. There are city

Finding an address

Addresses are written as: c/Picasso 2, 4° – which means Picasso street (carrer) number two, fourth floor. You may also see *esquerra*, meaning 'left-hand' (apartment or office); *dreta* is right; *centro* centre. C/Picasso s/n means the building has no number (*sense numero*). In the gridded streets of the Eixample, **building numbers** run from south to north (ie lower numbers at the Plaça de Catalunya end) and from west to east (lower numbers at Plaça d'Espanya).

The main address **abbreviations** used in Barcelona (and this book) are: Avgda. (for *Avinguda*, avenue); c/ (for *carrer*, street); Pg. (for *Passeig*, more a boulevard than a street); Bxda. (for *Baixada*, alley); Ptge. (for *Passatge*, passage); and Pl. (for *Plaça*, square).

Party time

Decorated floats are inching down the crowded streets, teams of red-shirted men are clambering on each other's shoulders, sweets are being hurled to children, fireworks are bursting into the sky and the drummers are going crazy – yes, it's festival time in Barcelona, and you can forget about a decent night's sleep. Whichever month you visit, there will be something going on, though it's worth planning ahead to coincide with the major annual events, like Sant Joan festivities or the Sónar electronic music bash (both June), Gràcia's Festa Major (Aug) and the citywide Festa de la Mercè (Sept). New Year's Eve, the pre-Lent Carnaval, Easter and Christmas have their own distinctive traditions, too, from sombre processions to serial grape-eating; other special events and festivals bring live bands and performers onto the streets at the drop of a hat; while the summer-long Grec festival is an annual celebration of all that's best in the theatre, music and dance world. So you may as well pack your gladrags and prepare to party – and remember, no one toots a horn quite like a festive Catalan.

beaches right along the waterfront, from Barceloneta to **Poble Nou** – site of the 2004 Universal Forum expo – and it's here that Barcelona's inhabitants come to relax at weekends. Visitors, meanwhile, tend to gravitate at some point towards the fortress-topped hill of **Montjuïc** (Chapter 3) to the southwest, where the city's best museums and gardens, and the main Olympic stadium, are sited.

At the top of the Ramblas, **Plaça de Catalunya** marks the start of the gridded nineteenth-century extension of the city, the **Eixample** (Chapter 4), a symbol of the thrusting expansionism of Barcelona's early industrial age. No visit to Barcelona is complete without at least a day spent in the Eixample, as it's here that some of Europe's most extraordinary architecture – including Gaudí's **Sagrada Família** – is located. Beyond the Eixample lie the **northern suburbs** (Chapter 5), like **Gràcia**, with its small squares and lively bars, or the parks, museums and sights of **Horta**, **Sarrià**

and **Pedralbes**. Gaudí left his mark in these areas, too, particularly in the hallucinatory **Parc Güell**, but also in a series of embellished buildings, private houses and unfinished chapels, which the enthusiast will find simple to track down. It's worth making for the hills, too, where you can join the crowds at Barcelona's famous **Tibidabo** amusement park – or escape them with a walk through the woods in the peaceful **Parc de Collserola**.

The good public transport links also make it easy to head further **out of the city** (Chapter 6). The mountain top monastery of **Montserrat** is the most obvious day-trip to make, not least for the extraordinary ride up to the monastic eyrie by cable car or mountain railway. **Sitges** is the local beach town *par excellence*, while with more time you can follow various trails around the local **wine country**, head south to the Roman town of **Tarragona**, or north to medieval **Girona** or the Dalí museum in **Figueres**.

When to go

The best times to go to Barcelona are late **spring** and early **autumn**, when the weather is still comfortably warm (around 21–25°C) and walking the streets isn't a chore. In **summer**, the city can be unbearably hot and humid, with temperatures averaging 28°C (but often a lot more). August, especially, is a month to be avoided, since the climate is at its most unwelcoming and many shops, bars and restaurants close as local inhabitants head out of the city in droves. It's worth considering a **winter** break in the city, as long as you don't mind the prospect of occasional rain. It's generally still warm enough to sit out at a café, even in December, when the temperature hovers around 13°C.

Out of the city, the weather varies enormously from region to region. On the coast either side of Barcelona it's best – naturally enough – in summer, though from June to September tourist resorts like **Sitges** are packed. **Tarragona**, too, can be extremely hot and busy in summer, though it's worth knowing that **Girona** is considered to have a much more equable summer climate, and escaping from the coast for a few cool days is easy.

Temperature chart

Average maximum temperatures

	JAN	FEB	MAR	APR	MAY	JUNE	JULY	AUG	SEPT	OCT	NOV	DEC
DEGREES °C	13	14	16	18	21	25	28	28	25	21	16	13

things not to miss

It's not possible to see everything that Barcelona has to offer on a short trip – and we don't suggest you try. What follows is therefore a subjective selection of the city's highlights, from modernista masterpieces and laidback café life, to tranquil parks and great day-trip destinations around Catalunya – all arranged in five colour-coded categories to help you find the very best things to see, do and experience. All entries have a page reference to take you straight into the guide, where you can find out more.

01 Bars of the Old Town Page **199** • Some of the city's most atmospheric bars are hidden in the Barri Gòtic.

02 Girona Page **141** • This medieval walled city, an hour from Barcelona, has a beautiful riverside setting and one of Catalunya's finest Gothic cathedrals.

03 **Las Ramblas** Page **44** • A stroll down Barcelona's famous thoroughfare is a must for both tourists and locals alike.

04 **Montserrat** Page **128** • For centuries this mountain and monastery have been a place of pilgrimage – and now make a great day-trip from the city.

05 **Montjuïc** Page **81** • The largest green space in the city, with a host of fascinating museums and the impressive buildings from the 1992 Olympics.

06 **Parc de la Ciutadella** Page **68** • Barcelona's favourite park and a Sunday afternoon rendezvous for families, friends and ducks.

07 *Modernista* architecture

Modernisme was Catalunya's version of Art Nouveau and an architectural response to the nineteenth-century economic revival in the region. The big three names of the movement, Gaudí, Domènech i Montaner and Puig i Cadafalch, were all active from the 1870s onwards, creating the weird and wonderful buildings that are still a draw for the city's visitors today. Most of the important and many of the minor *modernista* works in Barcelona are covered in Chapter 4, while below is a checklist of the buildings and works by the architects mentioned above.

Gaudí Casa Batlló p.97; Torre Bellesguard p.119; **Casa Calvet** p.103; **Casa Milà/ La Pedrera** p.99; Casa Vicens p.111; Collegi Santa Teresa p.119; Colònia Güell p.133; Finca Güell p.117; **La Sagrada Família** p.103; Palau Güell p.62; Parc de la Ciutadella fountain and gates p.68; Parc Güell p.112.

Domènech i Montaner Casa Fuster p.112; **Casa Lleó Morera** p.97; Casa Montaner i Simon p.98; Casa Thomas p.102; Hospital de la Santa Creu i de Sant Pau p.105; Hotel España p.63; Palau de la Música Catalana p.64.

Puig i Cadafalch Casa Amatller p.97; **Casa Macaya** p.102; Casa Martí/Els Quatre Gats p.58; **Casa de les Punxes** p.102; Palau Quadras p.102.

△ Casa Calvet

△ Casa Batlló

△ Casa de les Punxes

△ Casa Lleó Morera

△ Casa Milà/La Pedrera

△ La Sagrada Família

△ Casa Macaya

08 **Camp Nou** Page **115** • Home of FC Barcelona, one of Europe's premier sides, with a cabinet full of trophies to prove it.

09 **La Seu** Page **53** • Built from the thirteenth to fifteenth centuries on the site of a Roman temple, La Seu is one of the great Gothic cathedrals in Spain.

10 **Fundació Joan Miró** Page **90** • The adventurous Fundació Joan Miró celebrates the work of one of the greatest Catalan artists.

11 **La Boqueria** Page **47** • This cavernous iron and glass market in the city centre, filled with fresh produce and colourful characters, is the perfect place to get picnic provisions.

12 **Shopping** Page **230** • Barcelona has the best shopping in Spain, with everything from designer outlets to traditional family speciality shops.

13 **Sónar** Page **208** • This cutting-edge electronic music festival in June is the highlight of Barcelona's contemporary music scene.

14 **Barri Gòtic** Page **48** • The Barri Gòtic's evocative narrow streets were once the centre of Barcelona's medieval prosperity.

15 **MACBA** Page **59** • Barcelona's luminous contemporary arts museum was designed to "create a dialogue" with its surrounding working-class neighbourhood.

16 Barceloneta Page **77** • Busy neighbourhood which retains its village atmosphere amidst the best seafood restaurants in town.

17 Tibidabo Page **119** • Scale the heights of Mount Tibidabo for fantastic views and a wonderful amusement park.

19 Sitges Page **125** • Very popular "Barcelona-on-sea", Sitges is an easy day-trip from the city and frequented by families and gay visitors in equal numbers.

18 Festivals Page **221** • The *castellers*, or human tower-builders, draws crowds at several of Barcelona's traditional festivals.

20 Street-café life Page **171** • Sitting outside, nursing a drink and watching the world go by is one of the pleasures of Barcelona.

Contents

Using this Rough Guide

We've tried to make this Rough Guide a good read and easy to use. The book is divided into eight main sections, and you should be able to find whatever you want in one of them.

Front section

The front **colour section** offers a quick tour of **Barcelona**. The **introduction** aims to give you a feel for the place and tells you the best times to go. Next, our author rounds up his favourite aspects of Barcelona in the **things not to miss** section – whether it's great food, amazing sights or a unique neighbourhood. After this comes a full **contents** list.

Basics

The Basics section covers all the **pre-departure** nitty-gritty to help you plan your trip and the practicalities you'll want to know once there. This is where to find out how to get there, about money and costs, Internet access, transport, car rental and local media – in fact just about every piece of **general practical information** you might need.

The city

This is the heart of the Rough Guide, divided into user-friendly chapters, each of which covers a city district or day-trip destination. Every chapter starts with an **introduction** that helps you to decide where to go, followed by an extensive tour of the sights.

Listings

Listings contain all the consumer information needed to make the most of your stay, with chapters on **accommodation**, places to **eat** and drink, **nightlife** and **culture spots**, **shopping** and **sports**.

Contexts

Read Contexts to get a deeper understanding of what makes Barcelona tick. We include a brief **history**, and a section on **Catalan cookery**, as well as a further-reading section reviewing dozens of **books** relating to the city.

Language

The **language** section offers useful guidance for speaking Catalan and Castilian and pulls together all the vocabulary you might need on your trip, including a comprehensive **menu reader**. Here you'll also find a **glossary** of words and terms peculiar to Barcelona.

Index + small print

Apart from a **full index**, which includes maps as well as places, this section covers publishing information, credits and acknowledgements, and also has our contact details in case you want to send us updates, corrections or suggestions for improving the book.

Colour maps

The back colour section contains ten detailed **maps and plans** to help you explore the city up close and locate every place recommended in the guide.

Chapter list

Contents

Contexts

247–273

Language

275–287

Adverts

288–308

Index and small print

310–320

Colour maps

Basics

Basics

Getting there

It's never been easier to reach Barcelona by air from the UK, with a variety of budget, "no-frills" airlines competing with the national carriers Iberia and British Airways to get you directly to the city, quickly and cheaply. There's also a fair amount of choice from North America, though you may have to fly via Madrid or another European city to get the best fare. There's a second gateway to the city at Girona (an hour north of Barcelona by train or bus), which is used mainly by British charter flights due to its proximity to resorts on the Costa Brava. The other charter airport in the region is at Reus, west of Tarragona, ninety minutes from Barcelona by bus or train.

How much you pay to get there depends on the **season**, with the highest fares being from May to September (dropping during the "**shoulder**" seasons, March–April and October–November) with the cheapest prices usually during the **low** season, December to February. At Christmas, New Year and Easter prices are hiked up and seats are at a premium. Note also that flying on **weekends** usually adds to the round-trip fare; price ranges quoted here assume mid-week travel. In addition, to get the very cheapest fares advertised by the budget airlines you'll need to book weeks, if not months, in advance.

You can often cut costs by going through a **specialist flight agent**, who in addition to dealing with discounted flights may also offer student and youth fares and a range of other travel-related services such as travel insurance, rail passes, car rental and tours. Some agents specialize in **charter flights**, which may be cheaper than anything available on a scheduled flight, but departure dates are fixed and withdrawal penalties are high.

Other options are to visit the city on a **package tour** or **city break**, which are easily arranged in Britain, Ireland or North America. Or you can travel from Europe by **train or bus**, but this inevitably takes much longer than flying and often works out no cheaper. However, if Barcelona and Spain are part of a longer European trip it can be an interesting proposition, in which case you might want to check out details of the **Eurail** or **InterRail** passes, which must be purchased in advance of your trip and can get you by train from anywhere in Europe to Barcelona.

Booking flights online

Many airlines and discount travel websites offer you the opportunity to book your tickets online, which may cut out the costs of agents and middlemen. Good deals can often be found through discount or auction sites, as well as through the airlines' own websites.

Online booking agents and general travel sites

@**travel.yahoo.com** Incorporates a lot of Rough Guide material in its coverage of destination countries and cities across the world, with information about places to eat, sleep, etc.

@**www.cheapflights.co.uk** Bookings from the UK and Ireland only (for US, @ www.cheapflights.com; for Canada, @ www.cheapflights.ca; for Australia, @ www.cheapflights.com.au). Flight deals, travel agents, plus links to other travel sites.

@**www.cheaptickets.com** Discount flight specialists (US only).

@**www.ebookers.com** Discount flight specialists (for UK; for Republic of Ireland, @ www.ebookers.ie).

@**www.etn.nl/discount.htm** A hub of consolidator and discount agent Web links, maintained by the nonprofit European Travel Network.

@**www.expedia.com** Discount airfares, all-airline search engine and daily deals (US only; for the UK, @ www.expedia.co.uk; for Canada, @ www.expedia.ca).

@**www.flynow.com** Online air travel info and reservations site.

Ⓦwww.gaytravel.com Gay online travel agent, offering accommodation, cruises, tours and more.

Ⓦwww.hotwire.com Bookings from the US only. Last-minute savings of up to forty percent on regular published fares. Travellers must be at least 18 and there are no refunds, transfers or changes allowed.

Ⓦwww.lastminute.com Offers good last-minute holiday package and flight-only deals (UK only; for Australia, Ⓦwww.lastminute.com.au).

Ⓦwww.priceline.com Name-your-own-price website that has deals at around forty percent off standard fares. You cannot specify flight times (although you do specify dates) and the tickets are non-refundable, non-transferable and non-changeable (US only; for the UK, Ⓦwww.priceline.co.uk).

Ⓦwww.skyauction.com Bookings from the US only. Auctions tickets and travel packages using a "second bid" scheme.

Ⓦwww.smilinjack.com/airlines.htm An up-to-date compilation of airline website addresses.

Ⓦwww.travelocity.com Destination guides, hot Web fares and best deals for car rental, accommodation and lodging.

Ⓦwww.travelshop.com.au Australian website offering discounted flights, packages, insurance and online bookings.

Flights and tours from the UK and Ireland

Flying to Barcelona from the UK takes about two hours, and around thirty minutes more than this from Ireland. Note that some budget airlines (including Ryanair) fly to Girona, despite their advertising of flights to "Barcelona", so it's always worth double-checking your precise destination before buying. Full-time **students** and anyone **under 26** can usually qualify for special discounts on standard BA and Iberia tickets – consult one of the specialist agents listed opposite.

Scheduled flights

The cheapest deals direct to Barcelona/Girona are with the **budget "no-frills" airlines**, like bmibaby, easyJet, Jet2.com, Monarch and Ryanair, from a variety of British regional airports. There are daily departures on most routes, though timetables are sometimes cut back in winter. Prices vary – rising the closer you get to your chosen date of departure – but tickets can start as low as £20 one way, £40 return, plus taxes, though around the £100–120 return mark is more realistic. Some seasonal sales even offer free, or virtually free, flights (though, again, plus taxes). The cheapest tickets sell out fast so you should book as far in advance as possible. These tickets can be bought over the phone or online (often working out slightly cheaper) and cannot usually be changed or cancelled.

The alternative is to fly with Spain's national airline, **Iberia**, or with **British Airways**, which between them have a wide range of direct scheduled services to Barcelona from London, Manchester and Birmingham. This will rarely be the cheapest option – high-season fares start around £200–250 return – but BA and Iberia special offers sometimes prove competitive (the websites have up-to-date details). The least expensive tickets with Iberia or BA are usually valid for one or two months, require you to stay at least one Saturday night, and don't allow for change or cancellation. For a **more flexible ticket** (valid for one year, fully refundable, return date left open), you're looking at up to £500 return.

There are also services to Barcelona from London with other major airlines (Air France, KLM, etc), but in all instances you'll be routed through their respective European hubs, adding considerably to your travel time.

The cheapest direct scheduled services **from Ireland** are with Jetmagic from Cork to Barcelona or Ryanair from Dublin to Girona, from as little as €100 return if you book far enough in advance or coincide with a special offer. Jet2.com has services from Belfast to Leeds Bradford, where you can pick up their low-cost service to Barcelona. Otherwise, Aer Lingus has a direct scheduled service from Dublin to Barcelona (from €170 return), as does Iberia (from around €300 return in summer, less in the low season). With other airlines you'll have to route through London or other European hubs to reach Barcelona.

Charter flights

Charter flights – either to Girona or Reus – are usually block-booked by package-holiday firms, but even in the middle of August spare seats are sold off at discounts.

Departures are from a wide range of British regional airports and Dublin, and – unlike the budget airlines – if you're prepared to book at the last minute you'll often get pretty good deals, though obviously you can't guarantee the departure date you want. The cheapest fares can cost as little as £79/€120 return, though they're more likely to be £150–180/€220–270 in the height of summer. For current prices and availability, contact any high-street travel agent or one of the charter operators listed below.

The major disadvantage of a charter flight is the **fixed return date** – a maximum of four weeks from the outward journey. This isn't a problem for most short trips to Barcelona, but for more flexibility you'll have to travel on a scheduled flight.

City breaks and specialist holidays

Three-night **city breaks** to Barcelona start at around £350 flying from London or Manchester, or from about €450 from Dublin. The price includes return flights, transfers and bed-and-breakfast in a centrally located three-star hotel. You can occasionally find cheaper deals than this, while adding extra nights or upgrading your hotel is possible, usually at a fairly reasonable cost. Three nights in the five-star *Hotel Claris*, for example, cost from around £550. Ask your travel agent for the best deals, or check the tour operators listed below. If you book online you'll often qualify for a discount. A few operators offer rather more **specialist holidays** in and around Barcelona, concentrating on things like art and architecture, cooking classes, wine tours or rural Catalunya. We've picked out some of the better options in the list on p.12, where there are further details of prices.

Airlines

Aer Lingus UK ☎0845/084 4444, Republic of Ireland ☎0818/365 000, ⊛www.aerlingus.ie. Scheduled flights to Barcelona from Dublin (with connections from Cork).
Air 2000 ☎0870/240 1402, ⊛www.air2000.com. Charter flights to Girona from Gatwick, Manchester, Birmingham and Glasgow.
Avro ☎0870/458 2841, ⊛www.avro.com. Charter flights to Girona from Gatwick and Manchester.
bmibaby UK ☎0870/264 2229, Republic of

Ireland ☎01/236 6130, ⊛www.bmibaby.com. Scheduled flights to Barcelona from East Midlands and Manchester.
British Airways UK ☎0845/773 3377, Republic of Ireland ☎1800/626 747, ⊛www.ba.com. Scheduled flights to Barcelona from Heathrow, Gatwick, Manchester and Birmingham.
easyJet UK ☎0870/600 0000, ⊛www.easyjet.com. Scheduled flights to Barcelona from Bristol, East Midlands, Liverpool, Gatwick, Luton, Stansted and Newcastle.
Iberia Airlines UK ☎0845/601 2854, Republic of Ireland ☎01/407 3017, ⊛www.iberia.co.uk. Scheduled flights to Barcelona from Heathrow, Gatwick, Manchester, Birmingham and Dublin.
Jet2.com UK ☎0870/737 8282, ⊛www.jet2.com. Scheduled flights to Barcelona from Leeds Bradford; connections available from Belfast.
Jetmagic Republic of Ireland ☎0818/200 135, ⊛www.jetmagic.com. Scheduled flights from Cork to Barcelona.
JMC ☎0870/010 0434, ⊛www.jmc.com. Charter flights to Girona from Gatwick, Manchester and Newcastle.
Monarch ☎0870/040 5040, ⊛www.fly-crown.com. Scheduled flights to Barcelona from Manchester; charter flights to Reus from Gatwick, Luton, Manchester and Dublin.
Ryanair UK ☎0871/246 0000, Republic of Ireland ☎0818/303 030, ⊛www.ryanair.com. Scheduled flights to Girona from Stansted, Bournemouth, Birmingham, Liverpool, Glasgow and Dublin; and to Reus from Stansted.
Virgin Express UK ☎020/7744 0004, ⊛www.virgin-express.com. Scheduled, indirect flights to Barcelona from London City via Brussels.

Discount flight agents

UK

Co-op Travel Care ☎0870/112 0099, ⊛www.travelcareonline.com. Flights and holidays around the world.
Flightbookers ☎0870/010 7000, ⊛www.ebookers.com. Low fares on an extensive selection of scheduled flights.
Flynow ☎0870/444 0045, ⊛www.flynow.com. Large range of discounted tickets.
North South Travel ☎01245/608 291, ⊛www.northsouthtravel.co.uk. Competitive travel agency, offering discounted fares worldwide – profits are used to support projects in the developing world, especially the promotion of sustainable tourism.
STA Travel ☎0870/1600 599, ⊛www.statravel.co.uk. Worldwide specialists in

low-cost flights and tours for students and under-26s, though other customers welcome.
Trailfinders ☏020/7628 7628,
🖳www.trailfinders.co.uk. One of the best-informed and most efficient agents for independent travellers.
Travel Cuts ☏0207/255 2082 or 255 1944,
🖳www.travelcuts.co.uk. Specializing in budget, student and youth travel.

Ireland

CIE Tours International Republic of Ireland ☏01/703 1888, 🖳www.cietours.ie. General flight and tour agent.
Joe Walsh Tours Republic of Ireland ☏01/676 0991, 🖳www.joewalshtours.ie. General budget fares agent.
McCarthy's Travel Republic of Ireland ☏021/427 0127, 🖳www.mccarthystravel.ie. General flight agent.
Premier Travel Northern Ireland ☏028/7126 3333, 🖳www.premiertravel.uk.com. Discount flight specialists.
Student & Group Travel Republic of Ireland ☏01/677 7834. Student and group specialists, mostly to Europe.
Trailfinders Republic of Ireland ☏01/677 7888, 🖳www.trailfinders.ie. One of the best-informed and most efficient agents for independent travellers.
usit NOW Republic of Ireland ☏01/602 1600, Northern Ireland ☏028/9032 7111,
🖳www.usitnow.ie. Student and youth specialists for flights and trains.

City-break and tour operators

UK and Spain

Arblaster & Clarke ☏01730/893344,
🖳www.arblasterandclarke.com. Annual four-night wine tours of Barcelona, and the Penedès and Priorato regions, with expert in tow, plus tours, tastings and meals (£899).
Cox & Kings ☏0208/873 5027,
🖳www.coxandkings.co.uk. Select, annual art tours of Barcelona (3 nights, £675).
Culinary Adventures ☏932 654 071 or 915 316 489, 🖳www.atasteofspain.com. Interesting food-based tours from a company with offices in Barcelona and Madrid – from one-day cooking-and-market excursions from Barcelona (€220) to a seven-day culinary Catalan tour (land-only, €2455).
Exodus ☏0208/675 5550, 🖳www.exodus.co.uk. Small, escorted tours of Catalunya, starting and finishing in Barcelona, using public transport with optional walks (7 nights, from £465).
Madrid and Beyond Spain ☏917 580 063,

🖳www.madridand.beyond.com. Madrid-based specialist operator with a wide variety of Barcelona hotels on its database, plus city breaks and tailor-made itineraries.
Magic of Spain ☏0870/888 0228, 🖳www.magictravelgroup.co.uk. High-quality tour operator offering Barcelona holidays, Sitges and Catalunya side-trips, plus flight and car-rental travel services.
Martin Randall Travel ☏0208/742 3355,
🖳www.martinrandall.com. Experts lead small groups on annual, all-inclusive tours to Spain, concentrating on things like Gaudí and the Guggenheim (6 nights, £1200) or Barcelona at Christmas (5 nights, £1100).
Mundi Color ☏0207/828 6021,
🖳www.mundicolor.co.uk. Spanish specialists for flights, accommodation, tours and city breaks.
My Travel UK ☏0870/238 7777,
🖳www.uk.mytravel.com. Large tour company offering city breaks, flights, car rental and more.
Saga Holidays ☏0130/377 1111,
🖳www.saga.co.uk. The country's most established specialist in tours and holidays aimed at older people – see Barcelona as part of a wider "Iberian capitals" tour, or visit rural Catalunya.
Simply Spain ☏0208/541 2208, 🖳www.simply-travel.com. Upmarket tour company for Barcelona city breaks, either arranged as stand-alone holidays or in conjunction with a wider Spain tour.
Spanish Travel Services ☏0207/387 5337,
🖳www.apatraveluk.com. Spanish flight, city-break, package-tour and car-rental specialists.
Sports Travel International ☏01279/661700,
🖳www.stisport.com. Organizes holidays for sports teams, including arranging friendlies with local clubs and tickets for league matches.
Thomas Cook Holidays ☏0870/010 0437,
🖳www.thomascook.com. Wide range of Barcelona hotels available in their city-break programme.
Travellers Way ☏01527/559000,
🖳www.travellersway.co.uk. Tailor-made holidays and city breaks, perhaps combining Barcelona with the Costa Brava.

Ireland

Citiescapes Republic of Ireland ☏01/677 5533,
🖳www.citiescapes.ie. Barcelona city breaks.
Flying Visits Republic of Ireland ☏062/51019,
🖳www.flyingvisits.ie. City breaks from Dublin airport.
Go Holidays Republic of Ireland ☏01/874 4126,
🖳www.goholidays.ie. City breaks, plus two-centre holidays (Barcelona/Madrid), package tours and fly-drives.
Lee Travel Republic of Ireland ☏021/277 111,
🖳www.leetravel.ie. Flights and holidays.

Neenan Travel Republic of Ireland ☎ 01/607 9900, ⊛ www.neenantrav.ie. Hotels, holidays, city breaks and car rental.
Rosetta Travel Northern Ireland ☎ 028/9064 4996, ⊛ www.rosettatravel.com. General flight and holiday agent.

Flights and tours from the USA and Canada

Most **direct scheduled services** to Spain from North America are to Madrid, from where you'll fly on (or make a local connection) to Barcelona. Only Delta has a direct Barcelona service, daily in high season from New York and Atlanta. European-based airlines (Air France, British Airways, Lufthansa, KLM, TAP, etc) can also get you to Barcelona, though you'll be routed through their respective European hubs – Iberia, the Spanish national airline, and Air Europa tend to have the best connections through Madrid. Flying time from New York is around seven hours to Madrid, though with the onward connection it can take as much as eleven hours to reach Barcelona.

Return **fares** run as much as US$1000/CAN$1400 in summer, though in low season you should be able to fly for under US$600-800/CAN$1000. Special promotional deals can undercut these prices, while it might pay you to buy a cheap flight to London and travel on to Barcelona from there with one of the budget airlines (see "Flights and tours from the UK and Ireland", p.10). The widest range of deals is on the New York–London route, where competition is intense, so look out for bargains, especially out of the summer season.

Plenty of **tour companies** include a couple of days in Barcelona as part of a whirlwind escorted itinerary around Spain, costing from US$1500 to $2000 for a standard two-week tour, or up to $4000 for something more luxurious. Some specialize in food and wine tours, or concentrate on art and architecture, and you may be able to find a tour that spends more time than usual in Barcelona/Catalunya, spending up to $3000 for a week's specialist escorted tour. However, for an in-depth Barcelona experience you'll really want the flexibility of a **city break**. A typical three-night stay in a central Barcelona three-star hotel costs from around

US$600–750, depending on the season – these prices include breakfast, transfers and usually a half-day tour or equivalent, with flights to Barcelona usually charged as extra. Inclusive three-night city breaks with flights included tend to start at around $1000, rising to around $2000 for a week's stay in the city.

Airlines

Air Europa ☎ 1-800/238-7672, ⊛ www.air-europa.com. Direct flights from New York to Madrid, with daily connections to Barcelona.
Air France US ☎ 1-800/237-2747, ⊛ www.airfrance.com, Canada ☎ 1-800/667-2747, ⊛ www.airfrance.ca. Direct flights from major US and Canadian cities to Madrid and Barcelona, via Paris.
American Airlines ☎ 1-800/433-7300, ⊛ www.aa.com. Direct flights from Miami and Chicago to Madrid.
British Airways ☎ 1-800/247-9297, ⊛ www.british-airways.com. Flights to Barcelona via London from Montréal, Toronto and Vancouver plus 21 gateway cities in the US.
Continental Airlines ☎ 1-800/231-0856, ⊛ www.continental.com. Direct flights from New York to Madrid with onward connections to Barcelona.
Delta Air Lines ☎ 1-800/241-4141, ⊛ www.delta.com. Direct flights from New York and Atlanta to Barcelona, with connections from most other major North American cities.
Iberia ☎ 1-800/772-4642, ⊛ www.iberia.com. Direct flights from New York, Chicago and Miami to Madrid with connecting flights to Barcelona.
Lufthansa US ☎ 1-800/645-3880, Canada ☎ 1-800/563-5954, ⊛ www.lufthansa-usa.com. Direct flights from several US cities to Madrid and Barcelona via Frankfurt.
Northwest/KLM Airlines ☎ 1-800/447-4747, ⊛ www.nwa.com, ⊛ www.klm.com. From major US and Canadian cities to Madrid and Barcelona via Amsterdam.
TAP Air Portugal ☎ 1-800/221-7370, ⊛ www.tap-airportugal.pt. Flights from New York and Boston to Barcelona via Lisbon.
United Airlines ☎ 1-800/538-2929, ⊛ www.ual.com. Direct flights from Washington, DC, to Madrid.

Discount flight agents

Airtech ☎ 212/219-7000, ⊛ www.airtech.com. Standby seat broker.
Council Travel ☎ 1-800/2COUNCIL, ⊛ www.counciltravel.com. Nationwide organization

that mostly specializes in student/budget travel. Flights from the US only.

Educational Travel Center ☎1-800/747-5551 or 608/256-5551, ⊛www.edtrav.com. Student/youth discount agent.

New Frontiers ☎1-800/677-0720 or 310/670-7318, ⊛www.newfrontiers.com. Discount-travel firm based in Los Angeles.

STA Travel US ☎1-800/781-4040, Canada 1-888/427-5639, ⊛www.sta-travel.com. Worldwide specialists in independent travel; also student IDs, travel insurance, car rental, rail passes, etc.

Student Flights ☎1-800/255-8000 or 480/951-1177, ⊛www.isecard.com. Student/youth fares, student IDs.

TFI Tours ☎1-800/745-8000 or 212/736-1140, ⊛www.lowestairprice.com. Consolidator.

Travac ☎1-800/TRAV-800, ⊛www.thetravelsite.com. Consolidator and charter broker with offices in New York City and Orlando.

Travel Cuts Canada ☎1-800/667-2887, US ☎1-866/246-9762, ⊛www.travelcuts.com. Canadian student-travel organization.

Worldtek Travel ☎1-800/243-1723, ⊛www.worldtek.com. Discount travel agency for worldwide travel.

Tour operators

American Express ☎1-800/346 3607, ⊛www.travel.americanexpress.com. City breaks and packages.

Delta Vacations ☎1-800/654-6559, ⊛www.deltavacations.com. City breaks with options such as car rental and city tours.

EC Tours ☎1-800/388-0877, ⊛www.ectours.com. Themed Spain tours (Spain by Train, Museum Treasures) that have a Barcelona element.

Far & Wide ☎866/FAR-WIDE, ⊛www.farandwide.com. Group and independent tours, offering Barcelona city breaks, or twin-centre holidays combining Barcelona with Madrid, Costa del Sol or the Balearics.

Food and Wine Trails ☎1-800/367-5348, ⊛www.foodandwinetrails.com. Their "Catalan Cuisine" tour spends two nights in Barcelona and four on the Costa Brava, visiting markets, taking cooking classes, touring and eating.

Maupintour ☎1-800/255-4266, ⊛www.maupintour.com. Luxury Spain tours and Barcelona city breaks.

New Frontiers ☎1-800/677-0720 or 310/670-7318, ⊛www.newfrontiers.com. Five-night Barcelona package available, or customize your own trip.

Olé Spain ☎1-888/869-7156, ⊛www.olespain.com. Eight-day cultural walking

tours in Catalunya, beginning and ending in Barcelona, with time to explore the city.

Petrabax ☎1-888/427-7246, ⊛www.epetrabax.com. City breaks and tours with a Spanish specialist, plus independent travel services – accommodation, car rental, etc.

Rick Steve's ☎425/771-8303, ⊛www.ricksteves.com. Fully guided six-night Barcelona tours, including side-trips, guides and some meals.

Saranjan Tours ☎1-800/858-9594, ⊛www.saranjan.com. Upscale, fully guided, customized tours concentrating on unusual combos, like Barcelona and its nearby wine country, or a two-centre Barcelona/Bilbao holiday.

Sports Travel International ☎1-888/STI-7997, ⊛www.stisport.com/usa.htm. Organizes tours for sports teams including arranging friendly games with local clubs and tickets for league soccer matches.

Flights from Australia and New Zealand

There are **no direct flights to Spain** from Australia or New Zealand. However, a number of airlines do fly to Barcelona with a stopover elsewhere in Europe or Asia (flights via Asia are generally the cheaper option). Another possibility is to fly to Madrid, from where you can pick up a connecting flight or train. It's best to discuss your route and preferences with a specialist agent, especially if your visit to Barcelona is part of a wider Spanish trip – in which case, you might be better off buying a **Round-The-World** (RTW) ticket. Otherwise, the lowest standard **return fare** from eastern Australia to Spain is around A\$1800 in low season and up to A\$2800 in high season; from New Zealand, you're looking at NZ\$2400/\$3000. If you'd rather someone else made all the arrangements, talk to one of the special **tour operators** who can arrange an organized visit to Barcelona, sorting out your accommodation, guided tours and car rental.

Airlines

Air France Australia ☎02/9244 2100, New Zealand ☎09/308 3352, ⊛www.airfrance.com.au.
Air New Zealand Australia ☎13 24 76, ⊛www.airnz.com.au, New Zealand ☎0800/737 000, ⊛www.airnz.co.nz.
Alitalia Australia ☎02/9244 2445, New Zealand ☎09/308 3357, ⊛www.alitalia.com.

14

American Airlines Australia ⓣ1300/130 757, New Zealand ⓣ09/309 9159, ⓦwww.aa.com.
British Airways Australia ⓣ1300/767 177, New Zealand ⓣ0800/274 847 or 09/356 8690, ⓦwww.britishairways.com.
Cathay Pacific Australia ⓣ13 17 47, ⓦwww.cathaypacific.com/au, New Zealand ⓣ09/379 0861 or 0508/800 454, ⓦwww.cathaypacific.com/nz.
KLM/Northwest Airlines Australia ⓣ1300/303 747, ⓦwww.klm.com/au_en, New Zealand ⓣ09/309 1782, ⓦwww.klm.com/nz_en.
Qantas Australia ⓣ13 13 13, ⓦwww.qantas.com.au, New Zealand ⓣ0800/808 767, ⓦwww.qantas.co.nz.
Singapore Airlines Australia ⓣ13 10 11, New Zealand ⓣ0800/808 909, ⓦwww.singaporeair.com.
TAP Air Portugal Australia ⓣ02/9244 2344, New Zealand ⓣ09/308 3373, ⓦwww.tap-airportugal.pt.
Thai Airways Australia ⓣ1300/651 960, New Zealand ⓣ09/377 0268, ⓦwww.thaiair.com.
United Airlines Australia ⓣ13 17 77, ⓦwww.unitedairlines.com.au, New Zealand ⓣ09/379 3800 or 0800/508 648, ⓦwww.unitedairlines.co.nz.
Virgin Atlantic Airways Australia ⓣ02/9244 2747, New Zealand ⓣ09/308 3377, ⓦwww.virgin-atlantic.com.

Discount flight agents

Flight Centre Australia ⓣ13 31 33 or 02/9235 3522, ⓦwww.flightcentre.com.au, New Zealand ⓣ0800 243 544 or 09/358 4310, ⓦwww.flightcentre.co.nz.
Holiday Shoppe New Zealand ⓣ0800/808 480, ⓦwww.holidayshoppe.co.nz.
New Zealand Destinations Unlimited New Zealand ⓣ09/414 1685 ⓦwww.holiday.co.nz.
Northern Gateway Australia ⓣ1800/174 800, ⓦwww.northerngateway.com.au.
STA Travel Australia ⓣ1300/733 035, ⓦwww.statravel.com.au, New Zealand ⓣ0508/782 872, ⓦwww.statravel.co.nz.
Student Uni Travel Australia ⓣ02/9232 8444, ⓦwww.sut.com.au, New Zealand ⓣ09/379 4224, ⓦwww.sut.co.nz.
Trailfinders Australia ⓣ02/9247 7666, ⓦwww.trailfinders.com.au.

Tour operators

Explore Holidays Australia ⓣ02/9423 8080, ⓦwww.exploreholidays.com.au. Can arrange three-night Barcelona stays, plus city tours, apartment and car rental.
Ibertours Australia ⓣ1800/500 016, ⓦwww.ibertours.com.au. Spanish specialist offering two-three-night Barcelona breaks, plus escorted tours, self-drive holidays and other options.
IB Tours Australia ⓣ02/9560 6722, ⓦwww.ib-tours.com.au. Villas in Spain, as well as car rental and city stays.
Spanish Tourism Promotions Australia ⓣ03/9650 7377 or 1800/817 855, ⓦwww.spanishtourism.com.au. A good first stop for Spain info – tours, city breaks, hotel bookings, car rental and more.
Tempo Holidays Australia ⓣ1300/362 844, ⓦwww.yallatours.com.au. General Mediterranean specialist offering city stays, packages, car rental, tours, and all transport arrangements.
travel.com.au/travel.co.nz Australia ⓣ1300/130 482 or 02/9249 5444, ⓦwww.travel.com.au, New Zealand ⓣ0800/468 332, ⓦwww.travel.co.nz. Comprehensive online travel company providing access to tours, packages, flights and car rental.

By rail from the UK

From London to Barcelona takes around 24 hours by train on the traditional cross-Channel route, though using the Eurostar service through the Channel tunnel to Paris and then the overnight "train-hotel" can shave up to seven hours off this. However, using Eurostar to kick-start your rail trip to Spain is expensive – you will almost certainly be able to fly all the way there for less. Indeed, rail tickets of all kinds to Barcelona can't compete with the cheapest fares from the budget airlines. Whichever route you choose will usually require a change of trains in Paris (from Gare du Nord to Gare d'Austerlitz). An amazingly useful website, ⓦwww.seat61.com, provides hugely detailed route, ticket, timetable and contact information for all European train services.

Routes and fares

The most straightforward option is to take the Eurostar service to Paris and then the overnight **Paris–Barcelona "train-hotel",** which stops in Girona at around 7am and arrives in Barcelona at around 8.30am. This is an all-sleeper service (with restaurant and café), with various classes and levels of comfort available. The cheapest ticket is in a four-berth compartment, costing between £200 and £260 return, depending on availability; you have to spend one Saturday night away and specify a return date. One- and two-berth first (including breakfast) and "gran clase" (breakfast and dinner) compartments are also available, with corresponding price hikes up to around £400 return. Under-26s/senior citizens qualify for small discounts, while InterRail holders (see "Rail passes" below) get a special rate on the sleeper section of the fare.

There are slightly cheaper alternatives, but they take longer and can be more complicated to arrange. Using the **cross-Channel ferries/Seacats** and the local trains to Paris could save you up to £50 on the Eurostar fare, and instead of the "train-hotel" there are regular overnight **couchette sleeper** services with SNCF (French Railways) as far as the French border, where you change onto the Spanish services. This way you have the choice of travelling down the main route via **Cerbère /Port Bou**, running to Barcelona by way of the Costa Brava, or going via Toulouse and **La Tour de Carol/Puigcerdà**, an exciting route which crosses the central Pyrenees and runs to Barcelona via Ripoll and Vic. The cheapest rail–sea–rail route from London to Barcelona costs around £165 return (small discounts for under-26s/senior citizens; tickets valid for two months), though for any comfort you'll need to add a couchette bed (£16 each way) for the overnight legs – no great saving on a good Eurostar deal booked well in advance.

You can also travel through France during the day by the high-speed **TGV service** from Paris, via Montpellier and Perpignan, which makes it to Barcelona in under ten hours.

You'll need to talk to a **rail agency** (see list below) to sort out all the options; you'll pay a £5–10 booking fee on top of the ticket price. Rail Europe can only make through-bookings to Barcelona with the Eurostar option, though they can make other French rail reservations, as can SNCF, which has a useful English-language version of its website. Eurostar often have good advance-purchase deals from London as far as Perpignan. For the rail–sea–rail routes, talk to FFestiniog Travel or Railbookers.

Rail passes

If you plan to travel extensively in Europe by train, a rail pass might prove a good investment. However, if you're just headed for Barcelona, InterRail and Eurail aren't necessarily a good deal, and even if you intend to travel around Catalunya by train, rail travel in that part of Spain is fairly limited (and fairly cheap), so you may not get your money's worth.

An **InterRail** pass (valid one month, available to anyone resident in Europe for at least six months) comes in two forms: either an all-zones pass, for unlimited standard-class travel in thirty European countries including Spain (£379, under-26s £265), or a zonal pass – you'll need a two-zone pass (£275, under-26s £195) to travel through France to Spain, which is also grouped with Portugal and Morocco. The passes don't include travel between Britain and the continent, though pass holders get up to fifty percent off cross-Channel services and qualify for special Eurostar return fares. The pass is available from Rail Europe and the other rail agencies listed below, from branches of STA Travel, from other independent travel agencies and from major UK train stations.

A **Eurailpass** must be purchased before arrival in Europe (and cannot be purchased by European residents). It allows unlimited free first-class travel in Spain and 23 other countries and is available in increments of 15 days, 21 days, 1 month, 2 months and 3 months. If you're under 26, you can save money with a **Eurailpass Youth** (valid for second-class travel), and there are other options too, like a **Eurailpass Flexi** (10 or 15 days' travel within a two-month period, also available in an under-26/second-class version). Prices, obviously, vary significantly, but any good travel agent can supply up-to-date information, or consult ⊛www.eurail.com or ⊛www.raileurope.com (North America), ⊛www.railplus.com.au (Australia) or ⊛www.railplus.co.nz (New Zealand).

Rail agencies

Eurostar ☎0870/160 6600, ⊛www.eurostar.com
FFestiniog Travel ☎01766/512400

Railbookers ☎0870/730 0720,
🌐www.railbookers.com
Rail Choice ☎0208/659 7300,
🌐www.railchoice.co.uk
Rail Europe ☎0870/584 8848,
🌐www.raileurope.co.uk
SNCF 🌐www.sncf.fr

By bus from the UK

Eurolines (☎08705/808080, 🌐www
.eurolines.co.uk) operates a year-round bus
service to Barcelona from London (currently
on Mon, Wed, Fri & Sat), which takes up to
27 hours. It's a long journey but quite bearable – just make sure you take along
enough to eat, drink and read. There are
stops for around twenty minutes every four
to five hours, and the routine is also broken
by the cross-Channel ferry (included in the
cost). Costing from £119 return (as little as
£69 return if you book the 15-day advance
fare), it's the cheapest regular fare you'll find
to Barcelona; under-26s/senior citizens
qualify for a small discount. There's also a
Eurolines Pass, available in 15-, 30- and 60-
day increments, which gives you unlimited
bus travel on Eurolines services throughout
Europe (including Barcelona). There's a
high-season (June–Sept) and low-season
price and, again, discounts for under-
26s/senior citizens.

Tickets are available from many high-street
travel agents. Or contact Eurolines directly,
which also sells tickets and through-
transport to London at all British National
Express bus terminals.

By car

It's about 1600km from London to
Barcelona, which, with stops, is going to take
you almost two full days to drive. Also, with
motorway tolls in France and Spain, fuel
costs and cross-Channel fares, it's certainly
not a cheap option. Motoring organizations
(AA, 🌐www.theaa.com; RAC, 🌐www.rac
.co.uk) provide useful route planners, including advice on how to avoid toll roads. For
more details about documentation and driving conditions in the city, see "City transport:
driving and vehicle rental", p.27.

Many people use the conventional **cross-
Channel ferry links** (principally Dover/
Folkestone–Calais/Bouolgne), though services from the southwestern ports to Brittany
or Normandy might be more convenient.
However, the quickest way of crossing the
Channel is to use the **Eurotunnel** service,
which operates trains 24 hours a day (every
15min at peak times) carrying cars, motorcycles, buses and their passengers, and taking
35 minutes between Folkestone and Calais.
Fares on all services vary enormously
according to the time of year, time of day,
length of stay and size of car, though special
offers often substantially undercut the published brochure prices. It's cheaper to travel
between 10pm and 6am, while the highest
fares are reserved for weekend departures
and returns in July and August. Your local
travel agent will have the latest ticket and
timetable details, or contact the operators
directly.

Alternatively, you can use one of the direct
ferry services from England to Spain, though
you won't get to Barcelona any quicker.
Brittany Ferries operates a car-passenger
ferry from **Plymouth to Santander** (twice
weekly; 24hr). From Santander, it's about
nine hours' drive to Barcelona, via Bilbao
and Zaragoza. Or there's the P&O service
from **Portsmouth to Bilbao** (twice weekly;
35hr), east of Santander in the Basque
country. Both services are very expensive,
especially in summer, when return fares can
cost as much as £700.

Eurotunnel

Eurotunnel ☎08705/353535,
🌐www3.eurotunnel.com.

Ferry operators

Brittany Ferries ☎08703/665333,
🌐www.brittanyferries.co.uk. Poole to Cherbourg;
Portsmouth to Caen and St Malo; Plymouth to
Roscoff and Santander.
Hoverspeed ☎0870/240 8070,
🌐www.hoverspeed.co.uk. Dover to Calais and
Ostend; Newhaven to Dieppe.
P&O Portsmouth ☎0870/242 4999,
🌐www.poportsmouth.com. Portsmouth to
Cherbourg, Le Havre and Bilbao.
P&O Stena Line ☎0870/600 0600 or 01304/864
003, 🌐www.posl.com. Dover to Calais.
Sea France ☎0870/571 1711,
🌐www.seafrance.com. Dover to Calais.

Red tape and visas

Citizens of EU countries, including Britain and Ireland, need only a valid national identity card or passport to enter Spain for up to ninety days. Other Europeans, and citizens of the United States, Canada, Australia and New Zealand, require a passport but no visa and can stay as a tourist for up to ninety days. Other nationalities may need to get a visa from a Spanish embassy or consulate before departure. Visa requirements do change and it's always advisable to check the current situation before leaving home.

EU nationals no longer need to apply for a residence permit to **stay longer**, as a valid passport or identity document now acts as a permit. This entitles EU citizens to reside as employees, self-employed or students; retired people or those of independent means will still have to apply for a residence permit. The British Embassy in Spain website (ⓦ www.ukinspain.com) has useful general information for EU citizens. US citizens can apply for one ninety-day extension, showing proof of funds, but this must be done from outside Spain. Other nationalities will need to get a special visa from a Spanish embassy or consulate before departure (see below for addresses).

For details of the office in Barcelona dealing with permits and trip extensions, see p.244. There's a list of **foreign consulates in Barcelona** on p.242.

Spanish embassies and consulates abroad

Australia ⓦ www.embaspain.com: 15 Arkana St, Yarralumla, ACT 2600 ⓣ 02/6273 3555.
Canada ⓦ www.docuweb.ca/SpainInCanada: 74 Stanley Ave, Ottawa, Ontario K1M 1P4 ⓣ 613/747-2252; 1 Westmount Square, Suite 1456, Montréal, Quebec H3Z 2P9 ⓣ 514/935-5235.
Ireland 17a Merlyn Park, Ballsbridge, Dublin 4 ⓣ 01/269 1640.
New Zealand No representative; contact the embassy in Australia.
UK ⓦ www.conspalon.org: 20 Draycott Place, London SW3 2RZ ⓣ 020/7589 8989; 63 Northcastle St, Edinburgh EH2 3LJ ⓣ 0131/220 1843; Brook House, 70 Spring Gardens, Manchester M22 2BQ ⓣ 0161/236 1233.

USA ⓦ www.spainemb.org: 2375 Pennsylvania Ave NW, Washington, DC 20037 ⓣ 202/728-2330; 545 Boylston St, Boston, MA 02116 ⓣ 617/536-2506; 180 N Michigan Ave, Chicago, IL 60601 ⓣ 312/782-4588; 1-800 Bering Drive, Houston, TX 77057 ⓣ 713/783-6200; 5055 Wilshire Blvd, Los Angeles, CA 90036 ⓣ 213/938-0158; 2655 Lejeune Rd, Miami, FL 33134 ⓣ 305/446-5511; 2102 World Trade Center, 2 Canal St, New Orleans, LA 70131 ⓣ 504/525-4951; 150 E 58th St, New York, NY 10155 ⓣ 212/355-4080; 1405 Sutter St, San Francisco, CA 94109 ⓣ 415/922-2995.

Customs

EU travellers returning home from Spain do not have to make a declaration to Customs at their place of entry. In other words, you can bring almost as many duty-paid Spanish cigarettes and as much wine or beer home as you can carry. The **guidance levels** are 10 litres of spirits, 90 litres of wine and 110 litres of beer, which should suffice for anyone's requirements – any more than this and you'll have to provide proof that it's for personal use only. The guidelines for tobacco are 800 cigarettes, 400 cigarillos, 200 cigars or 1kg of loose tobacco. If you're travelling to or from a non-EU country, you can still buy duty-free goods, but this perk no longer exists within the EU. The **duty-free allowances** are:
Tobacco: 200 cigarettes; or 100 cigarillos; or 50 cigars; or 250g of loose tobacco.
Alcohol: 2 litres of still wine plus 1 litre of drink over 22 percent alcohol, or 2 litres of alcoholic drinks not over 22 percent.
Perfumes: 60ml of perfume plus 250ml of toilet water.

Insurance

EU countries have reciprocal health agreements with Spain; British and Irish citizens need form E111, available from main post offices. However, even EU citizens – and certainly all other nationalities – would do well to take out an insurance policy before travelling to cover against theft, loss and illness or injury.

Before paying for a new policy, however, it's worth checking whether you are already covered: some all-risks home insurance policies may cover your possessions when overseas, and many private medical schemes include cover when abroad. Even so, you still might want to contact a specialist travel insurance company, or consider the travel insurance deal we offer (see below). A typical travel insurance policy usually provides cover for the loss of baggage, tickets and – up to a certain limit – cash or cheques, as well as cancellation or curtailment of your journey. Many policies can be chopped and changed to exclude coverage you don't need – for example, sickness and accident benefits can often be excluded or included at will. If you do take medical coverage, ascertain whether benefits will be paid as treatment proceeds or only after return home, and whether there is a 24-hour medical emergency number. When securing baggage cover, make sure that the per-article limit – typically under £500 – will cover your most valuable possession. If you need to make a claim, you should keep receipts for medicines and medical treatment, and in the event you have anything stolen you must obtain an official statement from the police.

Rough Guides travel insurance

Rough Guides offers its own travel insurance, customized for our readers by a leading UK broker and backed by a Lloyd's underwriter. It's available for anyone, of any nationality and any age, travelling anywhere in the world.

There are two main Rough Guide insurance plans: **Essential**, for basic, no-frills cover; and **Premier** – with more generous and extensive benefits. Alternatively, you can take out **annual multi-trip insurance**, which covers you for any number of trips throughout the year (with a maximum of 60 days for any one trip). Unlike many policies, the Rough Guides schemes are calculated by the day, so if you're travelling for 27 days rather than a month, that's all you pay for.

For a policy quote, call the Rough Guide Insurance Line on UK freephone ⓣ0800/015 0906; US toll-free ⓣ1-866/220 5588, or, if you're calling from elsewhere, ⓣ+44 1243/621 046. Alternatively, get an online quote or buy online at ⓦwww.roughguidesinsurance.com.

Arrival

There are two main, adjacent terminals (A and B) at Barcelona's airport, with taxis and airport buses found immediately outside each terminal and the airport train station a short distance away along the overhead walkway. The city's train stations – Barcelona Sants and Estació de França – and the Estació del Nord bus station are all more central, with convenient metro stations for onward travel. In most cases, you can be off the plane, train or bus and in your hotel room within the hour. Driving into Barcelona is also reasonably straightforward, with traffic only slow in the morning and evening rush hours. Parking, however, is a different matter altogether – rarely easy and not cheap. If your trip is just to the city and its surroundings, our advice is not to bother with a car at all.

Note that all transport contact telephone numbers and websites are listed in Chapter 17, "Directory".

By air

Barcelona's **airport** is 12km southwest of the city at El Prat de Llobregat. EasyJet uses Terminal A. British Airways and Iberia use Terminal B. There's a tourist office in each terminal, handling hotel bookings; there are also ATMs, exchange facilities and car-rental offices.

The **airport train** (6.13am–10.43pm; journey time 18min; €2.25; info on ☎902 240 202) runs every thirty minutes to Barcelona Sants and continues on to Plaça de Catalunya (best stop for the Ramblas and Barri Gòtic) and Arc de Triomf (convenient for La Ribera). There are metro stations at each of these stops too. Buy your ticket from the automatic vending machine at the airport station platform (you don't need the exact change) or at the ticket office.

There's also an **Aerobús** service (Mon–Fri 5.30am–11pm, Sat & Sun 6am–11.30pm; €3.45), which leaves every twelve minutes from outside both terminals, stopping in the city at Plaça d'Espanya, Gran Via de les Corts Catalanes (at c/Comte d'Urgell), Plaça Universitat, Plaça de Catalunya (in front of El Corte Inglés) and Passeig de Gràcia (at c/la Diputació). The bus takes around thirty minutes to reach Plaça de Catalunya, though allow longer in the rush hour. At night, local bus #106 takes over, leaving the airport at 10.15pm, 11.35pm, 12.50am, 2.05am and

3.20am and ending its run at Plaça d'Espanya (south of Barcelona Sants).

A **taxi** from the airport to the centre costs roughly €20–25, including the airport surcharge. The fares are metered, so as long as you take a taxi from the official rank outside (rather than anyone who may approach you), you'll have no problems. You will, however, be charged more after 10pm and at weekends, and there's a surcharge for any luggage that goes in the boot.

By train

The main station for national and some international arrivals is **Barcelona Sants**, 3km west of the city centre. There's a tourist office here (with an accommodation booking service), as well as ATMs, an exchange office, car-rental outlets, a police station and left-luggage facilities. The metro station (accessed from inside Barcelona Sants) is called Sants Estació – line 3 from here runs direct to Liceu (for the Ramblas), Catalunya (Plaça de Catalunya) and Passeig de Gràcia, while line 5 runs to Diagonal.

Estació de França, near Parc de la Ciutadella, 1km east of the Ramblas, handles many of the long-distance arrivals and departures: essentially, this means services from Madrid, Sevilla and Malaga, intercity services from other major Spanish cities, and international trains from Paris, Zürich, Milan and Geneva. However, many trains stop at both Sants and França – check the timetable first. From Estació de França you can either take the metro (line 4) from nearby

Barceloneta or simply walk into the Barri Gòtic, up Via Laietana and into c/Jaume I.

Other possible arrival points by train are the stations at: **Plaça de Catalunya**, at the top of the Ramblas (for trains from coastal towns north of the city, the airport, and towns on the Puigcerdà–Vic line); **Plaça d'Espanya** (from Montserrat); and **Passeig de Gràcia** (from Lleida, Tarragona, Port Bou, Figueres and Girona).

By bus

The main bus terminal, used by long-distance and provincial buses, is the **Estació del Nord** on Avinguda Vilanova (main entrance on c/Ali-Bei; ⓜArc de Triomf), three blocks north of Parc de la Ciutadella. There's a bus information desk on the ground floor (daily 7am–9pm), plus an ATM, shops and luggage lockers, with the ticket offices above at street level. Some intercity buses also make a stop at the bus terminal behind **Barcelona Sants** station at Plaça Joan Peiró (ⓜSants Estació), while international buses tend to stop only at Barcelona Sants. Either way, you're only a short metro ride from the city centre.

By ferry

Ferries from the Balearics dock at the **Estació Marítima**, Moll de Barcelona, Port Vell, located at the bottom of Avinguda Paral.lel (ⓜDrassanes). There are ticket offices inside the terminal, and taxis nearby, though no other services, but you're only a short walk from Drassanes metro station at the bottom of the Ramblas.

By car

Coming into Barcelona along any one of the *autopistes*, head for the Ronda Litoral, the southern half of the city's ring road. Following signs for the Port will take you towards the main exit for the old town, "Port Vell".

There are many indoor **car parks** in the city centre, linked to display boards that indicate where there are free spaces. Central locations include Plaça de Catalunya, Plaça Urquinaona, Arc de Triomf, Passeig de Gràcia, Plaça dels Angels/MACBA and Avinguda Paral.lel, and though parking in one of these is convenient it's also fairly expensive (from €1.60 per hr, or €17.50–20 for 24hr). There's a cheaper **park-and-ride** facility for day visitors at Plaça de les Gloriés in the eastern Eixample (junction of Avgda. Diagonal and Gran Via de les Corts Catalanes; ⓜGloriés); the fee includes a ticket for unlimited travel on the city's public transport. **Street parking** is permitted in most areas, but it can be tough to find spaces, especially in the old town (where it's nearly all residents' parking only) and Gràcia. In the Eixample the ubiquitous blue meter-zones are for pay-and-display parking, usually with a two-hour maximum stay. Don't be tempted to double-park, leave your car in loading zones or otherwise park illegally – the cost of being towed can exceed €120, and no mercy is shown to foreign-plated vehicles.

Information, websites and maps

The Spanish National Tourist Office (SNTO) has international offices in Europe and North America, and can send you a variety of maps, pamphlets and special-interest leaflets on Barcelona before you leave. If there's no representation in your home country, the SNTO's website (ⓦwww.tourspain.es) is a useful first call, while specialist tour operators dealing with Barcelona (see "Getting there", p.9) should be able to answer most of your questions. Once in the city, it is very easy to pick up leaflets and brochures, either at your point of entry or from one of the city-centre information offices.

SNTO offices abroad

Britain and Ireland 22–23 Manchester Square, London W1U 3PX ☎0207/486 8077, ⓦwww.tourspain.co.uk.
Canada 2 Bloor St W, Toronto, Ontario M4W 3E2 ☎416/961-3131, ⓦwww.tourspain.toronto.on.ca.
USA 666 5th Ave, New York, NY 10103 ☎212/265-8822; 8383 Wilshire Blvd, Suite 956, Beverly Hills, CA 90211 ☎323/658-7188; 845 N Michigan Ave, Chicago, IL 60611 ☎312/642-1992; 1221 Brickell Ave, Suite 1850, Miami, FL 33131 ☎305/358-1992; ⓦwww.okspain.org.

Information in Barcelona

Offices under the auspices of **Turisme de Barcelona**, the city's tourist board – at the airport, Barcelona Sants station, Plaça de Catalunya and Plaça de Sant Jaume – are most useful for information about the city itself. As well as picking up free maps and brochures, you can book accommodation, buy **discount cards** (see box opposite), reserve space on guided tours and access other facilities. In summer (July–Sept) there is a temporary information kiosk in front of the Sagrada Família, while in the most touristed areas – such as along the Ramblas – you will also come across wandering **tourist information officers**, who can be picked out by their red jackets. For information about travelling in the wider province of Catalunya, you need the Generalitat's information centre (Centre d'Informació de Catalunya) at **Palau Robert**, while events, concerts, exhibitions, festivals and other cultural diversions are covered in full at the Institut de Cultura in the **Palau de la Virreina** on the Ramblas.

For anything else you might need to know, you can try the city's ☎**010 telephone enquiries service** (Mon–Sat 8am–10pm). They'll be able to help with questions about transport, public services and other matters, and there are English-speaking staff available. The city government's website (ⓦ**www.bcn.es**) is also a mine of information about every aspect of cultural, social and working life in Barcelona, useful for tracking down everything from sports centres to festival dates; it has an English-language version.

Information offices

Turisme de Barcelona ☎906 301 282 if calling from within Spain, ☎933 698 730 if calling from abroad, ⓦwww.barcelonaturisme.com. Main office, Pl. de Catalunya 17, ⓂCatalunya (daily 9am–9pm); also at Pl. de Sant Jaume, entrance at c/Ciutat 2, Barri Gòtic, ⓂJaume I (Mon–Fri 9am–8pm, Sat 10am–8pm, Sun & hols 10am–2pm); Airport Terminals A & B (daily 9am–9pm); and Barcelona Sants, Pl. dels Països Catalans, ⓂSants Estació (Mon–Fri 8am–8pm, Sat, Sun & hols 8am–2pm; April–Sept daily 8am–8pm). The main Pl. de Catalunya office is always busy; it's down the steps in the southeast corner of the square. There's a money exchange service, separate accommodation desk (personal callers only; no phone accommodation bookings) and a gift shop.

Institut de Cultura Palau de la Virreina, Ramblas 99, ⓂLiceu ☎933 017 775, ⓦwww.bcn.es/cultura (Mon–Sat 10am–8pm, Sun 11am–3pm). Cultural information office, with fliers and advance information on everything that's happening in the city; ticket sales here too.

Centre d'Informació de Catalunya Palau Robert, Pg. de Gràcia 107, Eixample, ⓂDiagonal ☎932 384 000, ⓦwww.gencat.net/probert (Mon–Sat 10am–7.30pm, Sun & hols 10am–2.30pm). For information about travel in Catalunya, providing maps, details of how to get around and lists of places to stay. Also guidebook sales.

Centre d'Informació per a Joves c/de Ferran 32, Barri Gòtic, ⓂLiceu ☎934 027 800, ⓦwww.bcn.es/ciaj (Mon–Fri 10am–2pm & 4–8pm). The city's drop-in youth information service (some English spoken), with a useful library, noticeboard, cultural and gig info, and photocopying/Internet service.

Barcelona Informació (Oficina d'Atenció als Ciutadans) Pl. de Sant Miquel, Barri Gòtic, ⓂJaume I ☎932 702 429, ⓦwww.bcn.es (Mon–Fri 8.30am–6pm). Citizens' information office, around the back of the Ajuntament in the new building. Not really for tourists, but invariably helpful (though no English spoken).

Barcelona on the Internet

There's plenty of information available on the Web about Barcelona. The city tourist office website (ⓦwww.barcelonaturisme.com) is a good place to start and, along with those operated by the city hall (Ajuntament;

Discount cards

If you're going to do a lot of sightseeing, you can save yourself money by buying one of the available discount cards.

• **Barcelona Card:** gives reductions of up to fifty percent on entry into many museums and attractions, and between ten percent and thirty percent in some shops, theatres and restaurants. The card also permits free public transport and provides discounts on the Aerobus to the airport, on the Montjuïc cable car and the Tomb Bus shopping service. It's valid for 1 day (€17), 2 days (€20), 3 days (€23), 4 days (€25) or 5 days (€27) and is available at the Plaça de Catalunya and airport tourist offices, Estació del Nord bus station, El Corte Inglés stores, the Aquarium and Poble Espanyol.

• **Articket** (€15; valid three months; ⑩ www.articketbcn.com): provides half-price admission into six major art centres and galleries (MNAC, MACBA, CCCB, Fundació Antoni Tàpies, Fundació Joan Miró, and Centre Cultural Caixa Catalunya at La Pedrera). It's a good saving if you're going to visit all half-dozen, and you can buy the ticket at the participating centres and galleries, and at Plaça de Catalunya and Barcelona Sants tourist offices.

• **Ruta del Modernisme** (€3; valid one month): a map and guide to the city's *modernista* sites, which also gets you fifty percent discounts at four specific attractions (saving you around €9). Currently, the discounted attractions are the tour of the Palau de la Música Catalana and entry to the Fundació Antoni Tàpies, the Museu de Zoologia and the Museu d'Art Modern (though, as this last collection will relocate to the Museu Nacional d'Art de Catalunya at Montjuïc in 2004, it's unclear if it will continue to be included in the *Ruta*). In addition, you can join a free English-language tour of the façades at the Mansana de la Discòrdia. It's available at the Centre del Modernisme in the Casa Amatller, Pg. de Gràcia 41 (see p.97).

⑩ www.bcn.es) and local government (Generalitat; ⑩ www.gencat.es), has a full English-language version. From these three alone you'll be able to find out about museum opening hours, bus routes, local politics, all-night pharmacies, festivals, sports, theatres and much, much more. The sites listed below offer either a less official view or more specialized information.

Art and architecture

⑩ **www.bcn.fjmiro.es** The Joan Miró Foundation's official website is the main source for the artist – a complete biography, plus clickable art, a round-up of his works in the city and elsewhere, and exhibition news.

⑩ **www.gaudiclub.com** The best first stop for Antoni Gaudí and his works, with plenty of links to other sites, plus Gaudí-related gifts, games, news, books and tours.

⑩ **www.qdq.com** Every building in the city has been photographed – click on "Callejero Fotografiico", then click on the map or type in the street name.

General

⑩ **www.barcelona-on-line.es** Packed with information in English on Barcelona, with searchable listings, entertainment guide, accommodation-booking service, what's-on details and more.

⑩ **www.catalanencyclopaedia.com**. English-language online encyclopaedia, for everything you ever wanted to know about Catalan people, history, buildings, economy, climate and geography, with links to a Catalan dictionary and an Internet bookshop for Catalan books.

⑩ **www.red2000.com/spain** General, thumbnail information for visitors in English, with a few nice touches – like links to colour photographs of all the major Gaudí buildings.

⑩ **www.vilaweb.com** Online newspaper, directory and portal, updated daily, with excellent links to Catalan sites, many in English. Also links to a huge variety of Barcelona webcams.

Language

⑩ **www.intercat.gencat.es/guia** The University of Barcelona's excellent online English–Catalan phrasebook, with an audio option.

ⓦ**www.travlang.com/languages/** Select "Catalan" or "Spanish" and you're presented with the tools for picking up a bit of the language before you set off.

Listings, news and reviews

ⓦ**www.diaridebarcelona.com** Up-to-the-minute city news, views, reviews, weather and listing (in Catalan), with links to all the other daily newspapers.
ⓦ**www.guiadelociobcn.es** Website of the weekly Barcelona listings magazine, *Guia del Ocio*. Mainly in Spanish, though with some English information.
ⓦ**www.lanetro.com** Spanish-only site for full cultural, entertainment, restaurant and shopping listings.
ⓦ**www.lavanguardia.es** Online version of the daily *La Vanguardia* newspaper, with listings, news and reviews for Barcelona.

Miscellaneous

ⓦ**www.barcelonareview.com** Internet-only literary magazine presenting international short fiction, poetry, reviews, essays and interviews. There's plenty in the archive on Spanish/Catalan writers, art, culture and life.
ⓦ**www.paginasamarillas.es** The Spanish Yellow Pages (find any business in Barcelona), with links to the *Paginas Blancas* (White Pages – find a person) and a Barcelona street-finder.

Sport

ⓦ**www.marca.com** The Madrid-based sports newspaper *Marca* gives you the lowdown (in Spanish) on the latest in Barça–Real rivalry, plus news, scores and stats for all other national sports.
ⓦ**www.soccer-spain.com** English-language football news, views, fixtures and results from La Liga.

Style

ⓦ**www.b-guided.com** Painfully chic website of Barcelona's coolest mag, for fashion, art, design, architecture, food and nightlife.

Maps

You can pick up a free city map from any tourist office, and from major hotels, which together with the maps in this book will be more than enough to help you find your way around. For an excellent fold-out **street plan** on tough, waterproof paper, look no further

than *Barcelona: The Rough Guide Map* (Penguin), which also includes full practical information, and dining, lodging and shopping listings. Map and travel shops in your home country (see below) should be able to supply a copy of this, as well a **road map** of Catalunya or northern Spain by Michelin, Firestone or Rand McNally. In Barcelona, you'll find a good selection of maps in most bookshops (see p.232) and at street kiosks or petrol stations.

Map outlets

UK

Blackwell's Map and Travel Shop 50 Broad St, Oxford OX1 3BQ ☏01865/793 550, ⓦwww.maps.blackwell.co.uk.
Heffers Map and Travel 20 Trinity St, Cambridge CB2 1TJ ☏01865/333 536, ⓦwww.heffers.co.uk.
Newcastle Map Centre 55 Grey St, Newcastle-upon-Tyne, NE1 6EF ☏0191/261 5622.
Stanfords 12–14 Long Acre, WC2E 9LP ☏020/7836 1321, ⓦwww.stanfords.co.uk, ⓔsales@stanfords.co.uk.
The Travel Bookshop 13–15 Blenheim Crescent, W11 2EE ☏020/7229 5260, ⓦwww.thetravelbookshop.co.uk.

Ireland

Easons Bookshop 40 O'Connell St, Dublin 1 ☏01/858 3881, ⓦwww.eason.ie.
Hodges Figgis Bookshop 56–58 Dawson St, Dublin 2 ☏01/677 4754, ⓦwww.hodgesfiggis.com.

US

Adventurous Traveler.com ☏1-800/282-3963, ⓦadventuroustraveler.com.
Distant Lands 56 S Raymond Ave, Pasadena, CA 91105 ☏1-800/310-3220, ⓦwww.distantlands.com.
Elliot Bay Book Company 101 S Main St, Seattle, WA 98104 ☏1-800/962-5311, ⓦwww.elliotbaybook.com.
Globe Corner Bookstore 28 Church St, Cambridge, MA 02138 ☏1-800/358-6013, ⓦwww.globe-corner.com.
Map Link 30 S La Patera Lane, Unit 5, Santa Barbara, CA 93117 ☏1-800/962-1394, ⓦwww.maplink.com.
Rand McNally ☏1-800/333-0136, ⓦwww.randmcnally.com. Around thirty stores across the US; check the website for the nearest location.

Canada

Travel Bug Bookstore 2667 W Broadway, Vancouver V6K 2G2 ☏604/737-1122, ⓦ www.swifty.com/tbug.
World of Maps 1235 Wellington St, Ottawa, Ontario K1Y 3A3 ☏1-800/214-8524, ⓦ www.worldofmaps.com.

Australia

The Map Shop 6–10 Peel St, Adelaide, SA 5000 ☏08/8231 2033, ⓦ www.mapshop.net.au.

Mapland 372 Little Bourke St, Melbourne, Victoria 3000 ☏03/9670 4383, ⓦ www.mapland.com.au.
Perth Map Centre 900 Hay St, Perth, WA 6000 ☏08/9322 5733, ⓦ www.perthmap.com.au.

New Zealand

MapWorld 173 Gloucester St, Christchurch ☏0800/627 967 or 03/374 5399, ⓦ www.mapworld.co.nz.
Specialty Maps 46 Albert St, Auckland ☏09/307 2217, ⓦ www.specialtymaps.co.nz.

City transport

Apart from the medieval Barri Gòtic, where you'll want to (and have to) walk, you'll need to use Barcelona's excellent integrated transport system to make the most of what the city has to offer. The system comprises the metro, buses, local FGC and RENFE Rodiales trains, plus a network of funiculars and cable cars. There's an invaluable free public transport map (*Guia d'Autobusos Urbanos de Barcelona*), available at the customer service centres (see box below) of Transports Metropolitans de Barcelona (TMB) and, usually, at any of the city tourist offices. The map and ticket information is also posted at major bus stops and all metro stations. Detailed transport information is available by telephone (☏010) and on the Internet (ⓦ www.tmb.net). Our public transport map is in the colour pages at the back of the book.

Tickets and travel passes

A transit plan divides the province into six zones, but as the entire metropolitan area of Barcelona falls within Zone 1, that's the only one you'll need to worry about on a day-to-day basis. On all the city's public transport you can buy a **single ticket** every time you ride (€1.10), but even over only a couple of days it's much cheaper to buy a *targeta* – a discount ticket strip which you pass through

TMB customer service centres

Barcelona Sants station (RENFE Vestibul): Mon–Fri 7am–9pm, Sat 9am–7pm, Sun 9am–2pm
ⓂDiagonal: Mon–Fri 8am–8pm
ⓂSagrada Família: Mon–Fri 7am–9pm
ⓂUniversitat: Mon–Fri 8am–8pm

the box on top of the metro/train barrier or punch in the machine on the bus. The *targetes* are valid for travel on the metro, city buses (including night buses), and local trains and funiculars, and are available at metro and train stations (at ticket windows or vending machines), but not on the buses.

The best general deal for most people is the **T-10** ("tay day-oo" in Catalan) *targeta* (€6), valid for ten separate journeys, with changes between methods of transport allowed within 75 minutes. The ticket can also be used by more than one person at a time – just make sure you punch it the same number of times as there are people travelling. It's also available at newsstands and tobacconists.

Other useful (single-person) *targetes* for Zone 1 include: the T-Dia ("tay dee-ah"; 1 day's unlimited travel; €4.60), plus combos up to the 5-Dies (5 days; €18.20); the

T-50/30 (50 trips within a 30-day period; €25); or the T-Mes (1 month; €38.80) – for the latter, the station ticket office will need to see some form of ID (driving licence or passport). The **Barcelona Card** (see p.23) also offers free city transport for between 1 and 5 days.

Heading for the airport, Sitges, the northern coast, Montserrat and other out-of-town destinations, you'll need to buy a specific ticket as Zone 1 *targetes* don't run that far. Anyone caught **without a valid ticket** anywhere on the system is liable to an on-the-spot fine of €40.

The metro

The quickest way of getting around Barcelona is by the modern and efficient metro system, which runs on five lines; entrances are marked with a red diamond sign with an "M". Its **hours of operation** are Monday until Thursday 5am to midnight; Friday, Saturday and the day before a public holiday 5am to 2am; Sunday and public holidays 6am to midnight. There's a colour **metro map** at the back of this book, or you can pick up a little fold-out one at metro stations (ask for *una guia del metro*).

The system is perfectly safe, though many of the train carriages are heavily graffitied. Buskers and beggars are common, zipping from one carriage to the next at stations. Theoretically, it's no smoking on the metro system, though that doesn't stop Catalans lighting up on the escalators and platforms. You might also be surprised by the services on offer at metro stations – not only are there bars at many, but you can buy lottery tickets from little booths and even books from some vending machines.

Buses

Bus routes in the city are easy to master if you get hold of a copy of the public transport map and remember that the routes are colour-coded: **city-centre buses** are red and always stop at one of three central squares (Catalunya, Universitat or Urquinaona); **cross-city buses** are yellow; green buses run on all the **peripheral routes** outside the city centre; and **night buses** (*autobusos nocturns* or simply *Nitbus*) are blue (and always stop near or in Plaça de

Catalunya). In addition, the route is marked at each bus stop, along with a timetable – useful bus routes are detailed in the text.

Most buses **operate daily**, roughly from 4am or 5am until 10.30pm, though some lines stop earlier and some run on until after midnight. The night buses fill in the gaps on all the main routes, with services every 20 to 60 minutes from around 10pm to 4am.

Useful Catalan words to look out for on **timetables** are *diari* (daily), *feiners* (workdays, including Saturday), and *diumenge* or *festius* (Sunday and holidays).

Trains

The city has a cheap and efficient commuter train line, the **Ferrocarrils de la Generalitat de Catalunya** (FGC; ☎932 051 515, ⓦwww.fgc.es), with its main stations at Plaça de Catalunya and Plaça d'Espanya. You'll use this going to places like Sarrià, Vallvidrera, Tibidabo and Montserrat, and details are given in the text where appropriate. **Travel passes** (*targetes*) are valid as far as the Zone 1 city limits, which in practice is everywhere you're likely to want to go except for Montserrat.

The national rail service, operated by **RENFE** (☎902 240 202, ⓦwww.renfe.es), runs all the other services out of Barcelona, with local lines – north to the Coasta Maresme and south to Sitges – designated as *Rodiales/Cercanías*. The hub is Barcelona Sants station, with services also passing through Plaça de Catalunya (heading north) and Passeig de Gràcia (south). Arrive in plenty of time to buy a ticket, as queues are often horrendous, though for most regional destinations you can use the automatic vending machines instead.

Funiculars, cable cars, trams and trolleys

An array of other transport options in the city provides some fun ways of getting around. Details of hours of operation and prices are given in the relevant sections of the text.

Several **funicular railways** still operate in the city, most notably to Montjuïc, Tibidabo and Vallvidrera. Weekend visits to Tibidabo also combine a funicular trip with a ride on the antique **tram**, the Tramvia Blau. There are two **cable car** (*telefèric*) rides you can make: from Barceloneta across the harbour to Montjuïc, and then from the top station of the Montjuïc funicular right the way up to the castle. Both aerial rides are pretty good experiences, worth doing just for the views alone. Finally, a train-trolley, the **Tren Turístic de Montjuïc**, trundles around the Montjuïc area during the summer months.

Taxis

Black-and-yellow taxis (with a green roof-light on when available for hire) are inexpensive, plentiful and well worth using, especially late at night. There's a minimum charge of €1.15 (€1.30 after 10pm, weekends and holidays) and after that it's currently €0.69/0.88 per kilometre, with small surcharges for baggage, picking up from Barcelona Sants station and the airport, and a multitude of other things. However, the taxis have meters, so charges are transparent – if not, asking for a receipt (*rebut* in Catalan, *recibo* in Spanish) should ensure that the price is fair. Most short journeys across town run to around €5 or €6. There are **taxi ranks** outside major train and metro stations, in main squares, near large hotels and at places along the main avenues. To call a taxi in advance, see "Directory", p.244 for a list of cab companies (few of the operators speak English) – you'll be charged around an extra €3 on top of the fare for calling a cab.

Driving and vehicle rental

You don't need a car to get around Barcelona, but you may want to rent one if you plan to see anything else of the region. However, in summer the coastal roads in particular are a nightmare, so if all you aim to do is zip to the beach or wine region for the day, it's far better to stick to the local trains. Driving in the city itself is not for the faint-hearted either, with opinion divided on whether it's worse negotiating impossibly narrow, old streets, or the racetrack avenues of the Eixample. It comes as no surprise to discover that Spain has one of the highest traffic accident rates in Europe. Moreover, fuel prices are only marginally lower than in Britain and almost double US prices, while you'll probably have to pay extra for parking (which is notoriously difficult in the city cen-

tre; see "Arrival: by car", p.21). **Vehicle crime** is rampant – never leave anything visible in the car.

Most foreign **driving licences** are honoured in Spain – including all EU, US and Canadian ones – or you can take an **International Driver's Licence** (available from recognized driving organizations). If you're bringing your own car, you must have a **green card** from your insurers, and a bail bond or extra coverage for legal costs is also worth having, since if you do have an accident it'll be seen as your fault as a foreigner, regardless of the circumstances. Without a bail bond both you and the car could be locked up pending investigation. Carry your licence and insurance documents with you at all times in the car.

Remember that you **drive on the right** in Spain; and away from main roads you yield to vehicles approaching from the right. **Speed limits** are posted – maximum on urban roads is 60kph, other roads 90kph, motorways 120kph. Wearing **seatbelts** is compulsory. If you're stopped for any violation, the Spanish police can and usually will levy a stiff on-the-spot fine before letting you go on your way, especially since as a foreigner you're unlikely to want, or be able, to appear in court.

Vehicle rental

It's usually cheapest to arrange **car rental** in advance of your trip, either through the main rental agencies (see list overleaf) or with one of the tour operators or airlines (see "Getting there" p.9 for contact details) when booking your holiday. Depending on the time of year, renting an economy car should run at £150–200/US$220–300 per week, including unlimited mileage, Collision Damage Waiver, insurance and tax. If you leave it until you arrive **in Barcelona**, you'll need to contact one of the rental companies listed in "Directory" on p.242, which have inclusive rates from around €40 per day for an economy car (less by the week, and often with better rates at the weekend). Drivers need to be at least 21 (23 with some companies) and to have been driving for at least a year.

Some of the Barcelona rental outlets also have **mopeds and motorcycles** available, though given the traffic conditions (and the good public transport system) it's not really recommended as a means of getting around the city. You have to be 14 to ride a machine under 75cc, 18 for one over 75cc, and crash helmets are compulsory. Note that mopeds and motorcycles are often rented out with insurance that doesn't include theft – always check with the company first. You will generally be asked to produce a driving licence as a deposit.

Car-rental agencies

Auto Europe US ☎1-800/223-5555; Canada ☎1-888/223-5555, ☎www.autoeurope.com.
Avis UK ☎0870/606 0100, ☎www.avis.co.uk; US ☎1-800/331-1084; Canada ☎1-800/272-5871, ☎www.avis.com; Northern Ireland ☎028/9024 0404; Republic of Ireland ☎01/605 7500, ☎www.avis.ie; Australia ☎13 63 33 or 02/9353 9000, ☎www.avis.com.au; New Zealand ☎09/526 2847 or 0800/655 111, ☎www.avis.co.nz.
Budget UK ☎0800/181 181, ☎www.budget.co.uk; US ☎1-800/527-0700, ☎www.budgetrentacar.com; Republic of Ireland ☎0903/277 11, ☎www.budget.ie; Australia ☎1300/362 848, ☎www.budget.com.au; New Zealand ☎09/976 2222, ☎www.budget.co.nz.
Dollar US ☎1-800/800-4000, ☎www.dollar.com; Australia ☎02/9223 1444, ☎www.dollarcar.com.au.
Europcar UK ☎0845/722 2525, ☎www.europcar.co.uk; US and Canada ☎1-877/940-6900, ☎www.europcar.com; Northern Ireland ☎028/9442 3444; Republic of Ireland ☎01/614 2888, ☎www.europcar.ie; Australia ☎1300/131 390, ☎www.deltaeuropcar.com.au.
Europe by Car US ☎1-800/223-1516, ☎www.europebycar.com.
Hertz UK ☎0870/844 8844, ☎www.hertz.co.uk; US ☎1-800/654-3001; Canada ☎1-800/263-0600, ☎www.hertz.com; Republic of Ireland ☎01/676 7476, ☎www.hertz.ie; Australia ☎13 30 39 or 03/9698 2555, ☎www.hertz.com.au; New Zealand ☎0800/654 321, ☎www.hertz.co.nz.
Holiday Autos UK ☎0870/400 0099, ☎www.holidayautos.co.uk; US ☎1-800/422-7737, ☎www.holidayautos.com; Republic of Ireland ☎01/872 9366, ☎www.holidayautos.ie; Australia ☎1300/554 432, ☎www.holidayautos.com.au; New Zealand ☎0800/144 040, ☎www.holidayautos.co.nz.
National UK ☎0870/536 5365, ☎www.nationalcar.co.uk; US ☎1-800/227-7368, ☎www.nationalcar.com; Australia ☎13 10 45, ☎www.nationalcar.com.au; New Zealand ☎0800/800 115, ☎www.nationalcar.co.nz.
Suncars UK ☎0870/500 5566, ☎www.suncars.co.uk; Republic of Ireland ☎1850/201406, ☎www.suncars.ie.
Thrifty UK ☎01494/751 600, ☎www.thrifty.co.uk; US ☎1-800/367-2277, ☎www.thrifty.com; Republic of Ireland ☎1800/515 800, ☎www.thrifty.ie; Australia ☎1300/367 227, ☎www.thrifty.com.au; New Zealand ☎09/309 0111, ☎www.thrifty.co.nz.

City tours

Although you can find your way around the city easily enough with a map and a guidebook, taking a tour is a good way to orientate yourself on arrival. Highest profile belongs to the two tour-bus operators, whose board-at-will open-top services can drop you outside virtually every attraction in the city. Otherwise, Barcelona has some particularly good walking tours, showing you parts of the old town you might not find otherwise, while guided bike tours and sightseeing boats offer a different view of the city.

Bike tours

Biciclot c/Sant Joan de Malta 1 ☎933 077 475, ☎www.biciclot.net; ⓂClot. Bike-rental outfit that offers two-hour city tours (Sat & Sun 11am, €18) as well as a Friday-night "Gaudí de Nit" cycle tour (Fri 10pm, €18). Bikes and local guide included in the price; reservations essential.
Mike's Bike Tours ☎933 013 612,

@ info@mikesbiketoursbarcelona.com. Four-hour city bike tours (€22, bike included) through the old town, port area, beach and Sagrada Família. Tours run once or twice daily March to mid-Dec (meeting at the Columbus monument at the bottom of the Ramblas); call for times (English-speaking) and off-season schedules.

Bus and trolley tours

Barcelona Tours The orange-coloured rival to Bus Turístic, with buses making a circular 3hr sweep through the city from Pl. de Catalunya (daily: May–Sept 9am–9pm, rest of the year until 8pm; departures every 15min). Tickets are bought on board: 1-day €16, 2-day €20 (under-14s €10/13 respectively).

Bus Turístic Sightseeing service (daily 9am–7pm; departures every 6–30min), starting at Pl. de Catalunya and linking all the main sights and tourist destinations, including the Sagrada Família, Parc Güell and the Poble Espanyol; a full circuit takes 2hr. Buses are colour-coded: red destination boards for northbound services and blue for southbound. Tickets cost €16 for 1 day, €20 for 2 days (children aged 4–12 €10/13 respectively). The ticket also gives discounts at various sights and on the tram to Tibidabo. Buy it on board the bus or at the Pl. de Catalunya tourist office.

Tren Turístic de Montjuïc The train-trolley leaves from Pl. d'Espanya (mid-June to mid-Sept daily; otherwise April–Oct Sat & Sun only 10am–8.30pm; every 30min; €3) and runs to all the major sights on Montjuïc, including the castle. The round trip lasts about 1hr and your ticket allows you to complete the full circuit once, getting on and off where you like.

Walking tours

Barcelona Walking Tours ☎ 906 301 282, @ www.barcelonaturisme.com. Advance booking advised (at Pl. de Catalunya tourist office) for the popular historical walking tour of the Barri Gòtic (Sat & Sun all year, in English at 10am; plus April–Sept Thurs & Fri at 10am; €8); tour lasts 90min. Also "Picasso Tours" (Sat & Sun all year, in English at 10.30am; €10, includes entry to Picasso Museum), concentrating on sights and buildings associated with Picasso in Barcelona.

Museu d'Historia de la Ciutat Pl. del Rei, Barri Gòtic ☎ 933 151 111, @ www.museuhistoria.bcn.es; Ⓜ Jaume I. The museum organizes a programme of walking tours (usually in Catalan, but other languages by arrangement) around the buildings it's responsible for, principally the Plaça del Rei ensemble and Pedralbes monastery. Tours usually last 2hr and cost €5–7.

My Favourite Things ☎ 933 295 351 or 637 265 405, @ www.myft.net. Highly individual tours which reveal the city in a new light – whether it's bohemian Barcelona, furniture and fashion, where and what the locals eat, or the signature tour "My Favourite Fusion", which gives an insider's view of the city. Tours (in English) cost €25 per person and last around 4hr, and there's always time for anecdotes, diversions, workshop visits and café visits. Tour numbers are limited to ten, and departures are flexible, so call or email Katrien and Caroline for latest information or tailor-made requests.

Travel Bar c/Boqueria 27, Barri Gòtic ☎ 933 425 252, @ www.travelbar.com; Ⓜ Liceu. The travellers' bar organizes a variety of year-round, youth-oriented tours, including an old-town walking tour (€12), evening bar crawl (€26, includes drinks), tapas bar tour (€33, includes food), bike tour (€58, includes bike, meal and drink) and kayaking on the harbour (June–Sept only; €23). Also excursions to nearby towns, cities and the Pyrenees. Call at the bar for a current schedule.

Water tours

Catamaran Orsom ☎ 932 258 260, @ www.barcelona-orsom.com. Barcelona from the sea: three daily afternoon departures (€12) from the quayside opposite the Columbus statue, at the bottom of the Ramblas (Ⓜ Drassanes) – there's a ticket kiosk there, or phone and reserve the day before. Also summer evening jazz cruises (June, July & Aug; €12).

Las Golondrinas ☎ 934 423 106, @ www.lasgolondrinas.com. Daily sightseeing boat departures from Pl. Portal de la Pau, behind the Columbus monument (Ⓜ Drassanes) – either around the port (35min; €3.70), or port and coast including the Port Olímpic (1hr 30min; €8.80). Departures at least hourly June–Sept; less frequently Oct–May.

The media

You'll be able to keep up with the news while you're away since British, European and American newspapers are sold at street kiosks on the Ramblas and elsewhere (see "Directory", p.243 for locations). Many have special European editions (including the *Guardian*, *Independent* and *Wall Street Journal*), so they're on sale the same day from around 10am. The city also has some English-language publications, and useful listings magazines – for these, and a rundown of the local Spanish press, see below. If you have a short-wave radio you'll be able to tune into the BBC World Service (®www.bbc.co.uk/worldservice) or Voice of America (®www.voa.gov), whose websites list their frequencies around the globe.

Newspapers and magazines

Of the Spanish newspapers the best is the Barcelona edition of the liberal **El País** – the only one with much serious analysis or foreign news coverage, plus good supplements on entertainment (Friday) and the arts (Saturday). The Barcelona paper **La Vanguardia** is conservative; it also has a good listings section on Friday. **El Periodico** is more tabloid in style, with big headlines and lots of photos. **Avui** is the chief nationalist paper, printed in Catalan. You can also pick up two free daily papers outside metro stations on weekdays, **Metro** and **20 Minutos**, both with useful local listings. For wall-to-wall coverage of sport (for which, in Barcelona, read FC Barcelona), buy the specialist dailies **Mundo Deportivo** or **Sport** – Madrid's **Marca** carries news of the old enemy, Real Madrid. If you are looking for an apartment, job or anything secondhand, you should pick up the classifieds newspaper **Primeramà**, which comes out on Mondays and Thursdays.

The most useful listings publication is the weekly **Guia del Ocio** (every Thurs), a small paperback-book-sized magazine, available at kiosks all over the city. It's in Spanish but is easily deciphered. Quality English-language publications include **Barcelona Metropolitan**, a free monthly magazine for English speakers living in Barcelona, available from hotels, bars, cinemas showing English-language films and other outlets; and **b-guided**, a quarterly style magazine on sale at newsagents. You'll also see copies of the monthly **Barcelona Business** – for Catalan business news in English – the free weekly **Sports Matter**, and the free monthly newsletter **Barcelona Connect**, the latter containing an idiosyncratic mixture of news, views and classified ads.

Televison

In Catalunya you can pick up **two national TV channels**, TVE1 and La 2, a couple of **Catalan-language channels**, TV3 and Canal 33, and the **private** Antena 3 and Tele 5 channels. In Barcelona you can also get the city-run **Barcelona TV**, which is useful for information about local events, and news programmes on the otherwise subscriber-only Canal Plus channel. TVs in most pensions and small hotels tend to offer these stations, with cable and satellite channels only available in higher-rated hotels.

The programming is a fairly entertaining mixture of grim game shows, tacky song-and-dance revues, news and sports. Soaps are a particular speciality, whether Catalan, Spanish or South American, while locally produced sitcoms and series compete with dubbed versions of North American favourites like *Will and Grace* and *"Los Simpson"*. Some foreign films and shows are broadcast in *dual* (simultaneously in the original and dubbed); undubbed films are marked "V.O. (*versión original*)" in listings (usually late-night only). Sports fans are well catered for, with regular live coverage of local and national basketball and football matches – in the football season, you can watch two or three live matches a week. The best local **weather** forecasting is on TV3.

Costs, money and banks

Although people still think of Spain as a budget destination, Barcelona is not a particularly cheap place to visit. Hotel prices have increased considerably over the last few years, while some major museums and attractions have steep admission charges. However, when balanced with the cost of visiting cities in core European countries, such as Britain, France or Germany, Barcelona still rates as pretty good value, especially when it comes to dining out or getting around on public transport. Only if you do all your shopping in designer stores, and all your eating and drinking in fusion restaurants and style bars, can you expect to spend as much as you would at home, if not more.

Average costs

Your single biggest daily expense by far will be accommodation, with the very cheapest double rooms starting at around €35–40. Snacks and meals, on the other hand, are still extremely good value, with a three-course lunch anywhere in the city available for under €9, while a one-day public transport pass gives you the freedom of the city for under €5.

If you're prepared to stay in inexpensive pensions, stick to basic restaurants and bars, and pick and choose your sightseeing, you could get by on €45 a day. Upgrade your accommodation, see all the museums, eat fancier meals and experience the Barcelona nightlife, and you'll need more like €90–100 a day – though, of course, if you're planning to stay in a four-star Ramblas or Eixample hotel, this figure might not even cover your room. For more detailed accommodation costs, see Chapter 7.

Currency, cash, cards and cheques

Spain's currency is the euro (€), with notes issued in **denominations** of 5, 10, 20, 50, 100, 200 and 500 euros, and coins in denominations of 1, 2, 5, 10, 20 and 50 cents, and 1 and 2 euros. The **exchange rate** currently fluctuates around €1.45 to £1 (€1 equals 70p) and €0.85 to US$1 (€1 equals $1.20).

By far the easiest way to get money in Barcelona is to use your bank debit card to withdraw cash from an **ATM** (cash machine). You'll find them all over the city, including the airport and major train stations, and you can usually withdraw up to €300 a day depending on the status of your account. Instructions are offered in English once you insert your card. The amounts withdrawn are not liable to interest payments, and the flat transaction fee is usually quite small – your

Budget Barcelona

Here's how to keep costs to a minimum in Barcelona.

- Eat your main meal of the day at lunchtime, when the *menú del día* offers fantastic value (p.170).
- Buy a public transport travel pass (see p.25), which will save you around 40 percent on every ride.
- Visit museums and galleries on the first Sunday of the month if you can, when admission is usually free.
- Drink and eat *inside* cafés – there's usually a surcharge for terrace service.

- Take any student/youth/senior citizen cards you're entitled to carry, as they often attract discounts on museum, gallery and attraction charges.
- Take advantage of the discount nights at the cinema (Mon and sometimes Wed), and at the theatre (Tues).
- Go to the Ramblas, La Seu, Parc de la Ciutadella, Parc de la Collserola, Port Olímpic, city beaches, Olympic stadium, Caixa Forum and Parc Güell – all free.

bank will be able to advise on this. Make sure you have a personal identification number (PIN) that's designed to work overseas, and take a note of your bank's emergency contact number in case the machine swallows the card.

Credit cards are a handy backup source of funds, and can be used either in ATMs or over the counter. MasterCard, Visa and American Express are accepted just about everywhere. Remember that all cash advances on credit cards are treated as loans, with interest accruing daily from the date of withdrawal; there may be a transaction fee on top of this.

Travellers' cheques are no longer the cheapest nor most convenient option, although they do offer protection against loss or theft. There's usually a fee for buying the cheques, and then a commission (sometimes quite large) charged to change them. Obviously, buying cheques in euros is the best option, since these can be cashed without incurring exchange service charges, though sterling and American dollars cheques will be accepted in all banks and exchange offices.

In an emergency, you might have to consider having money wired from home, though this is never a cheap way to access funds. **American Express** (see p.241 for Barcelona contact details) has a 24-hour money transfer service, while **Western Union** (ⓦwww.westernunion.com) can transfer cash to and from various locations in the city, including most main post offices.

Banks and exchange offices

Spanish banks (*bancos*) and savings banks (*caixas*) have branches throughout Barcelona, with concentrations down the Ramblas and around Plaça de Catalunya. Normal **banking hours** in Barcelona are Monday to Friday from 8.30am to 2pm, although from October until May most institutions also open Thursday 4pm to 6.30pm (savings banks) or Saturday 9am to 1pm (banks). Outside these hours you can use *bureaux de change* or an **exchange office**

(*cambio*). Some useful locations are listed in the "Directory" on p.241, and you'll find others along the Ramblas and elsewhere, often open well after midnight. Exchange offices don't always charge commission, though their rates aren't usually as good as the banks. Other exchange options are the automatic currency exchange machines (available at the airport, Barcelona Sants and outside some banks) or one of the larger hotels or travel agents, though again rates can be variable.

Taxes and tipping

Local sales tax, **IVA**, is seven percent in hotels and restaurants, and sixteen percent in shops. It's usually included in the price though not always, so some hotel or restaurant bills can come as a bit of a surprise – though quoted prices should always make it clear whether or not tax is included.

In most restaurants and bars service is considered to be included in the price of meals and drinks (hence the premium you pay for sitting at a terrace). **Tipping** is more a recognition that service was good or exceptional than an expected part of the server's wage. Locals actually tip very little, leaving a few cents or rounding up the change for a coffee or a drink, and a euro or two for most meals. Anything beyond is considered excessive, certainly the ten or fifteen percent that most visitors are used to at home. However, fancy restaurants may specifically indicate that service is not included, in which case you will be expected to leave ten to fifteen percent. Taxi drivers usually get around five percent, more if they have helped you with bags or been similarly useful, while hotel porters and toilet attendants should be tipped a euro or two for their assistance.

To cancel **lost or stolen credit cards**, call the following 24-hour numbers:
American Express ☏902 375 637
Diners Club ☏934 670 145
MasterCard ☏900 971 231
Visa ☏900 991 216

Mail, phones and email

You'll have no trouble keeping in touch whilst in Barcelona. Stamps are widely sold, public telephones are plentiful and there is a growing number of Internet cafés where you can check your email.

Post offices and mail

The main **post office** in Barcelona, near the harbour in the old town, is open daily, including Sunday, while other central branches have long weekday hours; see "Directory", p.244, for all the relevant details. However, if all you need are **stamps** it's much easier to visit a tobacconist (look for the brown-and-yellow *tabac* sign), found on virtually every street. These can also usually weigh letters and small parcels, advise about postal rates, and send mail "urgente" (worth a try if you need to speed things up a little). Use the yellow on-street **postboxes** and put your mail in the flap marked *províncies i estranger* or *altres destins*. Letters or cards take around three to four days to European countries, five days to a week to North America.

Letters can be sent **poste restante** (general delivery) to Barcelona's main post office: they should be addressed (preferably with the surname underlined and in capitals) to *Lista de Correos* followed by the city name and province (Catalunya). To collect, take along your passport and ask the clerk to check under all of your names – letters are often to be found filed under first or middle names. Alternatively, American Express in Barcelona will hold mail for a month for members.

Public phones and phone centres

Spanish **public telephones** have instructions in English, and you'll find plenty of *cabinas* on the street. They accept coins, credit cards and phone cards, while dialling codes

Telephone information

Spanish regional prefixes are an integral part of the nine-digit telephone numbers. Thus, in Barcelona, the first two digits of all phone numbers are 93, and it is necessary to dial these digits even when calling from within the city. Spanish mobile numbers begin with a 6, freephone numbers begin 900, while other 90-plus-digit numbers are special-rate services.

Useful numbers
Directory enquiries ☏1003
International operator (Europe) ☏1008
International operator (rest of the world) ☏1005
Weather forecast ☏932 211 600
Road conditions ☏938 892 211
The time ☏093
Alarm call ☏096

Phoning abroad from Barcelona
to Australia: dial ☏00, then 61 + area code minus first 0 + number
to Britain: dial ☏00, then 44 + area code minus first 0 + number

to Ireland: dial ☏00, then 353 + area code + number
to New Zealand: dial ☏00, then 64 + area code minus first 0 + number
to US and Canada: dial ☏00, then 1 + area code + number

Phoning Barcelona from abroad
from Australia: dial ☏0011 +34 + number
from Britain: dial ☏00 + 34 + number
from Ireland: dial ☏00 + 34 + number
from New Zealand: dial ☏00 +34 + number
from US and Canada: dial ☏011 + 34 + number

(Spanish provincial and overseas) and other information are displayed in the cabins. **Phone cards** are available in tobacconists, newsagents and post offices, issued either by Telefónica (the dominant operator) or one of its rivals. Credit cards are not recommended for local and national calls, since most have a minimum charge which is far more than a normal call is likely to cost. The **ringing tone** is long; **engaged** is shorter and rapid; the standard Spanish response is *¿diga?* (speak) or in Barcelona, a less linguistically committal *¿si?*.

You can also make calls from the old-style telephones in cafés and bars, though their rates are higher and you can't make anything except a simple coin call. If possible, avoid making any calls from your hotel room, as even local calls will be slapped with a heavy surcharge, and "no charge" calls to international operators may be charged as well.

For **international calls,** you can use any of the street cabins, paying with coins, phone card, credit card or **charge card** issued by your domestic telephone company. This way, all calls made from overseas will automatically be billed to your home account. Contact your home provider, which will provide you with a number that you can dial free from cabins and which will connect you directly with one of their operators in your home country. However, the cheapest way to make an international call is to go to one of the ubiquitous phone centres, or **locutorios**, which specialize in discounted overseas connections – you'll find them scattered through the old city, particularly in the Raval and Ribera. If the rates to the country that you want to call are not posted, just ask. You'll then be assigned a cabin to make your calls, and afterwards you pay in cash.

Mobile phones

Most European-subscribed **mobile phones** will work in Barcelona, though if you are planning to take your phone with you it's worth checking with your provider whether you need to get international access switched on and what the charges will be. You will be charged higher rates for making calls when abroad and also for *receiving* calls, though you can often choose to pay a small premium while away which brings the charges down a little. You may also have to ask your provider for a new access code if you want to retrieve messages from your voice mail while in Barcelona.

If you plan to use your mobile phone a lot, or you're spending some time in the city, it's almost certainly better to **buy a Spanish mobile**. The cheapest rechargeable pre-paid phones cost around €60, which usually includes €20 or so of free calls. Price plans vary, but charges of around €0.28 a minute for daytime use are standard. You can buy top-up cards, or have them recharged for you, in phone shops and post offices.

Email

One of the best ways to keep in touch while travelling is to sign up for a free **Internet email address** that can be accessed from anywhere – for example, YahooMail (@www.yahoo.com) or Hotmail (@www.hotmail.com). Once you've set up an account, you can use these sites to pick up and send mail from any place with online access. There are **Internet shops and cafés** all over Barcelona (some of the main ones are listed on p.242), while an increasing number of youth hostels and pensions provide cheap or free Internet access for their guests. Hotel Internet access is usually more expensive (whether in the hotel's business centre or in bedrooms wired for access), as hotel call charges are so high.

Admission to museums, galleries and churches

Most of the showpiece museums and galleries in Barcelona open all day, from 10am to 7 or 8pm, though some of the smaller collections and attractions close over lunchtime between 1 and 4pm. On Sundays most open in the morning only and on Mondays most are closed all day. On public holidays (see p.36), most museums and galleries have Sunday opening hours, while everything is closed on Christmas and New Year's Day.

Museum opening hours tend to stay the same from year to year, perhaps varying by half an hour here and there. We've included current opening hours for all attractions listed in the guide, and you can check any changes in the "Museos y fundaciones" section of the weekly *Guia del Ocio* listings magazine or on the websites of the museums and galleries themselves.

Admission charges for all attractions vary from between €3 and €12, though most museums cost around €5 or €6. Many offer **free admission** on the first Sunday of every month, and there's usually a reduction or free entrance if you show a student/youth/senior citizen card. There are also several

discount cards available (see p.23), which give heavily reduced admission to Barcelona's museums and galleries – worth considering if you're planning to see everything that the city has to offer.

Apart from the cathedral (La Seu) and the Sagrada Família – the two **churches** you're most likely to visit, which have tourist-friendly opening hours – other churches are usually kept locked, opening only for worship in the early morning (around 7–8am) and/or the evening (around 6–9pm). The Sagrada Família is the only church to charge an admission fee, though for all churches "decorous" dress is required, ie no shorts or bare shoulders.

Forum Barcelona 2004

Barcelona is hosting the **Universal Forum of Cultures** (🌐 www.barcelona2004.org) from May 9 to September 26, 2004. The closing ceremony will coincide with the traditional end of the annual Mercè festival, the city's biggest party. Best described as a peace, cultural diversity and sustainability Expo, the Forum is being held in the recently developed Poble Nou area of the city, with twenty weeks of activities, exhibitions, workshops, festivals, debates, games, markets, installations, concerts and other performances. Most of these events are being held in the new plaza, buildings and conference centre at the site, though the city's museums and cultural institutions will play a role too.

Admission fees will be charged for entry to the main Forum site, and to other related events and activities, with **tickets** costing €21 (1 day), €42 (3 days) or €169 (season pass); there are discounts for senior citizens and children under 16; under-7s get in free. Tickets are available in advance from Plaça de Catalunya tourist office, the cultural information office at Palau Virreina, Ramblas 99, and at the Generalitat's information office at Palau Robert (see "Information offices", p.22, for all contact details), or you can buy them on the gate after the Forum opening. There's more information on the website, including a full programme of events.

Opening hours and public holidays

Basic working hours in Barcelona are Monday to Saturday 9.30/10am to 1.30pm and 4.30 to 8/9pm, though many offices and shops don't open on Saturday afternoons. However, local cafés, bars and markets open earlier, usually from around 7am, while shopping centres, major stores and large supermarkets tend to remain open all day from 10am to 9pm, with some even opening on Sunday these days.

In the lazy days of summer everything becomes a bit more relaxed, with offices working until around 3pm and many shops and restaurants closing for part or the whole of **August**. Conversely, while Barcelona seems semi-deserted, it can prove nearly impossible to find a free bed in the nearby coastal and mountain resorts in August; similarly, seats on planes, trains and buses should be booked well in advance.

Official **public holidays** can also disrupt your travel plans, though not all public and bank holidays in Spain are observed in Catalunya, and vice versa. On the days listed below, and during the many local festivals (see Chapter 00), you'll find most shops closed, though bars and restaurants tend to stay open.

Barcelona's public holidays

January 1 Cap d'Any, New Year's Day
January 6 Epifanía, Epiphany
Easter Good Friday & Easter Monday
May 1 Dia del Treball, May Day/Labour Day
June 24 Dia de Sant Joan, St John's Day
August 15 L'Assumpció, Assumption of the Virgin
September 11 La Diada, Catalan National Day
September 24 Festa de la Mercè, Our Lady of Mercè, Barcelona's patron saint
October 12 Día de la Hispanidad, Spanish National Day
November 1 Tots Sants, All Saints' Day
December 6 Dia de la Constitució, Constitution Day
December 8 La Imaculada, Immaculate Conception
December 25 Nadal, Christmas Day
December 26 Sant Esteve, St Stephen's Day

Crime and personal safety

Barcelona has a reputation as a city plagued by petty crime. Popular prejudice blames the crime rate on immigration, but as usual this is a gross distortion of the facts. More to the point is that, because robbery without injury is treated as a misdemeanour under Spanish law, bag-snatchers and other thieves know that they can operate with near impunity. Tourists should stay alert to possible threats, and follow the basic security strategies outlined below. You will certainly encounter begging in Barcelona – people come here from other Spanish cities to beg – and while you can take many beggars at face value (whether or not you give them money), you should beware of people accosting you or who in any other manner try to distract you.

However, don't be unduly paranoid. Most of Barcelona is as safe as any other city you may be used to – and the potential for violent street crime is much lower than in Britain and the United States. Away from the city, in the Catalan countryside, most of the region is rural, friendly and safe, though do be on your guard at all times against bag-snatching.

Avoiding trouble

Almost all the problems tourists in Barcelona encounter are to do with **petty crime** – pickpocketing and bag-snatching – rather than more serious physical confrontations. Sensible precautions include: carrying bags slung across your body, not off one shoulder; not carrying anything in zipped pockets which you can't keep an eye on; having photocopies of your passport, leaving the original and any tickets in the hotel safe; never leaving your wallet in your back pocket; and noting down travellers' cheque and credit card numbers. Don't depend on moneybelts – good thieves know how they are carried and how to remove them.

The bottom end of the Ramblas and the medieval streets to either side are where you most need to be on your guard. Take the usual precautions at night: avoid unlit streets and dark alleys, don't go out brimming with valuables, and don't flash fancy cameras or look hopelessly lost in run-down areas. Other places to be especially wary are around the Sagrada Família and on the metro. Thieves often work in pairs, so watch out for people standing unusually close; keep a hand on your wallet or bag if it appears you're being distracted.

Some things to be aware of include:

• Being distracted by some very sophisticated operators, like the "helpful" person pointing out bird shit (shaving cream or something similar) on your jacket while someone relieves you of your money; the card or paper you're invited to read to distract your attention; the person trying to give you or sell you flowers, herbs, or small Catalan-flag stickers.

• In cafés and on *terrassas*, never leave your bags unzipped or on a neighbouring chair – place them where you can see or feel them, and loop a chair leg through a shoulder strap. Be careful of someone in a café making a move for your drink with one hand – the other hand will be in your bag as you react to save your drink.

• Don't leave anything in view in your car when you park it; take the radio with you. Vehicles are rarely stolen, but luggage and valuables left in cars do make a tempting target and rental cars are easy to spot. When driving in the city, keep all car doors locked, as thieves can easily snatch a bag from a car's back seat and run off, leaving the driver stranded. On Catalan highways, take precautions before pulling over to help apparently stranded motorists – in recent years foreigners have been robbed having been lured to pull over.

• Looking for hotel rooms, don't leave any bags unattended anywhere. This applies especially to buildings where the hotel or *hostal* is on the higher floors and you're tempted to leave baggage in the hallway or ground-floor lobby. Don't assume that your fellow dorm mates or travellers are honest just because they speak your language.

What to do if you're robbed

If you're robbed, you need to **go to the police** to report it, not least because your insurance company will require a police report. Don't expect a great deal of concern if your loss is relatively small – but do expect the process of completing forms and formalities to take ages.

In the unlikely event that you're **mugged**, or otherwise threatened, *never* resist; hand over what's wanted and run straight to the police, who will be more sympathetic on these occasions. For details of the main **police stations in Barcelona**, see p.244.

The police

There are four types of **police** – the Guàrdia Civil, the Policía Nacional, the municipal police known as the Guàrdia Urbana, and the Catalan Mossos d'Esquadra – all of them armed.

The **Guàrdia Civil**, in green uniforms and sometimes sporting black three-cornered hats, are a national police force and are formally a military organization but also investigate crime on a national (and, in some places, local) level. Traditionally associated with the oppressive Franco regime, their role in Catalunya has been gradually limited, though they can still be seen guarding some public buildings, and at airports and border crossings.

The **Policía Nacional** wear uniforms resembling blue combat gear and will normally only be seen in Barcelona. Here they operate primarily as an anti-crime force, which includes street patrols, investigations, checking papers of suspected illegal immigrants, and crowd control. If you are mugged or robbed in Barcelona, it is the Policía Nacional who will take your statement.

More visible on the streets of Barcelona and generally more sympathetic are the **Guàrdia Urbana**, in blue shirts and navy jackets, who are responsible for controlling the traffic. They are likely to be the first to respond to calls for help. They also guard the Ajuntament installations.

Catalunya also has its own autonomous police force, the **Mossos d'Esquadra**, whose navy-blue uniforms with red trim give them the aspect of bellhops rather than police. In Barcelona you'll see them guarding buildings that belong to the Generalitat, but in the countryside they are gradually taking over highway patrol and investigative duties from the Guàrdia Civil, as well as from the Policía Nacional in some large towns.

Sexual harassment

Sexual harassment is certainly a possibility in Barcelona but is probably no worse than in other European tourist destinations. In fact, Barcelona often seems a much safer place for women to walk the streets than London or New York, and there is little of the pestering that you have to contend with in, say, the larger French or Italian cities. However, without a very clear understanding of Catalan or Spanish it can be hard to deal with situations that do arise which you'd cope with quite routinely at home. Common sense should help you avoid getting into such situations in the first place, while using taxis to go home late at night (they are cheap and widely available) is always a good idea.

Offences

There are a few **offences** you might commit unwittingly that it's as well to be aware of.

• In theory you're supposed to carry some kind of **identification** at all times, and the police can stop you in the street and demand it. In practice they're rarely bothered if you're clearly a foreigner.

• While the **rules of the road** seem to be barely observed, to say the least, if you have an accident you can bet that, as a foreigner, it will be your fault. Try not to make a statement to anyone who doesn't speak fluent English.

• In theory at least, **drug** use is forbidden. You'll see signs in some bars saying "*no porros*" (no joints), which you should heed. However, in practice the police are little worried about personal use. Larger quantities (and any other drugs) are a very different matter.

Should you be **arrested** on any charge, you have the right to contact your **consulate** (see p.242 for the address), and although they're notoriously reluctant to get involved they are required to assist you to some degree if you have your passport stolen or lose all your money. If you've been detained for a drugs offence, don't expect any sympathy or help from your consulate.

Travellers with disabilities

Travellers with disabilities will find it easier to get around Barcelona than most other Spanish cities, but that's not saying a great deal. However, there are plenty of accessible hotels in Barcelona, while ramps and other forms of access are gradually being added to museums, sites and sports facilities. By law, all new public buildings are required to be fully accessible.

Planning a holiday

There are **organized tours** and holidays specifically for people with disabilities – the contacts below will be able to put you in touch with any specialists for trips to Barcelona. Remember, if you use a wheelchair, to have it serviced before you go and carry a repair kit.

Read your travel insurance small print carefully to make sure that people with a pre-existing medical condition are not excluded. And use your travel agent to make your journey simpler: airline or bus companies can cope better if they are expecting you, with a wheelchair provided at airports and staff primed to help. A medical certificate of your fitness to travel, provided by your doctor, is also extremely useful; some airlines or insurance companies may insist on it. Make sure that you have extra supplies of any drugs you need – carried with you if you fly – and a prescription including the generic name in case of emergency. Carry spares of any clothing or equipment that might be hard to find; if there's an association representing people with your disability, contact them early in the planning process.

In Barcelona

Arriving in Barcelona is reasonably straightforward. Barcelona's **airport** is fully accessible to travellers in wheelchairs, with adapted toilets, lifts to the various levels, and special lifts for access to and from the planes. The **Aerobús** is also equipped to take wheelchairs.

Getting around the city is more problematic since the **metro** system is perhaps the least wheelchair-friendly that can be imagined. Only line 2 is easily accessible, with elevators at major stations (including Universitat, Paral.lel, Passeig de Gràcia and Sagrada Família) from the street to the platforms. At **Barcelona Sants** there are no access ramps for the trains themselves, and the steps/escalators are fairly steep, but there are access ramps at Estació de França and a lift to the platforms at Plaça de Catalunya station. In addition, many city **buses** have been adapted for wheelchair use, with automatic ramps/steps and a designated wheelchair-space inside; simply ring the bell on the bus door. Some of the more useful wheelchair accessible lines are #24 (Carmel–Manso), #33 (Pedralbes–Verneda), #44 (Sants-Estació–Badalona), #47 (Canyelles–Plaça de Catalunya), #59 (Maria Cristina–Barceloneta) and #72 (Maria Cristina–Zona Franca). All night buses are also wheelchair-accessible. Hertz has **rental cars** with hand controls available in Barcelona (with advance notice), while if you need a **taxi** that's wheelchair-accessible, call Barna Taxi (℡933 577 755) or Taxi Móvil (℡933 581 111). Out on the **streets**, the only acoustic traffic-light signals are on Rambla de Catalunya and Plaça d'Espanya; and only some of the pavements in the newly renovated parts of town have graduated slopes at crossing points.

Most of the fully **wheelchair-accessible hotels** in Barcelona are in the more expensive price categories, though several others will do their best to accommodate travellers who are less mobile. The city tourist offices and information lines can provide accommodation suggestions, but you're strongly recommended to check on facilities directly with individual hotels in advance of your trip.

The **Institut Municipal de Disminuïts**, c/Llacuna 161, 3°, (Ⓜ Llacuna ℡932 918

400), has information on most aspects of life and travel in the city for disabled residents and visitors. It produces a booklet called *Guia d'Accessibilitat*, available from tourist offices, which, among other things, details the number and height of steps, width of doors, availability of ramps, lifts and adapted transport for a variety of museums, theatres, cinemas and other attractions in the city. If you're coming for the showpiece **attractions**, note that only the Fundacío Joan Miró, Fundacío Antoni Tàpies, La Pedrera, Caixa Forum, the Museu de la Ciència, Museu d'Història de Catalunya and the Palau de la Música are fully accessible; most old-town attractions, including the Museu Picasso, have steps or other impediments to access. The **city information line** – on ☎010 – also has accessibility information for hotels, restaurants, museums, bars and stores in Barcelona. And you can obtain a map showing accessible routes for disabled tourists from the Ajuntament information office in Plaça Sant Miquel, or the Transports Metropolitans de Barcelona (TMB) office in Universitat metro station.

The **Organización Nacional de Ciegos de España (ONCE)**, c/Calabria 66–76, Barcelona 08015 (☎933 259 200), sells a braille guidebook to Barcelona, provides information about restaurants that have braille menus, and can arrange trips for blind and visually impaired people; write for details.

Contacts for travellers with disabilities

UK and Ireland

Access Travel ☎01942/888844, ⓦwww.access-travel.co.uk. Tour operator that can arrange flights, transfer and accommodation, personally checking out places before recommendation.
Accessible City Breaks ☎01452/729739, ⓦwww.accessiblecitybreaks.co.uk. Organizes city breaks to Barcelona for wheelchair users, the

sensory impaired and slow walkers. Accessible accommodation guaranteed.
Holiday Care ☎0845/124 9971, ⓦwww.holidaycare.org.uk. Provides free lists of accessible accommodation abroad.
Irish Wheelchair Association Dublin ☎01/818 6400, ⓦwww.iwa.ie. Useful information provided about travelling abroad with a wheelchair.
Tripscope ☎0845/7585 641, ⓦwww.tripscope.org.uk. This registered charity provides a national telephone information service offering free advice on UK and international transport for those with a mobility problem.

US and Canada

Access-Able ⓦwww.access-able.com. Online resource for travellers with disabilities.
Directions Unlimited ☎1-800/533-5343 or 914/241-1700. Travel agency specializing in bookings for people with disabilities.
Mobility International USA ☎541/343-1284, ⓦwww.miusa.org. Information and referral services, access guides, tours and exchange programmes. Annual membership US$35 (includes quarterly newsletter).
Society for the Advancement of Travelers with Handicaps (SATH) ☎212/447-7284, ⓦwww.sath.org. Non-profit educational organization that has actively represented travellers with disabilities since 1976.
Wheels Up! ☎1-888/38-WHEELS, ⓦwww.wheelsup.com. Provides discounted airfare, tour and cruise prices for disabled travellers; also publishes a free monthly newsletter and has a comprehensive website.

Australia and New Zealand

ACROD (Australian Council for Rehabilitation of the Disabled) ☎02/6282 4333, ⓦwww.acrod.org.au. Provides lists of travel agencies and tour operators for people with disabilities.
Disabled Persons Assembly ☎04/801 9100, ⓦwww.dpa.org.nz. New Zealand resource centre with lists of travel agencies and tour operators for people with disabilities.

The City

The City

The Ramblas and the Old Town

t is a telling comment on Barcelona's character that one can recommend a single street – the **Ramblas** – as a highlight. No day in the city seems complete without a stroll down at least part of what, for Lorca, was "the only street in the world which I wish would never end". Lined with cafés, shops, restaurants and newspaper kiosks, and thronged by tourists, locals, buskers and performance artists, it's at the heart of Barcelona's life and self-image. There are important buildings and monuments along the way, but undoubtedly it's the street life which is the greatest attraction – and which you're a part of every time you set foot on Spain's most famous thoroughfare.

On either side of the Ramblas spreads Barcelona's **old town** (*ciutat vella*), bordered by Parc de la Ciutadella to the east and the slopes of Montjuïc to the west. Contained within this jumble of streets is a series of neighbourhoods – originally separate medieval parishes – that retain certain distinct characteristics today. By far the greatest concentration of interest is in the highly picturesque **Barri Gòtic**, east of the Ramblas, which curls out from around the cathedral. Here, the city's finest medieval buildings and churches are tucked into arcaded squares and skinny alleys, alongside several fascinating museums and the surviving portions of walls and buildings dating back to Roman times. On the west side of the Ramblas is **El Raval**, less of an obvious draw for tourists since it's traditionally been known as the city's red-light area. The neighbourhood still has some very dingy streets and seedy corners, though it's changing rapidly, particularly in the "upper Raval" around Barcelona's notable contemporary art museum, from which ripple out cutting-edge galleries, see-and-be-seen restaurants and fashionable bars.

East of the Barri Gòtic across the broad Via Laietana lie the other two old-town neighbourhoods, split by c/de la Princesa. **Sant Pere**, to the north, is in the throes of development around its revamped market, while **La Ribera**, to the south, has been transformed utterly in the last decade. Tourists always came down here to visit two of Barcelona's most popular sights – the graceful church of Santa María del Mar and the showpiece Museu Picasso – but the neighbourhood is possibly even better known now for the galleries, workshops, bars and restaurants of the **Born** district, which attract a hip, moneyed, local crowd. At the edge of La Ribera spreads **Parc de la Ciutadella**, the city's favourite park, loved by locals and tourists alike for its ornamental lake and gardens, palm-houses, museums and zoo. On lazy summer days here, the old town's historic intrigues and labyrinthine alleys seem a world away.

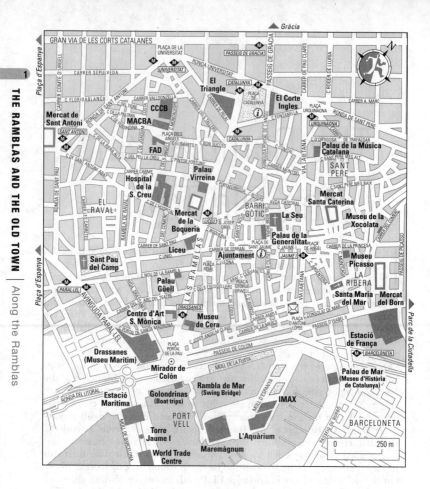

Along the Ramblas

Everyone starts with the **Ramblas**, the city's most famous feature. The name, derived from the Arabic *ramla* (or "sand"), refers to the bed of the seasonal stream which once flowed here. In the dry season, the channel was used as a road, and by the fourteenth century this had been paved over in recognition of its use as a link between the harbour and the old town. In the nineteenth century, benches and decorative trees were added, overlooked by stately balconied buildings, and today – in a city choked with traffic – this wide tree-lined swath is still given over to pedestrians, with cars forced up the narrow strips of road on either side. There are **metro stops** at Catalunya (top of the Ramblas), Liceu (middle) and Drassanes (bottom), or you can walk the entire length in about twenty minutes.

The first eccentricity is that the Ramblas are actually five separate streets strung head to tail – from north to south, Rambla Canaletes, Estudis, Sant Josep, Caputxins and Santa Mònica – though no one treats (or refers to) them as such. However, you will notice changes as you walk down the Ramblas, primarily that the streets on either side become a little less polished – seedier even – as you get closer to the harbour. The shops, meanwhile, reflect the mixed clientele, from patisseries to pizza takeaways, and stores selling hand-crafted jewellery to shops full of *sombreros*, bullfight posters ("your name here"), Simpsons T-shirts and Gaudí ashtrays. On the central avenue under the plane trees you'll find pet canaries, rabbits, tropical fish, flowers, plants, postcards and books. You can buy sunglasses from a blanket stretched out on the ground, cig-arettes from itinerant salespeople, have your palm read and your portrait paint-ed, or just listen to the buskers and watch the pavement artists. Human statues are much in evidence and will take any coins you can spare; card and dice sharps, operating from foldaway tables and cardboard boxes, will skin you for much more if you let them.

The show goes on at night, too, as people stroll arm in arm from newspaper stall to café before heading off for a meal or a drink. Later, in the small hours, there are still plenty of folk around, drinking in the late-opening bars or chat-ting on the street. Drag yourself home with the dawn, and you'll rub shoulders with the street cleaners hosing down the pavements, watchful policemen and bleary-eyed stallholders. If you're around when Barça wins an important match you'll catch the Ramblas at its best: the street erupts with instant and infectious excitement, as fans drive up and down with their hands on the horn, cars bedecked with Catalan flags, and pedestrians wave champagne bottles.

> ### The Ramblas statues
>
> You can't move for human statues on the Ramblas, and there's no end either to the inventiveness of the protagonists or to the enthusiasm of the general public for this most inexplicable of art forms. As fads and fashions change, Greek statues and Charlie Chaplins have given way to movie characters from *Planet of the Apes* or *Gladiator*, standing immobile on their little home-made plinths, daring you to catch them out in a blink. Some join in the fun – "Mr Burns" and "Lisa Simpson" posing jauntily for photographs, "Matador" swirling a cape for the camera, "Orange Twirly Girl" windmilling her streamers as money is dropped in front of her. Many are actors (or at least waiters who say they're actors), and others make a claim to art – how else to begin to explain "Silver Cowboy", lounging on the railings at Liceu metro, or "Tree Sprite", clinging chameleon-like to one of the Ramblas plane trees. Then there's the plain weird, like "Lady Under Rock", her bottom half crushed under a boulder, issuing plaintive shrieks at passers-by. And for the truly annoying, look no further than "Manuel" from *Fawlty Towers*, astride an ostrich – of course – who has a nasty habit of creeping up behind you and shouting in your ear. They all put in long hours on the Ramblas, gratefully receiving small change, though tourists or no tourists, many of them would probably just turn up anyway, lock the bicycle, put down the battered suitcase and strike the pose. What else is a statue going to do?

Plaça de Catalunya

The huge **Plaça de Catalunya** is many people's first real view of Barcelona, with trains from the airport depositing visitors at the underground station on its western flank. Laid out in its present form in the 1920s, the pigeon-choked square is right at the heart of the city, with the old town and port below it, and the planned Eixample above and beyond. The central gardens, statues, circular fountains, main city tourist office, and bus and metro stops, make it something of a tourist magnet, yet it's also the focal point for local festivals and demon-strations. The most prominent monument is the towering angular slab and bust dedicated to **Francesc Macià**, leader of the Republican Left, parliamentary deputy for Barcelona and first president of the Generalitat, who died in office in 1933. It was commissioned from the pioneer of Catalan avant-garde sculpture, Josep María Subirachs, perhaps best known for his continuing work on the Sagrada Família.

For most visitors, an initial orientation point is the massive white-faced **El Corte Inglés** department store on the eastern side of the square, whose ninth-floor cafeteria has some stupendous views. On the southwest side, over the road from the top of the Ramblas, **El Triangle** shopping centre makes another landmark. Incorporated in its ground floor is the **Café Zurich**, a traditional Barcelona meeting place, whose ranks of outdoor tables – patrolled by supercilious waiters – are a day-long draw for beggars, buskers and pan-pipe bands.

Rambla Canaletes and Estudis

Heading down from Plaça de Catalunya, the first two stretches of the Ramblas are **Rambla Canaletes**, with its iron fountain (a drink from which supposedly means you'll never leave Barcelona), and **Rambla Estudis**, named after the university (L'Estudi General) that was sited here until the beginning of the eighteenth century. This part is also known locally as "Rambla dels Ocells", as it contains a bird market, the little captives squawking away from a line of cages on either side of the street.

It seems hard to believe, but the Ramblas was a war zone during the Spanish Civil War as the city erupted into factionalism. **Café Moka** (on the left, at no. 126) was occupied in 1937 by the Guàrdia Civil, whose members were sniped at by George Orwell and his POUM colleagues from across the street. Further down on the right, the restored **Església de Betlem** was begun in 1681, built in Baroque style for the Jesuits, but destroyed inside during the Civil War. Consequently, the interior is plain in the extreme, though the main facade on c/del Carme sports a fine sculpted portal and relief. Opposite the church, the arcaded **Palau Moja** at no. 188 (Tues–Sat 10am–8pm, Sun 10am–3pm; free) dates from the late eighteenth century and still retains an exterior staircase and elegant great hall. The ground floor of the building, restored by the Generalitat, is now a cultural bookshop, while the interior is open for exhibitions – the entrance is around the corner in c/Portaferrissa. Take a look, too, at the illustrated tiles above the **fountain** at the start of c/Portaferrissa, which show the medieval gate (the *Porta Ferriça*) and market that once stood here. The streets west of here, towards Avinguda del Portal del Àngel, are good for shopping, especially for clothes.

Palau de la Virreina

The graceful eighteenth-century **Palau de la Virreina** stands at no. 99 (ⓂLiceu), on the corner of c/del Carme, set back slightly from the Ramblas. Commissioned by a Peruvian viceroy, Manuel Amat, and named after the wife who survived him, its five Ramblas-facing bays are adorned with pilasters and Rococo windows. Today the building is used to house changing exhibitions of art and photography – during the Mercè festival celebrations in September it's here that pictures of the previous year's celebration are displayed. Walk through the entrance to where glassed-in arches display some of the Carnival giants (*gegants vells*), once used to entertain the city's orphans but now an integral part of Barcelona's festival parades. The ground floor of the palace also has a good shop (Tues–Sat 10am–8.30pm), featuring locally produced *objets d'art* and other items relating to the city, and there is a walk-in **information centre** and ticket office (see p.213) for cultural events run by the Ajuntament.

La Boqueria and around

Beyond the Palau de la Virreina starts **Rambla Sant Josep**, the switch in names marked by the sudden profusion of flower stalls – it's sometimes known as "Rambla de les Flors". The city's glorious main food market is over to the right, officially the Mercat Sant Josep though referred to locally as **La Boqueria** (Mon–Sat 6am–8pm; Ⓦ www.ac-boqueria.com). Built on the site of a former convent between 1836 and 1840, the cavernous hall stretches back from the high wrought-iron entrance arch facing the Ramblas. It's a riot of noise and colour, as popular with locals who come here to shop daily as with snap-happy tourists. Everything radiates out from the central banks of fish and seafood stalls – great piles of fruit and vegetables, bunches of herbs and pots of spices, baskets of wild mushrooms, mounds of cheese and sausage, racks of bread, hanging hams, and meat counters dripping blood into the gutters below. If you're going to buy, do some browsing first, as the flagship fruit and veg stalls by the entrance tend to have higher prices than those further inside. There are also some excellent stand-up snack bars in here, like the *Bar Central La Boqueria* (see p.177), while for Boqueria cooking classes see p.183.

Past the market is the part of the Ramblas known as **Plaça de la Boqueria** marked (in the middle of the pavement) by a large round **mosaic by Joan Miró**, just one of a number of the artist's city works. Here too are a couple of *modernista*-decorated buildings, rare enough in this part of town to be worth a second glance. On the left, at no. 82, Josep Vilaseca's **Casa Bruno Quadros** was built in the 1890s to house an umbrella store – its unusual facade is decorated with a green dragon and Oriental designs, and scattered with parasols. On the other side of the Ramblas, a *farmàcia* and a cake shop get the treatment: the Genové at no. 77 (from 1911) and, more impressively, the **Antiga Casa Figueras** at no. 83. Redesigned in 1902, the latter overdoses on stained glass and mosaics, and sports a corner relief of a female reaper.

Gran Teatre del Liceu

Facing the Ramblas at c/de Sant Pau is the restored **Gran Teatre del Liceu** (ⓂLiceu), Barcelona's celebrated opera house, which burned down for the third time in 1994, when a worker's blowtorch set fire to the scenery during last-minute alterations to an opera set (many believe the accident was staged and that arson was the cause). The building has had an unfortunate history, to say the least. Founded in 1847, it was first rebuilt after a fire in 1861 to become Spain's grandest opera house. Regarded as a bastion of the city's late nineteenth-century commercial and intellectual classes, the Liceu was devastated again in 1893, when an anarchist threw two bombs into the stalls during a production of *William Tell*. He was acting in revenge for the recent execution of a fellow anarchist assassin – twenty people died in the bombing. More recently, Montserrat Caballé, widely acknowledged as Spain's greatest living soprano, won a court battle to become one of the first women to join the 150-year-old all-male Cercle del Liceu club at the opera house. The singer, who has appeared more than a hundred times at the Liceu and contributed to its restoration, used Spain's equal opportunities laws to change entrance rules to the club.

The latest restoration added a rather large and unsightly extension, the Espai Liceu, which runs south along the Ramblas. It's from here that you embark on tours of the opera house (daily 10am, 11am, noon & 1pm; €5.50; ⓦwww.liceubarcelona.com), which show you the lavishly decorated auditorium. Or you can simply contemplate the exterior from across the way, in the famous Café de l'Opera. This drinking spot has long been a fashionable meeting place and a favourite for post-performance refreshments for audience and performers alike. Inside, it's not as pricey as you might imagine from the period furnishings and white-coated waiters, though if you score an outside table on the Ramblas you can expect to pay a little more than usual for your drinks.

From the Liceu to the harbour

After the Liceu, attractions just off the Ramblas include the Palau Güell down c/Nou de la Rambla (see p.62) and, on the opposite side, the lovely Plaça Reial (see p.52). Sticking with the Ramblas itself, the avenue widens out as it heads for the harbour, with the two final attractions sited on the last named stretch of the Ramblas, the Rambla de Santa Mònica (ⓜDrassanes). On the right, at no. 7, a seventeenth-century convent houses the Centre d'Art Santa Mònica (Tues–Sat 11am–8pm, Sun 11am–3pm; free), approached by a ramp, which displays temporary exhibitions of contemporary art. Pavement artists and palm readers occasionally set up stalls outside here on the Ramblas, augmented on weekend afternoons by a small street market selling jewellery and ornaments.

The city's wax museum, the Museu de Cera (July–Sept daily 10am–10pm; Oct–June Mon–Fri 10am–1.30pm & 4–7.30pm, Sat & Sun 11am–2pm & 4.30–8.30pm; €6.65; ⓦwww.museocerabcn.com), is located on the opposite side of the Ramblas, at nos. 4–6, in an impressive nineteenth-century bank building; the entrance is along Ptge. de Banca. You might get dragged in by your children but, otherwise, you could resist its lure since it's of little relevance to Barcelona, or even Spain, being the usual trawl through the internationally famous and infamous, plus dated film characters, a mixed bag of public figures from Mother Teresa to Yasser Arafat, and underwater and space capsule simulations. However, it is worth poking your head into the museum's extraordinary bar, the *Bosc de les Fades* (see p.199), while for true kitsch value there are night visits every Saturday at 8.30pm and 9.30pm (€12, drink included; Spanish only) with actors and special effects ratcheting up the atmosphere.

By now, you've almost reached the foot of the Ramblas, passing Drassanes metro station to be confronted by the column at the very bottom of the avenue that's topped by a statue of Columbus. For this, the neighbouring maritime museum and the rest of the harbour area, see the next chapter.

The Barri Gòtic

The Barri Gòtic, or Gothic Quarter (ⓜJaume I), forms the very heart of the old town, spreading out from the east side of the Ramblas. Within lies a remarkable concentration of beautiful medieval buildings dating principally from the fourteenth and fifteenth centuries, when Barcelona reached the height of her commercial prosperity before being absorbed into the burgeoning kingdom of Castile. It will take the best part of a day to see everything here, with the cathedral – La Seu – a particular highlight, and you certainly won't want to miss the archeological remains at the Museu d'Història de la Ciutat or the unclassifiable collections of the Museu Frederic Marès. That said, sauntering through the medieval alleys and hogging a café table in one of the lovely squares is just as much an attraction.

The picture-postcard images of the Barri Gòtic are largely based on the streets north of c/de Ferran and c/de Jaume I, where tourists throng the boutiques, bars, restaurants, museums and galleries. South of here – from Plaça Reial and c/d'Avinyo to the harbour – the Barri Gòtic is rather more traditional (or sometimes just plain run-down). There are no specific sights or museums in this section, though there are plenty of great cafés, tapas bars and restaurants – just take care at night in the poorly lit streets.

Plaça de Sant Jaume

The quarter is centred on **Plaça de Sant Jaume**, a spacious square at the end of the main c/de Ferran, which runs east from the Ramblas. Once the site of Barcelona's Roman forum and marketplace, it's now one venue for the weekly dancing by local people of the Catalan folk dance, the *sardana* (Sun at 6.30pm), as well as the traditional site of demonstrations and gatherings.

The square contains two of the city's most significant buildings. On the south side stands the restored town hall, the **Ajuntament**, parts of which date from as early as 1373 though the Neoclassical facade is nineteenth-century, added when the square was laid out. You get a much better idea of the grandeur of the original structure by nipping around the corner, down c/de la Ciutat, for a view of the former main entrance. It's a typically exuberant Catalan-Gothic facade, but was badly damaged during renovations in the nineteenth century. Entering the building from Plaça de Sant Jaume, you can take a look at the lovely wall paintings, the work of Catalan artist Albert Rafols Casamada. On Sundays (10am–2pm; free) you're allowed further into the building, particularly to see the most interesting part, the restored fourteenth-century council chamber, the **Saló de Cent**, on the first floor.

Right across the square rises the **Palau de la Generalitat**, traditional home of the Catalan government, from where the short-lived Catalan Republic was proclaimed in April 1931. Begun in 1418, this presents its best – or at least its oldest – aspect around the side on c/del Bisbe, where the early fifteenth-century facade by Marc Safont contains a spirited medallion portraying St George and the Dragon. (Incidentally, the enclosed Gothic bridge across the narrow street – the so-called Bridge of Sighs – is an anachronism, added in 1928, though it's at one with its surroundings and features on many a postcard of the "Gothic" quarter.) Through the palace's Renaissance main entrance, facing the square, there's a beautiful cloister on the first floor with superb coffered ceilings, while opening off this gallery are two fine rooms – the chapel and salon of **Sant Jordi** (St George, patron saint of Catalunya as well as England), also by Safont – and other chambers of the former law courts. You can visit the interior on a **guided tour** (frequently in English) on the second and fourth Sunday of each month (every 20min 10am–2pm; free). The Generalitat is also traditionally open to the public on April 23 (expect a 2hr wait) – the **Dia de Sant Jordi** – when the whole square is festooned with bookstalls and flower sellers. Celebrated as a nationalist holiday in Catalunya, St George's Day is also a kind of local Valentine's Day: tradition has it that men give their sweethearts a rose and receive a book in return. Consequently, the stalls set up on Plaça de Sant Jaume and the Ramblas are mobbed all day with customers.

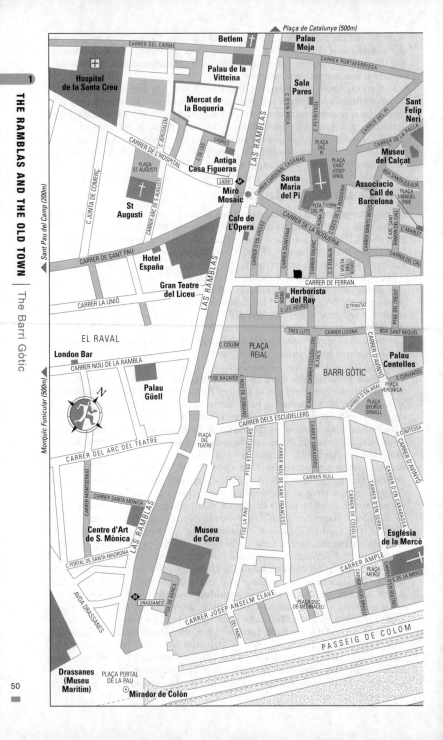

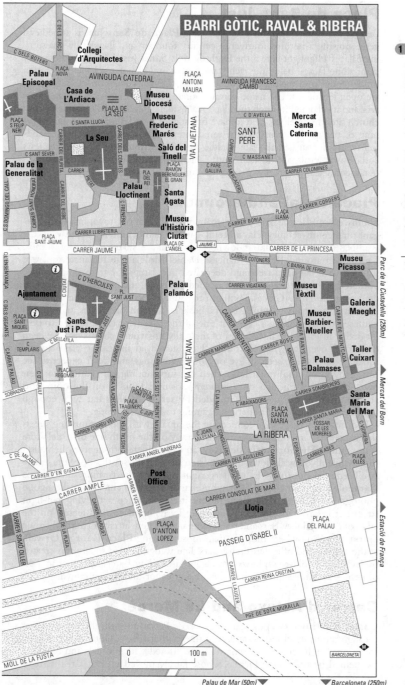

BARRI GÒTIC, RAVAL & RIBERA

C DELS BOTERS

C DELS ARCS

Collegi d'Arquitectes

PLAÇA NOVA

Palau Episcopal

AVINGUDA CATEDRAL

PLAÇA ANTONI MAURA

AVINGUDA FRANCESC CAMBO

Casa de L'Ardiaca

Museu Diocesá

C D'AVELLA

Mercat Santa Caterina

PLAÇA DE LA SEU

PLAÇA S FELIP NERI

C SANTA LLUCIA

Museu Frederic Marés

SANT PERE

C MASSANET

La Seu

C SANT SEVER

C SANTA LLUCIA

Saló del Tinell

CARRER COLOMINES

Palau de la Generalitat

CARRER DELS COMTES

PLAÇA RAMON BERENGUER EL GRAN

C PARE GALLIFA

CARRER CORDERS

CARRER DEL BISBE

Palau Lloctinent

PLA. DEL REI

Santa Agata

PLAÇA LLANA

CARRER BORIA

CS DOMINGO DEL CALL

CARRER SANT HONORAT

C FRENERIA

Museu d'Història Ciutat

PLAÇA SANT JAUME

CARRER LLIBRETERIA

PLAÇA DE L'ANGEL

JAUME I

CARRER DE LA PRINCESA

CARRER JAUME I

Museu Picasso

Parc de la Ciutadella (250m)

CARRER COTONERS

C.BARRA DE FERRO

C D'HERCULES

C DAGUERIA

Palau Palamós

CARRER VIGATANS

C CARASSA

Museu Tèxtil

C L'ENSENYANÇA

PL. SANT JUST

Galeria Maeght

Ajuntament

C DELS GEGANTS

PLAÇA SANT MIQUEL

Sants Just i Pastor

C PALMA SANT JUST

CARRER GRUNYI

Museu Barbier-Mueller

CARRER DE MONTCADA

CARRER ARGENTERIA

CARRER BANYS VELLS

Taller Cuixart

Mercat del Born

C BELLAFILA

C TEMPLARIS

CARRER DELS MIRALLERS

Palau Dalmases

CARRER ROSIC

CARRER PALAU

PLAÇA REGOMIR

CARRER MANRESA

Santa Maria del Mar

SOBRADIEL

C D'ATAULF

CARRER POU DE FIGA

PLAÇA TRAGINERS

C JUPI

CARRER SOMBRERERS

C VIDRIERA

C REGOMIR

HISTAL D'EN SOL

TINENT NAVARRO

C LA NAU

C ABAIXADORS

PLAÇA SANTA MARIA

CARRER SANTA MARIA

PLAÇA OLLES

C DE MILANS

CARRER CORREU VELL

C JOAN MASSANA

FOSSAR DE LES MORERES

CARRER D'EN GIGNAS

CARRER ANGEL BAIXERAS

CONSELLERS

LA RIBERA

CARRER ASES

CARRER MIRALLERS

C CANVIS VELLS

CESPASERIA

CARRER AMPLE

Post Office

CARRER DELS AGULLERS

Estació de França

CARRER SIMÓ OLLER

CARRER DE LA PLATA

CARRER MARQUET

CARRER FUSTERIA

PLAÇA D'ANTONI LOPEZ

CARRER CONSOLAT DE MAR

Llotja

PLAÇA DEL PALAU

PASSEIG D'ISABEL II

CARRER LAUDER

CARRER REINA CRISTINA

MOLL DE LA FUSTA

PGE DE SOTA MURALLA

BARCELONETA

0   100 m

Palau de Mar (50m) ▼   ▼ Barceloneta (250m)

Plaça de Sant Just

Behind the Ajuntament, off c/de la Ciutat, **Plaça de Sant Just** is a medieval gem, sporting a restored fourteenth-century fountain and flanked by unassuming palaces. Highlight here is the **Església dels Sants Just i Pastor**, whose very plain stone facade belies the rich stained glass and elaborate chapel decoration inside (enter from the back, at c/de la Ciutat; the main doors on Pl. de Sant Just are open less often). The name commemorates the city's earliest Christian martyrs, and it's claimed (though there's no real evidence) that this is the oldest parish church site in Barcelona, held to have first supported a foundation at the beginning of the ninth century; the restored interior, though, dates from the mid-fourteenth century. In the late Middle Ages it was the only place where Jews could swear legal oaths in deals with Christians, and even today a last will and testament declared verbally here has the full force of a written document.

Plaça Reial and around

Southwest of Plaça de Sant Jaume, many people's first old-town halt is the elegant nineteenth-century **Plaça Reial** – it's hidden behind an archway, off the Ramblas (to the left, walking down; ⓂLiceu) and is surprisingly easy to miss. Laid out in around 1850 by Francesc Daniel Molina, the Italianate square is studded with tall palm trees and decorated iron lamps (by the young Gaudí), bordered by high, pastel-coloured arcaded buildings, and centred on a fountain depicting the Three Graces. Taking in the sun at one of the benches puts you in strange company – punks, bikers, buskers, Catalan eccentrics, tramps and bemused tourists taking a coffee at one of the pavement cafés. It used to be a bit dodgy in Plaça Reial, but most of the really unsavoury characters have been driven off over the years as tourists have staked an increasing claim to the square. Nonetheless, keep an eye on your belongings, and don't expect to see too many locals until night falls, when the surrounding bars come into their own. If you pass through on a Sunday morning, look in on the **coin and stamp market** (10am–2pm), attended by serious dealers but with enough lightweight exhibits and frenetic bargaining to be entertaining.

The arcaded passageways connecting the square with the surrounding streets throw up a few interesting sights. Tucked away on the north side on c/del Vidre is the quirky **Herboristeria del Rey**, an early nineteenth-century herbalist's shop, while if you walk down the opposing alley on the south side of the square you'll emerge on c/dels Escudellers, right opposite the turning spits of **Los Caracoles** restaurant (see p.183), whose ranks of grilled chickens make a good photograph. **Carrer dels Escudellers** itself was once a thriving red-light street but it has gradually hauled itself up by its bootlaces and teeters on the edge of respectability. Bars and restaurants around here attract a youthful crowd on the whole, nowhere more so than those flanking **Plaça George Orwell**, at the eastern end of c/dels Escudellers. The wedge-shaped square was created by levelling an old-town block – a favoured tactic in Barcelona to let in a bit of light – and it has quickly become a hangout for the grunge crowd.

Carrer d'Avinyo and La Mercè

Carrer d'Avinyo, running south from c/de Ferran towards the harbour, cuts through the most atmospheric part of the southern Barri Gòtic. Again, it used to be a red-light district of some renown, littered with brothels and bars, and frequented by the young Picasso, whose family moved into the area in 1895 (see box on p.66). It still looks the part – a narrow thoroughfare lined with dark overhanging buildings – but the fashionable cafés and boutiques tell the story of its recent gentrification. The locals aren't overly enamoured of the influx of bar-crawling fun-seekers – banners and notices along the length of this and neighbouring streets plead with visitors to keep the noise down.

Carrer d'Avinyo ends at the junction with **Carrer Ample** ("wide street"), the latter an aristocratic address in the eighteenth century. Here, in the neighbourhood known as **La Mercè**, lived nobles and merchants enriched by Barcelona's maritime trade, though most fashionable families took the opportunity to move north to the Eixample later in the nineteenth century. The streets of La Mercè – just a block from the harbour – took on an earthier hue, and for years this has been a place to come and frequent the characteristic old-style **taverns** known as *tascas* or *bodegas*. Carrers Ample, Mercè and d'en Gignas sport a fine array of these (see p.177 for reviews of the best), most of them defiantly unfashionable, though even here are signs of encroaching yuppiedom.

At Plaça de la Mercè, the eighteenth-century **Església de la Mercè** is the focus of one of the city's biggest annual celebrations, the Festa de la Mercè every September, dedicated to the patroness of Barcelona. The church was burned in 1936 but the gilt side-chapels, stained-glass medallions and apse murals have been authentically restored. The square outside was remodelled in the twentieth century around its statue of Neptune, though the more pleasing local square is the older **Plaça Duc de Medinaceli**, a block to the west, with its palms and commemorative cast-iron column saluting a Catalan admiral.

La Seu

North of Plaça de Sant Jaume, Barcelona's cathedral, **La Seu** (daily 8am–1.30pm & 4–7.30pm; Sat & Sun opens 1hr later in the afternoon; free), is one of the great Gothic buildings of Spain. Located just behind the Generalitat, on a site previously occupied by a Roman temple, it was begun in 1298 and finished in 1448, with one notable exception commented on by Richard Ford in 1845: "The principal facade is unfinished, with a bold front poorly painted in stucco, although the rich chapter have for three centuries received a fee on every marriage for this very purpose of completing it." Perhaps goaded into action, the authorities set to and completed the facade within a ten-year period in the 1880s. Some critics complain that this delay cost the cathedral its architectural harmony, though the facade is Gothic enough for most tastes – and is seen to startling effect at night when it's floodlit.

The **interior** used to have a reputation for being gloomy and ponderous, the result of a shortage of windows in the clerestory. Artificial lighting, however, has transformed the place, replacing the dank mystery with a soaring airiness to echo the grandeur of the exterior. The cathedral is dedicated to Santa Eulàlia, who was martyred by the Romans for daring to prefer Christianity, and her tomb rests in a crypt beneath the high altar; if you put money in the slot the whole thing lights up.

See, too, the rich altarpieces, and carved tombs of the 29 side-chapels. Among the finest of these are the painted wooden tombs reputedly belonging to Ramon Berenguer I (Count of Barcelona from 1035 to 1076) and his wife Almodis, but which actually hold the remains of an earlier count and Petronila, the Aragonese princess whose betrothal to Ramon Berenguer IV united Aragon and Barcelona. Ramon Berenguer I is revered for having established many of the *usatges*, the first codified Catalan laws, although these were in fact drafted by Ramon Berenguer IV, who cleverly claimed that they dated back earlier, in order to stifle criticism. The colossal Muslim's head below the organ is a replacement for one that used to vomit sweets on *el Día dels Inocents* (Feast of the Holy Innocents, Dec 28), the Spanish equivalent of April Fool's Day.

The most renowned part of the cathedral is its magnificent fourteenth-century **cloister** (daily 8.45am–1.15pm & 4–7pm; free), which looks over a lush tropical garden complete with soaring palm trees and – more unusually – honking white geese. If they disturb the tranquillity of the scene, they do so for a purpose: geese have been kept here for over five hundred years, either (depending on which story you believe) to reflect the virginity of Santa Eulàlia or as a reminder of the erstwhile Roman splendour of Barcelona (geese having been kept on the Capitoline Hill in Rome). The cloister opens onto various small chapels and church offices, as well as the small **Museu de la Catedral** (daily 10am–1pm & 5–7pm; €1). This incorporates the Sala Capitular (Chapter House), with its ageing leather seats and assorted and unexceptional fifteenth-century religious paintings.

Plaça de la Seu and Plaça Nova

Outside the cathedral on **Plaça de la Seu**, occupying a renovated fourth-century Roman tower, is the **Museu Diocesà-La Pia Almonia** (Tues–Sat 10am–2pm & 5–8pm, Sun 11am–2pm; €2). This is a small and impressive collection of religious art and artefacts from around Barcelona, including the frescoes of the Apocalypse from a church in Polinyà and some great retables, including one of St Bartholomew being skinned alive. In front of here, the wide, pedestrianized Avinguda de la Catedral hosts an **antiques market** every Thursday, and there's a **Christmas craft fair** held here every December.

Flanking the cathedral, on the west side of Plaça de la Seu, are two fifteenth-century buildings closely associated with it. The **Casa de l'Ardiaca** (once the archdeacon's residence, now the city archives) boasts a tiny cloistered and tiled courtyard with a small fountain, while the **Palau Episcopal**, just beyond on c/del Bisbe, was the bishop's palace and built on a grander scale altogether. Though you're not allowed inside either building, you can go as far as both courtyards to see their fine outdoor stairways, a frequent local feature; there's a patio at the top of the Palau Episcopal's stairway with Romanesque wall paintings. Next to the Palau Episcopal, some of the city's remaining **Roman walls** are clearly visible – they once entirely enclosed the Barri Gòtic, though were largely pulled down in the nineteenth century.

The large **Plaça Nova**, facing the cathedral, marks one of the medieval entrances to the old town – north of it, you're fast entering the wider streets and more regular contours of the modern city. Even if you're sticking with the Barri Gòtic for now, walk over to study the frieze surmounting the modern College of Architects, the **Collegi d'Arquitectes** (Mon–Fri 10am–9pm, Sat 10am–2pm; free) on the other side of the square. Designed in 1960 from sketches supplied by Picasso, it has a crude, almost graffiti-like quality, at odds with the more stately buildings to the side. Picasso himself refused to come to Spain to oversee the work, unwilling to return to his home country while Franco was still in power. Temporary exhibitions inside the college concentrate on architectural matters.

Plaça del Rei and around

The cathedral and its associated buildings aside, the most concentrated batch of historic monuments in the Barri Gòtic is the grouping around the neat **Plaça del Rei**, behind the cathedral apse. The square was once the courtyard of the

△ Fountain head in the Barri Gòtic

rambling palace of the counts of Barcelona, and across it stairs climb to the great fourteenth-century **Saló del Tinell**, the palace's main hall. It was on the steps leading from the Saló del Tinell into the Plaça del Rei that Ferdinand and Isabella stood to receive Columbus on his triumphant return from his famous voyage of 1492. With the old town streets packed, Columbus advanced in procession with the monarchs to the palace, where he presented the queen with booty from the trip – exotic birds, sweet potatoes and six "Indians" (actually Haitians, taken on board on Columbus' return). The hall itself is a fine, spacious example of secular Gothic architecture, with interior arches spanning 17m. At one time the Spanish Inquisition met here, taking full advantage of the popular belief that the walls would move if a lie was spoken. Nowadays it hosts temporary exhibitions, while concerts are occasionally held in the hall or outside in the square. The palace buildings also include the romantic Renaissance **Torre del Rei Martí,** which rises above one corner of the square, as well as the beautiful fourteenth-century **Capella de Santa Agata**, with its tall single nave and fine Gothic retable. All can be seen more closely during a visit to the Museu d'Història de la Ciutat (see below), though the tower is currently closed for restoration.

The mid-sixteenth-century **Palau del Lloctinent**, the former viceroy's palace, has a facade facing the Plaça del Rei and another fine courtyard with staircase and coffered ceiling (enter on c/dels Comtes). Around the corner from here, down c/Paradís at no. 10, the little interior courtyard of the Centre Excursionista de Catalunya conceals some original Corinthian columns from the city's **Temple Romà d'Agusti**. To see the best-preserved sections of Barcelona's **Roman city walls**, walk around to Plaça Ramon Berenguer el Gran, at Via Laietana. Some of the fourth-century walls and towers here are over 13m high, and back onto the chapel of Santa Agata on Plaça del Rei.

Museu d'Història de la Ciutat

The building that closes off the rest of Plaça del Rei is the Casa Clariana-Padellás, a fifteenth-century mansion moved here brick by brick from nearby c/Mercaders in the early 1930s. It houses the splendid **Museu d'Història de la Ciutat** (June–Sept Tues–Sat 10am–8pm, Sun 10am–3pm; Oct–May Tues–Sat 10am–2pm & 4–8pm, Sun 10am–2pm; €4, first Sat of the month free; ⓦwww.museuhistoria.bcn.es), which is entered from c/del Veguer. Quite apart from the chance to see the interiors of the Plaça del Rei's finest buildings, and learn something of the city's long history from its exhibitions, the museum's crucial draw is its underground archeological section – nothing less than the extensive remains of the Roman city of Barcino. Descending in the elevator (the floor indicator shows "12 BC"), you are deposited onto walkways that run along the 4000 square metres excavated thus far, stretching under Plaça del Rei and the surrounding streets as far as the cathedral. The remains date from the first century BC to the sixth century AD and reflect the transition from Roman to Visigothic rule – at the end of the sixth century, a church was erected on top of the old Roman salt-fish factory, the foundations of which are preserved down here almost in its entirety. Not much survives above chest height, but explanatory diagrams show the extent of the streets, walls and buildings – from lookout towers to laundries – while models, mosaics, murals and displays of excavated goods help flesh out the reality of daily life in Barcino. This really is one not to miss.

Museu Frederic Marès

Another extraordinary display greets visitors in the **Museu Frederic Marès** (Tues–Sat 10am–7pm, Sun 10am–3pm; €3, Wed afternoon & first Sun of month free; ⓦ www.museumares.bcn.es), which occupies a further wing of the old royal palace, behind Plaça del Rei; the entrance is through Plaça de Sant Iu, off c/dels Comtes. The large arcaded courtyard, studded with orange trees, is one of the most romantic in the old town, and the summer café here (see p.174) makes a perfect place to take a break from sightseeing.

Frederic Marès (1893–1991) was a sculptor, painter and restorer who more or less single-handedly (like France's Viollet-le-Duc) restored, often not entirely accurately, Catalunya's decaying medieval treasures in the early twentieth century. The ground and basement floors of the museum consist of his personal collection of medieval sculpture – an important body of work that includes a comprehensive collection of wooden crucifixes showing the stylistic development of this form from the twelfth to the fifteenth centuries. There are also antiquities, from Roman busts to Hellenistic terracotta lamps, while the craftsmanship of medieval masons is displayed in a series of rooms focusing on carved doorways, cloister fragments, sculpted capitals and alabaster tombs. However, it's the upper two floors, housing Marès' personal collectibles, that tend to make jaws drop. These present an incredible retrospective jumble gathered during fifty years of travel, with entire rooms devoted to keys and locks, pipes, cigarette cards and snuffboxes, fans, gloves and brooches, playing cards, draughtsmen's tools, walking sticks, dolls' houses, toy theatres, old gramophones and archaic bicycles, to list just a sample of what's on show. In the artist's library on the second floor, some of Marès' own reclining nudes, penitent saints and bridling stags give an insight into his more orthodox work.

Santa María del Pi and around

With the cathedral area and Plaça del Rei sucking in every visitor at some point during the day, the third focus of attraction is to the west, around the church of Santa María del Pi – five minutes' walk from the cathedral or just two minutes from the Ramblas (ⓜLiceu).

The fourteenth-century **Església de Santa María del Pi** stands at the heart of three delightful little squares. Burned out in 1936, and restored in the 1960s, the church boasts a Romanesque door but is mainly Catalan-Gothic in style, with just a single nave with chapels between the buttresses. The rather plain interior only serves to set off some marvellous stained glass, the most impressive of which is contained within a huge rose window, often claimed (rather boldly) as the largest in the world. The church stands on the middle square, **Plaça Sant Josep Oriol**, the prettiest of the three, overhung with balconies and scattered with seats from the *Bar del Pi*. Buskers and street performers often appear in the square, while the whole area becomes an **artists' market** at the weekend (Sat 11am–8pm, Sun 11am–2pm). Incidentally, the squares on either side – Plaça del Pi and Placeta del Pi – are named, like the church, for the pine tree that once stood here.

Head east from Plaça Sant Josep Oriol, back towards the cathedral, and behind the Palau Episcopal you'll stumble upon **Plaça Sant Felip Neri**, scarred by a bomb dropped during the Civil War and now used as a playground by the children at the square's school. Antoni Gaudí walked here every evening after work at the Sagrada Família to hear Mass at the eighteenth-century church of Sant Felip Neri. Many of the other buildings that now hedge in the small square come from other points in the city and have been reassembled here over the last fifty years. One of these, the former headquarters of the city's shoemakers' guild, houses a footwear museum, the **Museu del Calçat** (Tues–Sun 11am–2pm; €1.80). Although not Barcelona's best museum, the collection of reproductions (models dating back as far as the first century) and originals (from as early as the 1600s) is of some interest, not least the giant shoe made for the Columbus statue and hailed by Guinness as the world's biggest. Foot-fetishists can also admire shoes of famous Catalans like Pau Casals.

North towards Plaça de Catalunya

Beyond Plaça Sant Josep Oriol, two or three diversions on the way north to Plaça de Catalunya make it worthwhile to stick to the backstreets, avoiding the Ramblas. Much of the area is devoted to antique shops and art galleries: one of the most famous is at c/de Petritxol 5, where the **Sala Pares** was already well established when Picasso and Miró were young; it still deals exclusively in nineteenth- and twentieth-century Catalan art. Carrer de Petritxol is also the place to come for a hot chocolate in one of the traditional cafés that still thrive here.

Across c/de Portaferrissa, the landscaped **Plaça Vila de Madrid** features some well-preserved Roman tombs in its sunken garden, while further north, off the shopping street of c/de Santa Anna, lies the **Església de Santa Anna**, one of the oldest religious foundations in the city. A monastery was established here as early as the twelfth century and a fine fifteenth-century cloister survived the turmoil of the Civil War.

Cross busy, pedestrianized Avinguda del Portal de l'Angel from here to find c/Montsió and **Els Quatre Gats** (The Four Cats), on your left at no. 3, the bar opened by Pere Romeu and other *modernista* artists in 1897 as a gathering place for their contemporaries. The building itself is gloriously decorated inside – it was the architect Puig i Cadafalch's first commission – and *Els Quatre Gats* soon thrived as the birthplace of *modernista* magazines, the scene of poetry readings and shadow-puppet theatre and, in 1901, the setting for Picasso's first public exhibition. Today's restaurant (see p.183) provides rather grand surroundings for a meal, overseen by a copy of Ramon Casas' famous wall painting of himself and Pere Romeu on a tandem bicycle.

El Raval

The old-town area west of the Ramblas is known as **El Raval** (from the Arabic word for "suburb"). Standing outside the medieval city walls, this has always formed a world apart from the power and nobility of the Barri Gòtic. In medieval times it was the site of hospitals, churches and monasteries and, later, of trades and industries that had no place in the Gothic quarter. Many of the street names still tell the story, like c/de l'Hospital or c/dels Tallers (named for the district's slaughterhouses). By the twentieth century the area south of c/de l'Hospital had acquired a more sinister reputation as the city's main red-light area, known to all (for obscure reasons) as the Barrio Chino, or Barri Xinès in Catalan – "China Town". According to the Barcelona chronicler Manuel Vázquez Montalbán, in the days when Jean Genet crawled its streets – an experience he recounted in his *Thief's Journal* – the district "housed . . . theatrical homosexuals and anarcho-syndicalist, revolutionary meeting places; women's prisons . . . condom shops and brothels which smelled of liquor and groins". George Orwell later related how, after the 1936 Workers' Uprising, "in the streets were coloured posters appealing to prostitutes to stop being prostitutes". These more unsavoury aspects of the Raval were much in evidence until relatively recently, and even today in the backstreets around c/de Sant Pau and c/Nou de la Rambla are found pockets of sleaze. Meanwhile, a handful of old bars – the *Bar Pastis*, *London Bar*, *Marsella* and *Almirall* (all reviewed on pp.200–201) – trade on their former reputations as bohemian hangouts.

However, El Raval is changing rapidly. The 1992 Olympics and then European Union funding achieved what Franco never could, and cleaned up large parts of the neighbourhood almost overnight. North of c/de l'Hospital the main engine of change was the building of the contemporary art museum, MACBA, around which entire city blocks were demolished, open spaces created and old buildings cleaned up. To the south, between c/de l'Hospital and c/de Sant Pau, a new boulevard – the **Rambla de Raval** – has been gouged through the former tenements and alleys, providing a huge new pedestrianized area. The local character of the neighbourhood is changing perceptibly, too. The new, young, more affluent and arty residents rub shoulders with the area's older, more traditional population, though this in turn is being supplanted by a growing influx of immigrants from the Indian subcontinent and North Africa. Alongside the surviving spit-and-sawdust bars you'll find new restaurants, galleries and boutiques, not to mention a burgeoning number of specialist grocery stores, *halal* butchers and hole-in-the-wall telephone offices advertising cheap international calls.

You'd hesitate to call El Raval gentrified, as it clearly still has its rough edges. You needn't be unduly concerned during the day as you make your way around, but it's as well to keep your wits about you at night, particularly in the southernmost streets.

Museu d'Art Contemporani de Barcelona and around

Reached along c/del Bonsuccés and c/d'Elisabets from the Ramblas, and anchoring the northern reaches of the Raval, is the **Museu d'Art Contemporani de Barcelona**, or **MACBA**, in Plaça dels Angels (June–Sept Mon & Wed–Sat 10am–8pm, Sun 10am–3pm; Oct–May Mon & Wed–Fri 11am–7.30pm, Sat 10am–8pm, Sun 10am–3pm; general entrance €7, Wed €3, special exhibitions €4; ⓦwww.macba.es; ⓂCatalunya/Universitat). The contrast between the huge, white, almost luminous, structure of the museum and the buildings around it couldn't be more stark and it has inevitably been the subject of some controversy amongst locals since it opened in 1995. The aim of the architect, American Richard Meier, was to make as much use of natural light as possible and to "create a dialogue" between the museum and its surroundings; this is reflected in the front side of the building, which is entirely of glass. Once inside, you go from the ground to the fourth floor up a series of swooping ramps which afford continuous views of the square below – usually full of careering skateboarders – and the sixteenth-century Convent dels Àngels.

The **collection** represents the main movements in contemporary art since 1945, mainly in Catalunya and Spain but with a good smattering of foreign artists as well. The pieces are not shown together in a permanent space but in smaller rotating exhibitions, so, depending on when you visit, you may catch works by major names such as Joan Miró, Antoni Tàpies, Eduardo Chillida, Alexander Calder, Robert Rauschenberg or Paul Klee. Joan Brossa, leading light of the Catalan Dau al Set group of the 1950s, has work here too, as do Catalan conceptual artists like the Grup de Treball, Muntadas and Francesc Torres. There's also a broad collection of abstract and kinetic sculpture, and cutting-edge work by Spanish and Catalan artists using audiovisual techniques and other new technologies. For **guided tours** of the exhibitions (by appointment only), call ☎934 121 413. There's also a good museum shop for browsing and a café around the back.

Across the square, part of the former Convent dels Àngels now houses the headquarters of the **Foment de les Artes Décoratives** (**FAD**; ⓦwww.fad-web.com), whose exhibition spaces (including the former convent chapel) are dedicated to industrial and graphic design, arts, crafts, architecture, contemporary jewellery and fashion. While you're in the vicinity, it's worth looking around the other small private galleries or having a drink in one of the new bars that have sprung up in the wake of MACBA, especially on c/del Pintor Fortuny, c/de Ferlandina, c/dels Angels and c/del Dr Joaquim Dou. There are some excellent restaurants around here, too – the best are reviewed on p.187. For a sit-down in one of Barcelona's nicest traffic-free squares, head back along c/d'Elisabets to the arcaded **Plaça de Vicenç Martorell**, where *Kasparo's* tables overlook a popular children's playground.

Centre de Cultura Contemporània de Barcelona

Adjoining the MACBA building, up c/Montalegre, is the **Centre de Cultura Contemporània de Barcelona**, or **CCCB** (Tues, Thurs & Fri 11am–2pm & 4–8pm, Wed & Sat 11am–8pm, Sun 11am–7pm; €4 or €5.50 depending on number of exhibitions you see; ⓦwww.cccb.org; ⓂCatalunya/Universitat), which hosts temporary art and city-related exhibitions as well as supporting a cinema and a varied concert programme. The building is a prime example of the juxtaposition of old and new; built as the Casa de la Caritat in 1714 on the site of a fourteenth-century Augustine convent, and added to in the late eighteenth and nineteenth centuries, it was for hundreds of years an infamous workhouse and lunatic asylum. In the entrance to the centre, in what is now called the Plaça de les Dones, you can see the old tile panels and facade in a patio presided over by a small statue of Sant Jordi (patron saint of Catalunya) – the glass side of the square gives views of the patio as you go up the escalators

△ Newsagents on the Ramblas

to the exhibition spaces inside the new part of the building. At the back of the building there is a nice **café** (Mon–Fri 9am–7pm, Sat & Sun 11am–6pm) with a *terrassa* on the modern square joining the CCCB to the MACBA. Further up on c/Montalegre is another eighteenth-century patio, the arcaded and tiled **Pati Manning**, used for occasional open-air concerts.

Hospital de la Santa Creu and around

The district's most substantial historic relic is the **Hospital de la Santa Creu** (Ⓜ Liceu), which occupies a huge site between c/del Carme and c/de l'Hospital. The attractive complex of Gothic buildings was founded as the city's main hospital in 1402, a role that it assumed until 1930, when the hospital shifted site to Domènech i Montaner's new creation in the Eixample. The complex was subsequently converted for cultural and educational use, and now holds an artisanal school and two libraries, housed in the spacious fifteenth-century hospital wards. Visitors can wander freely through the pleasant interior **garden** (daily 10am–dusk; access from either street), with its orange trees and lovely medieval cloister. From c/de l'Hospital you get the best views of the building's facade, while just inside the c/del Carme entrance (on the right) are some superb seventeenth-century *azulejos* of various religious scenes and a tiled Reniassance courtyard. Plans are afoot to restore and reopen the eighteenth-century Academia de Medicina, whose lecture theatre holds a revolving marble dissection table, but for now the building remains closed. The hospital's former chapel, **La Capella de l'Antic Hospital** (Tues–Sat noon–2pm & 4–8pm, Sun 11am–2pm; free), entered separately from c/l'Hospital, is an exhibition space featuring a changing programme of works by young Barcelona artists.

Walking west along c/de l'Hospital, it's 100m or so to the bottom of **c/de la Riera Baixa**, a narrow street that's at the centre of the city's secondhand/vintage clothing scene. The **Rambla de Raval** is then just a few steps beyond, where you can pull up a chair at a pavement café and consider the merits of the latest urban boulevard to be driven through the old town. Walking the other way down c/de l'Hospital, back towards the Ramblas, one of the Raval's prettiest squares reveals itself, **Plaça de Sant Agusti**, backed by the Catalan Baroque bulk of the Església de Sant Agusti, an Augustinian foundation from 1728. Turning north, up c/de Jerusalem, you soon find yourself at the back of the Boqueria market, another area in which hip bars have proliferated recently. A couple overlook the **Jardins Dr Fleming**, a children's playground tucked into an exterior corner of the Hospital de la Santa Creu on c/del Carme.

Palau Güell and around

Much of Antoni Gaudí's early career was spent constructing elaborate follies for wealthy patrons. The most important patron was Eusebi Güell, a shipowner and industrialist, who in 1885 commissioned the **Palau Güell** (Mon–Sat 10am–1pm & 4–7pm; €3; Ⓜ Drassanes/Liceu), at c/Nou de la Rambla 3, as an extension of the family's townhouse located on the Ramblas. The first modern building to be declared a World Heritage Site by UNESCO, the Palau Güell is now a museum, so unusually you can visit the interior: most of the Gaudí houses are still privately owned. Here, Gaudí's feel for different materials is remarkable. At a time when architects sought to conceal the iron supports within buildings, Gaudí turned them to his advantage, displaying them as attractive decorative features in the rooms on the main floor. The roof terrace, too, makes a virtue of its functionalism, since the chimneys and other outlets are decorated with glazed tiles, while inside, columns, arches and ceilings are all shaped and twisted in an elaborate style that was to become the hallmark of Gaudí's later works. You have to see the building on one of the frequent, mandatory, guided tours (in English), and queues form early – having waited in line, you might well be given a later time-slot, as visitor numbers are limited.

Modernista buildings are fairly rare in the Raval, though the **London Bar**, further down c/Nou de la Rambla from Palau Güell at no. 34, is a nearby example. Best known, however, is the **Hotel España** at c/Sant Pau 9–11, five minutes up and off the Ramblas from Palau Güell. This has a hugely attractive tiled dining room designed by Domènech i Montaner, a bar with amazing marble fireplace by Eusebi Arnau, and a ballroom whose marine murals are by Ramon Casas. You can have a good look for the price of lunch (see p.189) or even stay here overnight (p.160).

Sant Pau del Camp

Carrer de Sant Pau cuts west through the Raval to the church of **Sant Pau del Camp** (St Paul of the Field; Mon & Wed–Sun 11.30am–1pm & 6–7.30pm, Tues 11.30am–12.30pm; free; ⓜParal.lel), its name a reminder that it once stood in open fields beyond the city walls. The oldest and one of the most interesting churches in Barcelona, Sant Pau was a Benedictine foundation of the tenth century, built after its predecessor was destroyed in a Muslim raid of 985 AD and constructed on a Greek cross plan. Sitting in a small courtyard studded with trees, it has been well restored. Above the main entrance are curious, primitive (and faded) thirteenth-century carvings of fish, birds and faces, while other animal forms adorn the capitals of the twelfth-century cloister; at the back of the church the delicately curved apses are worth a detour, too. Inside, the church is dark and rather plain, enlivened only by tiny arrow-slit windows and small stained-glass circles high up in the central dome.

Mercat de Sant Antoni to Paral.lel

The Raval's western edge is defined by the Ronda de Sant Pau and the Ronda de Sant Antoni, and where the two meet stands the handsome **Mercat de Sant Antoni** (Mon–Thurs & Sat 7am–2.30pm & 5.30–8.30pm, Fri 7am–8.30pm; ⓜSant Antoni), the neighbourhood's major produce market, dating from 1876. It makes a nice contrast to the Boqueria – there are not nearly so many tourists, for a start – and unlike the other city markets, it's surrounded by enclosed aisles packed with stalls selling cheap shoes, underwear, T-shirts, children's clothes, bed linen, towels and other household goods. Come on Sunday and there's a **book and coin market** (10am–2pm) here instead. The traditional breakfast, lunch and drinks spot is **Els Tres Tombs**, the café across the road on the corner of Ronda de Sant Antoni, open from 6am until late for a good-natured mix of market traders, locals, students and tourists.

Three blocks west of the market, lies **Avinguda Paral.lel**, one of Barcelona's major thoroughfares, which runs from the port to Plaça d'Espanya. The street was once the hub of Barcelona nightlife, famed for its cabarets, theatres and dance halls, only a few of which have survived the city's changing taste in entertainment. On the other side of the avenue lies the working-class district of Poble Sec (see p.88), while if you walk down Paral.lel towards the harbour you'll pass the **funicular station** for Montjuïc (access is through ⓜParal.lel) and then skirt the surviving **medieval walls** of the former shipyards (now the Museu Marítim; see p.73).

Sant Pere

The Barri Gòtic is bordered on its eastern side by Via Laietana, which was cut through the old town at the beginning of the twentieth century. Across it to the east stretches the quiet neighbourhood of **Sant Pere**, named after its medieval monastic church, Sant Pere de les Puelles. Visits to the *barri* tend to concentrate on its one remarkable building, the **Palau de la Música Catalana** (see below), just off the northern end of Via Laietana, but the neighbourhood rewards a slow stroll through on your way to the richer tourist area of La Ribera. This also gives you the opportunity to swing by one of Barcelona's more esoteric museums, devoted entirely to chocolate.

Three old streets, carrers de Sant Pere Més Alt (upper), Mitja (middle) and Baix (lower), contain the bulk of the district's finest medieval buildings and the nicest shops, and they converge to the east at **Plaça de Sant Pere**, site of the much-restored church. To the south, **Plaça de Sant Agusti Vell** makes a great target for lunch, with either *Bar Mundial* or *Restaurant L'Economic* offering a great deal. Meanwhile, west of here, in the very centre of the neighbourhood, work has continued to spruce up the streets and squares around the restored mid-nineteenth-century **Mercat Santa Caterina** (ⓂJaume I), another of Barcelona's attractive central market buildings. The discovery of the foundations of a major medieval convent held up its renovation for a while, but it's expected to be open again to the public during 2004. The shady medieval streets below here are a bit of a maze but, with a keen sense of direction and a touch of luck, you'll end up on c/de la Princesa, within shouting distance of c/de Montcada and the Picasso museum.

Palau de la Música Catalana

Domènech i Montaner's stupendous **Palau de la Música Catalana** (ⓂUrquinaona) doesn't seem to have enough breathing space in the tiny c/Sant Pere Més Alt. Built in 1908 for the Orfeo Català choral group, its bare brick structure is smothered in tiles and mosaics, the highly elaborate facade resting on three great columns, like elephant's legs; the corner sculpture, by Miquel Blay, represents Catalan popular song. The dramatic tiled lobby provides a taster of the stunning interior, which incorporates a bulbous stained-glass skylight capping the second-storey auditorium – which contemporary critics claimed to be an engineering impossibility.

Fifty-minute-long **guided tours** of the interior (daily 10am–3.30pm, in English on the hour; €7; ☎932 957 200, ⓦwww.palaumusica.org) are offered, but as visitor numbers are limited you'll almost certainly have to book in advance, which you can do in person or by phone at the box office or at the nearby gift shop, Les Muses del Palau, c/Sant Pere Mes Alt 1 (daily 9.30–3pm; no phone). If you can also get a ticket for one of the many fine concerts here, so much the better.

Museu de la Xocolata

Barcelona's engaging **Museu de la Xocolata** (Mon & Wed–Sat 10am–7pm, Sun 10am–3pm; €3.80, ⓦwww.museudelaxocolata.com; ⓂJaume I), on the eastern edge of Sant Pere, at c/del Comerç 36, is housed in the former Convent de Sant Agusti. The thirteenth-century cloister, rediscovered when the building was renovated, can still be viewed through the building's main doors. The museum itself recounts the history of chocolate, from its origins as a sacred and medicinal product of prehistoric Central America through to its introduction to Europe as a confection in the sixteenth century. It's a fascinating topic, well covered here, with some local relevance – in that the Bourbon army, which was once quartered in this building, demanded the provision of chocolate for its sweet-toothed troops. As you might expect, the museum café serves a mean cup of hot chocolate – and the shop and *choccie* counter is something to behold too – while at the adjacent Escola de Patisseria, glass windows allow you to look onto the students learning their craft in the kitchens.

La Ribera and the Born

Last of the old-town neighbourhoods, **La Ribera** – bordered by Via Laietana to the west, c/de la Princesa to the north and Parc de la Ciutadella to the east – is also one of the most visited, by virtue of the presence of the **Museu Picasso**, Barcelona's biggest single tourist attraction. This lies on c/de Montcada, a handsome street of medieval mansions, which runs down to the church of **Santa María del Mar**, the city's most perfect expression of the Catalan-Gothic style. The sheer number of tourists in this neighbourhood rivals the busiest streets of the Barri Gòtic, and this has had a knock-on effect in terms of the bars, shops and restaurants found here. Over the last decade it's also become the location of choice for designers, artists and craftspeople, whose boutiques and workshops lend the neighbourhood an air of creativity. The *barri* is at its most hip, and most enjoyable, in the area around the Passeig del Born, the pleasant elongated square leading from Santa María church to the old **Born market**. This is one of the city's premier nightlife centres – widely known as **the Born** – but even during the day the cafés at the far end are a nice place to call a halt to the day's sightseeing.

Museu Picasso

The **Museu Picasso**, at c/Montcada 15–23 (Tues–Sat & hols 10am–8pm, Sun 10am–3pm; €5, first Sun of month free; ⓦwww.museupicasso.bcn.es; ⓜJaume I), occupies five adjoining medieval palaces converted specifically to house the artist's celebrated works. It's one of the most important collections of Picasso's work in the world, but even so some visitors are disappointed: the museum isn't thoroughly representative, it contains none of his best-known works, and few in the Cubist style. But what is here provides a unique opportunity to trace Picasso's development from his early paintings as a young boy to the major works of later years. It's always thronged with visitors, though arriving when it opens is a good way to beat the worst of the crowds. A **café** with a *terrassa* in one of the palace courtyards offers refreshments, and there is of course a **shop**, stuffed full of Picasso-related gifts.

The collection

The museum opened in 1963 with a collection based largely on the donations of Jaime Sabartes, friend and former secretary to the artist. On Sabartes' death in 1968, Picasso himself added a large number of works – above all the 58 works of the Meninas series – and in 1970 he donated a further vast number of watercolours, drawings and paintings.

Picasso in Barcelona

Although born in Málaga, **Pablo Picasso** (1881–1973) spent much of his youth – from the age of 14 to 23 – in Barcelona. He maintained close links with Barcelona and his Catalan friends even when he left for Paris in 1904, and is said to have always thought of himself as Catalan rather than *andaluz*. The time Picasso spent in Barcelona encompassed the whole of his Blue Period (1901–04) and provided many of the formative influences on his art.

Apart from the Museu Picasso, there are echoes of the great artist at various sites throughout the old town. Not too far from the museum, you can still see many of the buildings in which Picasso lived and worked, notably the **Escola de Belles Arts de Llotja** (c/Consolat del Mar, near Estació de França), where his father taught drawing and where Picasso himself absorbed an academic training. The **apartments** where the family lived when they first arrived in Barcelona – Pg. d'Isabel II 4 and c/Reina Cristina 3, both near the Escola – can also be seen, though only from the outside, while Picasso's first real **studio** (in 1896) was located over on c/de la Plata at no. 4. A few years later, many of his Blue Period works were finished at a studio at c/del Comerç 28. His first **public exhibition** was in 1901 at *Els Quatre Gats* bar/restaurant (c/Montsió 3, Barri Gòtic); you can still have a drink there today. Less tangible traces line **c/Avinyó** in the Barri Gòtic, which cuts south from c/Ferran to c/Ample. Large houses along here were converted into brothels at the beginning of the last century, and Picasso used to haunt the street sketching what he saw. Some accounts of his life – based on Picasso's own testimony, it has to be said – claim that he had his first sexual experience here at the age of 14, but certainly the women at one of the brothels inspired his seminal Cubist work, *Les Demoiselles d'Avignon*.

It's extremely well laid out, following the artist's development chronologically. The **early drawings**, particularly, are fascinating, in which Picasso – still signing with his full name, Pablo Ruiz Picasso attempted to copy the nature paintings in which his father specialized. There are also many studies from his art-school days. Even at the ages of 15 and 16 (by which time he was living in Barcelona), he was painting major works – including a self-portrait and a portrait of his mother from 1896. Indeed, it's the early periods that are the best represented. Some works in the style of Toulouse-Lautrec, like the menu Picasso did for *Els Quatre Gats* restaurant in 1900, reflect his interest in Parisian art at the turn of the century; while other selected works show graphically Picasso's development of his own style. There are paintings here from the famous **Blue Period** (1901–04), the Pink Period (1904–06), and from his Cubist (1907–20) and Neoclassical (1920–25) stages.

The large gaps in the main collection (for example, nothing from 1905 until the celebrated *Harlequin* of 1917) only underline Picasso's extraordinary changes of style and mood. This is best illustrated by the large jump after 1917 – to 1957, a year represented by two rooms on the first floor that contain the fascinating works Picasso himself donated to the museum, his fifty-odd interpretations of Velázquez's masterpiece, **Las Meninas**. In addition, the museum's **minor works** – sketches, drawings and prints – cover in detail most phases of the artist's career up until 1972, with the top floor incorporating various studies of Jacqueline, his wife, along with 41 pieces of pottery, which she donated in 1981.

Along Carrer de Montcada

The street that the Museu Picasso is on – **Carrer de Montcada** – is one of the best-looking in the city. It was laid out in the fourteenth century and, until the Eixample was planned almost five hundred years later, was home to most of the city's leading citizens. They occupied spacious mansions built around central courtyards, from which external staircases climbed to the living rooms on the first floor; the facades facing the street were all endowed with huge gated doors that could be swung open to allow coaches access to the interior.

Almost opposite the Museu Picasso, at no. 12, the fourteenth-century Palau de Lló and its next-door neighbour contain the extensive collections of the **Museu Textil i d'Indumentaria** (Tues–Sat 10am–6pm, Sun 10am–3pm; €3.50, first Sun of month free; @www.museutextil.bcn.es). There are over four thousand items altogether including textiles from the fourth century onwards and costumes from the sixteenth onwards, plus dolls, shoes, fans and other accessories. Special exhibitions here are well regarded (for which there's usually a separate charge), while the courtyard café (see p.175) is one of the nicest in the old town. A joint ticket system also allows you entry to the ceramics and decorative arts museum at Pedralbes (see p.116) or to the adjacent **Museu Barbier–Mueller** on c/de Montcada (Tues–Sat 10am–6pm, Sun 10am–3pm; €3, first Sun of month free), a collection of pre-Columbian art housed in the renovated sixteenth-century Palau Nadal. The collection, entrusted to the Barcelona municipality by the Barbier–Mueller museum in Geneva, contains some beautiful pieces of sculpture, pottery, jewellery and textiles from early Mesoamerican cultures from Mexico to Peru.

Next door again, the **Sala Montcada**, c/de Montcada 14 (Tues–Sat 11am–8pm, Sun 11am–3pm; free), hosts changing contemporary art shows, while further down at no. 20, the **Palau Dalmases** is a handsome Baroque building of the seventeenth century, remodelled from its fifteenth-century roots. This is open in the evenings as a rather grand Baroque bar, *Espai Barroc* (see p.201 for details). At no. 25 a private gallery, the **Galeria Maeght** (Tues–Sat 10am–2pm & 4–8pm; free), spreads across two floors of the former Palau dels Cervelló, while at the end of the street, in the little Placeta Montcada, **Taller Cuixart BCN** (Tues–Sat 11am–3pm & 5–8pm, Sun 11am–3pm; €3, free on Tues; @www.cuixart.org) is a collection of the works of Catalan artist Modest Cuixart, co-creator of the influential magazine and art movement Dau al Set. Four rooms trace the development of his work, from early surrealism in the 1940s and 1950s to the sober, abstract landscapes of the 1990s.

At the bottom of c/de Montcada, the graceful lines of Santa María church impose themselves, but before you move on, and for a change of tack from palaces and art, drop into the lavishly tiled **El Xampanyet** bar at c/de Montcada 22 (see p.178), serving champagne, cider and tapas.

Santa María del Mar

The church of **Santa María del Mar** (daily 9am–1.30pm & 4.30–8pm; Sun choral Mass at 1pm; @Jaume I/Barceloneta) was begun on the order of King Jaume II in 1324, and finished in only five years. Built on what was the seashore in the fourteenth century, the church was at the heart of the medieval city's maritime and trading district (c/Argentería, named after the silversmiths who worked there, still runs from the church square to the city walls of the Barri Gòtic), and it came to embody supremacy of the Crown of Aragon (of which Barcelona was capital) in Mediterranean commerce. Built quickly, and therefore consistent in style, it's an exquisite example of Catalan-Gothic architecture, with a wide nave and high, narrow aisles, and for all its restrained exterior decoration is still much dearer to the heart of the average local than the cathedral, the only other church in the city with which it compares. The Baroque trappings were destroyed during the Civil War, which is probably all to the good, since the long-term restoration work has concentrated on showing off the simple spaces of the interior; the stained glass, especially, is beautiful.

Behind the church is the square known as **Fossar de les Moreres**, which was formally opened in 1989 to mark the spot where, following the defeat of Barcelona on September 11, 1714, Catalan martyrs fighting for independence against the King of Spain, Felipe V, were executed. A red steel scimitar with an eternal flame commemorates the fallen.

Passeig del Born and around

Fronting the church of Santa María is the fashionable **Passeig del Born**, once the site of medieval fairs and tournaments and now lined with a parade of plane trees shading a host of classy bars and shops. Boutiques and craft work-shops in this area provide one reason for a visit (see p.230 for more), while cafés at the eastern end put out tables in front of the old **Mercat del Born** (1873–76), once the biggest of Barcelona's nineteenth-century city market halls. The massive rectangular steel and iron construction, topped with a perky little cupola, is now empty, but works are underway to refit it as a public library. The streets all around this area harbour some excellent restaurants, while the nicest place to sit outside for a drink or lunch, other than the Born itself, is pretty little **Plaça de les Olles**, just to the south.

Parc de la Ciutadella and around

The Bourbons took no chances after the War of the Spanish Succession. Barcelona had put up a spirited resistance, and to quell any further dissent Felipe V ordered the building of a star-shaped citadel close to the water, on the edge of the old town. A great part of La Ribera was destroyed, and a garrison, parade ground and defensive walls were constructed over a twenty-year peri-od in the mid-eighteenth century. This Bourbon symbol of authority survived uneasily until 1869, when the military moved base. Many of the buildings were subsequently demolished and the surrounding area made into a park, the **Parc de la Ciutadella**. In 1888, the park was chosen as the site of the **Universal Exhibition** and the city's *modernista* architects, including the young Gaudí, left their mark here in a series of eye-catching buildings and monuments.

The Parc de la Ciutadella is still the largest green space in the city centre, home to a splendid fountain, large lake, plant houses, two museums and the city zoo. It's a very popular place for a stroll, and Sundays especially see couples and families taking time out here, while a younger crowd assembles in various spots for a bit of vigorous didgeridooing or bongo-work. The only surviving por-tion of the citadel, the much-altered Arsenal in the southeastern reaches of the park, has since 1980 housed Catalunya's legislative assembly, the **Parlament** (no public access – see Contexts, p.262, for more on the institution). Until recently, the building also contained the art collections of the Museu d'Art Modern de Catalunya, now transferred to new galleries in Montjuïc's Museu Nacional d'Art de Catalunya. Near the park, within short walking distance, are a couple of other attractions, including one of the city's most peculiar muse-ums, devoted to funeral carriages.

The park's **main gates** are on Passeig de Picasso (ⓂBarceloneta), and there's also an entrance on Passeig de Pujades (ⓂArc de Triomf); only use ⓂCiutadella-Vila Olímpica if you're going directly to the zoo, as there's no access to the park itself from that side.

Inside the park

Perhaps the most notable of the park's sights is the **Cascada**, the monumental fountain in the northeast corner. Designed by Josep Fontseré i Mestrès, the architect chosen to oversee the conversion of the former citadel grounds into a park, this was the first of the major projects undertaken here. Fontseré's assistant in the work was the young Antoni Gaudí, then a student: the Baroque extravagance of the Cascada is suggestive of the flamboyant decoration that was later to become Gaudí's trademark. The best place to contemplate it is from the small **open-air café** just to the south. Here you'll also find a lake, where for a few euros you can **rent a rowboat** and paddle about among the ducks. Gaudí is also thought to have had a hand in the design of the Ciutadella's iron park gates.

Just inside the northern entrance of the park, Domènech i Montaner designed a castle-like building intended for use as the exhibition's café-restaurant. Dubbed the *Castell dels Tres Dragons*, it became a centre for *modernista* arts and crafts, and many of Domènech's contemporaries spent time here experimenting with new materials and refining their techniques. It's now the **Museu de Zoologia** (Tues, Wed & Fri–Sun 10am–2pm, Thurs 10am–6.30pm; €3, first Sun of month free), whose decorated red-brick exterior knocks spots off the rather more mundane interior and its formulaic collections of stuffed birds and animals.

Beyond the museum you pass the attractive late nineteenth-century **Hivernacle** (conservatory) – which houses a pleasant bar (see p.201) – and **Umbracle** (palmhouse), between which sits the park's other museum, the **Museu de Geologia** (same hours and price as Museu de Zoologia), designed by Josep Fontseré, the park's original architect. Inside, you're due for an educational tour past a collection of geological and paleontological bits and pieces, including 120-million-year-old fossils.

Parc Zoològic

Ciutadella's most popular attraction by far is the city's zoo, the **Parc Zoològic** (daily: May–Aug 9.30am–7.30pm; April & Sept 10am–7pm; March & Oct 10am–6pm; Nov–Feb 10am–5pm; €12.90; ⓦwww.zoobarcelona.com), taking up most of the southeastern part of the park. There's an entrance on c/Wellington (closest if you've arrived at ⓂCiutadella-Vila Olímpica), as well as one inside Ciutadella. For years, the zoo's star exhibit was the pure-white albino gorilla Snowflake, who died of old age in November 2003. A baby male gorilla, his grandson, maintains the family line. Other notable endangered species found at the zoo include the Iberian wolf, and big cats such as the Sumatran tiger, Sri Lanka leopard and snow leopard. Otherwise, the jungle bird aviary, permanent gorilla exhibition and comprehensive collection of reptiles are the main attractions, while small children enjoy the petting zoo, which has typical Spanish farm animals. There are daily dolphin shows, too.

However, the zoo's days here in its current form are numbered – the powers that be perhaps having finally appreciated the irony of its juxtaposition next to the Parlament, and grown weary of explaining to visiting dignitaries the source of the strong smell pervading the area. There are advanced plans to move the marine animals at least to a new coastal zoo and wetlands area (by 2008) being laid out at the new Diagonal Mar seashore at Besós.

Arc de Triomf and around

From the northern entrance of the Parc de la Ciutadella, the wide Passeig Lluís Companys runs up to Josep Vilaseca i Casanoves' giant brick **Arc de Triomf** (ⓂArc de Triomf). Studded with ceramic figures and motifs, and topped by two pairs of bulbous domes, this announces the architectural efforts to come in the park itself – the reliefs on the main facade show the city of Barcelona welcoming visitors to the 1888 Universal Exhibition.

To the east lies the **Estacío del Nord** bus station, behind which stretches the undistinguished **Parc de l'Estacío del Nord**, which cuts across several city blocks as far as Avinguda Meridiana, ten minutes from the arch. The only reason to walk or ride out this way would be to present yourself at the front desk of the Serveis Funeraris (funerary services) de Barcelona, a few metres along c/Sancho de Ávila from the avenue (by the blue Banc Sabadell sign). You'll be escorted into the bowels of the building and the lights will be thrown on in the **Museu de Carrosses Fúnebres** (Mon–Fri 10am–1pm & 4–6pm, Sat & Sun 10am–1pm; free; ⓂMarina) to reveal a staggering set of 22 funerary carriages, each parked on its own cobbled stage, complete with ghostly attendants, horses and riders suspended in frozen animation. Used for city funeral processions from the end of the nineteenth century onwards, most of the carriages and hearses are extravagantly decorated in gilt, black or white – the service was mechanized in the 1950s, when the silver Buick, also on display, came into use. Old photographs show some of the carriages in use in the city's streets, while showcases highlight antique uniforms, mourning wear and formal riding gear.

The waterfront: Port Vell to Poble Nou

Perhaps the greatest recent transformation in the city has been along the **waterfront**, where harbour and Mediterranean have once again been placed at the heart of Barcelona. Dramatic changes here over the last two decades have shifted the cargo and container trade away to the south, opened up the old docksides as promenades and entertainment areas, and landscaped the city's beaches to the north – it's as if a theatre curtain has been lifted to reveal that, all along, Barcelona had an urban waterfront of which it could be proud.

Reaching the bottom of the Ramblas puts you within strolling distance of some heavyweight tourist attractions, including the **Mirador de Colón** (Columbus statue), **Museu Marítim**, the sightseeing harbour **boat trips**, and the boardwalks and promenades of the inner harbour, known as **Port Vell**. The old wharves and warehouses have been replaced by an entertainment zone that encompasses the **Maremàgnum** shopping and nightlife centre, the city's high-profile aquarium and IMAX screens and, across the marina, the impressive **Museu d'Història de Catalunya**. The wedge of land backing the marina is **Barceloneta**, an eighteenth-century fishing quarter that's the most popular place to come and sample the fish and seafood dishes of which Barcelona is most proud.

From Barceloneta six interlinked **beaches** stretch up the coast, backed by an attractive promenade. The city's inhabitants have taken to these in a big way, strolling, jogging and skating their length and descending in force at the weekend for a leisurely lunch at a nearby restaurant. The main development is around the **Port Olímpic**, filled with places to eat, drink and shop, and although fewer tourists keep on as far as the old working-class neighbourhood of **Poble Nou**, its beaches, historic cemetery and pretty *rambla* make for an interesting diversion. This is also the site of Forum 2004, the cultural diversity and sustainability Expo, whose new buildings and leisure facilities have helped reshape the neighbourhood.

You can reach all the areas covered below by **metro**, though there's a fair amount of walking required between neighbourhoods – from the bottom of the Ramblas to Poble Nou (the entire extent of this chapter) would take an hour. In addition, **buses** #17 (from Pl. de Catalunya) and #64 (from Avgda. Paral.lel and Pg. de Colom) run to Barceloneta's Passeig Joan de Borbó (the restaurant strip) and on to the Sant Sebastià cable-car station. The #45 (from Via Laietana) and #59 (from the Ramblas) run through Barceloneta and out to the Port Olímpic. The #71 connects Passeig Marítim to Poble Nou metro.

Map labels:
Museu de Carrosses Fúnebres
LLACUNA (M)
POBLE NOU
Estació del Nord
MARINA (M)
BOGATELL (M)
Cementiri de Poble Nou
Mar Bella
Bogatell
Palau de Justicia
VILA OLIMPICA
ARC DE TRIOMF
Arc de Triomf
Parc de la Ciutadella
Parlament de Catalunya
Torre Mapfre
MOLL DE MESTRAL
MOLL DE GREGAL
Port Olimpic
Museu de Zoologia
Hivernacle
Museu Geologia
Mercat del Born
Parc Zoològic
CIUTADELLA-VILA OLIMPICA (M)
Hotel Arts
Nova Icaria
Museu Picasso
Estació de França
JAUME I (M)
Santa Maria del Mar
Parc de la Barceloneta
RONDA LITORAL
PASSEIG DE JOAN DE BORBÓ
Barceloneta
BARRI GOTIC
Pl. de Catalunya
BARCELONETA (M)
PLAÇA D'ANTONI LOPEZ
MAQUINISTA
PL. BARCELONETA
Palau del Mar
BARCELONETA
Sant Sebastià
PORT VELL
IMAX
ADMIRALL
PASSEIG JOAN DE BORBÓ
DRASSANES (M)
Mirador de Colón
PLAÇA PORTAL DE LA PAU
L'Aquàrium
Drassanes (Museu Marítim)
Maremàgnum
MOLL DE BARCELONA
Torre Sant Sebastià
Montjuïc
Teleféric
Torre Jaume I
MAR MEDITERRÁNEO
MOLL DE PONIENTE
N
0   500 m

Plaça Portal de la Pau and around

The Ramblas at **Plaça Portal de la Pau** ((M)Drassanes), coming up hard against the teeming traffic that runs along the harbourside road. The maritime museum is over to the right, and the Columbus monument straight ahead in the middle of the traffic circle, with the quayside square beyond flanked by rather pompous **Port de Barcelona** (Port Authority) and **Duana** (Customs House) buildings. Away to the south (right) is the Moll de Barcelona, a landscaped wharf leading to the Torre de Jaume I cable-car station (see feature on p.78) and the **Estació Marítima,** where ferries leave for the Balearics. The large, bulbous building perched in the centre of the wharf is the city's **World Trade Centre,** where a luxury hotel complements the complex of offices, convention halls, shops and restaurants.

From the quayside just beyond the foot of the Columbus monument, **Las Golondrinas** sightseeing boats and the **Catamaran Orsom** depart on regular trips throughout the year around the inner harbour – all the details are on p.29.

Mirador de Colón

Inaugurated just before the Universal Exhibition of 1888, the **Mirador de Colón** (June–Sept daily 9am–8.30pm; Oct–March Mon–Fri 10am–1.30pm & 3.30–6.30pm, Sat & Sun 10am–6.30pm; April & May daily until 7.30pm; €2) commemorates the visit made by Christopher Columbus to Barcelona in June 1493. The Italian-born navigator was received in style by the Catholic monarchs Ferdinand and Isabella, who had supported his voyage of exploration a year earlier, when Columbus had set out to chart a passage west to the Orient. Famously, he failed in this, as he failed also to reach the North American mainland (instead "discovering" the Bahamas, Cuba and Haiti), but Columbus did enough to enhance his reputation and made three more exploratory voyages by 1504. Later, nineteenth-century Catalan nationalists took the navigator to their hearts – if he wasn't exactly Catalan, he was the closest they had to a local Vasco da Gama, and so they put him on the pedestal that they thought he deserved. Awkwardly for the locals, the statue is actually pointing in the general direction of Libya, not North America, but, as historian Robert Hughes puts it, at least "the sea is Catalan".

Columbus himself tops a grandiose, iron column, 52m high, guarded by lions at the base, around which unfold reliefs telling the story of his life and travels – here, if nowhere else, the old mercenary is still the "discoverer of America". On the harbour side of the column, steps lead down to a ticket office and lift, which you ride up to the enclosed *mirador* at Columbus' feet. The 360-degree views are terrific but the narrow viewing platform, which tilts perceptibly outwards and downwards, is emphatically not for anyone without a head for heights.

The Drassanes: Museu Marítim

Opposite Columbus, set back from the avenue, are the **Drassanes,** unique medieval shipyards dating from the thirteenth century. Originally used as a dry dock to fit and arm Catalunya's war fleet in the days when the Catalan-Aragonese crown was vying with Venice and Genoa for control of the Mediterranean, the shipyards were in continuous use until well into the eighteenth century. The basic structure – long parallel halls facing the sea – has changed little, however; its singular size and position couldn't be bettered, whether the shipbuilders were fitting out medieval warships or eighteenth-century trading vessels destined for South America.

The huge, stone-vaulted buildings make a fitting home for the **Museu Marítim** (daily 10am–7pm; €5.40; ⓦwww.diba.es/mmaritim; ⓂDrassanes), whose centrepiece is a copy of the sixteenth-century Royal Galley (*Galera Reial*), a red-and-gold barge which was originally constructed here and was present at the great naval victory over the Ottoman Turks at Lepanto in 1571.

It's surrounded by smaller models, fishing skiffs, sailing boats, figureheads, old maps and charts, ship portraits, navigation instruments and other nautical bits and pieces – none of which, worthy though they are, can really compete with the soaring building itself. There is also a permanent exhibition about the dangers of the sea that's great for kids, the "Gran Aventura del Mar", in which you can take a virtual-reality trip in a Catalan submarine (see box) or experience a storm-tossed sea at first hand.

Moored over on the Moll de la Fusta (on the other side of the harbour's swing bridge), the **Santa Eulàlia** (Tues–Fri noon–5.30pm, Sat & Sun 10am–5.30pm; €2.40) is another of the museum's showpiece exhibits. Dating from 1908, the three-masted schooner once made the run between Barcelona and Cuba. It's only the first in a series of ships that the museum intends to station here.

Port Vell

Barcelona's inner harbour has been rebranded as **Port Vell** (Old Port; ⓂDrassanes/Barceloneta), an area that encompasses the Moll d'Espanya wharf, the adjacent marina and the Palau de Mar development at the northwestern head of the Barceloneta district. It has its local critics – it's undoubtedly tourist-orientated, showy and expensive – but there's no denying the improvement made to what was formerly a largely neglected, decaying port area. The city's old timber wharf was among the first to be prettified. Backed by sedate nineteenth-century buildings along the Passeig de Colom, the **Moll de la Fusta** is a landscaped promenade with a note of humour injected by the addition of a giant crayfish, by Catalan designer Xavier Mariscal, topping what used to be a bar. From the Columbus-statue end of the wharf, the wooden **Rambla de Mar** swing bridge strides across the harbour to the **Moll d'Espanya**, whose main features are the leisure complex known as Maremàgnum – jammed with fast-food joints, shops, restaurants and bars – plus the aquarium and IMAX cinema. The eastern arm of the Moll d'Espanya connects back to the Moll de la Fusta, providing pedestrian access to the **Palau de Mar** at the northern end of Barceloneta's Passeig Joan de Borbó. This old warehouse has been beautifully restored, with a series of restaurants in the lower arcade overlooking the marina and the regional history museum occupying the upper floors.

Maremàgnum and the Moll d'Espanya

Maremàgnum (daily 11am–11pm; ⓦwww.maremagnum.es; ⓂDrassanes) is a typically bold piece of Catalan design, the soaring glass lines of the complex tempered by the surrounding undulating wooden walkways. Inside are two floors of gift shops and boutiques, plus a range of bars and restaurants with harbourside seating and high prices. It's a fun place to come at night, though no self-respecting local would rate the food as anything but ordinary. Outside, benches and park areas provide scintillating views back across the harbour to the city.

Anchoring Moll d'Espanya, **L'Aquàrium** (daily: July & Aug 9.30am–11pm; Sept–June 9.30am–9pm, until 9.30pm at weekends; €13.50; ⓦwww.aquariumbcn.com; ⓂDrassanes) drags in families and school parties throughout the year to see "a magical world, full of mystery".

Or, to be more precise, to see fish and sea creatures in 21 themed tanks representing underwater caves, tidal areas, tropical reefs, the planet's oceans and other maritime habitats. It's vastly overpriced, it has to be said, and despite the claims of excellence it offers few new experiences, save perhaps the eighty-metre-long walk-through underwater tunnel which brings you face to face with gliding rays and cruising sharks. Some child-centred displays and activities, and a nod towards ecology and conservation matters, pad out the attractions, before you're tipped out in the aquarium shop so they can part you from even more of your money.

IMAX Port Vell (☎932 251 111, ⊛www.imaxportvell.com) stands next to the aquarium, with three screens showing films virtually hourly in 3D or in giant format. Tickets are fairly reasonably priced (€7 or €10, depending on the film) given the technology and spectacle, but you'll find that the films are in Spanish or

---

Monturiol and the Catalan submarine

Narcís Monturiol i Estarriol (1819–1885) was born in Figueres in northeastern Catalunya but studied in Barcelona, soon falling in with radicals and revolutionaries. Although a law graduate, he never practised, turning his energetic talents instead to writing and publishing, setting up his first publishing company in 1846 (the year he married Emilia; they later had eight children). A series of journals and pamphlets followed, all espousing Monturiol's radical beliefs – in feminism, pacifism and utopian communism – and it was no surprise when one of his publications was suppressed by the government in the heady revolutionary days of 1848. Monturiol was forced briefly into exile and on his return to Barcelona, with the government now curtailing his publishing activities, he turned his hand instead to self-taught science and engineering.

It was a period where scientific progress and social justice appeared as two sides of the same coin to utopians like Monturiol – indeed, his friend, the civil engineer Ildefons Cerdà, would later mastermind the building of Barcelona's Eixample on socially useful grounds. Monturiol's mind turned to more immediately practical matters and, inspired by the harsh conditions in which the coral fishermen of Cadaques worked, he conceived the idea of a man-powered submarine. It would improve their lot, he had no doubt, though Monturiol's grander vision was of an underwater machine to explore the oceans and expand human knowledge.

The **Ictineo** – the "fish-boat" – made its maiden voyage in Barcelona harbour on June 28, 1859. At 7m long, it could carry four or five men, and eventually made more than fifty dives at depths of up to 20m. An improved design was started in 1862 – *Ictineo II* – a seventeen-metre-long vessel designed to be propelled by up to sixteen men. Trials in 1865 soon showed that human power wasn't sufficient for the job, so Monturiol installed a steam engine instead near the stern. This, the world's first steam-powered submarine, was launched on October 22, 1867 and dived to depths of up to 30m on thirteen separate runs (the longest lasting for over 7hr). However, Monturiol's financial backers had finally run out of patience with a machine that, though technically brilliant, couldn't yet pay its way. They withdrew their support and the submarine was seized by creditors and sold for scrap – the engine ended up in a paper mill.

Monturiol spent the rest of his life in a variety of jobs, but continued to come up with new inventions. With the *Ictineo*, he had pioneered the use of the double hull, a technique still used today, while Monturiol also claimed advances in the manufacture of glues and gums, copying documents, commercial cigarette production and steam engine efficiency. He died in relative obscurity in 1885 and was buried in Barcelona, though his remains were later transferred to his home town. There's a memorial there, while others to Monturiol's pioneering invention, the *Ictineo*, are scattered throughout Barcelona. Monturiol himself is remembered in the city by a simple plaque at the Cementiri de Poble Nou.

△ The beach, Barceloneta

Catalan only. Instead, you might saunter down to the sloping lawn nearby, where there's usually a school party examining the replica of the strange fish-shaped submarine, the **Ictineo**, a genuine Catalan curiosity (see box, p.75). From here, it's only a ten-minute walk down the *moll*, past the towering Roy Lichtenstein sculpture, and around the marina to the Palau de Mar and Barceloneta.

Palau de Mar: Museu d'Història de Catalunya

The only surviving warehouse on the Port Vell harbourside is known as the **Palau de Mar**, home to the **Museu d'Història de Catalunya** (Tues & Thurs–Sat 10am–7pm, Wed 10am–8pm, Sun 10am–2.30pm; €3, first Sun of month and public holidays free; ⓂBarceloneta), which traces the history of Catalunya from the Stone Age to the twentieth century. It's a spacious exhibition area wrapped around a wide atrium, with temporary shows on the ground floor and a lift to take you to the permanent displays on the upper floors: second floor for year dot to the Industrial Revolution, and third for periods and events up to 1980 (though later coverage is planned). You can pick up full English notes at the desk, and there's plenty to get your teeth into, whether it's poking around the interior of a Roman grain ship or comparing the rival nineteenth-century architectural plans for the Eixample. There's a dramatic Civil War section, while other fascinating asides shed light on matters as diverse as housing in the 1960s or the origins of the design of the Catalan flag. On the fourth floor, the café-bar boasts a glorious view from its huge terrace of the harbour, Tibidabo, Montjuïc and the city skyline – you don't need a museum ticket to visit this.

The fish and seafood **restaurants** in the Palau de Mar arcade are some of the most popular in the city, especially at weekends. Here you overlook the packed **marina**, where Catalans park their yachts like they park their cars – impossibly tightly – fronted in summer by hawkers spreading blankets on the ground to sell jewellery and sunglasses. A boat near the Palau de Mar in the marina has been converted into a floating bar, the *Luz de Gas* (see p.202).

Barceloneta

Barceloneta (ⓂBarceloneta) was laid out in 1755 – a classic eighteenth-century grid of streets where previously there had been mud flats – to replace part of La Ribera that was destroyed to make way for the Ciutadella fortress to the north. Bound by the harbour on one side and the Mediterranean on the other, the long, narrow streets are still very much as they were planned, broken at intervals by small squares and lined with abundantly windowed houses designed to give the sailors and fishing folk who originally lived here plenty of sun and fresh air. These days, it's the neighbourhood's many fish and seafood restaurants that are its *raison d'être*, found scattered right across the tight grid of streets but most characteristically lined along the harbourside **Passeig Joan de Borbó**. The best are reviewed on p.190.

Modern apartment building has scarred the neighbourhood's eighteenth-century proportions, but here and there survive a few reminders of the old days. Some original houses still venture a decorative flourish, a sculpted balcony or a carved lintel, while in the central **Plaça de la Barceloneta** is an

The cross-harbour cable car

The most thrilling ride in the city centre is across the inner harbour on the **cable car**, which sweeps right across the water from the **Torre de Sant Sebastiá**, at the foot of Barceloneta, to Montjuïc, with a stop in the middle at **Torre de Jaume I**, in front of the World Trade Centre on the Moll de Barcelona. The views are stunning, approaching either Montjuïc or Barceloneta, and you can pick out with ease the familiar towers of the cathedral and Sagrada Família, while the trees lining the Ramblas look like the forked tongue of a serpent.

Departures are every fifteen minutes (daily 10.45am–7pm), though in summer and at weekends you may have to wait for a while at the top of the towers for a ride as the cars only carry about twenty people at a time. **Tickets** cost €7.50 one way or €9 return for the whole journey, or €7.50 one way/return if you join at the middle station, Torre de Jaume I.

eighteenth-century fountain and the Neoclassical church of Sant Miquel del Port. The *Can Ganassa* café here puts out tables in the summer and, though you're just a couple of blocks from the tourist-filled restaurants of the *passeig*, the atmosphere remains resolutely local – people filling water-bottles or simply passing the time of day, kids riding bikes and playing ball. The adjacent Plaça de la Font holds the neighbourhood **Mercat de la Barceloneta** (Mon–Sat 7am–3pm, plus Fri except Aug 4.30–8.30pm).

Recent development has been most marked on the seaward side of Barceloneta. The beachside snack bars and simple restaurants – *xiringuitos* – that used to line this stretch disappeared in the Olympic cleanup (though some of the more famous establishments upped sticks to new locations elsewhere). In their place, Barceloneta acquired a beach, much improved from the days when it was a scrappy fishermen's strand, now furnished with boardwalks, showers, benches, climbing frames, water fountains and public art.

Platja de Sant Sebastià is the first in a series of beaches that stretches north along the coast to the River Besòs. A double row of palms backs the **Passeig Marítim**, a sweeping stone esplanade which runs as far as the Port Olímpic, a fifteen-minute walk away. On the way, just before the hospital and port, you'll pass the **Parc de la Barceloneta**, a rather plain expanse enlivened only by its whimsical *modernista* water tower (1905), rising like a minaret above the palms.

Vila Olímpica and the Port Olímpic

From any point along the Passeig Marítim, the soaring twin towers of the Olympic village and port impose themselves upon the skyline, while a shimmering golden mirage above the promenade slowly reveals itself to be a huge copper fish (courtesy of North American Frank Gehry, architect of the Bilbao Guggenheim). These are the showpiece manifestations of the huge seafront development constructed for the 1992 Olympics. The **Vila Olímpica** (Olympic Village) housed the 15,000 competitors and support staff, with the apartment buildings and residential complexes converted into permanent housing after the Games. It was a controversial plan, not least because the local population from the old industrial neighbourhood of Poble Nou – part of which was destroyed in the process – were excluded as property prices here later soared. Generally agreed to have been more beneficial is the **Port Olímpic**, site of the Olympic marina and many of the watersports events. Backed by the city's two tallest buildings – the **Torre Mapfre** and the steel-framed **Hotel Arts Barcelona**, both 154m high – the port area has filled up with restaurants, bars, shops and nightspots, and is a major target for visitors and city dwellers at weekends and on summer nights. Two wharves contain the bulk of the action: the Moll de Mestral has a lower deck by the marina lined with cafés, bars and *terrassas*, while the Moll de Gregal sports a double-decker tier of seafood restaurants. Beyond here, on the far side of the port, **Nova Icària** and **Bogatell** beaches – each with a beachside café, play facilities, showers and loungers – stretch up to the Poble Nou neighbourhood, now also in the throes of major development.

It's another fifteen minutes' walk from the port to the end of Bogatell beach and Poble Nou. Heading back into the city, the entrance to Ⓜ Ciutadella-Vila Olímpica lies over the main Ronda del Litoral, behind the port.

Poble Nou

Next neighbourhood along from the Port Olímpic is **Poble Nou** (New Village), a largely nineteenth-century industrial area that has long been slated for redevelopment. Since the early 1990s its transformation has formed part of the overall scheme that envisions turning the 5km of shoreline from Barceloneta to the River Besòs into a hi-tech business, leisure and residential corridor. The controversial extension of Avinguda Diagonal to the sea, north of Poble Nou, has provided the necessary rebranding, and it's as **Diagonal Mar** that the area hopes to prosper. Development here has been boosted by the neighbourhood's hosting of the Universal Forum of Cultures (May–Sept 2004; see p.35), a sort of cultural and environmental Expo, which is bringing new amenities in its wake – convention centre, marina, green zones, new beaches, housing, a business district, university campus, metro links and even an improved site for part of the city's zoo. It's on a grand scale: the convention centre is the biggest in southern Europe, while the boast about the main Forum open space – the **Plaza** – is that it's the second largest square in the world (150,000 square metres) after Beijing's Tiananmen Square. As with the Vila Olímpica before it, the redevelopment has its critics amongst the locals, who feel they're being pushed out as the money floods in – "Poble Nou is not for sale" reads the ubiquitous graffiti, though it's an increasingly forlorn cry.

It will be some time before the new Poble Nou is fully on the tourist circuit, though a few more traditional attractions are easily seen by anyone with a couple of hours to spare. The spruced-up **beaches** – Bogatell, Mar Bella and Nova Mar Bella – are easily reached along the promenade from the Port Olímpic, while crossing the main highway backing Bogatell beach puts you at the bottom of the pretty, traffic-free, tree-lined **Rambla Poble Nou**. This runs inland through the most attractive part of nineteenth-century Poble Nou and is entirely local in character – no cardsharps or human statues here. Stop off for an *orxata* or a crushed lemon drink at *El Tío Ché* (see p.176), or lunch at *Els Pescadors* (p.192) – Ⓜ Poble Nou (yellow line 4) is at the top of the *rambla* and a block over to the right, and will take you back to Ciutadella, Barceloneta or the city centre.

Back near the beach, it's also worth taking the time to stroll around the long walls to the entrance of the **Cementiri de Poble Nou** (daily 8am–6pm), at the northern end of Avinguda d'Icaria. This vast nineteenth-century mausoleum has its tombs set in walls 7m high, tended by families who have to climb great stepladders to reach the uppermost tiers. With traffic noise muted by the high walls, and birdsong accompanying a stroll around the flower-lined pavements, quiet courtyards, sculpted angels and tiny chapels, this village of the dead is a rare haven of peace in contemporary Barcelona.

Montjuïc

R ising over the city to the southwest, the steep hill of **Montjuïc** is by far the largest green area in Barcelona, and you'll need to reserve an entire day, perhaps even longer, to see its substantial attractions. It takes its name from the Jewish community that once settled on its slopes, and there's been a castle on the heights since the mid-seventeenth century, which says much about the hill's obvious historical defensive role. But it's as a cultural and leisure park that contemporary Montjuïc is positioned, anchored around the heavyweight art collections in the **Museu Nacional d'Art de Catalunya** (**MNAC**). This unsurpassed national collection of Catalan art is supplemented by other superb galleries on Montjuïc, devoted to international contemporary art in the **Caixa Forum** and, in the **Fundació Joan Miró**, to the work of the Catalan artist perhaps most associated with the city. In addition, there are separate (though minor) archeological, ethnological, military and theatrical **museums**, quite apart from the buildings and stadiums associated with the 1992 **Olympics**, which was centred on the heights of Montjuïc.

As late as the 1890s, the hill was nothing more than a collection of private farms and woodland on the edge of the old town, though some landscaping had already taken place by the time Montjuïc was chosen as the site of the **International Exhibition** of 1929. The slopes were then laid with gardens, terraces and fountains, while monumental Neoclassical buildings were added to the north side, many of them later adapted as museums. The famous **Poble Espanyol** (Spanish Village) – a hybrid park of collected Spanish buildings – is the most extraordinary relic of the Exhibition, while the various lush **gardens** still provide enjoyment and respite from the crowds. Above all, perhaps, there are the **views** to savour from this most favoured of Barcelona's hills: from the steps in front of the Museu Nacional, from the castle ramparts, from the Olympic terraces, or from the cable cars which zigzag up the steepest slopes of Montjuïc.

The hill covers a wide area, so it's vital to plan your visit carefully around the various opening times. If you're intent on covering everything, it might be better to see Montjuïc in two separate visits – art museums, Poble Espanyol and Olympic area on one day, and Fundació Joan Miró, cable car and castle on the other. There are several approaches to Montjuïc, depending on where you want to start, and various means of **transport** around the hill: the box p.83 has all the details. The Barcelona Card and Articket (see p.23), and Bus Turístic pass (p.29), provide discounted entry into some of Montjuïc's museums, galleries and attractions, or there's the **Montjuïc Card** (one day; €20), which gives free entry to everything plus complimentary rides on the tourist train and cable car. It's available from participating attractions, including the upper station of the Funicular de Montjuïc. Places to eat are thin on the ground, though there are good **cafés** in Caixa Forum and the Fundació Joan Miró, outdoor snack bars at the castle and on the slopes below the Museu Nacional d'Art, and decent **restaurants** in the neighbouring *barri* of Poble Sec (see p.189).

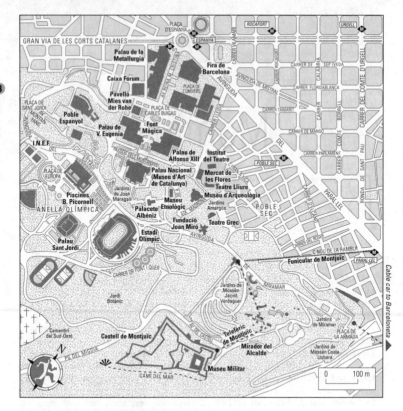

Around Plaça d'Espanya

Gateway to the 1929 International Exhibition was the vast **Plaça d'Espanya**, based on plans by noted architect Josep Puig i Cadalfach. Arranged around a huge Neoclassical fountain, and offset by the existing Moorish-style bullring on the northern side (no longer in use), the square is unlike any other in Barcelona, and a radical departure from the *modernisme* so in vogue elsewhere in the contemporary city. Striking twin towers, 47m high, stand at the foot of the imposing **Avinguda de la Reina Maria Cristina**, which heads up towards Montjuïc, the avenue lined by huge exhibition halls still used for trade fairs. At the end of the avenue is Plaça de Carles Buïgas, from where monumental steps (and modern escalators) ascend the hill to the Palau Nacional, past water cascades and under the flanking walls, busts and roofline "kiosks" of two grand Viennese-style pavilions. It's an overtly showy approach to Montjuïc, hugely impressive in its way, but almost anti-Catalan in spirit if not scale – evocative, more than anything, of Eastern Bloc vainglory. There's little whimsy in evidence, save for the **Font Màgica**, at the foot of the steps, which, on selected evenings (May–Sept Thurs–Sun 8pm–midnight, music starts 9.30pm; Oct–April Fri & Sat only at 7pm & 8pm; free), becomes the centrepiece of an impressive if slightly kitsch sound-and-light show – the brightly coloured water appears to dance to the strains of Holst and Abba.

Montjuïc transport

Getting there

- ⓂEspanya deposits you at the foot of Avinguda de la Reina Maria Cristina, for easy access to Caixa Forum, Poble Espanyol and the Museu Nacional d'Art (MNAC). The Olympic area can then be reached by escalators behind MNAC.
- The **Funicular de Montjuïc** (daily 9am–10pm every 10min; normal city transport tickets and passes apply) departs from inside the station at ⓂParal·lel and takes a couple of minutes to ascend the hill. At the upper station on Avinguda de Miramar you can switch to the Montjuïc cable car (see "Getting around" below), or you're only a few minutes' walk from the Fundació Joan Miró.
- The **cross-harbour cable car** (see p.78) from Barceloneta drops you outside the Jardins de Miramar, on the far southeastern slopes. From here, it's a ten-minute walk to the Montjuïc cable-car and funicular stations.

Getting around

- **Walking**. It takes a good hour to walk on the road around the hill from Avinguda de la Reina Maria Cristina, past the Poble Espanyol, Olympic area and Fundació Joan Miró to the cross-harbour cable-car station at the far end of Montjuïc – and it's steep and shadeless in parts. Escalators up the hill between the Museu Nacional d'Art and the Olympic area cut out the worst of the slog. Walking up the steep hill all the way to the castle is not advised (though there are steps through the gardens and between the road) – use the cable car.
- **Buses**. From Plaça d'Espanya (Avgda. de la Reina Maria Cristina) take: bus #13 for Caixa Forum and the Poble Espanyol; #50 for Caixa Forum, Poble Espanyol, Olympic area, funicular and cable-car stations; or bus #PM (Parc de Montjuïc; weekends only) for the same route plus the castle. The Bus Turístic (see p.29) also stops at the main Montjuïc attractions.
- **Tren Turístic de Montjuïc**. The train-trolley leaves from Plaça d'Espanya (mid-June to mid-Sept daily; otherwise April to mid-June & mid-Sept to Oct Sat & Sun only 10am–8.30pm; every 30min; €3.20) and runs to all the major sights on Montjuïc, including the castle. The return trip lasts about an hour and your ticket allows you to complete the full circuit once, getting on and off where you like.
- **Telefèric de Montjuïc**. The Montjuïc cable car (June to mid-Sept daily 11am–9pm; April, May & mid-Sept to Oct daily 11am–7pm; rest of the year weekends only 11am–7pm; €3.60 one way, €5 return), from Avinguda de Miramar, whisks you up to the castle and back in little four-person gondolas.

Caixa Forum

To the right of the fountain (before climbing the steps/escalators), and hidden from view until you turn the corner around Avinguda del Marquès de Comillas, is **Caixa Forum** (Tues–Sun 10am–8pm; free; ☎902 223 040, Ⓦwww.fundacio .lacaixa.es), an arts and cultural centre set within the old Casamarona textile factory. Constructed in 1911 in the finest modernist stylings of Puig i Cadafalch, the factory shut down in 1920 and lay abandoned until pressed into service as a police building after the Civil War. The subsequent renovation and expansion under the auspices of the Fundacío La Caixa has produced a remarkable building, entered beneath twin iron-and-glass canopies representing spreading trees. You descend into a palatial white marble foyer, where a vibrant Sol LeWitt mural splashes across one wall. Beyond here are found the exhibition halls, fashioned within the former factory buildings, whose external structure has been left untouched – original girders, pillars and stanchions, factory brickwork and crenellated walls appear at every turn. The Casamarona tower, etched in blue and yellow tiling, rises high above the walls, as readily recognizable as the huge Miró starfish logos emblazoned across the building.

The centre houses the foundation's celebrated **contemporary art collection**, focusing on the period from the 1980s to the present, with hundreds of artists represented, from Antoni Abad to Rachel Whiteread. Works are shown in partial rotation, along with touring exhibitions. There's also a library and resource centre, the Mediateca multimedia space, regular children's activities, and a 400-seat auditorium with a full programme of music, art, poetry and literary events. The **café** is a nice spot, too – an airy converted space within the old factory walls, serving sandwiches, snacks and lunch.

Pavelló Mies van der Rohe

Immediately across Avinguda del Marquès de Comillas from Caixa Forum, set back from the road, is the 1986 reconstruction by Catalan architects of the **Pavelló Mies van der Rohe** (daily 10am–8pm; €3.40; Ⓦwww.miesbcn .com), which recalls part of the German contribution to the 1929 Exhibition. Originally designed by Mies van der Rohe, and used as a reception room during the Exhibition, it's considered a major example of modern rationalist architecture. The pavilion has a startlingly beautiful conjunction of hard straight lines with watery surfaces, its dark-green polished onyx alternating with shining glass. It's open to visitors but unless there's an exhibition in place (a fairly regular occurrence) there is nothing to see inside, though you can buy postcards and books from the small shop and debate quite how much you want a Mies mousepad or a "Less is More" T-shirt.

Poble Espanyol

A five-minute walk up Avinguda del Marquès de Comillas brings you to the **Poble Espanyol**, or "Spanish Village" (Mon 9am–8pm, Tues–Thurs 9am–2am, Fri & Sat 9am–4am, Sun 9am–midnight; €7; Ⓦwww.poble-espanyol.com). A complete village consisting of streets and squares with reconstructions of famous or characteristic buildings from all over Spain – such as the fairy-tale medieval walls of Ávila through which you enter – this was an inspired concept for the International Exhibition (and since then copied world over). "Get to know Spain in one hour" is what's promised and it's nowhere near as cheesy as you might think. It works well as a crash-course introduction to Spanish architecture – everything is well labelled and at least reasonably accurate. The echoing main square is lined with cafés, while the surrounding streets, alleys and buildings contain around forty workshops, where you can see engraving, weaving, pottery and other crafts. Inevitably, it's all one huge shopping experience – castanets to Lladró porcelain, religious icons to Barcelona soccer shirts – and prices are inflated, but children will love it (and you can let them run free as there's no traffic). Your ticket also gets you entry to the **Fran Daurel Col.leccío d'Art Contemporani** (daily 10am–7pm), so you might as well look in. Among the minor Tàpies and Miró lithographs is a series of Picasso ceramics – a jug with the face of a woman, plates with painted and relief faces and assorted decorated tiles.

Get to the village as it opens if you want to enjoy it in relatively crowd-free circumstances – once the tour groups arrive, it becomes a bit of a scrum. You could, of course, always come at the other end of the day, when the village transforms into a vibrant and exciting centre of Barcelona nightlife. Two of Barcelona's hippest designers, Alfredo Arribas and Xavier Mariscal, installed a club, the *Torres de Avila*, in the Ávila gate in the early 1990s. Other fashionable venues followed and, this being Barcelona, the whole complex now stays open until the small hours.

Museu Nacional d'Art de Catalunya

The towering, domed **Palau Nacional**, set back on Montjuïc at the top of the long flight of steps from the fountains, was the flagship building of Barcelona's 1929 International Exhibition. Partly the work of Pere Domènech i Roura (son of the more famous Domènech i Montaner), its massive frescoed oval hall hosted the opening ceremony of the Exhibition, providing a fittingly grandiose backdrop for the city's biggest show since the Universal Exhibition of 1888. The palace was due to be demolished once the exhibition was over, but gained a reprieve and ultimately became home to one of Spain's great museums, devoted to Catalan art.

This, the **Museu Nacional d'Art de Catalunya** (**MNAC**; Tues–Sat 10am–7pm, Sun 10am–2.30pm; €4.80, first Thurs of the month free; ⓦwww.mnac.es), has undergone a major refit over the last few years, designed to bring together collections previously held in different buildings. In addition to the medieval art collection – already beautifully displayed here for some time – new sections have been added for MNAC's impressive holdings of European Renaissance and Baroque art, as well as for the collection of nineteenth- and twentieth-century Catalan art (until the 1940s) formerly housed in the Parc de la Ciutadella – everything from the 1950s and later is covered by the MACBA (see p.59). In addition to these major areas of interest, there is also a collection of drawings and engravings (Gabinet de Dibuixos i Gravats; Tues & Thurs 10am–2pm) dominated by Catalan pieces from the last three centuries but including works from elsewhere in Europe; a numismatic section (Gabinete Numismàtic de Catalunya; by appointment only, Mon–Fri 9am–2pm); and a photographic collection, again primarily Catalan. Items from these more specialist collections sometimes appear in **temporary exhibitions** on the lower level (separate entry €4.20, joint admission with main museum €6), which change every two to four months.

Faced with this wealth of art, it can be difficult to know where to start, but if time is limited it's recommended that you concentrate on the medieval collection. It's split into two main sections, one dedicated to Romanesque art and the other to Gothic – periods in which Catalunya's artists were pre-eminent in Spain. The collection of Romanesque frescoes in particular is the museum's pride and joy, and is perhaps the best collection of its kind in the world.

Modern art collection

The modern art collection (ie of nineteenth- and twentieth-century Catalan art) will be transferred to MNAC in the second half of 2004, with the gallery inauguration expected in December 2004.

The Romanesque collection

Great numbers of Romanesque churches were built in the Catalan Pyrenees as the Christian conquest spread, though there are far fewer further south, where Christianity arrived later. Medieval Catalan studios concentrated on decorating the churches with frescoes depicting biblical events, and even the most remote Pyrenean valleys could boast lavish masterpieces of great skill. However, by the nineteenth century many of these churches and their decorative frescoes had either been ruined by later renovations or lay abandoned, prone to theft and damage. Not until 1919 was a concerted effort made to remove the frescoes to the museum, where they could be better preserved and displayed.

Six remarkable sections present the frescoes in a reconstruction of their original setting, so you can see their size and where they would have been placed in the church buildings. Full explanatory notes (in English) cover the artistic techniques, interpretation and iconography of the paintings, which for the most part have a vibrant, raw quality, best exemplified by those taken from churches in the Boí valley in the Catalan Pyrenees. In the apse of the early twelfth-century church of Sant Climent in Taüll, the so-called **Master of Taüll** painted an extraordinarily powerful Christ in Majesty, combining a Byzantine hierarchical composition with the imposing colours and strong outlines of contemporary manuscript illuminators. Look out for details such as the leper, to the left of the Sant Climent altar, patiently allowing a dog to lick his sores. Frescoes from other churches explore a variety of themes, from heaven to hell, with the displays complemented by sculptures, altar panels, woodcarvings, religious objects and furniture retrieved from the mouldering churches themselves.

The Gothic collection

The Gothic collection is also extensive, ranging over the whole of Spain and particularly good on Catalunya, Valencia and Aragón. Again the pieces are laid out chronologically with a well-written commentary in each section, explaining the development of artistic movements from the thirteenth to the fifteenth centuries and the influence of other European styles on Catalan art. The evolution from the Romanesque to the Gothic period was marked by a move from mural painting to painting on wood, and by the depiction of more naturalistic figures in scenes showing the lives of the saints, and later in portraits of kings and patrons of the arts. In the early part of the period, the Catalan and Valencian schools particularly were influenced by contemporary Italian styles, and you'll see some outstanding altarpieces, tombs and church decoration as well as colourful, if less refined, paintings. Later began the International Gothic or "1400" style in which the influences became more widespread; the important figures of this movement were the fifteenth-century artists **Jaume Huguet** and **Lluís Dalmau**. Works from the end of this period show the strong influence of contemporary Flemish painting, in the use of denser colours, the depiction of crowd scenes and a concern for perspective. The last Catalan artist of note here is the so-called **Master of La Seu d'Urgell**, represented by a number of works, including a fine series of six paintings (Christ, the Virgin Mary, saints Peter, Paul and Sebastian, and Mary Magdalene) which once formed the covers of the organ in La Seu's cathedral. The section concludes with examples of funerary art – tombs, sarcophagi and sepulchres of the fourteenth and fifteenth centuries – and cases of religious gold and silverware.

The Renaissance, Baroque and modern collections

Many of the **Renaissance** and **Baroque** works on display originally formed part of the Col.leccío Cambó, named after the early twentieth-century Catalan politician who bequeathed his personal collection to the city of Barcelona. Major European artists from the fifteenth to eighteenth centuries are represented, and though there are no real masterpieces you will find works by Lucas

Cranach, Quentin Massys, Peter Paul Rubens, Giovanni Battista Tiepolo, Jean Honoré Fragonard, Francisco de Goya, El Greco, Diego Velázquez and others.

These act as a taster for the **nineteenth- and twentieth-century Catalan art** collection, which as you might expect is particularly good on *modernista* and *noucentista* painting and sculpture, the two dominant schools of the period. The collection starts with works by Marià Fortuny i Marsal, who specialized in minutely detailed, very highly finished canvases, often of exotic subjects – including his *Battle of Tetuan*, based on a visit to Morocco in 1859 to observe the war there. Although he died young, in 1874, Fortuny is often regarded as the earliest *modernista* artist; he was certainly the first Catalan painter known widely abroad, having exhibited to great acclaim in Paris and Rome. The master of nineteenth-century Catalan landscape painting was Joaquim Veyreda i Vila, founder of the so-called "Olot School" (Olot being a town in northern Catalunya), whose members were influenced both by the work of the early Impressionists and by the distinctive volcanic scenery of the Olot region. However, it wasn't until the later emergence of Ramon Casas i Carbó (whose work once hung on the walls of *Els Quatre Gats*) and Santiago Rusiñol i Prats that Catalan art acquired a progressive sheen, taking its cue from the very latest in European styles, whether the symbolism of Whistler or the vibrant social observation of Toulouse-Lautrec. Hot on their heels came a new generation of *modernista* artists – Josep Maria Sert, Marià Pidelaserra i Brias, Ricard Canals i Llambí and others – who were strongly influenced by the scene in contemporary Paris. The two brightest stars of the period, though, were Joaquim Mir i Trinxet, whose landscapes tended towards the abstract, and Isidre Nonell i Monturiol, who from 1902 until his early death in 1911 painted only naturalistic studies of impoverished gypsies and gypsy communities. *Noucentisme* was a style at once more classical and less consciously flamboyant than *modernisme* – Joaquim Sunyer i Miró, perhaps the best known *noucentista* artist, has several pieces here, though there are works by a host of others, including Xavier Nogués i Casas, Joaquim Torres-Garcia and the sculptors Pau Gargallo i Catalán and Enric Casanovas i Roy.

La Ciutat del Teatre and around

Downhill from the Palau Nacional, just to the east, steps descend the hillside to the theatre area known as **La Ciutat del Teatre**, which occupies a corner at the back of the old working-class neighbourhood of **Poble Sec**. A road, the Passeig de Santa Madrona, snakes down this way too, passing the **museums of ethnology and archeology** – the also-rans of Montjuïc really, though both are decent wet-weather targets – and the **Teatre Grec,** a reproduction of a Greek theatre cut into the hillside. This was built for the 1929 Exhibition and is now used during Barcelona's summer cultural Grec festival.

Museu Etnològic

The **Museu Etnològic** (Tues–Sun 10am–2pm; €3, first Sun of the month free; Ⓦwww.museuetnologic.bcn.es) boasts extensive cultural collections from Spain, Central and South America, Asia, Africa, Australia and the Middle East, housed in a series of glass hexagons. The collection itself is too big to exhibit at any one time, so the museum displays rotating exhibitions, which usually last for a year or two and focus on a particular subject or geographical area. The Spanish collections range across every province in the country, with exhibitions occasionally homing in on the minutiae of rural life and work, or examining medieval carving or early industrialization. Other artefacts from further afield are also worth looking out for, especially the Native Australian "X-ray" paintings, the collection of Afghan carpets and jewellery, and the Pre-Columbian ceramics from Peru and Ecuador.

Museu d'Arqueologia de Catalunya

More relevant to the region than the city's ethnological collections are those of the **Museu d'Arqueologia de Catalunya** (Tues–Sat 9.30am–7pm, Sun 10am–2.30pm; €2.40; ⓦwww.mac.es), lower down the hill. The museum has an impressive array of relics spanning the centuries from the Stone Age to the time of the Visigoths, with the Roman and Greek periods particularly well represented. Although some attempt has been made at chronology, the displays can at times be slightly confusing, partly a reflection of the complex mixture of cultures found in this part of Spain and partly a result of scanty labelling. However, it's worth persevering, especially for the finds from the Greek site at Empúries on the Costa Brava, some beautiful figures from the Carthaginian settlements in Ibiza and an interesting selection of Iberian ceramics from around Catalunya and further south, including tablets bearing inscriptions in the Iberian script, which is still indecipherable.

La Ciutat del Teatre and Poble Sec

The theatre buildings that make up La Ciutat del Teatre sit in a tight huddle off c/de Lleida, with the **Mercat de les Flores** – once a flower market – and **Teatre Lliure** occupying the spaghetti-western-style Palau de l'Agricultura premises built for the 1929 Exhibition. Walk through the terracotta arch from c/de Lleida, and off to the left is the far sleeker **Institut del Teatre**, whose contemporary sheer walls contrast markedly with the neighbourhood's cheap housing, whose laundry is strung just metres away from the gleaming "Theatre City". The institute brings together the city's major drama and dance schools, and various conservatories, libraries and study centres. In one of the wings, opening onto the remodelled square of Plaça de Margarida Xirgu, is the **Museu de les Arts Escèniques** (Tues–Sat 10am–1pm & 5–7.30pm, Sun 10am–2pm; €3, ⓦwww.diba.es/iteatre), though you'll have to be especially keen (and read Catalan) to get anything out of its changing exhibitions relating to Catalan theatre.

The streets to the south and east make up the neighbourhood of **Poble Sec**, or "dry village", so called because it had no water supply until the nineteenth century. Confined by the hill of Montjuïc on one side and the busy Avinguda del Paral.lel on the other, it's a complete contrast to the landscaped slopes behind it – a grid of down-to-earth grocery stores, bakeries, old-fashioned bars and good-value restaurants (see p.189). There's nothing to see, though you might walk through on your way back to the Raval and Barcelona's old-town areas, in which case it's worth negotiating the precipitous c/Nou de la Rambla for a drink in the *Bar Primavera* (closed Mon). It's an old cottage at the very top of the street, with partial views from its tables set on a vine-clad terrace. The **funicular** (from ⓜParal.lel to the cable-car station for the castle) departs from right at the other end of this street.

The Olympics on Montjuïc

From Poble Espanyol, the main road through Montjuïc climbs around the hill and up to the city's principal **Olympic area**, sometimes known as the Anella

△ Communications Tower, Montjuïc

Olímpica (Olympic Ring). The 1992 Olympics were the second planned for Montjuïc. The first, in 1936 – the so-called "People's Olympics" – were organized as an alternative to the Nazis' infamous Berlin games of that year, but the day before the official opening Franco's army revolt triggered the Civil War and scuppered the Barcelona games. Some of the 25,000 athletes and spectators who had turned up stayed on to join the Republican forces.

Avinguda del Estadi leads you right past some of Barcelona's most celebrated sporting edifices – like Ricardo Bofill's Institut Nacional d'Educació Física de Catalunya or **INEF** (a sort of sports university), the **Piscines Bernat Picornell** (swimming pools and sports complex) and the Japanese-designed, steel-and-glass **Palau Sant Jordi**. Opened in 1990 with Luciano Pavarotti in attendance, this sports and concert hall seats 17,000 people and is overshadowed only by the Olympic stadium itself, the **Estadi Olímpic**, which comfortably holds 65,000. Built originally for the 1929 Exhibition, and completely refitted to accommodate the 1992 opening and closing ceremonies, it's a marvellously spacious stadium, its original Neoclassical facade left untouched by the Catalan architects in charge of the project. There's usually a gate open if you just want a glimpse of the pitch (the city's other local soccer team, Espanyol, plays here), and you can get the same view from the self-service *Olympic Sports Café* inside the stadium.

At the stadium, the **Galeria Olímpica** (April–Sept Mon–Fri 10am–2pm & 4–7pm; Oct–March Mon–Fri 10am–1pm & 4–6pm; €2.70, ⓦwww .fundaciobarcelonaolimpica.es) exhibits assorted items from the opening and closing ceremonies, and shows videos of the Games themselves. Between the stadium and the Palau Sant Jordi, a vast *terrassa* provides one of the finest vantage points in the city. Long water-fed troughs break the concrete and marble expanse, while the confident, space-age curve of Santiago Calatrava's communications tower dominates the skyline.

Fundació Joan Miró

Montjuïc's highlight for many is the **Fundació Joan Miró** (Tues, Wed, Fri & Sat 10am–7pm, Thurs 10am–9.30pm, Sun 10am–2.30pm; €7.20, exhibitions €3.60; ⓦwww.bcn.fjmiro.es), possibly Barcelona's most adventurous art museum and certainly its most attractive. The impressive white structure is set in lovely gardens overlooking the city, and it lies just a few minutes' walk from either the Olympic stadium or the Montjuïc funicular and cable-car stations.

Joan Miró (1893–1983) was one of the greatest of Catalan artists, establishing an international reputation while never severing his links with his homeland. He had his first exhibition in 1918 and after that spent his summers in Catalunya and the rest of the time in France, before moving to Mallorca in 1956, where he died. His friend, the architect Josep-Luis Sert, designed the beautiful building that now houses the museum, which comprises a permanent collection of paintings, graphics, tapestries and sculptures donated by Miró himself and covering the period from 1914 to 1978. With good English notes available, and a layout that uses natural light and space to good effect, it's a museum that's a positive pleasure to negotiate.

Miró, meanwhile, has a grip on the city that's hard to ignore, whether it's T-shirts for tourists or branding for businesses. You'll notice his sculptures and designs littering the city: the starfish logo which he designed for the Caixa de Pensions; the España logo on Spanish National Tourist Board publications; his sculpture in the Parc Joan Miró; and the mosaic on the Ramblas.

The Fundació sponsors excellent temporary exhibitions, film shows, lectures and children's theatre: check the website or listings magazines, or consult the notices on display. There's also a **library**, with books and periodicals on contemporary art, a **bookshop** selling posters and a **bar-restaurant** with outdoor tables on a pleasant patio – you don't have to pay to get into the museum to use this.

The collection

The **paintings and drawings** are instantly recognizable, among the chief links between Surrealism and abstract art. Miró showed a childlike delight in colours and shapes and developed a free, highly decorative style – one of his favourite early techniques was to spill paint on the canvas and move his brush around in it. Much of the collection is, in fact, of his later works, since the museum was only proposed – and works specifically set aside – in the 1960s, when Miró had already been painting for almost fifty years. But there are early Realist works from before the mid-1920s, like the effervescent *Portrait of a Young Girl* (1919), while other gaps are filled by a collection later donated by Miró's widow, Pilar Juncosa, which demonstrates Miró's preoccupations in the 1930s and 1940s. Affectingly, these seem to have included his wife: *The Morning Star* from 1946 forms part of his Constellations series, dedicated to Juncosa. Perhaps the most moving works are those of the *Barcelona Series* (1939–44), fifty black-and-white lithographs executed in the immediate post-Civil War period. Miró's artistic appraisal of the war is a dark reflection of the turmoil of the period; snarling faces and great black shapes and shadows dominate. The most recent acquisitions – 23 Miró works on long-term loan from a Japanese collector – are on display in the museum's **Sala K**.

Perhaps the most innovative room of all is that full of work by other artists in homage to Miró, including fine pieces by Henri Matisse, Henry Moore, Robert Motherwell and the Basque sculptor Eduardo Chillida. The single most compelling exhibit, however, has to be Alexander Calder's **Mercury Fountain**, which he built for the Republican pavilion at the Paris Universal Exhibition of 1936–37 – the same exhibition for which Picasso painted *Guernica*. Like *Guernica*, it's a tribute to a town, this time the mercury-mining town of Almáden – its name spelled out in dangling metal letters above the fountain – which saw saturation bombing during the Civil War.

Other exhibits include Miró's enormous bright **tapestries** (he donated nine to the museum), pencil drawings (particularly of misshapen women and gawky ballerinas), and **sculpture** outside in the gardens. All these started life in the form of **sketches and notes**, and the museum has retained five thousand separate examples, of which it usually displays a selection. From a doodle on a scrap of old newspaper or on the back of a postcard, it's possible to trace the development of shapes and themes that later evolved into full-blown works of art.

Castell de Montjuïc and around

The Telefèric de Montjuïc tacks up the hillside, offering magnificent views on the way, before depositing you within the walls of the eighteenth-century **Castell de Montjuïc**. Built on seventeenth-century ruins, the fort's outer defences are constructed as a series of angular concentric perimeters, designed for artillery deflection, but the inner part is startlingly medieval in appearance, with its straight walls and square shape. The fort served as a military base and prison for many years after the Civil War, and it was here that the last president of the prewar Generalitat, Lluís Companys, was executed on Franco's orders on October 15, 1940 – he had been in exile in Paris, but had been handed over to Franco by the Germans upon their capture of the French capital.

You can walk along the ramparts, taking photographs from the various viewpoints, and there's a little outdoor café within the walls. Leave by the drawbridge and you can skirt the outer walls of the bastion as well, where the locals come at weekends to practise archery in the moat. You have to pay to go inside the inner keep, where you'll find Barcelona's **Museu Militar** (mid-March to mid-Nov Tues–Sun 9.30am–8pm; mid-Nov to mid-March Tues–Sun 9.30am–5pm; €2.50), containing models of the most famous Catalan castles and an excellent collection of swords and guns, medals, uniforms, maps and photographs, capped by a collection of suits of armour down in the lower level. Franco is paid anachronistic homage in an equestrian statue presiding over the collection of uniforms – a reminder of Spain's all-too-recent dictatorial past.

Below the castle walls, a panoramic pathway – the **Camí del Mar** – has been cut from the cliff edge, providing scintillating views, first across to Port Olímpic and the northern beaches, and then southwest as the path swings around the castle. This is an unfamiliar view of the city, of the sprawling docks and container yards, and cruise ships and tankers are usually visible negotiating the busy sea lanes. The path is just over 1km long and ends at the back of the castle battlements near the **Mirador del Migdia**, where a small house (weekends only) sells drinks and rents out bikes for use on the surrounding wooded trails. It's worth strolling through the trees to the *mirador* itself, a balcony with extensive views over the Baixa Llobregat industrial area. You can see across to the Olympic stadium from here, while in the immediate foreground is the extraordinary **Cementiri del Sud-Oest**, stretching along the ridge below, whose tombs are stacked like apartment blocks on great conifer-lined avenues.

The gardens of Montjuïc

Montjuïc's main gardens are scattered across the southern and eastern reaches of the hill, below the castle. Principal among them is the **Jardí Botànic de Barcelona** (daily: July, Aug & Nov–March 10am–3pm; April–June, Sept & Oct 10am–5pm; €3; ⓦwww.jardibotanic.bcn.es), on c/Dr Font i Quer, on the slopes behind the Olympic stadium, whose easy-to-follow paths wind through landscaped zones representing the flora of the Mediterranean, Canary Islands, California, Chile, South Africa and Australia. There are **tours** every weekend (not Aug) on the half-hour between 11am and 1.30pm.

East of here, the Montjuïc cable car passes over the **Jardins de Mossèn Jacint Verdaguer** (daily 10am–sunset; free), while the nearby **Jardins de Miramar** are currently undergoing restoration. Neither of these really warrants a separate visit, though it definitely is worth seeking out the entrance to the precipitous cactus gardens of the **Jardins de Mossèn Costa i Llobera** (daily 10am–sunset; free), which look out over the port. Steps lead down into the garden from a point close to the upper cross-harbour cable-car station, into flourishing stands of Central and South American, Indian and African cacti, some over 6m high. It's a dramatic scene, little experienced by most visitors to Montjuïc.

The Eixample

T he **Eixample** – the gridded, nineteenth-century new-town area north of Plaça de Catalunya – is the city's main shopping and business district. It covers a vast expanse, spreading north to the outlying hills and suburbs, though most of what there is to see lies within a few blocks of the two central, parallel thoroughfares, Passeig de Gràcia and Rambla de Catalunya. To visitors the district's regular blocks and seemingly endless streets can appear offputting, while many locals experience only a fraction of the district on a daily basis. Indeed, the Eixample can't really be said to be a neighbourhood at all – at least not in the same way that the old-town *barris* distinguish themselves – though its genesis lay in the increasingly crowded streets and alleys of the Ciutat Vella.

As Barcelona grew more industrialized throughout the nineteenth century, the old town became overcrowded and unsanitary. Conditions were such that in 1851 permission was given by the Spanish state to knock down the encircling walls so that the city could expand beyond its medieval limits, across the plain to the hills beyond the old town. The Barcelona authorities championed a fan-shaped plan by popular municipal architect **Antoni Rovira i Trias**, whose elegant if conventional design radiated out from the existing shape of the old town. However, much to local chagrin, this was passed over by the Spanish government in favour of a revolutionary blueprint drawn up by utopian engineer and urban planner **Ildefons Cerdà i Sunyer**. This envisaged a grid-shaped new town marching off to the north, intersected by broad avenues cut on the diagonal. Districts would be divided into mathematically defined groups of blocks, with buildings limited in height, and central gardens, schools, markets, hospitals and other services provided for the inhabitants. Work started in 1859 on what became known as the *Ensanche* in Castilian, and *Eixample* in Catalan – the "Extension" or "Widening". Space and light were part of the very fabric of the design, with Cerdà's characteristic wide streets and shaved corners of the blocks surviving today. However, he saw most of his more radical social proposals ignored, as the Eixample rapidly became a fashionable area in which to live. Speculators developed buildings on the proposed open spaces as the moneyed classes sought to move from their cramped quarters by the port in the old town to spacious new apartments and business addresses. As the money in the city moved north, so did a new class of **modernista architects**, who began to pepper the Eixample with ever-more-striking examples of their work, which were eagerly commissioned by status-conscious merchants and businessmen.

These extraordinary *modernista* buildings – most notably the work of Antoni Gaudí, Lluís Domènech i Montaner and Josep Puig i Cadafalch (see box p.96) – provide the main attraction for the visitor in the Eixample, turning it into a sort of open-air urban museum. The best-known examples are those in the famous block known as the "Mansana de la Discòrdia", as well as Gaudí's La Pedrera apartment building, all found on the attractive central spine of **Passeig de Gràcia**. Almost everything else you're likely to want to see is found to the east of here in the area known as **Dreta de l'Eixample** (the right-hand side), including Gaudí's extraordinary **Sagrada Família** church – the one building in the city to which a visit is virtually obligatory. Other attractions in the *Dreta* include museums concentrating on Egyptian antiquities, Catalan art and ceramics, and perfume, with a special draw provided by the gallery devoted to the works of Catalan artist Antoni Tàpies.

There's less to get excited about on the western, or left-hand side – the so-called **Esquerra de l'Eixample** – which houses many of the public buildings contained within Cerdà's nineteenth-century plan. Nevertheless, certain areas provide an interesting contrast with the *modernista* flourishes over the way, particularly the urban park projects close to Barcelona Sants train station.

As the Eixample covers a very large area, you're unlikely to be able to see everything described below as part of a single outing. You'll need to take **public transport** where you can to individual sites and then walk around the sur-

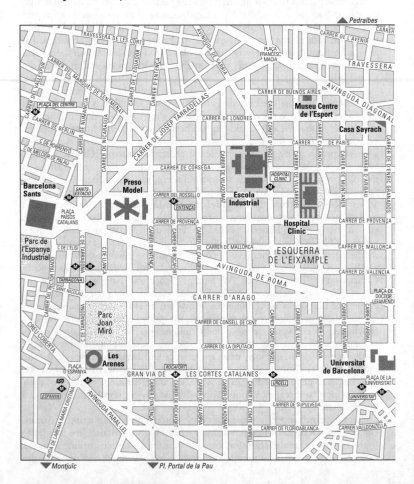

rounding area; all the relevant details are given in the text. For a map showing all the city's *modernista* sights, a guided tour of the Mansana de la Discòrdia facades and for other benefits, the **Ruta del Modernisme** package might be of interest, while the Barcelona Card or the Articket also offer useful discounts (see p.23 for details of all). You'll find plenty of reasonable places to stop for lunch, while you may well be in this part of town at night, too, since many of the city's designer bars and restaurants are found here – the relevant chapters have useful listings.

Along Passeig de Gràcia

If you want to walk in the Eixample, the section you'll get most out of is the wide **Passeig de Gràcia,** which runs northwest from Plaça de Catalunya as far as the southern reaches of Gràcia. Laid out in its present form in 1827, it's a splendid, showy avenue, bisected by the other two main

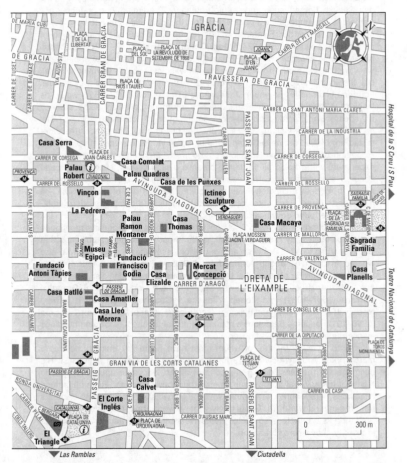

city boulevards, the Gran Via de les Corts Catalanes and Avinguda Diagonal. If you walk its length as far as the Diagonal (a 25min stroll) you'll get a view of some of the best of the city's *modernista* architecture, flaunted in a series of remarkable buildings on and just off the avenue. The *passeig* itself reveals the care taken at the turn of the last century to provide a complete environment for these buildings. At intervals you can rest at the elaborate benches and lamps designed in 1900 by the city's municipal architect, Pere Falqués.

Modernisme

Modernisme, the Catalan offshoot of Art Nouveau, was the expression of a renewed upsurge in Catalan nationalism in the 1870s. The early nineteenth-century economic recovery in Catalunya had provided the initial impetus, and the ensuing cultural renaissance in the region – the *Renaixença* – led to the fresh stirrings of a new Catalan awareness and identity after the dark years of Bourbon rule.

Lluís Domènech i Montaner (1850–1923) – perhaps the greatest *modernista* architect – was responsible for giving Catalan aspirations a definite direction with his appeal, in 1878, for a national style of architecture, drawing particularly on the rich Catalan Romanesque and Gothic traditions. The timing was perfect, since Barcelona was undergoing a huge expansion: the medieval walls had been pulled down, and the gridded Eixample was giving the city a new shape and plenty of new space to work in. By 1874 **Antoni Gaudí i Cornet** (1852–1926) had begun his architectural career. Born in Reus, near Tarragona, to a family of artisans, his work was never strictly *modernista* in style (it was never strictly anything in style), but the imaginative impetus he provided to the movement was incalculable. Fourteen years later the young **Josep Puig i Cadafalch** (1867–1957) would be inspired to become an architect (and later a reforming politician) as he watched the spectacularly rapid round-the-clock construction of Domènech's *Grand Hotel* on the Passeig de Colom. It was in another building by Domènech (the café-restaurant of the Parc de la Ciutadella) that a craft workshop was set up after the Exhibition of 1888, giving Barcelona's *modernista* architects the opportunity to experiment with traditional crafts like ceramic tiles, ironwork, stained glass and decorative stone carving. This combination of traditional methods with experiments in modern technology was to become the hallmark of *modernisme* – a marriage that produced some of the most fantastic and exciting modern architecture to be found anywhere in the world.

Most attention is usually focused on the three main protagonists mentioned above; certainly they provide the bulk of the most extraordinary buildings that Barcelona has to offer. But keep an eye out for lesser-known architects who also worked in the city. **Josep Maria Jujol i Gilbert** (1879–1949), renowned as Gaudí's collaborator on several of his most famous projects, can also boast a few complete constructions of his own; while the hard-working **Jeroni Granell i Barrera** (1867–1931) and **Josep Vilaseca i Casanoves** (1843–1910) were responsible for other minor buildings and works. **Josep Domènech i Estapa** (1858–1917) became Barcelona's main institutional architect, providing buildings as diverse as the prison and observatory.

It's Antoni Gaudí, though, of whom most have heard: by training, he was a metalworker, and by inclination a fervent Catholic and Catalan nationalist. His buildings are the most daring creations of all Art Nouveau, apparently lunatic flights of fantasy that at the same time are perfectly functional. His architectural influences were Moorish and Gothic, while he embellished his work with elements from the natural world. Yet Gaudí rarely wrote a word about the theory of his art, preferring its products to speak for themselves. Like all the *modernista* buildings in the city, they demand reaction.

Mansana de la Discòrdia

The most famous grouping of buildings, the so-called **Mansana de la Discòrdia**, or "Block of Discord" (Ⓜ Passeig de Gràcia), is just four blocks up from Plaça de Catalunya. It gets its name because the adjacent buildings – built within a decade of each other by three different architects – show off wildly varying manifestations of the *modernista* style and spirit.

Casa Lleó Morera and the Museu del Perfum

On the corner with c/Consell de Cent, at Pg. de Gràcia 35, the six-storey **Casa Lleó Morera** is by Domènech i Montaner, completed in 1906. It's the least appealing of the buildings in the block (in that it has the least extravagant exterior), and has suffered more than the others from "improvements" wrought by subsequent owners, which included removing the ground-floor arches and sculptures. A Loewe leather clothes and goods store occupies the whole of the ground floor, while the main entrance to the building is resolutely guarded to prevent more than a peek inside. This is a pity, because it has a rich Art Nouveau interior, flush with ceramics and wood, as well as exquisite stained glass, while its semicircular jutting balconies are quite distinctive.

An oddity a couple of doors up is the **Museu del Perfum** (Mon–Fri 10.30am–1.30pm & 5–8pm, Sat 11am–1.30pm; free; Ⓦ www.museodelperfume .com), in the back of the Regia perfume store at Pg. de Gràcia 39. They may have to turn the lights on for you, but there's no missing the exhibits as a rather cloying pong exudes from the room. It's a private collection of over five thousand perfume and essence bottles from Egyptian times onwards, and there are some exquisite pieces displayed, including Turkish filigree-and-crystal ware and bronze and silver Indian elephant flasks. More modern times are represented by scents made for Brigitte Bardot, Grace Kelly and Elizabeth Taylor, and if you're diligent enough to scan all the shelves you might be able to track down the perfume bottle designed by Salvador Dalí.

Casa Amatller

Puig i Cadafalch's striking **Casa Amatller** is at Pg. de Gràcia 41, an apartment building from 1900 created largely from the bones of an existing building and paid for by Antoni Amattler, a Catalan chocolate manufacturer. The facade rises in steps to a point, studded with coloured ceramic decoration and with heraldic sculptures over the doors and windows. Inside the hallway, the ceramic tiles continue along the walls, while twisted stone columns are interspersed by dragon lamps, all of which is further illuminated by fine stained-glass doors and an interior glass roof. The ground floor contains the small **Centre del Modernisme** (Mon–Sat 10am–7pm, Sun 10am–2pm; free), which is worth calling into to peruse its temporary exhibitions on the buildings and personalities of the *modernista* period. There's also an excellent selection of postcards for sale, while you can buy the useful *Ruta del Modernisme* ticket here (see p.23).

Casa Batlló

Perhaps the most extraordinary creation on the Block of Discord is at Pg. de Gràcia 43, where Gaudí's **Casa Batlló** (Mon–Sat 9am–2pm, Sun 9am–8pm; €10; ☎932 160 306) – designed for the industrialist Josep Batlló and finished in 1907 – was similarly wrought from an apartment building already in place but considered dull by contemporaries. Gaudí was hired to give it a face-lift and contrived to create an undulating facade that Dalí later compared to "the tranquil waters of a lake". There's an animal aspect at work here, too: the stone facade hangs in folds, like skin, and (from below), the twisted balcony railings resemble malevolent eyes. The higher part of the facade is less abstruse and more decorative, pockmarked with circular ceramic buttons laid on a bright mosaic background and finished with a little tower topped with a cross. The interior resembles the insides of some great organism, and self-guided audio tours show you the main floor, patio and rear facade – it's best to reserve a ticket in advance (by phone or in person) as this is a very popular attraction.

Fundació Antoni Tàpies

Turn the corner onto c/Aragó, and at no. 255 (just before Rambla de Catalunya) you'll find Domènech i Montaner's first important building, the **Casa Montaner i Simon**, finished in 1880. This was one of the earliest of all *modernista* projects in Barcelona: like Gaudí after him, the architect incorporated Moorish-style flourishes into his iron-framed work, which consists of two floors, supported by columns and with no dividing walls. The building originally served the publishing firm of Montaner i Simon, but, as the enormous aluminium tubular structure on the roof now announces, it's been converted to house the **Fundació Antoni Tàpies** (Tues–Sun 10am–8pm; €4.20; Ⓦ www.fundaciotapies.org; Ⓜ Passeig de Gràcia).

Born in the city in 1923 (on c/de la Canuda in the Barri Gòtic), Antoni Tàpies i Puig left school to study Law at the University of Barcelona in 1944, though he left before completing his degree. Drawn to art from an early age, and largely self-taught (though he studied briefly at Barcelona's Academia Valls), he was a founding member (1948) of the influential Dau al Set ("Die at Seven"), a grouping of seven artists producing a monthly avant-garde magazine of the same name which ran until 1956. His first major paintings date from as early as 1945, at which time he was interested in collage (using newspaper, cardboard, silver wrapping, string and wire) and engraving techniques. In the Dau al Set period, after coming into contact with Miró, among others, he underwent a brief Surreal phase (the fruits of which are displayed in the museum basement). However, after a stay in Paris he found his feet with an abstract style that matured in the Fifties, during which time he held his first major exhibitions, including shows in New York and Europe. His large works – many on show in the main gallery – are deceptively simple, though underlying messages and themes are signalled by the inclusion of everyday objects and symbols on the canvas. Tàpies has also continually experimented with unusual materials, like oil paint mixed with crushed marble, or employing sand, cloth or straw in his collages. His work became increasingly political during the Sixties and Seventies. The harsh colours of *In Memory of Salvador Puig Antich* commemorate a Catalan anarchist executed by Franco's regime, while slogans splashed across other works, or the frequent use of the red bars of the Catalan flag, leave no doubt about his affiliations.

Temporary exhibitions focus on selections of Tàpies' work from all these periods, and the foundation also includes a library and a collection of works by other contemporary artists (such as Mario Merz, Francis Picabia, Hans Haacke and Craigie Horsfield). In later years Tàpies himself has concentrated on public art and sculpture, contributing the murals to the Catalan pavilions at the Seville Expo of 1992. Important outdoor works in Barcelona include *Homenatge a Picasso* (Homage to Picasso; 1983), on Passeig de Picasso, outside the gates of the Parc de la Ciutadella, while the foundation building is capped by Tàpies' own striking sculpture, *Núvol i Cadira* ("Cloud and Chair"; 1990), a tangle of glass, wire and metal.

Museu Egipci de Barcelona

Half a block east of Passeig de Gràcia, the **Museu Egipci de Barcelona**, at c/de València 284 (Mon–Sat 10am–8pm, Sun 10am–2pm; €5.50; ⓦwww.fundclos.com; ⓂPasseig de Gràcia), is an exceptional private collection of artefacts from ancient Egypt, ranging from the earliest kingdoms to the era of Cleopatra. It was founded by hotelier Jordi Clos – whose *Hotel Claris*, a block away, still has its own private museum for guests – and displays a remarkable gathering of over 600 objects, amulets to sarcophagi. The emphasis is on the shape and character of Egyptian society, and visitors are given a hugely detailed English-language guidebook, which enables you to nail down specific periods and descriptions, case by case, if you so wish. But the real pleasure here is a serendipitous wander, turning up items like a wood-and-leather bed of the 1st and 2nd Dynasties (2920–2649 BC), some examples of cat mummies of the Late Period (715–332 BC) or a rare figurine of a spoonbill (ibis) representing an Egyptian god (though archeologists aren't yet sure which). If you'd like to know more, an egyptologist leads **guided tours** every Saturday at 11am and 5pm (included in the entry price). There are temporary exhibitions, a library and a good book and gift shop on the lower floor, and a terrace café upstairs. The museum also hosts a full programme of study sessions, children's activities and evening events – the reception desk can provide details.

Fundacío Francisco Godia

The building next door to the Egyptian museum on c/de València houses the private art collection of the **Fundacío Francisco Godia** (daily except Tues 10am–8pm; €4.50, joint admission with Museu Egipci €8.50; ⓦwww.fundacionfgodia.org; ⓂPasseig de Gràcia). Harnessing medieval art, ceramics and modern Catalan art, in many ways it serves as a taster for the huge collections at Montjuïc in MNAC, while its small size makes it immediately more accessible. The pieces here – displayed in hushed rooms where the only sound is the hum of the airconditioning – were collected by aesthete and Fifties racing driver Francisco Godia, whose medals and cups are the first things you encounter. Beyond lie selected Romanesque carvings and Gothic paintings, notably work by fifteenth-century artist Jaume Huguet, and then there's a jump to the *modernista* and *noucentista* paintings of Isidre Nonell, Santiago Rusiñol and Ramon Casas, among others. There's a varied selection of ceramics on show, too, from most of the historically important production centres in Spain. From fifteenth-century Valencia originate the *socarrats*, decorated terracotta panels used to stud ceilings. Not all of the collection can be shown at any one time, so pieces are rotated (and added) on occasion, while special exhibitions also run in tandem, to which there's usually no extra charge. For a guided tour of the exhibits, visit on Saturday or Sunday at noon.

La Pedrera

Gaudí's weird apartment building, the Casa Milà, at Pg. de Gràcia 92 (ⓂDiagonal), is simply not to be missed. Constructed between 1905 and 1911, and popularly known as **La Pedrera** – "The Stone Quarry" – it was declared a UNESCO World Heritage Site in 1984. Its hulking, rippled facade, curving around the street corner in one smooth sweep, is said to have been inspired by the mountain of Montserrat, while the apartments themselves, whose balconies of tangled metal drip over the facade, resemble eroded cave dwellings. Indeed,

△ Interior of La Pedrera

there's not a straight line to be seen – hence the contemporary joke that the new tenants would only be able to keep snakes as pets. The building, which Gaudí himself described as "more luminous than light", was his last secular commission – and one of his best – but even here he was injecting religious motifs and sculptures into the building until told to remove them. A sculpture of the Virgin Mary was planned to complete the roof, but the building's owners demurred, having been alarmed by the anti-religious fervour of the "Tragic Week" in Barcelona in 1909, when anarchist-sponsored rioting destroyed churches and religious foundations. Gaudí, by now working full-time on the Sagrada Família, was appalled, and determined in future to use his skills only for purely religious purposes.

Casa Milà is still split into private apartments and is administered by the Fundació Caixa de Catalunya. Through the grand main entrance of the building you can access the Fundació's first-floor **exhibition hall** (daily 10am–8pm; free; guided visits Mon–Fri at 6pm), which hosts temporary art shows of works by international artists. The side entrance on c/Provença – you can't miss the queues – is where you go in to **visit La Pedrera** itself (daily 10am–8pm; €7). This includes a trip up to the roof to see at close quarters the enigmatic chimneys, as well as an exhibition about Gaudí's work in the *golfes* (or top rooms) of the building; *El Pis* ("the apartment") is a re-creation of a *modernista*-era bourgeois apartment, with period furniture and decoration as well as displays on aspects of fin-de-siècle life in Barcelona. Perhaps the best way to see the building is by buying a ticket for **La Pedrera de Nit**, when you can enjoy the rooftop and night-time cityscape with a complimentary *cava* and music (June–Aug Fri & Sat only at 9.30pm; €10; ☎934 845 900) – advance booking at the ticket office is essential.

Casa Ramon Casas: Vinçon

Right next to La Pedrera, in the same block on Passeig de Gràcia, the **Casa Ramon Casas** dates from 1899, a huge building designed for the artist Ramon Casas, who maintained a home here. In 1941, the **Vinçon** store (Mon–Sat 10am–2pm & 4.30–8.30pm) was established in the building, which emerged in the Sixties as the country's pre-eminent purveyor of furniture and design, a reputation today's department store still maintains. There are several entrances – at Pg. de Gràcia 96, c/Provença 273 and c/Pau Claris 175 – and apart from checking out the extraordinary furniture floor, which gives access to a terrace with views of the interior of La Pedrera, you should try and make time for **La Sala Vinçon** (open same hours as the store). This is Vinçon's exhibition hall and art gallery, located in Casas' original studio, and it puts on excellent, regularly changing, shows of new design and furniture.

Dreta de l'Eixample

The right-hand side of the Eixample – the so-called **Dreta de l'Eixample** – sports a series of extraordinary buildings, mostly contained within the triangle east of Passeig de Gràcia formed by the *passeig*, **Avinguda Diagonal** and the Gran Via de les Corts Catalanes. Several are by the two hardest-working architects in the Eixample, Domènech i Montaner and Puig i Cadafalch, while

Gaudí's first apartment building, the **Casa Calvet**, is also here. Apart from the Casa Calvet, all the buildings are within a few blocks of each other, or you could pass most of them on a long walk further east to the **Sagrada Família**, Antoni Gaudi's most celebrated monument. There's more detail on the colour map at the back of the book.

4 Along Avinguda Diagonal

At the top of Passeig de Gràcia you'll find the **Palau Robert**, Pg. de Gràcia 107 (Mon–Sat 10am–7pm, Sun 10am–2.30pm; free; ⓂDiagonal), the information centre for the region of Catalunya, which hosts changing exhibitions on all matters Catalan; the pretty gardens around the back are a popular meeting point for the local nannies and their charges. Cross Avinguda Diagonal here and over to the right stands **Casa Comalat** (1909), Avgda. Diagonal 442, at the junction with c/de Corsega. It's a tricky corner plot, handled with aplomb by the architect Salvador Valeri i Pupurull, who gave it two very different *modernista* facades. On the other side of the avenue, at no. 373, Puig i Cadaflach's almost Gothic **Palau Quadras** from 1904 is typically intricate, with sculpted figures and emblems by Eusebi Arnau and a top row of windows that resemble miniature Swiss chalets. Further down Diagonal, on the left at nos. 416–420, is Puig i Cadafalch's largest work, the soaring Casa Terrades, more usually known as the **Casa de les Punxes** ("House of Spikes") because of its red-tiled turrets and steep gables. Built in 1903 for three sisters, and converted from three separate houses spreading around an entire corner of a block, the crenellated structure is almost northern European in style.

Keep to the avenue and you'll pass a sculpture of the **Ictineo** (Diagonal at c/de Provença), the world's earliest powered submarine, courtesy of the Catalans (see p.75), before turning up Passeig de Sant Joan for half a block to see Puig i Cadafalch's palatial **Casa Macaya** (ⓂVerdaguer). Dating from 1898–1900, it's a superbly ornamental building, rich in unusual exterior carvings and with a Gothic-inspired courtyard and canopied staircase from which griffins spring. You should at least be able to poke your head inside for a look, since the house has been used in the past as a gallery run by the Fundació La Caixa. You're only four blocks west of the Sagrada Família at this point, but you might as well stay with the Diagonal until you reach Josep Maria Jujol's **Casa Planells** at Avgda. Diagonal 332. Jujol was one of Gaudí's early collaborators, responsible for La Pedrera's undulating balconies and much of the mosaic work in the Parc Güell. Built in 1923–24, this apartment block – a sinuous solution to an acute-corner building – simplifies many of the themes that Gaudí exaggerated in his own work.

South of Avinguda Diagonal

The area around the junction of c/de Mallorca and c/Roger de Llúria (ⓂPasseig de Gràcia) boasts two contrasting Domènech i Montaner buildings, dating from the mid-1890s. The ground floor of the neo-Gothic **Casa Thomas** at c/de Mallorca 291, with its understated pale ceramic tiles, is given over to BD Ediciones de Diseño, a furniture-design showroom. A little way along, set back from the crossroads in a small garden, the **Palau Ramon de Montaner** (c/de Mallorca 278) is much plainer, though its severe facade is at least enlivened by rich mosaic pictures, while there's a fine interior staircase.

A block south, the **Casa Elizalde**, c/de Valencia 302 (Mon–Fri 5–8pm, Sat & Sun 11am–2pm & 5–8pm; free), hosts classical music concerts and maintains regular exhibitions and film shows about *modernisme* and related themes. Close by, to the east, stand the church and market of **La Concepció**, in between c/de Valencia and c/d'Aragó. The early fifteenth-century Gothic church and clois-ter once stood in the old town, part of a convent abandoned in the early nine-teenth century and then transferred here brick by brick in the 1870s by Jeroni Granell. The **market** (Mon 8am–3pm, Tues–Fri 8am–8pm, Sat 8am–4pm; July & Aug closes at 3pm) was added in 1888, its iron-and-glass tram-shed structure reminiscent of others in the city. Flowers and plants spill out of the entrance on c/de Valencia, and there are a couple of good snack bars just inside the market.

That's about it for the *modernista* highlights of the Dreta de l'Eixample, though Gaudí fans will want to walk the four blocks south, crossing the Gran Via de les Corts Catalanes, to tick off the great man's earliest commissioned townhouse building, erected for a prominent local textile family. **Casa Calvet**, at c/de Casp 48 (ⓂUrquinaona/Catalunya), dates from 1899 and, though fair-ly conventional in style, the Baroque inspiration on display in the sculpted facade and church-like lobby was to surface again in his later, more elaborate buildings on Passeig de Gràcia. If you want a closer look inside, you'll have to book a table in the restaurant (see p.193) that now occupies the premises.

Sagrada Família

However diverting, and occasionally provocative, the pockets of architectural interest throughout the Eixample, nothing prepares you for the impact of the city's most famous monument, Antoni Gaudí's great **Temple Expiatori de la Sagrada Família** (daily: April–Sept 9am–8pm; Oct–March 9am–6pm; €8, €11 including guided tour; ⓌMwww.sagradafamilia.org; ⓂSagrada Família), which occupies an entire block between c/de Mallorca and c/de Provença, north of the Diagonal.

In many ways this has become a kind of symbol for the city, and was one of the few churches (along with the cathedral) left untouched by the orgy of church-burning which accompanied both the 1909 "Tragic Week" rioting and the 1936 revolution. It's an essential stop on any visit to Barcelona, for, more than any building in the Barri Gòtic, it speaks volumes about the Catalan urge to glorify uniqueness and endeavour. It is the most fantastic of the modern architectural creations in which Barcelona excels – and is almost certain to set you on the trail of other *modernista* works. Even the coldest hearts will find the Sagrada Família inspirational in form and spirit.

Some history

Begun in 1882 by public subscription, the Sagrada Família was conceived orig-inally by its progenitor, the Catalan publisher Josep Bocabella, as an expiatory building that would atone for the city's increasingly revolutionary ideas. Bocabella appointed the architect Francesc de Paula Villar to the work, and his plan was for a modest church in an orthodox neo-Gothic style. Two years later, after arguments between the two men, Gaudí – only 31 years of age – took charge and changed the direction and scale of the project almost immediately, seeing in the Sagrada Família an opportunity to reflect his own deepening spir-itual and nationalist feelings. He spent most of the rest of his life working on the church. Indeed, after he finished the Parc Güell in 1911, Gaudí vowed never to work again on secular art, but to devote himself solely to the Sagrada Família (where, eventually, he lived in a workshop on site), and he was adapting the plans ceaselessly right up to his untimely death. Run over by a tram on the Gran Via on June 7, 1926, he died in hospital three days later – initially unrecognized, for he had become a virtual recluse, rarely leaving his small studio. His death was treated as a Catalan national disaster, and all of Barcelona turned out for his funeral procession. Following papal dispensation, he was buried in the Sagrada Família crypt.

Work on the church was slow, even in Gaudí's day, mainly due to a persistent lack of funds. It took four years to finish the crypt (1901) and the first full plan of the building wasn't published until 1917. The first tower was erected the following year, but by the time of Gaudí's death only one facade was complete. Although the church building survived the Civil War, Gaudí's plans and models were destroyed in 1936 by the anarchists, who regarded Gaudí and his church as conservative religious relics that the new Barcelona could do without: George Orwell – whose sympathies were very much with the anarchists during the Civil War – remarked that the Sagrada Família had been spared because of its supposed artistic value, but added that it was "one of the most hideous buildings in the world" and that the anarchists "showed bad taste in not blowing it up when they had the chance".

Work restarted in the late 1950s amid great controversy, and has continued ever since – as have the arguments. Some maintain that the Sagrada Família should be left incomplete as a memorial to Gaudí, others that the architect intended it to be the work of several generations, each continuing in its own style. The current work has attracted criticism for infringing Gaudí's original spirit, not least the work on the Passion facade, by sculptor Josep María Subirach, which has been ongoing since 1987. Certainly, contemporary methods and materials are being used – including computers and hi-tech construction techniques – but on balance it's probably safe enough to assume that Gaudí saw the struggle to finish the building as at least as important as the method and style. As the project draws inexorably towards realization (current projections predict a completion date of around 2017), a fresh set of arguments has arisen as to how to wrap the whole thing up – whether to continue with the design, which calls for an even taller central tower, or to go for a quicker but more modest alternative.

The building

The size alone is startling – Gaudí's original plan was to build a church capable of seating over 10,000 people. In particular, eight **spires** rise to over 100m. They have been likened to everything from perforated cigars to celestial billiard cues, but for Gaudí they were symbolic of the twelve apostles; he planned to build four more above the main facade and to add a 170-metre tower topped with a lamb (representing Jesus) over the transept, itself to be surrounded by four smaller towers symbolizing the evangelists.

A precise symbolism also pervades the **facades**, each of which is divided into three porches devoted to Faith, Hope and Charity, and each uniquely sculpted. Gaudí made extensive use of human, plant and animal models (posing them in his workshop), as well as taking casts and photographs, in order to produce exactly the likenesses he sought for the sculptural groups. The east facade further represents the Nativity and the Mysteries of Joy; the west (currently the main entrance, and nearing completion) depicts the Passion and the Mysteries of Affliction. Gaudí meant the south facade to be the culmination of the Temple – the Gloria, designed (he said), to show "the religious realities of present and future life . . . man's origin, his end." Everything from the creation to heaven and hell, in short, was to be included in one magnificent ensemble.

The reality is that the place often looks like a giant building site, with scaffolding, cranes, tarpaulins and fencing lying about. Construction of the vaults over the side-aisles began in 1995 and for the first time a recognizable church interior is starting to take shape. In early 2001 the roof over the central nave was finished, and the whole church is due to be roofed in due course. There's still an awfully long way to go, though, and engineering paraphernalia will continue to dominate the church for years to come. Once you climb inside the structure, however, all considerations except the building itself soon fall away. An **elevator** (open same hours as the church; €2) runs up one of the towers around the rose window, or you can make the long, steep climb to the top (a twisting 400 steps). Either way, you'll be rewarded by partial views of the city through an extraordinary jumble of latticed stonework, ceramic decoration, carved buttresses and sculpture.

Your entrance ticket also gives you access to the crypt, where a small **museum** (times as for the church) traces the career of the architect and the history of the church. Models, sketches and photographs help to make some sense of the work going on around you, and you can view sculptors and model-makers at work on the project. There's a film show about Gaudí's career, too, which is likely to set you on the trail of his earlier projects, all of which, astonishingly, date from before 1911.

Hospital de la Santa Creu i de Sant Pau

While you're in the neighbourhood, it would be a shame not to stroll from the Sagrada Família to Domènech i Montaner's innovative **Hospital de la Santa Creu i de Sant Pau** (Ⓜ️Hospital de Sant Pau), possibly the one building that can touch the church for size and invention within the limits defined by Cerdà's street plan. The building has its own metro stop, but it's far better to walk up the four-block-long diagonal Avinguda de Gaudí, which gives terrific views back over the spires of the Sagrada Família.

Work started on the hospital in 1902, the brief being to replace the medieval hospital buildings in the Raval (see p.59) with a modern series of departments and wards. Domènech i Montaner spent ten years working on the building and left his trademarks everywhere: cocking a snook at Cerdà, the buildings are aligned diagonally to the Eixample, surrounded by gardens; and everywhere, turrets and towers sport bright ceramic tiles and little domes. Domènech retired in 1912, once funds had run out, and the building wasn't fully completed until 1930, seven years after his death, though the latter stages were overseen by Domènech's son Pere, ensuring a certain continuity of style.

You are welcome to walk into the sloping landscaped **grounds**, past the whimsical **pavilions** that make up the hospital interior. Craftsmen adorned every inch with sculpture, mosaics, stained glass and ironwork, while much of the actual business of running a hospital was hidden away in a series of underground corridors that connects the buildings together. It's a stunning, harmonious achievement – that it's a hospital seems almost incidental, which is doubtless the effect that the architect intended. Naturally, given the demands now made upon them, the *modernista* hospital buildings are deemed to have served their purpose; behind them spreads the hi-tech central block of the new hospital, due to be fully operational by 2006. The pavilions will then probably be turned over to educational or cultural use (a Museum of Medicine is mooted), though in the meantime there are **guided tours** (in English/Spanish) of the complex (Sat & Sun, 10am–2pm every 30min; €4.20; ☎934 882 078, ⓦwww.santpau.es), which can tell you more about the 600-year history of the hospital.

Esquerra de l'Eixample

The long streets west of Passeig de Gràcia – making up the **Esquerra de l'Eixample** – are no competition when it comes to planning a route around the Eixample, and most visitors only ever travel this part of the city underground – on their way in and out of the centre by metro. This was the part of the Eixample intended by Cerdà for public buildings, institutions and industrial concerns, many of which still stand. The grand **Universitat de Barcelona**, at Plaça de la Universitat, built in the 1860s, is the one you're most likely to see in passing, a Neoclassical pile with attractive courtyards and gardens, but there are many other large-scale projects in the streets to the northwest. Their exteriors are typically eye-catching, while there are pockets of more particular interest – including some fine *modernista* houses and a small sports museum – that warrant a closer look. The westernmost boundary of *L'Esquerra* is marked by **Barcelona Sants** train station and, again, though most people see no further than its concourse, it's possible to use the station as the starting point of a short walk through the public spaces created in the style known as *nou urbanisme* – typified by a wish to transform former industrial sites into urban parks accessible to local people.

Around Avinguda Diagonal

The most interest lies in the *modernista* buildings on and off the upper reaches of Avinguda Diagonal (ⓂDiagonal), running northwest from Passeig de Gràcia. At the top of Rambla de Catalunya, Puig i Cadafalch's pseudo-medieval **Casa Serra** (1903) has been much altered, though it retains its tiles, canopies and jaunty tower. A bronze statue of Sant Jordi, patron saint of Catalunya, guards the Diagonal side of the building, now used as offices. Further up the Diagonal, also on the left, at no. 423 at the junction with c/Enric Granados, **Casa Sayrach** (1918) flows around its corner site, a vision of pink granite and marble, with a central tower topped by a cupola and a Pedrera-style roof.

Beyond here Avinguda Diagonal flows on to Plaça Francesc Macia and the business district, though you only need walk the three blocks to c/de Buenos Aires 56–58 to find the quirky **Museu i Centre d'Estudis de l'Esport** (Mon–Fri 10am–2pm & 4–8pm; free; ⓂHospital Clinic). Built as the Casa Companys in 1911 by Puig i Cadafalch, the little cream-coloured house contains probably the most unassuming sporting "Hall of Fame" found anywhere in the world. In a couple of quiet, wood-panelled rooms photographs of Twenties Catalan rally drivers and footballers are displayed alongside a motley collection of memorabilia, from a signed waterpolo ball used in the 1992 Olympics to Everest mountaineer Carles Vàlles' ice pick.

South of the museum stand several much larger examples of the *modernista* and Neoclassical spirit which infused public buildings of the nineteenth century. The Battló textile mill on the corner of c/del Comte d'Urgell and c/del Rossello underwent major refurbishment in 1908 to emerge as the **Escola Industrial** (Ⓜ Hospital Clinic). It occupies four entire Eixample blocks, with later academic buildings added in the Twenties, including a chapel by Joan Rubió i Bellvér, who worked with Antoni Gaudí. Students usually fill the courtyards, and no one minds if you take a stroll through. A block to the east is **Hospital Clinic** (1904), with its fine pedimented portico; while even the prison over to the west, the **Preso Model** (1881–1904), was constructed with care, down to its star-shaped cell blocks.

Contemporary architecture

It's easy to get sidetracked by the *modernista* architecture of the Eixample, and to forget that Barcelona also boasts plenty of contemporary wonders. Following the death of Franco, there was a feeling among architects that Barcelona had a lot of catching up to do, but the last three decades have seen the city take centre stage in the matter of urban design and renewal. Now the world looks to Barcelona for inspiration.

Even in the Franco years exciting work had taken place, particularly among the "rationalist" school of architects working from the Fifties through the Seventies. José Antonio Coderch produced such marvels as the dark curved-glass Trade Towers at Gran Vía de Carles III 86–94. Less dramatic but still very pleasing are his blocks of Mediterranean-style apartments at c/Raset 21–31 and those adorned with adjustable blinds and screens at c/Johann Sebastian Bach 7. From the latter part of this period, too, dates the earliest work by the Catalan architects – among them **Oriol Bohigas**, **Carlos Buxadé**, **Joan Margarit**, **Ricardo Bofill** and **Frederic Correa** – later to transform the very look and feel of the city. You can see Bohigas' Habitatges Treballadors Metal·lurgics, for example, at c/Pallars 301–319; Correa's Atalaia de Barcelona at Avgda. Sarrià 71; and Bofill's Bloc Residencial at c/Nicaragua 99.

The impetus for change on a substantial level came from hosting the **1992 Olympics**. Nothing less than the redesign of whole city neighbourhoods would do, with decaying industrial areas either swept away or transformed. While Correa, Margarit and Buxadé worked on the refit of the Estadi Olímpic, Bofill was in charge of INEF (the Sports University) and had a hand in the airport refit. Down at the harbour Bohigas and others were responsible for creating the visionary Vila Olímpica development, carving residential, commercial and leisure facilities out of abandoned industrial blackspots.

Attention later turned to other neglected areas, with signature buildings announcing a planned transformation of the local environment: Richard Meier's contemporary art museum, **MACBA**, in the Raval, and Helio Piñon and Alberto Viaplana's **Maremàgnum** complex at Port Vell, anchor those neighbourhoods' respective revivals. Meanwhile, the city acquired **new landmarks**, like Norman Foster's Torre de Collserola at Tibidabo, the twin towers of the *Hotel Arts* and Torre Mapfre at the Port Olímpic, and Bofill's Teatre Nacional de Catalalunya (TNC) at Plaça de les Glòries. The latter – resembling a Greek temple – was a fairly controversial work in an otherwise indistinct quarter of the Eixample, which has subsequently been joined in the vicinity by the even more eye-catching 140-metre-high Torre Agbar, a giant cigar of a building by Jean Nouvel. The former industrial area of Poble Nou has also been transformed, this time by the works associated with the Universal Forum of Cultures 2004. Jacques Herzog (architect of London's Tate Modern) has provided a centrepiece **Forum** that sits at the heart of a new commercial, cultural and leisure district, linking Barcelona with the once-desolate environs of the River Besòs. On the other side of the city, it's been left to Richard Rogers to revitalize the city's neglected bullring, **Les Arenes** at Plaça d'Espanya, which is destined to become a gateway landmark, incorporating a domed garden, viewing platform and leisure centre.

Barcelona Sants to Plaça d'Espanya

Directly in front of Barcelona Sants station (Ⓜ Sants Estació), **Plaça dels Països Catalans** features a series of walls, raised meshed roofs and coverings designed by Helio Piñon – a rather comfortless "park" in most people's eyes, more intimidating than welcoming.

It's easier to see the attraction of Basque architect Luis Peña Ganchegui's **Parc de l'Espanya Industrial**, two minutes' walk away around the southern side of the station. Built on the site of an old textile factory, it has a line of red-and-yellow-striped lighthouses at the top of glaring white steps, with an incongruously classical Neptune in the water below, seen to best effect at night. Altogether, six sculptors are represented here and, along with the boating lake, playground and sports facilities provided, the park takes a decent stab at reconciling local interests with the largely industrial nature of the surroundings.

To the south, down c/de Tarragona, **Parc Joan Miró** (Ⓜ Tarragona) was laid out on the site of the nineteenth-century municipal slaughterhouse. It features a raised piazza whose main feature is Joan Miró's gigantic mosaic sculpture *Dona i Ocell* ("Woman and Bird"), towering above a small lake. It's a familiar symbol if you've studied Miró's other works, but the sculpture is known locally by several other names – all of them easy to guess when you consider its erect, helmeted shape. Indeed, it was originally entitled "The Cock", until the city authorities suggested otherwise. The rest of the park is given over to games areas and landscaped sections, with a café found in among the trees.

The northern suburbs

U
ntil the Eixample stretched out across the plain to meet them, a string of small towns ringed the city to the north. Today, they're firmly entrenched as suburbs of Barcelona, but most still retain an individual identity worth investigating even on a short visit to the city. Some of the sights will figure on most people's tours of the city, while others are more specialized, but taken together they do help to counter the notion that Barcelona begins and ends in the Barri Gòtic.

Gràcia – the closest neighbourhood to the Eixample – is still very much the liberal, almost bohemian stronghold it was in the nineteenth century. Visits tend

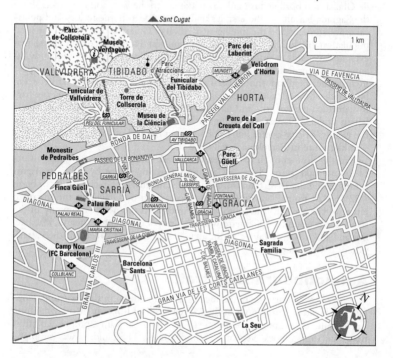

to revolve around browsing in the neighbourhood market or sipping a drink in one of the quiet squares, though Gràcia also has an active cultural scene and nightlife of its own. Gaudí's surreal **Parc Güell**, on the northeastern fringes of Gràcia, is the single biggest suburban draw, and there are more parks to the north in the neighbourhood of **Horta**, including the **Parc del Laberint** – and its renowned maze – set within a former country estate. To the northwest, **Pedralbes** features the most concentrated selection of attractions, from its Gothic monastery and royal palace to the equally hallowed precincts of **Camp Nou**, FC Barcelona's stupendous football stadium and museum.

Further out, beyond the ring road (the Ronda de Dalt), extend the Collserola hills whose highest peak – **Tibidabo**, reached by tram and funicular – should really be saved for a clear day. The views are the thing here, from the amusement park, peak-top church or nearby **Torre de Collserola**, while a pleasant walk winds west to **Vallvidrera**, a hilltop village with another funicular connection back towards the city. Finally, from the information centre of the nearby **Parc de Collserola**, you can hike in the pinewoods high above Barcelona and see scarcely a soul – perhaps the greatest surprise in this most surprising of cities.

Gràcia

Named after a fifteenth-century monastery (long destroyed), **Gràcia** was a village for much of its early existence before being annexed as a fully fledged suburb of the city in the late nineteenth century. Beginning at the top of Passeig de Gràcia, and bordered roughly by c/Balmes to the west and the streets above the Sagrada Família to the east, it's traditionally been home to arty and political types, students and the intelligentsia, though Gràcia also has a genuine local population (including one of the city's biggest Romany communities) that even today lends it an attractive small-town atmosphere. Consequently, its annual summer festival, the Festa Major every August (see p.223), has no peer in any other neighbourhood. Real guidebook sights are few and far between, but much of the pleasure to be had here is serendipitous – wandering the narrow, gridded eighteenth- and nineteenth-century streets, parking yourself on a bench under a plane tree, catching a film or otherwise taking time out from the rigours of city-centre life. You'll soon get the feel of a neighbourhood that – unlike some in Barcelona – still has a soul.

Gràcia is close enough to the centre to walk to if you wish – around a thirty-minute hike from Plaça de Catalunya. **Getting there** by public transport means taking the FGC train from Plaça de Catalunya to Gràcia station, or buses #22 or #24 from Plaça de Catalunya up c/Gran de Gràcia, or the metro to either ⓂDiagonal, to the south, or ⓂFontana, to the north. From any of the stations, it's around a 500-metre walk to Gràcia's two central squares, Plaça del Sol and Plaça Rius i Taulet, in the network of gridded streets off the eastern side of c/Gran de Gràcia.

A neighbourhood stroll

You may as well start where the locals start – first thing in the morning, shopping for bread and provisions in the **Mercat de la Llibertat** (Mon 8am–3pm, Tues–Thurs 8am–2pm & 5–8pm, Fri 7am–8pm, Sat 7am–3pm; closed afternoons in Aug), a block west of c/Gran de Gràcia. The building was revamped

GRÀCIA

▲ Parc Güell

▼ Pg. de Gràcia & Pl. Catalunya

in 1893 by Francesc Berenguer i Mestrès, a former pupil of Gaudí, who sheltered its food stalls under a *modernista* wrought-iron roof. Two blocks to the
north, **Rambla del Prat** has the finest surviving collection of *modernista*
townhouses in the district, while a couple of blocks further north again stands
Antoni Gaudí's first major private commission, the **Casa Vicens** (1883–85) at
c/les Carolines 24 (ⓂFontana). Here he took inspiration from the Moorish
style, covering the facade in linear green-and-white tiles with a flower motif.
The decorative iron railings are a reminder of Gaudí's early training as a met-
alsmith and, to further prove his versatility – and how Art Nouveau cuts across
art forms – Gaudí designed much of the mansion's furniture, too (though
unfortunately you can't get in to see it).

From Casa Vicens, it's a five-minute walk east along c/Santa Agata, c/de la
Providencia and then south into pretty **Plaça de la Virreina**, backed by its
much-restored parish church of Sant Joan. This is one of Gràcia's favourite
squares, with the *Virreina Bar* and others providing drinks and a place to rest and
admire the handsome houses, most notably **Casa Rubinat** (1909), c/de l'Or
44, the last major work of Francesc Berenguer. Another five minutes to the
southwest, **Plaça del Sol** is the beating heart of much of the district's nightlife,
though it's not quite so appealing during the day. It was redesigned rather soul-
lessly in the 1980s, losing much of its attraction for older locals at least. Far more
in keeping with Gràcia's overall tenor is **Plaça Rius i Taulet**, a couple of minutes to the south across Travessera de Gràcia. The thirty-metre-high clock tower
was a rallying point for nineteenth-century radicals – whose 21-century

counterparts prefer to meet for brunch at the popular café *terrassas*.

At Plaça Rius i Taulet you're just a minute or two's walk from the main c/Gran de Gràcia. Walk south, and where the street becomes Passeig de Gràcia stands the **Casa Fuster**, on the left at no. 132 (ⓂDiagonal). Designed by Domènech i Montaner in 1908, it allows you to see the development of his style from the early Casa Montaner i Simon (now the Fundació Antoni Tàpies), built nearly thirty years earlier. Here are many of Domènech's most characteristic design features: a multi-columned building with chunky floral capitals, and – designed to fit the awkward corner it's built on – one concave and one convex tower.

Parc Güell

From 1900 to 1914 Antoni Gaudí worked for Eusebi Güell (patron of Gaudí's Palau Güell, off the Ramblas) on the **Parc Güell** (daily: May–Aug 10am–9pm; April & Sept 10am–8pm; March & Oct 10am–7pm; Nov–Feb 10am–6pm; free), on the outskirts of Gràcia. This was Gaudí's most ambitious project after the Sagrada Família – on which he was engaged at the same time – commissioned as a private housing estate of sixty dwellings and furnished with paths, recreational areas and decorative monuments. It was conceived as a "garden city", of the type popular at the time in England – indeed, Gaudí's original plans used the English spelling "Park Güell". In the end, only two houses were actually built, and the park was officially opened to the public instead in 1922.

Laid out on a hill, which provides fabulous views back across the city, the park is an almost hallucinatory expression of the imagination. Pavilions of contorted stone, giant decorative lizards, meandering rustic viaducts, a vast Hall of Columns (intended to be the estate's market), carved stone trees – all combine in one manic swirl of ideas and excesses, reminiscent of an amusement park. The Hall of Columns, for example, was described by Sacheverell Sitwell (in *Spain*) as "at once a fun fair, a petrified forest, and the great temple of Amun at Karnak, itself drunk, and reeling in an eccentric earthquake". Perhaps the most famous element – certainly the most widely photographed – is the long, me-andering **ceramic bench** that snakes along the edge of the terrace above the columned hall. It's entirely decorated with a brightly coloured broken tile-and-glass mosaic (a method known as *trencadís*) that forms a dizzying sequence of abstract motifs, symbols, words and pictures.

You can take in the atmosphere and the views from the self-service café, which operates from one of the caverns adjoining the main (ceramic bench) terrace, but to escape the milling crowds you'll need to climb away from here, up into the wooded, landscaped gardens. At the very highest point – follow signs for "Turó de les Tres Creus" – on the spot where Gaudí had planned to place a chapel, three stone crosses top a stepped tumulus. It's from here that a 360-degree city panorama unfolds in all its glory.

The ceramic mosaics and decorations found throughout the park were mostly executed by Josep Maria Jujol, who assisted on several of Gaudí's projects, while one of Gaudí's other collaborators, Francesc Berenguer, designed and built a turreted house in the park in 1904, in which Gaudí was persuaded to live until he left to camp out at the Sagrada Família for good. The house is now the **Casa Museu Gaudí** (daily: April–Sept 10am–8pm; Oct–March 10am–6pm; €3), a diverting collection of some of the furniture he designed for other projects – a typical mixture of wild originality and

△ Parc Güell

brilliant engineering – as well as plans and objects related to the park and to Gaudí's life.

Park practicalities

If you have a choice, it's probably best to visit Parc Güell during the week, as weekends can be very busy indeed. The park straddles a steep hill and however you get there will involve an ascent on foot of some kind to reach the main section. The most direct route there is on **bus #24** from Plaça de Catalunya, Passeig de Gràcia or c/Gran de Gracia, which drops you on Carretera del Carmel at the eastern side gate by the car park. From Ⓜ Vallcarca you have to walk a few hundred metres down Avinguda de l'Hospital Militar until you see the mechanical escalators on your left, ascending Baixada de la Glòria. Follow these – and the short sections of stepped path in between – right to the western-side park entrance (15min in total), from where you wind down a path to the main terrace. **Walking from Gràcia** (and Ⓜ Lesseps), turn right along Travessera de Dalt and then left up steep c/Larrard, which leads (10min) straight to the main entrance of the park on c/Olot. The **Bus Turístic** (red circuit) stops at the bottom end of c/Larrard on c/la Mare de Deu de la Salut.

You'll have to walk back down c/Larrard to Travessera de Dalt for bus or metro connections back to the city, though **taxis** do hang about the main gates on c/Olot. There's a **café** with terrace seats in the park, rather pricey but, more to the point, often absolutely packed. Carrer Larrard has several other little cafés, if you want to refuel on your way up or down, as well as a mini-market for picnic supplies.

Horta and Vall d'Hebron

To the north of Parc Güell spreads the neighbourhood of **Horta**, named for the gardens and country estates that once characterized the area. It's been developed beyond recognition over the last century, though there are some quiet spots to seek out. The **Vall d'Hebron** area, just to the east, was the site of another of the city's Olympic developments, based around the Velòdrom d'Horta, Barcelona's cycle stadium. It's behind here that the most extraordinary rural relic still survives, the hillside gardens and maze of the Parc del Laberint.

Parc de la Creueta del Coll

There couldn't be a greater contrast with Parc Güell than Horta's **Parc de la Creueta del Coll** (May–Aug 10am–9pm; April & Sept 10am–8pm; March & Oct 10am–7pm; Nov–Feb 10am–6pm; free), a *nou urbanisme* development by Olympic architects Martorell and Mackay, which was laid out on the site of an old quarry. There's a stand of palm trees by a small artificial lake, and concrete promenades under the sheer quarry walls, but it's all been allowed to go to the dogs (and feral cats) a bit lately and could do with a spruce-up. Still, you're greeted at the top of the park steps by an Ellsworth Kelly metal spike, while suspended by steel cables over a water-filled quarry corner is a massive concrete claw by the Basque artist Eduardo Chillida. **Bus #28** from Plaça de Catalunya, up Passeig de Gràcia, stops just 100m from the park steps, or you can walk up Passeig de la Mare de Deu del Coll from Ⓜ Vallcarca in about twenty minutes (there's a neighbourhood map at the metro station).

Combining the park with a visit to Parc Güell is easy, too, though you'll need a keen sense of direction to find it from the rear exit of Parc Güell – it helps if you've climbed to the top of Güell's three-crosses hill and fixed in mind the quarry walls, which you can see across the valley. It's far easier to visit Parc de la Creueta del Coll first, then walk back down the main Passeig de la Mare de Deu del Coll until you see the signpost pointing down c/Balears (on your left) – from there, signposts guide you into Parc Güell the back way.

Parc del Laberint

Confronted by the roaring traffic on the Passeig Vall d'Hebron, it seems inconceivable that there's any kind of sanctuary to hand, but just a couple of minutes' walk from Ⓜ Mundet metro puts you at the gates of the **Parc del Laberint** (daily: May–Sept 10am–9pm; Oct–April 10am–6pm; €1.85, free on Wed & Sun). The former estate mansion is undergoing restoration, but the late eighteenth-century gardens are open for visits and present an enchanting spectacle. A series of paths, terraces, pavilions and water features embrace the hillside, merging with the pine forest beyond. At the very heart of the park is the famed topiary maze, *El Laberint*, created by the Marquis de Llupià i Alfarràs and designed as an Enlightenment puzzle concerning the forms of love. A statue of Eros in the centre is the reward for successfully negotiating the maze. Near the park entrance are found a drinks kiosk, picnic area and children's playground.

At Ⓜ Mundet, use the Passeig Vall d'Hebron (Muntanya) exit. Walk up the main road against the traffic flow for one minute and turn left into the car park and grounds of the Velòdrom – the park entrance is immediately behind the cycle stadium, up the green slope.

Camp Nou: Museu del Futbol Club Barcelona

Within the city's Diagonal area, behind the university buildings, the magnificent **Camp Nou** football stadium of **FC Barcelona** (Ⓜ Collblanc/Maria Cristina) will be high on the visiting list of any sports fan, and might well surprise even those indifferent to the game. Built in 1957, and enlarged to accommodate the 1982 World Cup semi-final, the stadium seats a staggering 98,000 people in three steep tiers that provide one of the best football-watching experiences in the world – on a par with the famous Maracaña stadium in Brazil. In the early 1990s, the club was the most successful in Spain, attracting the cream of international talent, winning the domestic league and cup on a regular basis, and lifting the European Cup in 1992. Times have changed and the pendulum has now swung decisively in favour of arch rivals Real Madrid, who rubbed Catalan noses in it by snatching Luis Figo from Barça (and, latterly, David Beckham from Manchester United). The first time Figo came back to the Camp Nou to play with his new team, Barça supporters were merciless: almost 100,000 people whistled and jeered his every touch, and when he came to take a corner a pig's head was thrown onto the pitch. Such reaction tells you something about the status of FC Barcelona – it's more than just a football club to most people in the city. During the Franco era, it stood as a Catalan symbol, around which people could rally, and perhaps as a consequence FC Barcelona has the world's largest soccer club membership. The matches (played mostly on Sunday) can be an invigorating introduction to Catalan passions, particularly the big games against Real Madrid or Valencia: if you can get a ticket (see p.226 for details), you're in for a treat.

Meanwhile, a visit to the club's **Museu del Futbol** (Mon–Sat 10am–6.30pm, Sun 10am–2pm; €5, guided tours €9; ⓦwww.fcbarcelona.com), entered through Gate 14, provides a splendid celebration of Spain's national sport. The rooms full of silverware become repetitive after a while, but not the view you're allowed from the directors' box. There's an excellent English-language photo-history, an audiovisual display of goals galore, team and match photos dating back to 1901, and a gallery of the celebrated foreign players who have graced Barça's books: as early as 1911, there were five British players in the team. You can also see an exhibition of football memorabilia, paintings and sculpture, and there's a souvenir shop and café at the ground.

Pedralbes

Northwest of the university and Avinguda Diagonal, the well-to-do residential neighbourhood of **Pedralbes** is one of wide avenues and fancy apartment buildings. Two interesting museums here (of decorative art and ceramics) occupy a former royal palace, the Palau Reial de Pedralbes, while a half-day's excursion can be made of the trip by walking from the palace, past an early Gaudí creation, to the Gothic Monestir de Pedralbes. This is a choice attraction in its own right, enhanced by the glorious art of the Col.leccíoThyssen-Bornemisza, on permanent display at the monastery.

Palau Reial de Pedralbes

Opposite the university, the formal grounds of the **Palau Reial de Pedralbes** (ⓜPalau Reial) stretch up to the Italianate palace itself – basically a large villa with pretensions. It was built for the use of the royal family on their visits to Barcelona, with the funds raised by public subscription, and received its first such visit in 1926, but within five years the king had abdicated and the palace somewhat lost its role. Franco kept it on as a presidential residence and it later passed to the city, which since 1990 has used its rooms to show off certain of its applied art collections. There are plans to shift the displays to a purpose-built design museum, but for the foreseeable future the palace contains separate **museums of ceramics and decorative arts** (Tues–Sat 10am–6pm, Sun 10am–3pm; €3.50, first Sun of the month free), both accessible on the same ticket, which you can also use within one month to get into the Museu Textil i d'Indumentària in La Ribera.

The bulk of the exhibits at the **Museu de Ceràmica** (ⓦwww.museuceramica.bcn.es) range from the thirteenth to the nineteenth centuries, and include fine Moorish-influenced tiles and plates from the Aragonese town of Teruel, as well as a series of fifteenth- and sixteenth-century *socarrats* (decorated terracotta panels) from Paterno displaying demons and erotic scenes. Catalunya, too, has a long ceramics tradition, and there are entire rooms here of Catalan water stoups, jars, dishes, plates and bowls. Perhaps the most vivid examples of the polychromatic work coming out of Barcelona and Lleida workshops of the time are the two extensive *azulejo* panels of 1710, one showing a Madrid bullfight, the other the feasting and dancing taking place at a party centred on the craze of the period – hot-chocolate-drinking. In the modern section, Picasso, Miró and the *modernista* artist Antoni Serra i Fiter are all represented. The whole display is considerably more interesting than the bare recital of exhibits suggests, particularly if you're already fascinated by the diverse ceramic designs and embellishments that adorn so many of the city's buildings, old and new.

Across the corridor, the rooms of the **Museu de les Arts Decoratives** (ⓦwww.museuartsdecoratives.bcn.es) are arranged around the upper gallery of the palace's former throne room. This is a fair old romp from Romanesque art through to contemporary Catalan design, but there are some beautiful pieces here, starting with a pair of delicate thirteenth-century Andalusian boxes showing clear Arabic traits – these are two of the very earliest pieces in the collection. Side rooms showcase the various periods under the spotlight, with displays of highly polished Baroque and Neoclassical furniture contrasting with the varied Art Deco and *modernista* holdings. Highlight here has to be the four-metre-high stained-glass window of 1900, depicting the *sardana* being danced in a scene that looks back to medieval times for its inspiration. The entire latter half of the gallery concentrates on contemporary Catalan *disseny* (design), from chairs to espresso machines, lighting to sink taps, though there's not much context provided and in the end it's a bit like walking through the *Vinçon* design store and not being allowed to buy anything. English-language notes are provided if you'd prefer to put some names to goods and objects.

Finca Güell

A block east of the Palau Reial gardens, Avinguda Pedralbes heads north off the Diagonal up to the Monestir de Pedralbes. Just a couple of minutes up the avenue, you'll pass Gaudí's **Finca Güell** on your left. Built as stables and a riding school for the family of Gaudí's old patron, Eusebi Güell, the architect completed the *finca* in 1887, at the same time as he was working on the Palau Güell in the old town. The brick and tile buildings are frothy, whimsical affairs with more than a Moorish element to them, and you are allowed no further than the gateway – but what a gateway. An extraordinary winged dragon of twisted iron snarls at the passers-by, its razor-toothed jaws spread wide in a fearsome roar. Backing up to pose for a photograph suddenly doesn't seem like such a good idea.

Monestir de Pedralbes

At the end of Avinguda Pedralbes, the Gothic **Monestir de Pedralbes** (Tues–Sun 10am–2pm; monastery €4, art collection €3.50, both €5.50, first Sun of the month free) is reached up a cobbled street that passes through a small archway set back from the road. Founded in 1326 for the nuns of the Order of St Claire (whose members still reside here), this is in effect an entire monastic village preserved on the outskirts of the city, within medieval walls and gateways that shut out completely the noise and clamour of the 21st century. It's a twenty-minute walk from ⓂPalau Reial, or you can come directly by **bus** from the city centre (30min): the #22 from Plaça de Catalunya and Passeig de Gràcia stops outside, while the #64 from Ronda Sant Antoni and c/Aribau ends its run at the monastery.

The monastery

It took the medieval craftsmen a little over a year to prepare Pedralbes (from the Latin *petras albas*, "white stones") for its first community of nuns. The speed of the initial construction, and the subsequent uninterrupted habitation by the Order, helps explain the monastery's extreme architectural harmony. The **cloisters** in particular are perhaps the finest in the city, built on three levels and adorned by the slenderest of columns. Rooms opening off the cloisters give the clearest impression of monastic life you're likely to see in Catalunya (much more than at, say, Poblet): there's a large refectory, a fully equipped kitchen, infirmary (complete with beds and water jugs), separate infirmary kitchen, and windows overlooking a well-tended kitchen garden. All around the cloisters, too, are alcoves and rooms displaying the monastery's treasures – frescoes, paintings, memorabilia and religious artefacts. The adjacent **church** is a simple, single-naved structure, which retains some of its original fourteenth-century stained glass. In the chancel, to the right of the altar, the foundation's sponsor, Elisenda de Montcada, wife of Jaume II, lies in a superb carved marble tomb. Widowed in 1327, six months after the inauguration of the monastery, Elisenda retired to an adjacent palace, where she lived until her death in 1364.

The Thyssen-Bornemisza collection

After a bidding skirmish by various European countries, the immense private art collection of Baron Heinrich Thyssen-Bornemisza came to Spain in 1989, and the bulk of it is displayed in Madrid's Villahermosa palace, but the promptings of the baron's Catalan wife ensured a cache of paintings found its way to Barcelona. This now forms the **Col.leccío Thyssen-Bornemisza**, on permanent view in one of the monastery's capacious old dormitories, which has been given a black marble floor and soaring oak-beamed ceiling. It's a small but superb body of work, including priceless pieces from five major movements in European art from the fourteenth to the eighteenth centuries, displayed more or less chronologically (though if you want explanatory details you'll have to buy the guidebook from the bookshop).

The collection begins with a series of medieval Italian religious paintings, mostly of the Madonna and Child, of which the undoubted highlight is the sublime *Madonna of Humility* by Fra Angelico, painted in 1433. Religious works give way slowly to portraits commissioned by the Renaissance wealthy, like the Bentivoglio family, depicted in Lorenzo Costa's masterful group portrait (1493) as singing from a musical score. Subsequent works range far and wide – a minor Canaletto here, a lesser-known Rubens there – but there are more pieces of genuine quality, including Titian's sensuous *Madonna and Child* and a famous Velázquez portrait of the bulbous-nosed Maria Anna of Austria. The mainly Italian collection is offset by a group of works from the Flemish and German schools, most important of which are the dark, sombre depictions of saints by Cranach the Elder, which stand in sharp contrast to the exuberance of the Italian works of the same period. St George, a popular subject for Catalans, whose patron saint he is, is presented here as the all-conquering hero – albeit standing over the puniest dragon imaginable. The collection also includes several sculptures, mainly medieval Italian, and a delightful pair of Italian Renaissance angels holding candelabra from the della Robbia workshop in Florence.

Sarrià

If *modernista* buildings are high on your agenda, the exteriors of a couple of other important Gaudí buildings can be seen in the **Sarrià** district, just to the east of Pedralbes. The **Torre Bellesguard** (c/Bellesguard 16–20), built from 1900 to 1909 on the site of the early fifteenth-century palace of King Martin I (the last of the Catalan kings), is a neo-Gothic house of unremarkable proportions; the **Col.legi Santa Teresa** (c/Ganduxer 85) was a convent school, embellished in 1888 by Gaudí with an iron gate and parabolic arches. Both buildings are reached from the FGC Bonanova station.

If you are going to poke around these nether reaches of Barcelona, you may as well continue up into the heart of Sarrià, whose narrow main street – c/Major de Sarrià (FGC Sarrià; c/Mare de Deu de Núria exit) – shows aspects of the independent small town that Sarrià once was. At its northern end, at **Plaça de Sarrià** (bus #64 from Pedralbes stops here on its way to and from the monastery), the much-restored church of Sant Vincenç flanks the main Passeig de la Reina Elisenda de Montcada, across which lies the neighbourhood **market**, housed in a *modernista* red-brick building of 1911. Traffic-free c/Major de Sarrià runs downhill from here, past other surviving old-town squares, prettiest of which is **Plaça Sant Vicenç** (off c/Mañe i Flaquer), where there's a statue of the saint and a nice little sandwich café-bar, the *Can Pau* (closed weekends). If you make it this way, don't miss the *Bar Tomás* (see p.180), just around the corner on c/Major de Sarrià, for the world's best *patatas bravas*.

Tibidabo and around

If the views from the Castell de Montjuïc are good, those from the 550-metre heights of **Tibidabo** – which forms the northwestern boundary of the city – are legendary. On one of those mythical clear days, you can see across to Montserrat and the Pyrenees, and out to sea even as far as Mallorca. The very name is based on this view, taken from the Temptations of Christ in the wilderness, when Satan led him to a high place and offered him everything which could be seen: *Haec omnia tibi dabo si cadens adoraberis me* ("All these things will I give thee, if thou wilt fall down and worship me").

At the summit there's a modern church topped with a huge statue of Christ, and – immediately adjacent – a wonderful amusement park, where the rides and attractions are scattered around several levels of the mountaintop, connected by landscaped paths and gardens. A short walk away there are more views from the observation deck of a communications tower, while the nearby village of Vallvidrera offers an alternative route back to the city. Meanwhile, the city's revamped science museum on the lower slopes of Tibidabo really requires a separate visit.

Tibidabo

The funicular drops you right outside the gates of the **Parc d'Atraccions** (mid-June to mid-Sept daily noon–10pm, until 1am at weekends; mid-Sept to mid-June Sat & Sun noon–6pm; hours sometimes vary, call ☎ 932 117 942 for exact times; €10 or €20), a mix of traditional rides and hi-tech attractions, at all of which large queues form at peak times. The most expensive entrance ticket allows unlimited access to everything, otherwise you're limited to a selection of the best rides and attractions, including the Museu d'Autòmates, a collection of coin-operated antique fairground machines in working order. If you want a real thrill, try the aeroplane ride, a Barcelona institution: it's been spinning since 1928.

You can get views of the city for free from the belvedere by the side of the park, and they are even more extensive if you climb the shining steps of the neighbouring **Templo Expiatorio de España** to the dramatic, wide balcony. Inside the church, also known as the Sagrat Cor (Sacred Heart), a lift (*ascensor*; daily 10am–2pm & 3–7pm; €1.50) takes you higher still, to just under the feet of Christ, from where the city, surrounding hills and sea shimmer in the distance.

Practicalities

Getting there can be a convoluted matter but also part of the attraction. First, take the FGC **train** (Tibidabo line) from the station at Plaça de Catalunya to Avinguda Tibidabo (the last stop). Emerging from the station escalators, cross the road to the tram/bus shelter at the bottom of the tree-lined avenue; the Bus Turistic stops here, too. An **antique tram** service (the *Tramvia Blau*; weekends and holidays 10am–5.45pm every 15–30min; €2.10 one way, €3.10 return) then runs you up the hill to Plaça Doctor Andreu; on weekdays there's a bus service instead (Mon–Fri 7.45am–8.40pm every 20min). Near the tram and bus stop on Plaça Doctor Andreu there are several café-bars and restaurants and a **funicular station**. When the Parc d'Atraccions is open, this has regular connections to Tibidabo at the top (€2 one way, €3 return). If the funicular isn't running, you could take a taxi from Avinguda Tibidabo instead, which will cost about €8 to Tibidabo.

Alternatively, the special **Tibibus** runs direct to Tibidabo from Plaça de Catalunya, outside El Corte Inglés (weekends & holidays year round every 30min; plus weekdays in summer, hourly; €2).

Drinks and meals inside the park are pricey. Immediately outside the upper funicular station and park there's another restaurant, which is packed with families on Sundays. It's not that great, though it does have outdoor terrace seats. Best choice for a sandwich or simple meal is the *Marisa*, an inexpensive bar-restaurant on the road to Vallvidrera just below the Tibidabo car park. It's a three-minute walk from the upper funicular station and has a little concrete patio to the side with sweeping views.

Torre de Collserola and Vallvidrera

Follow the road from the Tibidabo car park and it's only a few minutes' walk to Norman Foster's **Torre de Collserola** (Wed–Fri 11am–2.30pm & 3.30–6pm, Sat & Sun 11am–6pm; July–Sept Wed–Sun until 8pm; €4.60; ⓦwww.torredecollserola.com), a soaring communications tower high above the tree line, with a glass lift that whisks you up ten floors (115m) for yet more stunning views – 70km, they claim, on a good day.

Afterwards, you could just head back to Tibidabo for the funicular-and-tram ride back to the city, but to complete a circular tour it's more interesting to follow the large cobbled path near the tower's car park, which brings you out on the pine-clad edges of **Vallvidrera**, a wealthy suburban village perched on the flank of the Collserola hills – a twenty-minute walk all told from Tibidabo. There's another **funicular** station here, this time with a year-round service (6am–midnight every 6–10min), connecting to Peu del Funicular, an FGC station on the Sabadell and Terrassa line from Plaça de Catalunya.

Vallvidrera's main square isn't obviously found – if you turn left out of the funicular station and walk down the steep steps, Plaça de Vallvidrera is the traffic roundabout at the bottom. There are a couple of local **bar-restaurants** on its fringes, most striking being *Can Josean* (closed Tues), with a simple bar at the front and a dining room at the rear, with views out over the city from the back tables.

Museu de la Ciència

The city's science museum, the **Museu de la Ciència** (Wwww .nuevomuseodelaciencia.com), has undergone massive refurbishment and should be open again by the time you read this. The museum was previously housed in a converted *modernista* hospice, built in 1904–09 by Josep Domènech i Estapà. The new works have retained the original building, but surrounded it by a park and added four times as much exhibition space in a huge underground extension and stylish public entrance. You can expect a fully interactive experience, touching on all aspects of science, and tracing the history of matter from the origins of the universe onwards. Special exhibitions, talks and experiments are planned, and the popular planetarium from the original museum will be revived. The museum is on c/Teodor Roviralta and transport is via FGC train from Plaça de Catalunya to Avinguda Tibidabo, then the *Tramvia Blau*/service bus – meanwhile, up-to-date opening hours and admission prices are available from the city tourist offices.

Parc de Collserola

The **Parc de Collserola**, encompassing Tibidabo (its highest peak), is one of Barcelona's best-kept secrets. While many make the ascent to the amusement park and church, few realize that beyond stretches an area of peaks and wooded valleys roughly 17km by 18km, threaded by rivers, roads and paths. You can, in fact, walk into the park from Tibidabo and the Torre de Collserola, but it's better to start from the park's information centre, across to the east, above Vallvidrera, where hiking-trail leaflets and other information are available.

The **Centre d'Informació** (daily 9.30am–3pm; ☎932 803 552, Whttp://ParcCollserola.amb.es) lies in oak and pinewoods, an easy, signposted ten-minute stepped walk up through the trees from the FGC Baixada de Vallvidrera station (Sabadell or Terrassa line from Pl. de Catalunya; 15min). There's an exhibition here on the park's history, flora and fauna, while the staff hand out English-language leaflets detailing the various walks you can make from the centre, ranging from a fifteen-minute stroll to the Vallvidrera dam to a couple of hours circling the hills. A bar-restaurant (with an outdoor terrace) provides snacks and meals, and sells bottles of water for hikers.

If you're here at the weekend, before you head off you might as well have a quick look inside the **Museu Verdaguer** (Sat & Sun 10am–2pm; free), housed in the Villa Joana, which sits just below the information centre. Jacint Verdaguer, the Catalan Reniassance poet, lived here briefly before his death in 1902, and the house has been preserved as an example of well-to-do nineteenth-century Catalan life. Extracts from his poetry enliven the climb up from the FGC station to the information centre and house.

Well-marked **paths** radiate from the information centre into the hills and valleys. Some – like the oak-forest walk – soon gain height for marvellous views over the tree canopy, while others descend through the valley bottoms to springs and shaded picnic areas. The walk touted as the most diverse is that to the **Font de la Buderalla**, a landscaped spring deep in the woods, beneath the Torre de Collserola. It's about an hour all told if you circle back to the information centre from here, but a good idea is to follow the signs for the Torre de Collserola and Vallvidrera once you reach the *font* (another 20min). That way, you can return to Barcelona instead via the funicular from the village of Vallvidrera (see p.120), or even take in the views from the Collserola tower or Tibidabo before going back.

6

Out of the city

lthough there are plenty of traditional coastal bolt holes close to Barcelona, like the small towns of the **Costa Maresme** to the north, unquestionably the best local seaside destination is **Sitges**, 30km south along the Costa Daurada. It's a charming resort with an international reputation, extremely popular with gay visitors and chic city-dwellers. Otherwise, the one essential excursion is to **Montserrat**, the extraordinary mountain and monastery 40km northwest of Barcelona, reached by a precipitous cable-car or mountain railway ride. However short your trip to the city, this is worth making time for, as it's a place of great significance for Catalans,

not to mention being a terrific place for a hike in the hills.

If Barcelona's varied church architecture inspires you, there's more to come, starting with Gaudí's inspired work at the **Colònia Güell**, a late nineteenth-century idealistic community established by the architect's patron Eusebi Güell. This is a half-day's outing, while another half-day can be spent visiting the Benedictine monastery at **Sant Cugat del Vallès** and the complex of early medieval churches at **Terrassa**, all of them largely unsung and utterly fascinating. Another route out of the city, due west, leads through the wine-producing towns of **Sant Sadurní d'Anoia** and **Vilafranca del Penedès**, either of which can be seen in a pleasant day's excursion with enough time for a wine-tasting tour.

It's also straightforward to see something of Barcelona's neighbouring cities, all very different from the Catalan capital. To the south of Barcelona, beyond Sitges, lies **Tarragona**, with a compact old town and an amazing series of Roman remains; while to the north, inland from the coast, sits medieval **Girona**, perhaps the most beautiful of all Catalan cities, with its river, fortified walls and golden buildings. Both of these destinations are around an hour from Barcelona, and it's only the extreme northern town of **Figueres** that requires any lengthier a journey – entirely justified for anyone interested in seeing Catalunya's most indescribable museum, the renowned **Museu Dalí**.

Regional festivals

February/March
Carnaval: Sitges has Catalunya's best Carnaval celebrations.

May
11 Cremada del Dimoni at Badalona: demon-burning, dancing and fireworks.
Third week: Fires i Festes de la Santa Creu in Figueres – processions and music.
Corpus Christi (movable feast, sometimes falls in early June): Festa de Corpus Christi in Sitges – big processions and streets decorated with flowers.

June
24 Dia de Sant Joan celebrated everywhere; watch out for things shutting down for a day on either side.
Last week: Annual festival at Canet de Mar and Sant Cugat del Vallès.

July
Second week: Annual festival at Arenys de Mar.

August
15 Annual festival at Castelldefels.
19 Festa de Sant Magi in Tarragona.
Last week: Festa Major in Sitges, to honour the town's patron saint, Sant Bartolomeu.
29 & 30: Festa Major in Vilafranca del Penedès, dedicated to Sant Felix, with human towers, dancing and processions – continues into the first two days of September.

September
Second Sunday: Fira Gran in Sant Sadurní d'Anoia, the town's big annual festival.
23 Festa de Sant Tecla in Tarragona, with processions of *gigants* and human castles.

October
Second week: Setmana del Cava – a sort of *cava* festival – is held in Sant Sadurní d'Anoia, well worth going out of your way for.

Full **public transport** details are given below for each destination. Local and regional trains provide the most reliable service, and you can check current timetables with RENFE (☎902 240 202, ⓦwww.renfe.es) or FGC (☎932 051 515, ⓦwww.fgc.es). There are buses to most regional destinations, too, from the Estació del Nord bus station, though these usually take longer than the train. For one or two side-trips, you might as well go by public transport. It really isn't worth renting a car unless you want to see a lot of what's described above in a short time. Each account also includes some **café and restaurant** recommendations, while if you feel like spending the night away from Barcelona it's best to contact the local tourist offices, whose details are provided. A visit to Barcelona's **Centre d'Informació de Catalunya** at Palau Robert (see p.22) might also be in order, to pick up maps, information and advice before you go.

Costa Maresme

Immediately north of Barcelona, before you reach the Costa Brava, is a stretch of coast known as the **Costa Maresme**, accessed by trains from Barcelona Sants, stopping at Plaça de Catalunya (departures roughly every 15min, direction Maçanet). The first 30km are dominated by the grim industrial towns of Badalona and Mataró, and even beyond here – where the train hugs the coast – it's still far from pretty. Each stop has a strand of sorts and a promenade, but on the whole it's much less attractive than the Costa Brava itself, while proximity to the city means clogged-up roads and packed trains in the summer, as people head out in search of a change of scenery.

ARENYS DE MAR, 40km from Barcelona (55min by train) is the largest fishing port on the coast, and has a harbour and marina that bear investigation. The wide sands here stretch for 3km up to the next train stop of Canet de Mar, while on Saturdays a huge market fills the main street, good for cheap clothes, paella pans and a multitude of other things. To be honest, though, it's only **SANT POL DE MAR**, 45km from Barcelona (1hr), that has any degree of real charm, with a jumble of old streets above the station and a selection of rocky coves and decent beaches within walking distance. There are a few restaurants here, a small parish church, and sea views from the upper part of the village, though not too much else to get excited about. From Sant Pol, Blanes (the start of the Costa Brava proper) is another twenty minutes up the line.

Sitges

SITGES, 30km south of Barcelona, is definitely the highlight of the Costa Daurada – the great weekend escape for young Barcelonans, who have created a resort very much in their own image. It's also a noted gay holiday destination, with a nightlife to match, and between June and September it seems like there's one nonstop party going on – which, in a way, there is. During the heat of the day, though, the tempo drops as everyone hits the beach, while out of season Sitges is delightful: far less crowded (indeed, empty in midweek), and with a temperate climate that encourages promenade strolls and old-town

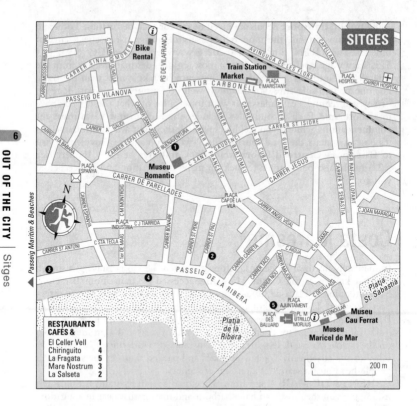

RESTAURANTS
CAFÉS &

El Celler Vell	1
Chiringuito	4
La Fragata	5
Mare Nostrum	3
La Salseta	2

exploration. As well as a certain style, the Barcelona trippers have brought with them the high prices from the Catalan capital, but you can still eat reasonably cheaply if you know where to look. Monday isn't the best day to come, as the three museums and many restaurants are closed.

The Town

It's the **beach** that brings most people to Sitges and it's not hard to find, with two strands right in town, to the west of the church. From here, a succession of beaches of varying quality and crowdedness stretches west as far as the *Hotel Terramar*, a couple of kilometres down the coast. The **Passeig Marítim** runs all the way there, with beach bars, restaurants, showers and water sports facilities along its length. Beyond the *Terramar*, following the rail line, you eventually reach the more notorious nudist beaches, a couple of which are exclusively gay.

Make the effort at some stage to climb up the knoll overlooking the beaches, topped by the Baroque **parish church** – known as La Punta – and a street of old whitewashed mansions. One house on c/Fonollar contains the **Museu Cau Ferrat** (July & Aug Tues–Sun 10am–2pm & 5–9pm; Sept–June Tues–Fri 10am–1.30pm & 3–6.30pm, Sat 10am–7pm, Sun 10am–3pm; €3), the former house and workshop of the artist and writer Santiago Rusiñol (1861–1931). Its two floors contain a massive jumble of his own paintings, as well as sculpture, painted tiles, drawings and various collected odds and ends – like the decorative ironwork Rusiñol brought back in bulk from the Pyrenees. The museum also contains works by the artist's friends (including Picasso), who used to meet in the *Quatre Gats* bar in Barcelona.

Next door, the **Museu Maricel de Mar** (same opening hours and price as Cau Ferrat) has other minor artworks, medieval to modern, and maintains an impressive collection of Catalan ceramics and sculpture. More entertaining is the **Museu Romàntic** (same opening hours and price as Cau Ferrat; guided tour every hour), right in the centre of town, at c/Sant Gaudenci 1, off c/Sant Josep, which aims to show the lifestyle of a rich Sitges family in the eighteenth and nineteenth centuries by displaying some of their furniture and possessions. A combination ticket (€5.41) is available for all three museums.

> ### Carnaval
>
> Carnaval in Sitges (*Carnestoltes* in Catalan; Feb/March) is outrageous, thanks large-ly to the gay populace. The official programme of parades and masked balls is com-plemented by an unwritten but widely recognized schedule of events. The climax is Tuesday's late-night parade (not in the official programme), in which exquisitely dressed drag queens swan about the streets in high heels, twirling lacy parasols and coyly fanning themselves. Bar doors stand wide open, bands play, and processions and celebrations go on until four in the morning.

Practicalities

Trains to Sitges leave Passeig de Gràcia or Barcelona Sants stations every 20 minutes, more frequently at peak times (destination Vilanova/St Vicenç), and it's a thirty- to forty-minute ride depending on the service. Although the Sitges nightlife might be legendary, the trains do you no favours, with the last departure back to Barcelona at around 10.30pm. A taxi will cost at least €40. The **Oficina Turisme** (July–Sept daily 9am–9pm; Oct–June Mon–Fri 9am–2pm & 4–6.30pm; ☎938 945 004, ⓦwww.sitges.org) is at the Oasis shopping centre, up Passeig de Vilafranca, five minutes' walk from the station. There's a second office on c/Fonollar, opposite the Museu Cau Ferrat (July–Sept daily 10am–1.30pm & 5–9pm; Oct–June Sat 11am–2pm & 4–7pm, Sun 11am–4pm; ☎938 110 611). You can pick up a town map, and restaurant and accommodation lists, from either office. There's **bike rental** from Sitges Bike (☎938 949 458, ⓦwww.sitgesbike.com), at the front of the Oasis shopping centre.

For picnic supplies, visit the town's **market** – the Mercat Nou – which is very close to the train station, on Avinguda Artur Carbonell. Areas to explore for **cafés and restaurants** are the side streets around the church, and the beach-front for the more expensive seafood restaurants. In town, *El Celler Vell*, c/Sant Buenaventura 21 (☎938 111 961; closed Tues night and all Wed), serves Catalan food in rustic surroundings and features a *menú del dia* for €7.60. *La Salseta*, c/Sant Pau 35 (☎938 110 419; closed Sun night and all Mon) also has a good local reputation. On the seafront there's a wide choice, starting with the *Chiringuito*, Pg. de la Ribera (☎938 947 596), claiming to be Spain's oldest beach bar and serving grilled sardines, fried *chipirones* and calamari, sandwich-es and snacks at budget prices. *Mare Nostrum*, Pg. de Ribeira 60 (☎938 943 393; closed Wed), is a long-established seafront fish restaurant with higher prices, while typical of the new wave of classier seafood places is *La Fragata*, Pg. de la Ribera 1 (☎938 941 086), serving inventive fish, shellfish, rice and *fideuà* dish-es at moderate to expensive prices.

Montserrat

The mountain of **Montserrat**, with its weirdly shaped crags of rock, vast monastery and deserted hermitage caves, stands just 40km northwest of Barcelona, off the road to Lleida. It is one of the most spectacular of all Spain's natural sights, a saw-toothed outcrop left exposed to erosion when the inland sea that covered this area around 25 million years ago was drained by progressive uplifts of the earth's crust. Legends hang easily upon it. Fifty years after the birth of Christ, St Peter is said to have deposited an image of the Virgin carved by St Luke in one of the mountain caves, and another tale makes this the spot in which the knight Parsifal discovered the Holy Grail.

It is the "Black Virgin" (*La Moreneta*), the icon supposedly hidden by St Peter, which is responsible for the existence of the **Monastery of Montserrat**. The legend is loosely wrought, but it appears the icon was lost in the early eighth century after being hidden during the Moorish invasion. It reappeared in 880, accompanied by the customary visions and celestial music and, in the first of its miracles, would not budge when the Bishop of Vic attempted to remove it. A chapel was built to house it, and in 976 this was superseded by a Benedictine monastery, set about three-quarters of the way up the mountain at an altitude of nearly 1000m. Miracles abounded and the Virgin of Montserrat soon became the chief cult-image of Catalunya and a pilgrimage centre second in Spain only to Santiago de Compostela – the main **pilgrimages** to Montserrat take place on April 27 and September 8. For centuries, the monastery enjoyed outrageous prosperity, having its own flag and a form of extraterritorial independence along the lines of the Vatican City, and its fortunes declined only in the nineteenth century. In 1811 Napoleon's troops devastated the buildings, stole many of the treasures and "hunted the hermits like chamois along the cliffs". In 1835 the monastery was suppressed for supporting the wrong side in the civil war known as the First Carlist War. Monks were allowed to return nine years later, but by 1882 their numbers had fallen to nineteen. In recent decades Montserrat's popularity has again become established; there are over three hundred brothers and, in addition to the tourists, tens of thousands of newly married couples come here to seek *La Moreneta*'s blessing on their union.

Quite apart from its spiritual significance, Montserrat has become an important **nationalist symbol** for Catalans. Montserrat's Abbot Marcel was a vigorous promoter of the Catalan language, creating a printing press in 1918, which published the Montserrat Bible in Catalan. During Franco's dictatorship books continued to be secretly and illegally printed here, and it was then and afterwards the site of massive Catalan nationalist demonstrations.

The monastery

The monastery itself is of no particular architectural interest, save perhaps in its monstrous bulk. Its various buildings – including hotel, post office, souvenir shop and even supermarket – fan out around an open square, and there are extraordinary mountain views from the terrace as well as from various other vantage points scattered around the complex.

Of the religious buildings, only the **Basilica** (daily 8–10.30am & noon–6.30pm; free), dating largely from 1560 to 1592, is open to the public. **La Moreneta**, blackened by the smoke of countless candles, stands above the high altar – reached from behind, by way of an entrance to the right of the basilica's main entrance. The approach to this beautiful icon reveals the enormous wealth of the monastery, as you queue along a corridor leading through the back of the basilica's rich side-chapels. Signs at head height command "SILENCE" in various languages, but nothing quietens the line which waits to climb the stairs behind the altar and kiss the image's hands and feet. Your appreciation of the icon's noble features is likely to be limited to a quick glimpse as you file by.

The best time to be here is at the chanting of Ave Maria, daily at 1pm (noon on Sun), when Montserrat's world-famous **boys' choir** sings. The boys belong to the Escolania, a choral school established in the thirteenth century and unchanged in musical style since its foundation.

Near the entrance to the basilica, the **Museu de Montserrat** (Mon–Fri 10am–6.45pm, Sat & Sun 9.30am–7.45pm; €5.50) presents a few archeological finds brought back by travelling monks together with painting and sculpture dating from as early as the thirteenth century, including works by Caravaggio, El Greco, Tiepolo, Picasso, Dalí, Monet and Degas. Religious items are in surprisingly short supply, as most of the monastery's valuables were carried off by Napoleon's troops. The joint ticket also gets you in the **Espai Audiovisual** (daily 9am–6pm), near the tourist office, which tells you something of the life of a Benedictine community.

Walks on the mountain

After you've poked around the monastery grounds, it's the walks around the woods and mountainside of Montserrat that are the real attraction. Following the tracks to various caves and the thirteen different hermitages, you can contemplate what Goethe wrote in 1816: "Nowhere but in his own Montserrat will a man find happiness and peace." The going is pretty good on all the tracks – most have been graded and some concreted – and the signposting is clear, but you do need to remember that you are on a mountain. Take water if you're hiking far, and keep away from the edges. A map with walking notes is available from the Montserrat tourist office (see p.130).

Montserrat: flora and fauna

The **vegetation** of the lower slopes of Montserrat is essentially Mediterranean forest, but a fire in 1986 left huge burned patches which have since been recolonized by Spanish gorse, rosemary and a profusion of grape hyacinths, early purple orchids and martagon lilies. Higher up, although apparently barren of vegetation, Montserrat's rounded turrets support a wide variety of fissure plants, not least of which is the lime-encrusting saxifrage *Saxifraga callosa* ssp. *catalaunica* – known to grow only at Montserrat and on the hills near Marseille. Plants more typical of the high Pyrenees also make their home here, including such botanical gems as ramonda and the handsome Pyrenean bellflower.

Birds of Montserrat include Bonelli's warblers, nightingales, serins and firecrests in the woodlands, while the burned areas provide refuge for Sardinian warblers and good hunting for Bonelli's eagles. Sant Jeroni, the high point of Montserrat, is an excellent place to watch for peregrines, crag martins and black redstarts all year round, with the addition of alpine swifts in the summer and alpine accentors in the winter. On sunny days Iberian wall lizards emerge from the crevices to bask on rock faces.

Two separate funiculars run from points close to the cable-car station, with departures every twenty minutes (daily 10am–6pm; weekends only in winter). One drops to the path for **Santa Cova** (€2.50 return), a seventeenth-century chapel built where the icon is said originally to have been found. It's an easy walk there and back, which takes less than an hour. The other funicular rises steeply to the hermitage of **Sant Joan** (€6.10 return), from where it's a tougher 45-minutes walk to the **Sant Jeroni** hermitage, and another fifteen minutes to the Sant Jeroni summit at 1236m. Several other walks are also possible from the Sant Joan funicular, perhaps the nicest the simple (but steep) circuit around the ridge that leads in 45 minutes all the way back down to the monastery.

Practicalities

FGC **trains** (line R5, direction Manresa; ⓦwww.fgc.net) leave from beneath Plaça d'Espanya daily from 8.36am at hourly intervals; get off at Montserrat Aeri (52min). From here, the connecting **cable car** (*Aeri*; every 15min, daily 9.25am–1.45pm & 2.20–6.45pm) completes the journey, a five-minute swoop up the sheer mountainside to a terrace just below the monastery – probably the most exhilarating ride in Catalunya. The alternative approach is by the *cremallera*, or cog-wheel **mountain railway** (ⓦwww.cremallerademontserrat com), which departs from Monistrol de Montserrat (the next stop after Montserrat Aeri, another 4min); this leaves every twenty to sixty minutes (depending on season), connecting with train arrivals from Barcelona, and takes twenty minutes to climb to the monastery. **Returning to Barcelona**, trains depart hourly from Monistrol de Montserrat (9.33am–11.33pm) and Montserrat Aeri (9.37am–11.37pm). **Drivers** should take the A2 motorway as far as Martorell, and then follow the N11 and C1411 before zigzagging up to the monastery.

A **return ticket** from Plaça d'Espanya costs €11.80 (train and cable car/train and *cremallera*), and there are also two combined tickets: the **Transmontserrat** (€20.50 return), which includes the metro, train, cable car/*cremallera* and unlimited use of the two mountain funiculars; and the **Totmontserrat** (€34.50), which includes the same plus museum/audiovisual entry and a self-service cafeteria lunch. The combined tickets are also available from any city FGC station. There is also a daily morning **bus service** (€7.40 return, weekends €8.40) from Barcelona to the monastery and full bus tour (€38), both with *Julia Tours* (information from any tourist office), but these can't compete for thrills with the train and aerial rides.

There's a tourist office at Montserrat, just up from the *cremallera* station, marked **Informació** (daily 9am–5.45pm, July–Sept until 7pm; ☎938 777 701, ⓦwww.abadiamontserrat.net), where you can pick up maps of the complex and mountain. They can also advise you about the accommodation options, from camping to staying at the three-star hotel.

There are plenty of places to eat, but all are relatively pricey and none particularly inspiring. They are also very busy at peak times. The most expensive **restaurant** is inside the *Hotel Abat Cisneros*, opposite the basilica, which is reasonably good but overpriced (the *menú del dia* is a whopping €25). Much cheaper, and boasting the best views, is the *Restaurant de Montserrat* (with *menús* at €12.60 and €19.80), in the cliff-edge building near the car park, though here and in the **self-service cafeteria** (*menú* €9.40), one floor up and with the same good views, there's no *à la carte* choice – that is, you have to have the full meal – and the food can best be described as adequate. The latter is where

△ The Black Madonna of Montserrat

you eat with the all-inclusive Tot Montserrat ticket. There's a cheaper self-service cafeteria near the upper cable-car station, a bar in the square further up, plus a patisserie and a supermarket, and there's a lot to be said for taking your own picnic and striking off up the mountainside. You might also want to try the fresh *mató* (curd cheese) and honey sold at stalls on the road up to the car park. Finally, there's the economical *Bar El Rincon*, for simple meals, behind the rail line down at Montserrat Aeri – this is also the only realistic place to kill time if you've missed a train connection.

Sant Cugat and Terrassa

A series of remarkable churches lies on the commuter line out of the city to the northwest, the first in the dormitory town of **Sant Cugat del Vallès** – just 25 minutes from Barcelona – and the second (actually a group of three) another fifteen minutes beyond in the industrial city of **Terrassa**. You can see all the churches easily in a morning, but throw in lunch and this just about stretches to a day-trip, and it's not a bad ride in any case – after Sarrià, the train emerges from the city tunnels and chugs down the wooded valley into Sant Cugat. FGC trains run on the S1 line from Plaça de Catalunya, also stopping in Gràcia, with departures every ten to fifteen minutes.

Sant Cugat del Vallès

At **SANT CUGAT DEL VALLÈS**, the Benedictine **Reial Monestir** (Mon–Sat 9am–noon & 6–8pm, Sun 9am–8pm; free) was founded as far back as the ninth century, though most of the surviving buildings date from three or four hundred years later. Its fawn stone facade and triple-decker bell tower make a lovely sight as you approach from the square outside, through the gate, past the renovated Bishop's Palace and under a splendid rose window. Finest of all, though, is the beautiful twelfth-century Romanesque **cloister** (under renovation at time of writing; admission charge), with noteworthy capital carvings of mythical beasts and biblical scenes. They have an unusual homogeneity, since they were all done by a single sculptor, Arnau Gatell. What were once the monastery's kitchen gardens lie across from the Bishop's Palace, though the formerly lush plots that sustained the brothers are now mere dusty gardens, albeit with views over the low walls to Tibidabo and the Collserola hills.

To reach the monastery, cross the road outside the train station and follow c/Valldoreix, taking the first right and then the first left (it's still c/Valldoreix), and then just keep straight along the shopping street until you see the monastery bell tower (10min). Plaça Octavia, outside the monastery, has a **café-restaurant** with outdoor seating, and you'll pass plenty of other places to eat on your way.

Terrassa

TERRASSA, a large city of 150,000 about 20km out of Barcelona, hides its treasures in the older part of town, a twenty-minute walk from the station (get off at Terrassa-Rambla, the last stop). Here, three pre-Romanesque churches, dating from the fifth to the tenth centuries, form an unusual complex built on the site of the former Roman town of Egara. It's known as the **Conjunt**

Monumental de les Esglésies de Sant Pere (Tues–Sat 10am–1.30pm & 4–7pm, Sun 11am–2pm; free) – not that you'll see any signs – and excavations are still ongoing, but the church doors are open for visits and someone should be around to give you an explanatory leaflet.

The largest church, **Sant Pere**, is the least interesting, with just a badly faded Gothic mural and a tenth-century mosaic fragment surviving the years. **Santa Maria** is far better endowed, starting with a mosaic pavement outside that dates from the fifth century. The same date is given to the sunken baptismal font inside, while much later Gothic (fourteenth- and fifteenth-century) murals and altarpieces – one by Catalan master Jaume Huguet – are also on display. But it's the intervening building, the fifth-century baptistry of **Sant Miquel**, that's the most fascinating here. A tiny, square building of rough masonry, steeped in gloom, it has eight assorted columns supporting the dome, each with carved Roman or Visigothic capitals. Underneath sits the partially reconstructed baptismal bath, once octagonal, while steps lead down into a simple crypt.

To get there, turn right out of the station (Rambla Egara exit) and immediately right again into Plaça de Clavé, following c/Major up to Plaça Vella, where there are some outdoor **cafés**. The route then crosses the square, turns up c/Gavatxons and follows c/Sant Pere, c/Nou de Sant Pere and c/de la Gran Creu, finally crossing a viaduct to arrive at the entrance to the church complex.

Colònia Güell

Before work at the Parc Güell (see p.112) got under way, Antoni Gaudí had already been charged with the design of parts of Eusebi Güell's earliest attempts to establish a Utopian industrial estate, or *colònia* (colony), on the western out-skirts of Barcelona. The **Colònia Güell** was very much of its time – more than seventy similar colonies were established along Catalan rivers in the late nine-teenth century, using water power to drive the textile mills – and the concept was a familiar one in Britain, where enlightened Victorian entrepreneurs had long created idealistic towns (Saltaire, Bournville) to house their workers.

The Colònia Güell at Santa Coloma de Cervelló was begun in 1890 and, by 1920, incorporated over one hundred houses, plus the chapel and crypt for which Gaudí was responsible. The buildings were predominantly of brick and iron, sporting typical *modernista* Gothic and Moorish-style flourishes, with a school, theatre, cultural association and other services provided. The Güell company was taken over in 1945 and the whole complex closed as a going concern in 1973, though the buildings have since been restored – and, indeed, many are still lived in today.

There's an interpretive exhibition (with English notes) at the visitor centre, but by far the best way of appreciating the site is simply to stroll the streets, past the rows of terraced houses, whose front gardens are tended lovingly by the current inhabitants. Brick towers, ceramic panels and stained glass elevate many of the houses above the ordinary – like the private Ca l'Espinal (1900) by Gaudí's con-temporary, Joan Rubió i Bellver. It is, though, Gaudí's **church** (mid-May–Oct Mon–Sat 10am–2pm & 3–7pm, Sun 10am–3pm; Nov to mid-May daily 10am–3pm), built into the pine-clad hillside above the colony, which alone deserves to be called a masterpiece. The crypt was designed to carry the weight of the chapel above, its palm-tree-like columns supporting a brick vault, and the whole resembling a labyrinth of caves fashioned from a variety of different stone and brick. The more extraordinary features of Gaudí's flights of fancy presage his later work on the Sagrada Família – like the original scalloped pews, the conch shells used as water stoups, the vivid stained glass, and the window that opens up like the wings of a butterfly. Despite appearances, the church was never actually finished – Gaudí stopped work on it in 1914 – and continuing restoration work aims to complete the outer walls, though Gaudí's planned 40-metre-high central dome is unlikely ever to be realized.

Practicalities

Take the **FGC train** S8 (direction Martorell; roughly every 15min) from Plaça d'Espanya to the small Colònia Güell station; the ride takes twenty minutes. From here, follow the painted blue footprints across the highway and into the *colònia* to the visitor centre (10min), the **Centre d'Acollida de Visitants** (mid-May to Oct Mon–Sat 9am–7pm, Sun 9am–3pm; Nov to mid-May daily 9am–3pm; ☎936 305 807). You can walk around the *colònia* and see the church from the outside for free, though to visit the church interior you'll have to buy a ticket (€4) at the visitor centre – the church is open during the hours detailed above, but closed for visits during Mass on Sundays (11am & 1pm). There are **guided tours** available daily throughout the year, of either the church and estate (€8; 2hr) or the church on its own (€5; 30min), but you'll need to call the visitor centre and reserve in advance.

It's a lived-in village, so you'll find a bank and pharmacy, as well as two or three cafés and restaurants.

The wine region: L'Alt Penedès

Trains (mon–Fri every 30min, Sat & Sun hourly) from Plaça de Catalunya or Barcelona Sants run west from Barcelona into **L'Alt Penedès**, a region roughly halfway between the city and Tarragona, devoted to wine production. It's the largest Catalan producer of still and sparkling wines, and boasts the most vineyards, too – this becomes increasingly clear the further the train heads into the region, with vines as far as the eye can see on both sides of the track. There are two main towns to visit, both of which can easily be seen in a single day by train: **Sant Sadurní d'Anoia**, the closer to Barcelona (35min), is the self-styled Capital del Cava, home to around fifty producers of sparkling wine; **Vilafranca del Penedès**, ten minutes down the line, is the region's administrative capital and produces mostly still wine.

If you're serious about **visiting vineyards**, it's a trip better done by car, as many of the more interesting boutique producers lie out in the sticks. Either of the towns' tourist offices can provide a good map pinpointing all the local vineyards as well as the rural farmhouse restaurants that are a feature of this region. However, there is a half-day **tour** (€4.80) offered of the Subirats winery region, a few kilometres to the southeast of Sant Sadurní d'Anoia. Tours (in Spanish) depart most Sundays and public holidays at 10am from the tourist office (☎938 993 499, ✉subiratstur@terra.es) at Lavern train station, a stop on the line between Sant Sadurní and Vilafranca. You can also pick up information here about walking and cycling trails, starting from the station, around the local vineyards.

Sant Sadurní d'Anoia

SANT SADURNÍ D'ANOIA, built on land watered by the Riu Noya, has been an important centre of wine production since the eighteenth century. When, at the end of the nineteenth century, French vineyards suffered heavily from disease, Sant Sadurní prospered, though later it too succumbed to the same wasting disease – something remembered still in the annual September festival by the parade of a representation of the feared Philoxera parasite. The production of *cava*, for which the town is now famous, began only in the 1870s – an industry that went hand in hand with the Catalan cork business, carried on in the forests of the hinterland. Today, a hundred million bottles a year of *cava* – the Catalan *méthode champenoise* – are turned out by dozens of companies, many of which are only too happy to escort you around their premises, show you the complicated fermentation process, and let you taste the odd glass or two as part of the bargain.

The town itself is of little interest, but it hardly matters, since most people never get any further than the most prominent and most famous company, **Freixenet** (☏938 917 000, ⓦwww.freixenet.es), whose building is right outside the train station. Free **tours** operate from Monday to Thursday 9am to 6pm, Friday 9am to 1pm, and it's best to call and reserve a place. Many of the other companies have similar arrangements, including the out-of-town **Codorníu** (☏938 183 232, ⓦwww.codorniu.com) – the region's earliest *cava* producer – which has a fine building by Puig i Cadafalch as an added attraction.

The town's **tourist office** (Mon–Fri 9am–1pm & 4–7pm, Sat 10am–1pm; ☏938 913 188, ⓦwww.santsadurni.org) is in the Ajuntament in the main square, Plaça Ajuntament. From the station, cross the river and walk up the hill, turning left at the top for the square. There are several restaurants in town, but *Vilafranca* is the better bet for lunch.

Vilafranca del Penedès

As a town, **VILAFRANCA DEL PENEDÈS** is rather more interesting than Sant Sadurní. Founded in the eleventh century in an attempt to attract settlers to land retaken from the expelled Moors, it became a prosperous market centre. This character is still in evidence today, with a compact old town at whose heart lie narrow streets and arcaded squares adorned with restored medieval mansions.

Cava

Cava is a naturally sparkling wine made using the *méthode champenoise*. The basic **grape** varieties of L'Alt Penedès are *macabeu*, *xarel.lo* and *parellada*, which are fermented to produce a wine base and then mixed with sugar and yeast before being bottled: a process known as **tiratge**. The bottles are then sealed hermetically – the **tapat** – and laid flat in cellars – the **criança** – for up to nine months, to ferment for a second time. The wine is later decanted to get rid of the sediment before being corked.

The *cava* is then **classified** according to the amount of sugar used in the fermentation: either *Brut* (less than 20g a litre) or *Sec* (20–30g); *Semisec* (30–50g) or *Dolç* (more than 50g). This is the first thing to take note of before buying or drinking: *Brut* and *Sec* are to most people's tastes and are excellent with almost any food; *Semisec* and *Dolç* are better used as dessert wines. To drink it at its best, serve *cava* at between 6° and 8°C, and remember – whatever your brain is telling you, and however swiggable that third bottle might be, it *is* alcoholic.

From the train station, walk up to the main Rambla de Nostra Senyora and cut to the right up c/de Sant Joan to the enclosed Plaça de Sant Joan, which has a small daily produce **market**. A rather larger affair takes place every Saturday, when the stalls also stock clothes, household goods, handicrafts and agricultural gear. There's a **tourist office** at the back of the square, at c/Cort 14 (Mon 4–7pm, Tues–Fri 9am–1pm & 4–7pm, Sat 10am–1pm; ☎938 920 358, ⊛www.ajvilafranca.es). Behind here, in Plaça Jaume I, opposite the much-restored Gothic church of Santa Maria, the **Museu de Vilafranca** (Tues–Sat 10am–2pm & 4–7pm, Sun 10am–2pm; €3) is housed in a twelfth-century palace and worth visiting largely for its section on the region's wine industry. The experience culminates with a visit to the museum's tavern for a tasting.

The vineyards of Vilafranca are all out of town, though the best known, **Torres** (Mon–Sat 9am–5pm, Sun 9am–1pm; ☎938 177 487, ⊛www.torres.es), is only a short, three-kilometre, taxi ride to the northwest, on the Sant Martí de Sarroca road. Torres make only still wines, but 1km further out on the same road at **Parés Baltà** (Mon–Fri 9am–1pm & 3–6pm, Sat 10am–2pm; ☎938 901 399, ⊛www.paresbalta.com) there's the opportunity to sample both still wine and *cava*.

The most agreeable place in town to **wine-taste** is *Inzolia*, c/de la Palma 21 (10am–2pm & 5–10pm, closed Mon morning and all Sun), just off c/de Sant Joan, where a range of *cavas* and wines are sold (cheaply) by the glass. Nibbles are available, and there's a good wine shop attached. There are plenty of **restaurants** – the tourist office has a list – with the moderately priced *L'Hereu*, c/Casal 1 (☎938 902 217) particularly recommended, serving generous country-style food with local wines from a very good-value €10 *menú del dia*. The restaurant is across the *rambla* from c/de Sant Joan, through the passageway.

The **Festa Major**, at the end of August and the first couple of days in September, brings the place to a standstill: dances and parades clog the streets, while the festival is most widely known for its display of *castellers* – teams of people competing to build human towers.

Tarragona

Majestically sited on a rocky hill, sheer above the sea, **TARRAGONA** is an ancient place: settled originally by Iberians and then Carthaginians, it was later used as the base for the Roman conquest of the peninsula, which began in 218 BC with Scipio's march south against Hannibal. The fortified city became an imperial resort and, under Augustus, "Tarraco" became capital of Rome's eastern Iberian province – the most elegant and cultured city of Roman Spain, boasting at its peak a quarter of a million inhabitants. The modern city provides a fine setting for some splendid Roman remains, and there's an attractive medieval part, too, while the rocky coastline below conceals a couple of reasonable beaches. It's worth noting that almost all Tarragona's sights and museums are **closed on Mondays**, though the old town and the exterior of some of the Roman remains can still be seen should you decide to visit then.

The City

Heart of the upper town is the sweeping **Rambla Nova**, a sturdy provincial rival to Barcelona's, lined with cafés and restaurants. Parallel, and to the east, lies

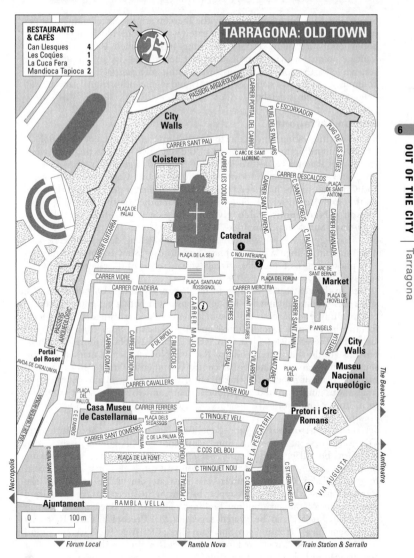

TARRAGONA: OLD TOWN

the **Rambla Vella**, marking – as its name suggests – the start of the old town. To either side of the *ramblas* are scattered a profusion of relics from Tarragona's Roman past, including various temples, and parts of the forum, theatre and amphitheatre.

For an overview of the city and its history, start at the **Passeig Arqueològic** (June–Sept Tues–Sat 9am–9pm, Sun 9am–3pm; Oct–May Tues–Sat 9am–5pm, Sun 10am–3pm; €2), a promenade that encircles the northernmost half of the old town. From the entrance at the Portal del Roser, a path runs between Roman walls of the third century BC and the sloping outer fortifications erected by the British in 1707 to secure the city during the War of the Spanish

Succession. Megalithic walls built by the Iberians are also excellently preserved in places, particularly two awesome gateways; the huge blocks used in their construction are quite distinct from the more refined Roman additions. Vantage points give views across the plain behind the city and around to the sea, while various objects are displayed within the *passeig* – several Roman columns, a fine bronze statue of Augustus, and eighteenth-century cannons still defending the city's heights.

Roman Tarragona

The most interesting remains in town are those of the ancient necropolis, a twenty-minute signposted walk out of the old town: walk to the northwestern end of Rambla Vella, turn left down Avinguda Pau Casals, cross Rambla Nova and continue straight down Avinguda Ramon i Cajal. Here, both pagan and Christian tombs have been uncovered, spanning a period from the third to the sixth centuries AD. They're now contained within the fascinating **Museu i Necropolis Paleocristians** (June–Sept Tues–Sat 10am–1pm & 4.30–8pm, Sun 10am–2pm; Oct–May Tues–Sat 10am–1.30pm & 3–5.30pm, Sun 10am–2pm; €2.40), whose entrance is on Passeig de la Independència. The museum is lined with sarcophagi and displays a few fragmented mosaics and photographs of the site, giving you a sense of Tarragona's erstwhile importance.

Back in the centre, the Roman forum has survived, too. Or rather forums, since – as provincial capital – Tarragona sustained both a ceremonial provincial forum (the scant remnants of which are close to the cathedral) and a local forum, the **Fòrum Local** (June–Sept Tues–Sat 9am–9pm, Sun 9am–3pm; Oct–May Tues–Sat 9am–5pm, Sun 10am–3pm; €2), whose more substantial remains are on the western side of Rambla Nova, near the market hall and square. This was the commercial centre of imperial Tarraco and the main meeting place for locals for three centuries. The site contains temples and small shops ranged around a porticoed square, and you'll also see a water cistern, house foundations, fragments of stone inscriptions and four elegant columns.

Tarragona's **Amfiteatre** (June–Sept Tues–Sat 9am–9pm, Sun 9am–3pm; Oct–May Tues–Sat 9am–5pm, Sun 10am–3pm; €2) is built into the green slopes of the hill beneath the *Imperial Tarraco* hotel. The tiered seats backing onto the sea are original, and from the top you can look north, up the coast, to the headland. On the Rambla Vella itself are the visible remains of the Roman Circus, whose vaults disappear back from the street into the gloom and under many of the surrounding buildings. The circus, as well as a Roman tower, the Pretori, can be visited together: the **Pretori i Circ Romans** (June–Sept Tues–Sat 9am–9pm, Sun 9am–3pm; Oct–May Tues–Sat 9am–5pm, Sun 10am–3pm; €2) is entered from Plaça del Rei. Built at the end of the first century AD to hold chariot races, the Circ has been restored and presented to spectacular effect. The rest of the complex contains computer-generated pictures of Roman Tarragona's buildings, while an elevator takes you up to the roof for the best views in Tarragona.

Perhaps the most remarkable (and least visited) of Tarragona's monuments stands outside the original city walls. This is the **Roman Aqueduct**, which brought water from the Riu Gayo, some 32km distant. The most impressive extant section, nearly 220m long and 26m high, lies in an overgrown valley, off the main road, in the middle of nowhere: take bus #5, marked "Sant Salvador" (every 20min from the stop outside Avgda. Prat de la Riba 11, off Avgda. Ramon i Cajal) – a ten-minute ride.

△ Roman Amphitheatre, Tarragona

The old town

For all its individual Roman monuments, the heart of Tarragona is the **medieval** old town, which spreads east of the Rambla Vella. The central c/Major climbs to the quarter's focal point, the **Catedral** (Mon–Sat: June to mid-Oct 10am–7pm; mid-Oct to mid-Nov 10am–5pm; mid-Nov to mid-March 10am–2pm; mid-March to May 10am–1pm & 4–7pm; €2.40), which sits at the top of a broad flight of steps. Quite apart from its own grand beauty, this is a perfect example of the transition from Romanesque to Gothic forms. You'll see the change highlighted in the main facade, where a soaring Gothic portal is framed by Romanesque doors, surmounted by a cross and an elaborate rose window. Except for during services, entrance to the cathedral is through the **cloisters** (*claustre*; signposted up a street to the left of the facade), themselves superbly executed with pointed Gothic arches softened by smaller round divisions. Among several oddly sculpted capitals here, one represents a cat's funeral being directed by rats. The ticket lets you proceed into the cathedral, and into its chapterhouse and sacristy, which together make up the **Museu Diocesa**, piled high with ecclesiastical treasures.

Strolling through the old town's streets will also enable you to track down Tarragona's excellent clutch of museums. The least obvious – but worth seeing for the setting inside one of the city's finest medieval mansions – is the **Casa Museu de Castellarnau** (June–Sept Tues–Sat 9am–9pm, Sun 9am–3pm; Oct–May Tues–Sat 9am–5pm, Sun 10am–3pm; €2) at c/Cavallers 14. The interior courtyard alone rewards a visit, with its arches and stone coats of arms built over Roman vaults. Otherwise, the small-scale collection is largely archeological and historical, rescued from banality by some rich eighteenth-century Catalan furniture and furnishings.

The splendid **Museu Nacional Arqueològic** (June–Sept Tues–Sat 10am–8pm, Sun 10am–2pm; Oct–May Tues–Sat 10am–1.30pm & 4–7pm, Sun 10am–2pm; €2.40), off Plaça del Rei, also shouldn't be missed. The huge collection is a marvellous reflection of the richness of imperial Tarraco, starting in the basement with a section of the old Roman wall preserved *in situ*. On other floors are thematic displays on the various remains and buildings around the city, accompanied by pictures, text and relics, as well as whole rooms devoted to inscriptions, mosaics, sculpture, ceramics and jewellery – even a series of anchors retrieved from the sea.

Tarragona's beaches

The closest beach to town is the long **Platja del Miracle**, over the rail lines below the amphitheatre – the water is filthy, but the sand is clean and there are two or three beach bars. The nicest beach is a couple of kilometres further up the coast, reached by taking Via Augusta (off the end of Rambla Vella) and turning right at the *Hotel Astari*. Don't despair upon the way: the main road and rail bridge eventually give way to a road that winds around the headland and down to **Platja Arrabassada**, an ultimately pleasant thirty-minute walk with gradually unfolding views of the beach. There are regular city buses (#3 or #9) from Rambla Vella. Arrabassada isn't anything very special, though it's roomy enough and has a few beach bars. Three coves further along (reached by the same buses) at **Platja Llarga**, a cluster of restaurants offers food at low prices.

Practicalities

There are trains every thirty minutes from Passeig de Gràcia and Barcelona Sants and the journey takes just over an hour. Tarragona's **train station** is in the lower town: turn right out of the station and climb the steps ahead of you and you'll emerge at the head of the Rambla Nova, by the statue of Roger de Lluria (10min), from where the Rambla Vella and the old town are just a short walk around the balcony promenade. There are **taxis** outside the station.

The **Oficina de Turisme** is at c/Major 39 in the old town (July–Sept daily 9am–9pm; Oct–June Mon–Sat 10am–2pm & 4–7pm, Sun 10am–2pm; ☎977 250 795). There are also seasonal information booths on Via Augusta and at Plaça Imperial Tarraco, at the end of Rambla Nova.

The head of Rambla Nova (by the Roger de Lluria statue), and the pretty old-town Plaça de la Font, are the best places for outdoor drinks. The latter in particular – traffic-free – features more than a dozen **cafés and restaurants** serving everything from *pinxtos* to pizzas, with *menús del dia* for around €7.50. Elsewhere in the old town, there's *Can Llesques*, c/Natzaret 6, on Plaça del Rei (☎977 222 906; closed Mon lunch), serving endless variations of *pa amb tomàquet* (Catalan toast-and-topping), accompanied by drinks dished up in ceramic pitchers. In summer you can eat at tables placed outside in the square. *Mandioca Tapioca*, c/Merceria 34 at Plaça del Forum (☎977 239 421), is a vegetarian restaurant with lots of choice. *La Cuca Fera*, Pl. Santiago Rossignol 5 (☎977 242 007; closed Mon) serves moderately priced Catalan dishes with tables in one of Tarragona's loveliest squares – there's a *menú del dia* for €9.50. Pricier is *Les Coques*, c/Nou Patriarca (☎977 228 300; closed Sun & July), at around €30 a head for fine dining.

You'll see the regional speciality, *romesco* sauce – served with fish – on many menus; it has a base of dry pepper, almonds and/or hazelnuts, olive oil, garlic and a glass of Priorato wine. Best place for this, and fish in general, is **Serrallo**, Tarragona's so-called "fishermen's quarter", a fifteen-minute walk west along the industrial harbourfront from the train station, where fish and seafood restaurants (moderate to expensive) are found along the main Moll Pescadores.

Girona

The ancient walled city of **GIRONA** stands on a fortress-like hill, high above the Riu Onyar. It's been fought over in almost every century since it was the Roman fortress of Gerunda on the Via Augusta and, perhaps more than any other place in Catalunya, it retains the distinct flavour of its erstwhile inhabitants. Following the Moorish conquest of Spain, Girona was an Arab town for over two hundred years, a fact apparent in the maze of narrow streets in the centre, and there was also a continuous Jewish presence here for six hundred years. By the eighteenth century, Girona had been besieged on 21 occasions, and in the nineteenth century it earned itself the nickname "Immortal" by surviving five attacks, of which the longest was a seven-month assault by the French in 1809. Not surprisingly, all this attention has bequeathed the city a hotchpotch of architectural styles, from Roman classicism to *modernisme*, yet the overall impression for the visitor is of an overwhelmingly beautiful medieval city. Its attraction is heightened by its setting, old and new towns divided by the river, which is crisscrossed by footbridges, with pastel-coloured houses reflected in the waters below.

The City

Although the bulk of modern Girona lies on the west side of the Riu Onyar, most visitors spend nearly all their time in the **old city**, over the river. This

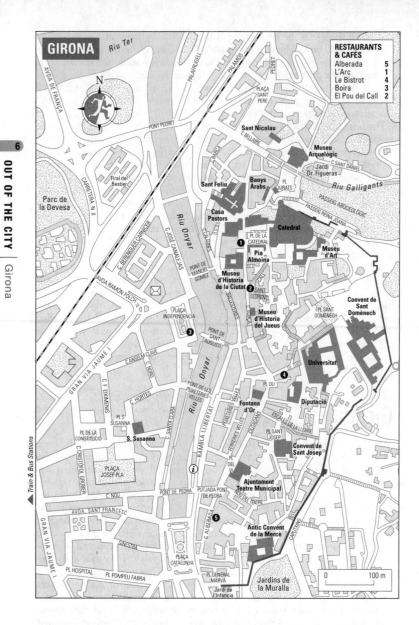

GIRONA

Riu Ter

RESTAURANTS
& CAFÉS
Alberada   5
L'Arc   1
Le Bistrot   4
Boira   3
El Pou del Call 2

thin wedge of land contains all the sights and monuments, and as it takes only half an hour or so to walk from end to end it's easy to explore thoroughly. It's worth noting that most of the museums and sights are **closed on Mondays**, though the city is emphatically still worth a visit if that's the only day you can manage.

The Catedral and Museu d'Art

The centrepiece of the old city is the **Catedral** (July–Sept Tues–Sat 10am–8pm; Oct–Feb Tues–Sat 10am–2pm & 4–6pm; March–June Tues–Sat 10am–2pm & 4–7pm; Sun all year 10am–2pm; €3), a mighty Gothic structure approached by a magnificent flight of seventeenth-century Baroque steps. This area has been a place of worship since Roman times, and a Moorish mosque stood on the site before the foundation of the cathedral in 1038. The main facade, remodelled in the eighteenth century, bursts with exuberant decoration: faces, bodies, coats of arms, and with SS Peter and Paul flanking the door. Inside, the cathedral is awesome – there are no aisles, just one tremendous Gothic nave vault with a span of 22m, the largest in the world. This emphasis on width and height is a feature of Catalan-Gothic, with its "hall churches", of which, unsurprisingly, Girona's is the ultimate example. The displayed treasures of the cathedral include a perfect *Beatus* illuminated by Mozarabic miniaturists in 975 and the famous eleventh- to twelfth-century *Creation Tapestry* – the best piece of Romanesque textile in existence, depicting in strong colours the months and seasons, and elements of the earth. But it's the exquisite Romanesque **cloisters** (1180–1210) that make the strongest impression, boasting minutely carved figures and scenes on double columns.

There's a separate **Museu d'Art** (March–Sept Tues–Sat 10am–7pm; Oct–Feb Tues–Sat 10am–6pm; Sun all year 10am–2pm; €2) housed on the southeastern side of the cathedral in the restored Episcopal Palace. The early rooms deal with Romanesque art taken from the province's churches, while among the manuscripts on display are an eleventh-century copy of Bede's works and an amazing martyrology from the monastery of Poblet.

Sant Feliu and the Banys Arabs

Climb back down the cathedral steps for a view of one of Girona's best-known landmarks, the blunt tower of the large church of **Sant Feliu**, whose huge bulk backs onto the narrow main street. Shortened by a lightning strike in 1581 and never rebuilt, the belfry tops a hemmed-in church that happily combines Romanesque, Gothic and Baroque styles; you can usually get in for a look around in the morning and late afternoon.

Close to Sant Feliu, through the twin-towered Portal de Sobreportas below the cathedral, are Girona's so-called **Banys Arabs** (July & Aug Mon–Sat 10am–8pm; April–June & Sept Mon–Sat 10am–7pm; Oct–March Mon–Sat 10am–2pm; Sun all year 10am–2pm; €1.50), a civil building probably designed by Moorish craftsmen in the thirteenth century, a couple of hundred years after the Moors' occupation of Girona had ended. They are the best-preserved ancient baths in Spain after those at Granada, featuring three principal rooms for different temperatures, with an underfloor heating system. The cooling room (the *frigidarium*) is the most interesting; niches (for storing clothes) and a stone bench provide seats for relaxation after the steam bath, while the room is lit, most unusually, by a central skylight-vault supported by octagonally arranged columns.

The Museu Arqueològic and the city walls

From the cathedral square, the main street, Pujada Rei Marti, leads downhill to the Riu Galligants, a small tributary of the Onyar. The **Museu Arqueològic** (June–Sept Tues–Sat 10.30am–1.30pm & 4–7pm, Sun 10am–2pm; Oct–May Tues–Sat 10am–2pm & 4–6pm, Sun 10am–2pm; €1.80) stands on the far bank in the former church of Sant Pere de Galligants, a harmonious setting for the varied exhibits. The church itself holds Roman statuary, sarcophagi and mosaics, while the beautiful Romanesque cloisters contain heavier medieval relics, such as inscribed tablets and stones, including some bearing Jewish inscriptions. The extensive rooms above the cloisters go on to outline rather methodically the region's history, from Paleolithic times to the Romanization of the area.

From the museum you can gain access to the **Passeig Arqueològic**, where steps and landscaped grounds lead up to the walls of the old city. There are fine views out over the rooftops and the cathedral, and endless little diversions into old watchtowers, down blind dead ends and around crumpled sections of masonry.

The Museu d'Història de la Ciutat

The other way from the cathedral, along c/de la Força, leads to the **Museu d'Història de la Ciutat** (Tues–Sat 10am–2pm & 5–7pm, Sun 10am–2pm; €2), at no. 27, housed in an eighteenth-century convent. Remains of the convent's cemetery are visible as you enter, with niches reserved for the preserved bodies of the inhabitants. The rest of the collection is fascinating, less for the insights into how Girona developed as a city – though this is explained efficiently through text, exhibits and photos – than for the strange, miscellaneous bits and pieces displayed. A circuit of the rooms shows you old radios from the 1930s, a 1925 Olivetti typewriter, a printing press, cameras, machine tools, engines and a dozen other mechanical and electrical delights.

Carrer de la Força and the Call

Quite apart from its Roman remains and Arab influences, Girona also contains the best-preserved **Jewish quarter** in Western Europe. There is evidence that Jews settled in Girona before the Moorish invasion, although the first mention of a real settlement – based in the streets around the cathedral – dates from the end of the ninth century. The area was known as the **Call** and at its height was home to around three hundred people who formed a sort of independent town within Girona, protected by the king in return for payment. From the eleventh century onwards, however, the Jewish community suffered systematic and escalating persecution: in 1391 a mob killed forty of the Call's residents, while the rest were locked up until the fury had subsided. For the next hundred years, until the expulsion of the Jews from Spain in 1492, the Call was effectively a ghetto, its residents restricted to its limits and forced to wear distinguishing clothing if they did leave.

For an idea of the layout of this sector of tall, narrow houses and maze-like interconnecting passages, visit the **Museu d'Història dels Jueus** (May–Oct Mon–Sat 10am–8pm; Nov–April Mon–Sat 10am–6pm; Sun all year 10am–3pm; €2), which is signposted (to "Call Jueu") up the skinniest of stepped streets off c/de la Força. Opened to the public in 1975, the complex of rooms, staircases, a courtyard and adjoining buildings off c/de Sant Llorenç is an attempt to give an impression of the cultural and social life of Girona's medieval Jewish community: this was the site of the synagogue, the butcher's shop and the community baths.

Practicalities

Trains run every hour from Barcelona Sants (currently at twenty past the hour), calling at Passeig de Gràcia station, and take between 1hr 15min and 1hr

30min. Girona's **train station** lies across the river in the modern part of the city – walk down to Gran Via Jaume I and then turn right down c/Nou to reach the Pont de Pedra and the base of the old town (10min). Or there's a taxi rank at the station.

The English-speaking **Oficina de Turisme** (Mon–Fri 8am–8pm, Sat 8am–2pm & 4–8pm, Sun 9am–2pm; ☎972 226 575, ⊛www.ajuntament.gi) is at Rambla de la Llibertat 1, on the river, near the Pont de Pedra. They can give you a useful map and have bus and train timetables for all onward and return services.

Girona's chic bars and restaurants are grouped on c/de la Força in the centre of the old city, as well as on and around Rambla de la Llibertat and on the parallel Plaça del Vi – the last two places being where you'll also find the best daytime cafés with outdoor seating. *L'Arc*, Pl. de la Catedral 9, is a friendly **bar** serving snacks and sandwiches at the foot of the cathedral steps. Favoured old-town **restaurants** – with weekday *menús del dia* for around €12 – include *El Pou del Call*, c/de la Força 14 (☎972 223 774; closed Sun dinner), right in the Jewish quarter, and the cheaper *Le Bistrot*, Pujada de Sant Domènec (☎972 218 803), which often has tables outside on the steps below the church. Considerably more expensive is the *Alberada*, c/Alberada 7 (☎972 226 002; closed all Sun, Mon dinner & Aug), for very fine Catalan dining. There's another little enclave of restaurants just over the river in pretty Plaça Independencia, best of which is the *Boira*, Pl. de la Independencia 17 (☎972 203 096), for very nice Catalan food – the weekday *menú* here is €9.80, drinks extra, and you can sit outside under the arcade.

Figueres and the Dalí museum

FIGUERES, a provincial town in the north of Catalunya with a population of some thirty thousand, would pass almost unnoticed were it not for the Museu Dalí, installed by Salvador Dalí in a building as surreal as the exhibits within. It's a popular day-trip from Barcelona, though you should make a reasonably early start since even the fastest trains take an hour and forty minutes to reach the town.

The museum is very much the main event in town (it's signposted from just about everywhere), though a circuit of the walls of the seventeenth-century Castell de Sant Fernand, 1km northwest of the centre, last bastion of the Republicans in the Civil War, helps fill in any spare time. In the centre, pavement cafés line the *rambla* and you can browse around the art galleries and gift shops in the streets and squares surrounding the church of Sant Pere. There are a couple of other museums, too. The Museu de l'Empordà has some local Roman finds and work by local artists, while the Museu de Joguets is a toy museum with over three thousand exhibits from all over Catalunya, but really these are small beer when compared to the Dalí extravaganza.

Museu Dalí

The **Museu Dalí** (July–Sept daily 9am–7.45pm, plus Aug also 10pm–1am; Oct–June Tues–Sun 10.30am–5.45pm; €9, night visits €10; ☎972 677 500; ⊛www.salvador-dali.org) is the most-visited museum in Spain after the Prado and Bilbao's Guggenheim, and appeals to everyone's innate love of fantasy,

FIGUERES

▲ Port Bou

◀ Castell de S. Fernand

◀ Albanyà

◀ Olot

▼ Barcelona & Girona

▼ Barcelona & Girona

▶ Roses

absurdity and participation. Although thematically arranged, the museum is not a collection of Dalí's "greatest hits" – those are scattered far and wide. Nonetheless, what you do get beggars description and is not to be missed. The very building (on Pl. Gala i Salvador Dalí) is an exhibit in itself, as it was designed to be. Topped by a huge metallic dome and decorated with luminous egg shapes, it gets even crazier inside. Here, the walls of the circular central well are adorned with stylized figures preparing to dive from the heights, while you can water the snail-encrusted occupants of a steamy Cadillac by feeding it with coins. There's also a soaring totem pole of car tyres topped with a boat and an umbrella. Climb inside to the main building and one of the rooms contains an unnerving portrait of Mae West, viewed by peering through a mirror at giant nostrils, red lips and hanging tresses. Other galleries on various levels contain such things as a complete life-sized orchestra, skeletal figures, adapted furniture

Salvador Dalí

Salvador Dalí (1904–89) was born in Figueres and gave his first exhibition in the town when he was just 14. Later expelled from the Royal Academy of Art in Madrid, he made his way to Paris, where he established himself at the forefront of the Surrealist movement. A celebrity artist in the US in the Forties and Fifties, he returned eventually to Europe where, among other projects, he set about reconstructing Figueres' old municipal theatre, where he had held his first boyhood exhibition. This opened as the Museu Dalí in 1974, which Dalí then fashioned into an inspired repository for some of his most bizarre works. A frail man by 1980, controversy surrounds the artist's final years, particularly after he suffered severe burns in a fire in 1984, following which he moved into the Torre Galatea, the tower adjacent to the museum. Spanish government officials and friends fear that, in his senile condition, he was being manipulated. In particular, it's alleged that he was made to sign blank canvases – and this has inevitably led to the questioning of the authenticity of some of his later works. Dalí died in Figueres on January 23, 1989. His body now lies behind a simple granite slab inside the museum.

(a bed with fish tails), and ranks of Surreal paintings. Some of the latter are less clamorous than others, but these are possibly more representative of his fabulous skill. One room, for example, is dominated by the huge feet of Dalí and Gala (his Russian wife and muse) painted on the ceiling, which means that beautiful pieces, such as a lithograph of Picasso in emperor's laurels or a haunting Dalí self-portrait, can go unnoticed. Higher floors also house paintings by other artists, the most notable being those by Antoni Pitxot, in which moss-covered stones portray various classical figures. Your ticket also allows admission to see the collection of extraordinary **Dalí jewels**, many originally designed in the Forties for an American millionaire and displayed here with Dalí's original drawings.

Practicalities

Trains depart hourly from Barcelona Sants and Passeig de Gràcia and take up to two hours to reach Figueres, depending on the service. Currently, the 7.50am, 9.20am or 10.20am from Sants (each taking 1hr 40min) are the best day-trip options. Alternatively, Figueres is just thirty to forty minutes by train from Girona, if you feel like combining the two towns. Arriving at the train station, you reach the centre of town simply by following the "Museu Dalí" signs (10min). There are small **tourist information** booths in Plaça Estació (July to mid-Sept Mon–Sat 10am–2pm & 4–6pm) and on Plaça de Dalí (July to mid-Sept Mon–Sat 9am–8pm, Sun 9am–3pm), with the main **Turisme** on Plaça del Sol (July–Sept Mon–Sat 9am–8pm, Sun 9am–3pm; reduced hours rest of the year but at least Mon–Fri 9am–3pm; ☎972 503 155, ⓦwww.figueresciutat.com), in front of the post office building.

A gaggle of tourist **restaurants** is crowded into the narrow streets around the Dalí museum, particularly along c/Jonquera. Here you'll be able to find a reasonably priced *menú del dia*, while the cafés on the *rambla* are good for snacks and sandwiches. For a food treat, head for the *Hotel Duran*, at c/Lausaca 5, at the top of the Rambla, where they serve generous regional dishes with a modern touch; it's expensive but has an excellent reputation.

Listings

Listings

Accommodation

H otel rooms in Barcelona are among the most expensive in Spain and finding a vacancy can be very difficult, especially at Easter, in summer and around the time of any festivals or trade fairs. You're advised to book in advance – several weeks at peak times – especially if you want to stay at a particular place. Either call the establishments direct (noting that English is by no means spoken everywhere) or use one of the reservations services detailed below.

Places to stay go under a bewildering array of names – *fonda, pension, residencia, hostal, alberg, hotel* – though these are mostly an anachronism and only **hotels and pensions** are recognized as official categories these days. Hotels and pensions in the city are all graded and star-rated, but the rating is not necessarily a guide to cost, facilities or ambience. To be absolutely certain of an en-suite bathroom, for example, you'll need to book into a hotel (rather than a pension), though our accommodation reviews make clear those pensions that also offer at least some rooms with private shower/bath. Private or en-suite "bathroom", incidentally, doesn't always mean exactly that, either – at least in the cheaper pensions where your private facility might be a shower stall stuck in the corner of the room or a small added-on shower-and-toilet room.

Room rates vary wildly. The absolute cheapest double rooms in a simple family-run pension, sharing an outside shower, cost around €30, though for anything bearable (and certainly for anything with an en-suite shower) you'll really need to budget on a minimum of €40–50 a night. If you want air conditioning, a TV, soundproofing and an elevator to your room, there's a fair amount of choice around the €60–90 mark, while up to €150 gets you the run of decent hotels in most city areas. For Barcelona's most fashionable and exclusive hotels, room rates are set at European capital norms – from €250 to €400 a night. Right at the other end of the scale is the burgeoning number of city **youth hostels**, where a dorm bed goes for between €15 and €20.

Breakfast isn't usually included in the price, unless specifically stated in our reviews. It's often available for an extra charge, though it can be better (and cheaper) to go out for your coffee and croissant. The other cost to be aware of is the seven percent **tax** (IVA) added to all accommodation bills. **Credit cards** are accepted almost everywhere, even in very modest places (though American Express isn't always) – we've highlighted any pensions or hotels that don't accept cards.

There's little change in prices throughout the year, since hotel owners can usually fill their rooms whatever the season. However, some cheaper places do still offer **discounts** in winter (Nov, Jan & Feb), or for longer stays, while larger hotels may have special rates in **August** (when business travel is scarce) or at **weekends** – it's always worth asking. All accommodation is required by law to

Balconies, views and noise

Almost all hotels and pensions in Barcelona have at least some rooms with a **balcony** over the street or square. These tend to be the lightest rooms in the building and, because of the obvious inherent attraction, they sometimes cost a little more than the other rooms. However, it can't be stressed enough that rooms facing onto Barcelona's streets are often noisy. Traffic is a constant presence (including the dawn street-cleaners) and, in a city where people are just getting ready to go out at 10pm, you can be assured of a fair amount of pedestrian noise too, particularly in the old town, and especially at weekends. Soundproofed windows and double glazing deal partly with the problem, but you tend not to have this luxury in cheaper pensions – where throwing open the windows may be the only way to get some air in the height of summer anyway. Bring earplugs if you're at all concerned about having a sleepless night.

Alternatively, ask for an **internal room** (*habitación interior*). It's true that most buildings are built around a central air/elevator shaft, and your view could simply be a lime-green wall 1m away and someone's washing line. But some places are built instead around an internal patio, so you might have light flooding down onto a pot-plant terrace or garden – and you shouldn't get any street noise.

post official rates, so if you think you're being overcharged, take it up first with the management; you can usually produce an immediate resolution by asking for the *llibre de reclamacions* (complaints book).

Finally, don't be afraid to **ask to see the room** before you part with any money – even the swankiest places won't balk at showing you around. Standards vary greatly between places in the same category and it does no harm to check that you're not being stuck at the back in an airless box.

Making a reservation

Barcelona's main tourist offices can supply accommodation lists, though these don't usually include the very cheapest places in the city. You can also book accommodation at the tourist offices, but only in person on the day – they do not make advance reservations, nor do they have a telephone reservation service. However, you can book online through the tourist office website, or contact one of the other **reservation agencies** listed below.

Some of the agencies specialize in **apartment rentals**, a growing business in Barcelona, with hundreds of apartments sleeping two to twelve, available by the night, week or month. Prices for these compare well with mid-range hotels (starting at around €70–100 a night), but make sure you're happy with the location (some are out in the more mundane suburbs) and understand all the costs – seasonal premiums, cleaning charges, utility bills and taxes can all push up the attractive quoted figure.

When booking directly at hotels and pensions, you may be asked for a **credit card** number to secure a room. At most hotels, the price won't be charged against your card until your stay, though some smaller pensions have been known to charge you in advance.

Reservation agencies

Barcelona Apartment Rentals UK ☎0117/907 3486, ⊛www.barcelonaapartmentrentals.co.uk.

A small range of quality apartments, mainly in the Eixample (some near the Sagrada Família) and Gràcia. Friendly, English-speaking service and advice from a born-and-bred *barcelonina*; airport pick-ups available.

Barcelona Living Barcelona ☎932 723 520 or 696 210 088, ⊛www.barcelonaliving.com. One-bed apartments in the Born (La Ribera), for short-term independent and corporate visitors.

Barcelona On-Line Barcelona ☎902 887 017 or 933 437 993, ⊛www.barcelona-on-line.es. Commission-free reservations for hotels, pensions and apartments in Barcelona and the local area. Call or use the online searchable database.

Hotels Abroad UK ☎0845/330 2500, from outside the UK (+44)1689 882 500, ⊛www.hotelsabroad.co.uk. Wide selection of Barcelona/Catalunya hotels.

Inside-BCN Barcelona ☎639 702 207, ⊛www.inside-bcn.com. Small selection of stylishly renovated apartments (sleeping two to six) available in the Born or on Plaça Reial.

My Favourite Things Barcelona ☎933 295 351 or 637 265 405, ⊛www.myft.net. Barcelona-based agency with an eye for unusual and offbeat accommodation, from boutique hotels to private bed and breakfasts in the city, or rural homestays and country retreats.

Turisme de Barcelona Offices in Barcelona at Pl. de Catalunya; Pl. de Sant Jaume; Barcelona Sants; Barcelona Airport ☎906 301 282, from abroad ☎933 689 730, ⊛www.barcelonaturisme .com. Same-day, commission-free accommodation bookings, in person only, or on the website. For office opening hours, see p.22.

Visit BCN.com Barcelona ☎933 424 534, ⊛www.visit-bcn.com. Wide range of private apartments for rent (by the night or longer), from lofts to *modernista* buildings.

Accommodation price codes

Accommodation listed in this chapter has been given a price code, which corresponds to one of the categories below. These reflect the **average cost of a double room** in each establishment (including the seven percent tax, IVA); the reviews make it clear if there are cheaper or more expensive rooms also available. Breakfast isn't included unless otherwise stated.

❶ Under €40	❹ €71–90	❼ €161–200
❷ €41–55	❺ €91–120	❽ €201–250
❸ €56–70	❻ €121–160	❾ Over €251

Hotels and pensions

Most of the cheapest accommodation in Barcelona is to be found in the old town, which is certainly a convenient and atmospheric place in which to base yourself. However, what may be atmospheric by day can sometimes seem a bit threatening after dark, and the further off the Ramblas you get, the less salubrious the surroundings. As a general rule, anything right on **the Ramblas** or near **the cathedral**, on the east side, should be reliable and safe – in fact these two particular areas contain some of the city's most charismatic old-town hotels. However, if you hanker after a Ramblas view in particular, you're going to pay heavily for the privilege.

The best hunting ground for out-and-out budget accommodation is in the **Barri Gòtic**, especially in the area bordered by c/dels Escudellers, Plaça de Sant Miquel and c/de la Boqueria, where there are loads of options, from basic pensions to three-star hotels. **Carrer de Ferran** and the area to the north, as far as **c/de Portaferrissa**, is usually considered quite safe; **south of c/de Ferran**, including the arcaded Plaça Reial, the streets are perfectly fine during the day, but can have a slight edge after dark – be careful with money and valuables, particularly in the streets closer to the harbour. East of

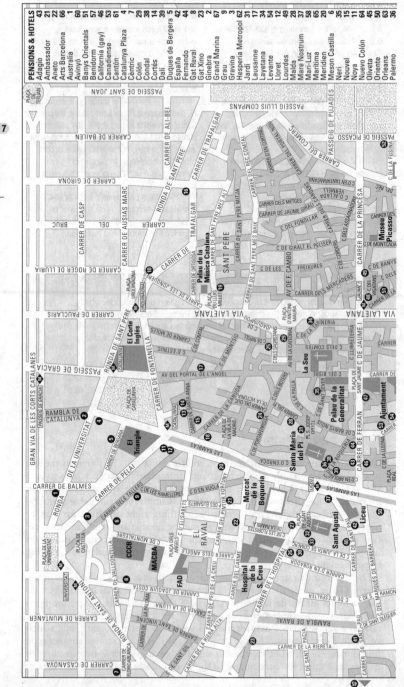

PENSIONS & HOTELS	
Adagio	43
Ambassador	21
Aneto	22
Arts Barcelona	66
Australia	1
Avinyó	60
Banys Orientals	51
Benidorm	57
California (gay)	46
Canadiense	53
Cantón	61
Catalunya Plaza	4
Cèntric	7
Colón	29
Condal	38
Cortés	14
Dalí	39
Duques de Bergara	5
España	42
Fernando	44
Gat Raval	8
Gat Xino	23
Ginebra	2
Grand Marina	67
Gravina	9
Grau	3
Hesperia Metropol	62
Jardí	31
Lausanne	17
Layetana	34
Levante	54
Lloret	12
Lourdes	49
Malda	28
Mare Nostrum	37
Mari-Luz	58
Marítima	65
Meridien	20
Meson Castilla	6
Neri	35
Noya	15
Nouvel	11
Nuevo Colón	64
Oliveta	45
Oriente	50
Orleans	63
Palermo	36

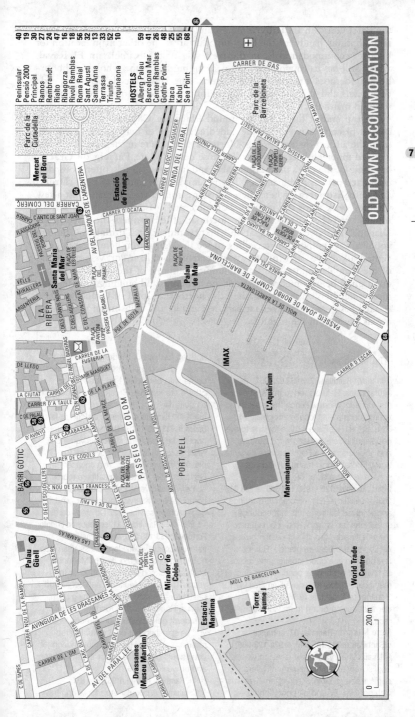

Peninsular	40
Pensió 2000	19
Principal	30
Ramos	27
Rembrandt	24
Rialto	47
Ribagorza	16
Rivoli Ramblas	18
Roma Reial	56
Sant Agustí	32
Santa Anna	13
Terrassa	33
Triunfo	52
Urquinaona	10

HOSTELS

Alberg Palau	59
Barcelona Mar	41
Center Ramblas	26
Gothic Point	48
Itaca	25
Kabul	55
Sea Point	68

Parc de la Ciutadella

Mercat del Born

CARRER DEL COMERÇ

C ANTIC DE SANT JOAN

FLASSADERS

PASSEIG DEL BORN

CARRER DE MONTCADA

Santa Maria del Mar

VELLS

MIRALLERS

ARGENTERIA

LA RIBERA

CORS CANVIS NOUS

CORS ANGELLS

C DEL CONSOLAT DE MAR

PLAÇA DE MAR LES OLLES

PLAÇA ANTONI LÓPEZ

PLAÇA DE ISABEL II

PGE DE SOTA MURALLA

Estació de França

CARRER DEL DOCTOR AIGUADER

CARRER D'OCATA

BARCELONETA

PLAÇA DE PAU VILA

Palau de Mar

RONDA DEL LITORAL

CARRER DELS PIZÓN

CARRER DE BALBOA

CARRER DE GINEBRA

CARRER DE LA MAQUINISTA

CARRER DE L'ATLÀNTIDA

CARRER DE SANT CARLES

CARRER DEL BALUARD

PLAÇA DE LA FONT

PLAÇA DE LA BARCELONETA

CARRER DE SANT CARLES

CARRER DE L'ALMIRALL CERVERA

CARRER DE L'ALMIRALL AIXADA

CARRER DEL JUDICI

CARRER DE GAS

Parc de la Barceloneta

PASSEIG MARÍTIM

PASSEIG DE SALVAT PAPASSEIT

PLAÇA DE LA MADRONERA

PLAÇA DE POMPEU GENER

CARRER DE PEPE ANDREU DÒRIA

PLAÇA DE LA BOTA

MOLL DE LA BARCELONETA

PASSEIG JOAN DE BORBÓ COMPTE DE BARCELONA

MOLL DE BOSCH I ALSINA

MOLL DE LA FUSTA

PASSEIG DE COLOM

PORT VELL

IMAX

L'Aquarium

Maremàgnum

MOLL DE BARCELONA

World Trade Centre

MOLL DEL BALEARS

CARRER D'ESCAR

DE LLEDO

CARRER DE LA FUSTERIA

CARRER DE REGOMIR MARQUET

PLAÇA REGOMIR

CARRER DE LA PLATA

CARRER D'EN GIGNAS

CARRER D'EN COMTAL

LA CIUTAT

CARRER D'A TAULE

C DE PALAU

D'AVINYÓ

BARRI GÒTIC

C DE CARABASSA

CARRER AMPLE

CARRER DE CÒDOLS

CARRER DE LA MERCÈ

C DELS ESCUDELLERS

C NOU DE SANT FRANCESC

PG DE LA PAU

C DE JOSEP ANSELM CLAVÉ

PLAÇA DEL DUC DE MEDINACELI

PLAÇA DEL PORTAL DE LA PAU

Mirador de Colón

Torre Jaume I

Estació Marítima

Palau Güell

LAS RAMBLAS

DRASSANES

C DE L'ARC DEL TEATRE

CARRER NOU DE LA RAMBLA

AVINGUDA DE LES DRASSANES

CARRER DEL PORTAL DE

CARRER NOU DE LA RAMBLA

C DE TAPES

C DE L'OM

CARRER DEL CID

C DE L'ARC DEL TEATRE

AV DEL PARAL·LEL

Drassanes (Museu Marítim)

200 m

0

155

the Barri Gòtic, in **La Ribera**, are a number of safely sited budget and mid-range options, handy for the Born nightlife area. The other main location for budget accommodation is on the west side of the Ramblas in **El Raval**, which still has its rough edges but is changing fast as the whole neighbourhood undergoes a massive face-lift. Look especially on c/de Sant Pau, c/de l'Hospital, and c/Junta del Comerç for a mix of bargain pensions and restored mansions.

The top end of the Ramblas, around **Plaça de Catalunya**, is a safe and central place to stay – with the added advantage of being reached directly from the airport by train or bus. North of here, you're in the Eixample – the gridded nineteenth-century city – whose central spine, **Passeig de Gràcia**, has some of the city's most fashionable and luxurious hotels, often housed in converted palaces and mansions. The Eixample itself splits into right (**Dreta**) and Left (**Esquerra**), where there are some comparative bargains just a few minutes' walk from the *modernista* architectural masterpieces. More serious money can be spent further north in the business hotels of the Diagonal/Pedralbes area, or at the luxury retreat at **Tibidabo** – though you're always going to be travelling to see the sights from here. There's more central luxury on offer in the two **waterfront** hotels: at Port Vell, at the end of the Ramblas, and at the Port Olímpic, southeast of the old town. If you don't mind being a metro ride from the museums and buildings, and like the idea of neighbourhood living, then the northern district of **Gràcia** makes a relaxed base – and its excellent bars, restaurants and clubs mean you're only a walk away from the nightlife.

The Ramblas

Benidorm Ramblas 37 ☏933 022 054; Ⓜ**Drassanes**. Refurbished rooms that offer real value for money, hence the tribes of young tourists – its location opposite Pl. Reial helps. Rooms available for one to five people, all nice and clean with bathtubs and showers, and a Ramblas view if you're lucky. English spoken and left-luggage service (€2) available. ❷

Lloret Ramblas 125 ☏933 173 366, ☏933 019 283; Ⓜ**Catalunya**. Gilt mirrors, old paintings and wrinkled leather sofas in the lounge speak of a faded glory, and rooms are on the elderly side, too, though bathrooms and tile floors have been upgraded. But it's a fine building in a good location; the rooms all have TV, heating/air conditioning, and many have balconies and a Ramblas view. Continental breakfast (€3) served in a Ramblas-facing dining room with sunny terrace. ❹

Mare Nostrum Ramblas 67, entrance on c/Sant Pau ☏933 185 340, ☏934 123 069; Ⓜ**Liceu**. Cheery two-star pension whose English-speaking management offers comfortable double or triple/family rooms with satellite TV and air conditioning –

nothing flashy, but modern, well kept and double-glazed against the noise. Some come with balconies and street views, others are internal. Breakfast included. ❸, en suite ❹

Marítima Ramblas 4, entrance on Ptge. de la Banca ☏933 023 152; Ⓜ**Drassanes**. Take this popular backpackers' choice as you find it, which is rough and ready but eager to please, and you'll not score a cheaper Ramblas view. Thirteen threadbare rooms, some with shower cubicles plonked in the corner, plus self-service laundry (€5) and luggage storage service (€2). No credit cards. ❶

Le Meridien Ramblas 111, entrance on c/Pintor Fortuny ☏933 186 200, ⓦwww.meridien-barcelona.com; Ⓜ**Catalunya**. Classy Ramblas hotel that's hosted the likes of Madonna, Michael Jackson and Pavarotti over the years. There are Mediterranean ochre-and-pastel tones inside, and a soothing hush, even in Ramblas-facing rooms – though you don't get a balcony or terrace unless you've splashed out on a suite. Posted rates are very high (€350 or so), though you should be able to better them in winter and at weekends. ❾

Noya Ramblas 133, 1° ☏933 014 831; Ⓜ**Catalunya**. A popular stop for young travellers, above a café-restaurant where you can get breakfast. Simple rooms – hot in summer, chilly in winter – all share a bathroom and the plumbing is a bit unreliable, but the reasonable prices and pleasant owners deflect most complaints. ❶

Oriente Ramblas 45 ☎933 022 558, ⓦwww.husa.es; ⓂLiceu. If you're looking for somewhere traditional on the Ramblas, this historic three-star is your best bet – mid-nineteenth-century style in the grand public rooms and tastefully updated bedrooms, some with Ramblas views. Single travellers and late bookers don't always do so well, so specify that you want space and light – not all rooms have these attributes. Special rates sometimes drop the price a category. Breakfast included. ❻

Rivoli Ramblas Ramblas 128 ☎934 817 676, ⓦwww.rivolihotels.com; ⓂCatalunya. Although incorporating a fine Art Deco interior, this is modern, hi-tech Barcelona. The elegant, soundproofed rooms come with satellite TV, the front ones with classic Ramblas views; there's a rooftop bar and safe parking provided at the nearby sister hotel in the Raval, the *Ambassador*. ❾

Barri Gòtic: c/de Ferran and c/de la Boqueria

Adagio c/de Ferran 21 ☎933 189 061, ⓦwww.adagiohotel.com; ⓂLiceu. Rooms on five floors (there's an elevator) have been given a thorough refurbishment – new beds, parquet floors, satellite TV, air conditioning, soundproofing and decent bathrooms – and a buffet breakfast is included, so prices aren't bad for the location (and drop by ten percent in winter). Front and side rooms have little balconies. Laundry service and car parking available on request. ❺

Condal c/de la Boqueria 23 ☎933 181 882, Ⓕ933 181 978; ⓂLiceu. Renovations have smartened up the rooms, and added a cafeteria, but they can't do much about the low ceilings and squeezed proportions – each has the feel of a ship's cabin. Still, you get a full bath, air conditioning and satellite TV, and a balcony with most rooms, while those on the top two floors get the morning light (and less noise). ❹

Dalí c/de la Boqueria 12 ☎ & Ⓕ933 185 580, Ⓔpensiondali@wanadoo.es; ⓂLiceu. The terracotta-tiled facade, sculpted doorway

and stained glass suggest a grandeur long lost. However, the rooms themselves are perfectly serviceable (and reasonably soundproofed if you get a street-side balcony), and there are a lot of them – with/without private shower, plus triples and quads, as well as a common room, Internet access, approachable management and parking. ❷

Fernando c/de Ferran 31 ☎933 017 993, ⓦwww.barcelona-on-line.es/fernando; ⓂLiceu. Rooms at these prices fill quickly around here; that they're also light, modern and well kept by friendly people is a real bonus. All come with sinks and TV, with or without attached shower, while dorm accommodation is available on the top floor for €19 per person – these rooms sleep four to eight, some have attached bathroom, and all are provided with lockers. All accommodation is a few euros cheaper in winter. ❷

Palermo c/de la Boqueria 21 ☎ & Ⓕ933 024 002; ⓂLiceu. Friendly, fairly spacious place with clean, high-ceilinged rooms with or without bath. Probably the most attractive of the low-to-moderate price places on this street, with a range of services available – laundry, safe box, beach-towel rental, etc. It's a bit overpriced in July and August, but outside these months rates come down by up to 25 percent. ❸, en suite ❹

Rialto c/de Ferran 42 ☎933 185 212, ⓦwww.gargallo-hotels.com; ⓂJaume I. Beyond the standard modern marble lobby, this turns out to be quite cosy inside – a three-star hotel that's more like a family-run concern, with carpeted corridors and heavy doors leading into updated period rooms with parquet flooring, oak furniture and country-style furnishings. The cellar restaurant is something to behold, too, and there's a good buffet breakfast included in the price. Internet access available. ❻

Barri Gòtic: south of c/de Ferran

Avinyó c/d'Avinyó 42 ☎933 187 945, ⓦwww.hostalavinyo.com; ⓂDrassanes. All the rooms here are furnished differently, and most are lighter than you'd expect on this street, either freshly painted or tiled, with and without private bath, and all boasting a ceiling fan. There's a fair amount of space and some rooms have little sofas. If you go for a street-side room, note that c/d'Avinyó is noisy at weekends. English-speaking management. No credit cards. ❶, en suite ❷

Canadiense Bxda. de Sant Miquel 1, 1° ☎933 017 461; Ⓜ Jaume I. Buzz your way in through the solid wooden doors into a quiet courtyard, where a friendly couple (no English spoken) oversee a decidedly old-school *hostal*. Everything has seen better days, and the prevailing colour is brown, but the clean rooms (some internal, some with street balconies) all have sinks, showers and a washing line strung at each window. One cheap single available. No credit cards. ❷

El Cantón c/Nou de Sant Francesc 40 ☎933 173 019, Ⓔ hostalcanton@retemail.es; Ⓜ Drassanes. The traffic-free but graffitied street looks (but isn't) a bit iffy, but you're only two blocks off the Ramblas and close to the harbour and Port Vell. It's a professionally run outfit on three floors, centrally heated in winter, with good-sized rooms – singles, doubles and triples – with shower and fridge. Family-sized "apartments" with kitchenette (for up to five people) also available by the night. ❷, apartments ❺

Hesperia Metropol c/Ample 31 ☎933 105 100, Ⓦ www.hesperia-metropol.com; Ⓜ Drassanes. Stylish conversion of an older building that – because it's slightly off the beaten old-town track – has remarkably good prices; certainly better value than similar places on the Ramblas. The lobby is a masterpiece of contemporary design, while rooms are understated but comfortable – street noise isn't too bad either, so opening the shutters onto c/Ample doesn't blast the earlugs first thing in the morning. Buffet breakfast €9. ❺

Levante Bxda. Sant Miquel 2 ☎933 179 565, Ⓦ www.hostallevante.com; Ⓜ Jaume I. A backpackers' favourite, with fifty rooms – singles, doubles, twins, triples – on two rambling floors. Even booking in advance can be a bit of lottery in determining which room you get, and, as some have newer pine furniture, attached bathrooms and balconies, you may want to switch after a first night if yours isn't up to scratch. Communal bathrooms get pretty busy, staff can be scatty, and the comings and goings aren't to everyone's liking ("*tranquilo*" it isn't), but prices are very reasonable. Six apartments with kitchen and washing machine also available, sleeping five to seven people

(charged at €30 per person a day). ❷, en suite ❸

Mari-Luz c/de la Palau 4, 2° ☎ & ☎933 173 463, Ⓔ pensionmariluz@menta.net; Ⓜ Jaume I. This old mansion, on a quieter than usual Barri Gòtic street, has six inexpensive doubles available, with shared bathrooms. Someone's been to IKEA for furniture and there are contemporary art prints on the walls, laundry facilities and a small kitchen. It's also very friendly – the drawback is that this is a hostel, too, with 35 dorm beds (€13–16 depending on season) in various other rooms, and it's a tight squeeze when full. You might prefer their sister place, *Fernando* (see p.157). ❷

Roma Reial Pl. Reial 11 ☎933 020 366, Ⓦ www.todobarcelona.com/romareial; Ⓜ Liceu. Its location, and the fact that some rooms look out onto the square, make this a popular choice and it's always busy, though sometimes with noisy groups. Bare-walled rooms all have smartish bathrooms, heating and air conditioning, and some can sleep up to four, but the jaded, multilingual staff don't do much for the atmosphere. Breakfast is available, but you wouldn't bother. Safety deposit boxes are charged by the day. ❸

Barri Gòtic: near the cathedral

Colón Avgda. Catedral 7 ☎933 011 404, Ⓦ www.hotelcolon.es; Ⓜ Jaume I. Splendidly situated four-star hotel, opposite the cathedral – rooms at the front throw open their windows to balconies with superb views, while a pavement *terrassa* takes full advantage of its position. It's an old-money kind of place, with faithful-retainer staff and huge public salons. "Superior" rooms have an Edwardian lounge area and highly floral decor, though other rooms are more contemporary. ❽, superior/cathedral view ❾

Jardí Pl. Sant Josep Oriol 1 ☎933 015 900, Ⓔ hoteljardi@retemail.es; Ⓜ Liceu. The location sells this place – overlooking the very attractive Pl. del Pi – which explains the steep prices for rooms that, though smart and modern, can be a bit bare and even poky. But the bathrooms have been nicely done and some rooms look directly onto the square. The lounge-diner also has views (and a small terrace) overlooking the square – breakfast here costs €5 – but it's a bit of a clinical space. Advance reservations essential. ❹

Layetana Pl. Ramon Berenguer el Gran 2, 1st floor ☎ & ℻ **933 192 012;** Ⓜ**Jaume I.** A fairly noisy location, though quieter in rooms round the side. Not much in the way of luxury (just a bed, small desk and chair), and elderly furnishings (check out the TV lounge with its velveteen high-back armchairs), but bathrooms have been upgraded and prices are very reasonable for this part of town – out of twenty rooms, just six have en-suite facilities and cost €12 more. ❷

Malda c/del Pi 5, 1° ☎**933 173 002;** Ⓜ**Liceu.** Not everyone likes this place, but it's one of the very cheapest deals in the Barri Gòtic (enter through the shopping arcade). Twenty-four rooms on one floor of a rambling, old-fashioned building, all with some kind of outlook and sharing communal bathrooms – single travellers might be offered the tiny tower above the roof for €10. There's a stuffed fox in the lounge, all kinds of knick-knackery and some very questionable paintings – family heirlooms all. No credit cards. ❶

Neri c/de Sant Sever 5 933 040 655, ℗**www.hotelneri.com.** Eighteenth-century palace close to the cathedral that's given the boutique treatment to its 22 stylish rooms and filled them with the latest mod cons – plasma-screen TV, movies on demand, Internet access and CD player. A tranquil roof terrace provides a nice escape, and there's a good Mediterranean restaurant attached; breakfast is €15. ❻, superior rooms ❼

Rembrandt c/Portaferrissa 23 ☎ & ℻ **933 181 011;** Ⓜ**Liceu.** The English-speaking owners are making a real effort to smarten this place up, adding prints to the walls, cane chairs to the rooms and an elevator. Doubles (with/without private bathroom) might have a balcony or little patio, while larger ones are more versatile – one has a gallery (with single bed above the double) and large corner bath, while a rather Victorian-looking "suite" (two rooms split by hanging net curtain) can sleep two or four. They'll serve you breakfast (€3), sell you a beer, or rent you a fan in summer if you need one. ❷, en suite ❹

La Ribera

Banys Orientals c/de l'Argenteria 37 ☎**932 688 460,** ℗**www.hotelbanysorientals.com;**

Ⓜ**Jaume I.** Funky boutique hotel with stylish rooms at decent prices. Hardwood floors, crisp white sheets, sharp marble bathrooms, urban-chic decor, and breakfast available for €9. Advance reservations essential. ❺

Lourdes c/Princesa 14 ☎ **933 193 372;** Ⓜ**Jaume I.** Absolutely basic backpackers' choice – "*habitaciones confortables*" is pushing it a bit, but as cheap as chips, especially for rooms without a bath. No credit cards. ❶, en suite ❷

Nuevo Colón Avgda. Marquès de l'Argentera 19, 1° ☎**933 195 077,** ℗**www.hostalnuevo-colon.com;** Ⓜ**Barceloneta.** In the hands of the same friendly family for over 70 years, with 26 spacious, hotel-quality rooms painted yellow and kitted out with directors' chairs, good beds, new tiling and double glazing. Front rooms are very sunny, as is the lounge and terrace, all with side views to Ciutadella park. There are small off-season discounts, and also three self-catering apartments available (by the night) in the same building, which sleep up to six. ❷, apartments ❺

Orleans Avgda. Marquès de l'Argentera 13, 1° ☎**933 197 382,** ℗**www.hostalorleans.com;** Ⓜ**Barceloneta.** Rooms on two floors of a tranquil family-run *hostal*. Public areas and rooms are kept spick-and-span, and twins and doubles have TV, desk and chair, and heating in winter. Front rooms with balconies face França station and the busy main road, so you'll get some noise here; other rooms are internal, while some sleep three or four. ❷

Triunfo Pg. de Picasso 22 ☎ & ℻ **933 150 860,** ℮**central@atriumhotels.com;** Ⓜ**Jaume I/Arc de Triomf.** Nice location for this small hotel in a pleasant building – right opposite Ciutadella park (your balcony view) and convenient for the Born nightlife. All rooms are en suite and air-conditioned and, though no breakfast is served, you're hardly pushed for options in this neighbourhood. ❸

Waterfront

Arts Barcelona c/Marina 19–21, Port Olímpic ☎**900 221 900 or 932 211 000,** ℗**www.ritz-carlton.com/hotels/barcelona;** Ⓜ**Ciutadella-Vila Olímpica.** Thirty-three floors of five-star designer luxury, with fabulous views of the port and sea from every angle. Service and standards are first-rate (there's a team of butlers on call) and the rooms are highly pleasing, with thick carpets and robes, marble bathrooms, fresh flowers, multi-entertainment centres and the rest. Two restaurants (including the highly rated *Newport Room*), café, two bars, gardens, gym, sauna and open-air pool complete the line-up. And, if you have to ask, you can't afford it. **⑨**

Grand Marina Hotel World Trade Centre, Moll de Barcelona, Port Vell ☎936 039 000, ⓦwww.grandmarinahotel.com; ⓜDrassanes. Five-star comforts on eight floors overlooking the port. It's very flash and most of the rooms have got enormous marble bathrooms with Jacuzzi baths, a separate dressing area, satellite TV and Internet connection. Public areas draw gasps, too, with commissioned works by Catalan artists and a rooftop pool with fantastic views. Winter-season and other special rates sometimes bring the price down to under €200. **⑨**

El Raval

Ambassador c/Pintor Fortuny 13 ☎933 426 180, ⓦwww.rivolihotels.com; ⓜCatalunya. Just a minute off the Ramblas, this has a sunny rooftop deck with loungers, tiny pool and spa. Rooms are very comfortable – air-conditioned and soundproofed – though the lilac colour scheme, dark wood panelling and earthy marble bathrooms won't be to everyone's taste. But the bar is great, an ornate cast-iron period piece in a contemporary setting. **⑧**

Aneto c/del Carme 38, 1° ☎933 019 989, ℻933 019 862; ⓜLiceu. Small, reasonably priced, one-star hotel in a good location – rooms at the front have balconies looking across to the Dr Fleming gardens and, though it's quieter at the rear, it's also darker. All rooms have TV, air conditioning and bathrooms with small bathtubs as well as showers. Breakfast included. **❹**

España c/de Sant Pau 9–11 ☎933 181 758, ⓦwww.hotelespanya.com; ⓜLiceu. The highlight of this elegant turn-of-the-century hotel – a few steps off the Ramblas – is undoubtedly the splendid *modernista* dining room, designed by Domènech i Montaner. Rooms are hardly in the same league, but some give onto a delightful internal patio garden, and they're all air-conditioned with decent enough bathrooms. Breakfast included. **❺**

Gat Raval c/Joaquín Costa 44, 2° ☎934 816

670, ⓦwww.gataccommodation.com; ⓜUniversitat. Going for the boutique end of the budget market, the *Gat Raval* has done its fashionable best with a rambling townhouse. Lime green is a recurring theme, from doors to bedspreads, while each room is broken down to fundamentals – folding chair, sink, wall-mounted TV, fan/heating, and signature back-lit street photograph/art-work that doubles as a reading light. Only six of the 24 rooms are en suite, but communal facilities are good, and there are internal or street/MACBA views, Internet access, drinks machine and 24hr access. At the nearby sister hotel, *Gat Xino*, c/Hospital 149–155, all the rooms are en suite. **❸**

Grau c/Ramelleres 27 ☎933 018 135, ⓦwww.hostalgrau.com; ⓜCatalunya. In a good location on the corner of c/dels Tallers, not far from MACBA, this is housed in a charming building above a café run by an accommodating English-speaking family. Soundproofed, centrally heated rooms with shutters come with or without bath, and there's an open-plan breakfast area and reading room, Internet access and laundry service, plus pay-parking nearby. Breakfast (not included) runs from tea and toast (€2.60) to a fry-up (€7). Three small private apartments in the same building (sleeping two, three or four, available by the night) offer a bit more independence. **❸**, apartments **❹**–**❻**

Meson Castilla c/Valldonzella 5 ☎933 182 182, ℻934 124 020; ⓜUniversitat. As quirky as it gets – contemporary Barcelona outside, Fifties rural Spain inside, with every inch carved, painted and stencilled, from the grandfather clock in reception to the wardrobe in your room. Large, air-conditioned rooms (some with terraces) filled with country furniture, a vast rustic dining room (buffet breakfast included) and – best of all – a lovely tiled rear patio on which to read in the sun. Parking available. **❻**

Peninsular c/de Sant Pau 34 ☎933 023 138, ℻934 123 699; ⓜLiceu. This interesting old building originally belonging to a priestly order, which explains the slightly cell-like quality of the rooms (available with/without private bathroom). There's nothing spartan about the public areas, which have been thoughtfully refurbished, including the attractive galleried inner courtyard (around which the rooms are ranged), hung with dozens of plants, and with breakfast served in the arcaded dining room. It's a big place, but fills quickly because it's such a good deal. Breakfast included. ❷, en suite ❸

Principal c/Junta del Comerç 8 ☏933 188 970, ⓦwww.hotelprincipal.es; Ⓜ Liceu. Rooms aren't huge but are adequate, and satellite TV, air conditioning and double glazing come as standard; you get a bit more contemporary style, and parquet floors, in the superior rooms. There's 24hr reception, Internet access and luggage storage available. Breakfast included. ❹, superior rooms ❻

Ramos c/Hospital 36 ☏933 020 723, ☏933 020 430; Ⓜ Liceu. The building's a treat, with the best rooms overlooking either the quiet marble internal patio or the attractive Pl. de Sant Agusti. Partitioning has spoiled the proportions of some rooms (those overlooking the square are the largest), but all have either half-size or full bathtubs, polished tile floors and TV. It's something of a haven and very popular; some English spoken. ❹

Sant Agustí Pl. Sant Agusti 3 ☏933 181 658, ⓦwww.hotelsa.com; Ⓜ Liceu. Barcelona's oldest hotel is housed in a former seventeenth-century convent building on a restored square, where the balconies overlook the trees and the namesake church. It's in a great location, and the appealing rooms have been modernized and air-conditioned, with the best located right in the eaves, from where there are rooftop views. Reservations essential. Breakfast included. ❻

La Terrassa c/Junta del Comerç 11 ☏933 025 174, ☏933 012 188; Ⓜ Liceu. Clean and friendly backpackers' favourite, with plain (really plain) rooms with a partition shower-toilet – those at the back overlook a large sunny terrace, open to all guests. However,

starting at the front, the owners are putting in proper little bathrooms, adding big closets and fitting mirrored double-glazed windows onto the street-side balconies. Prices are an absolute bargain, especially for the new rooms. Lockers available. Credit cards accepted, but for €100 minimum. ❶

Poble Sec

Oliveta c/Poeta Cabanyes 18 ☏933 292 316; Ⓜ Paral.lel. The sort of place that abounds in rural Spain or France, but is a bit of a rarity in the city – perfectly serviceable (if plain), spacious, tile-floor rooms with tidy bathrooms above a local bar and attached cheap neighbourhood restaurant. You're off the busy Avgda. Paral.lel, but not far from the metro and only a short walk from the Raval's bars and restaurants – and there's a great tapas bar, *Quimet i Quimet*, right over the road. Ask in the bar about the rooms. ❷

Around Pl. Universitat

Australia Ronda Universitat 11, 4° ☏933 174 177, ⓦwww.residenciaustralia.com; Ⓜ Universitat. The voluble Maria is well into her third decade looking after visitors and you'll need to reserve ahead – at least a fortnight in advance in summer. It's a bit old-fashioned, with elaborate bed headboards and clunky furniture, and a bit eccentric – you can only go up in the elevator, not down (don't ask). Rooms (one single and six doubles) will take a third person for an extra €12, or there's a more spacious one-bed suite with lounge, fridge and coffee-making machine in the next block of the Ronda. ❷, suite ❸

Cèntric c/Casanova 13 ☎934 267 573 or 902 014 881, ⓦwww.hostalcentric.com; ⓜUniversitat. Thirty hotel-quality rooms for pension prices in a convenient location. All rooms feature new panelling and furniture, decent beds, and plenty of light; cheaper ones on the upper floors (no elevator) share bathrooms, while some of the more expensive en-suite ones also have air conditioning. There's a sunny terrace at the rear, and Internet access. ❸, en suite ❹

Gravina c/Gravina 12 ☎933 016 868, ⓦwww.hotelh10gravina.com; ⓜUniversitat. The old-style facade deceives, for this is a contemporary update and pretty good value for the money. It's fairly quiet (off the main road), while comfort levels are high – toiletries, robes and hair driers in the bathrooms, neat little window-side armchairs, artwork in the sharply styled public areas, and a buffet breakfast included in the price. ❼

Around Pl. Catalunya

Catalunya Plaza Pl. de Catalunya 7 ☎933 177 171, ⓦwww.h10.es; ⓜCatalunya. The only hotel actually on the square, with twelve rooms that look directly onto the fountains, shops, traffic and pedestrians of Barcelona's busiest hub. Make sure you request a room well in advance. Otherwise, it's a contemporarily styled three-star establishment (set in a nineteenth-century mansion), with comfortable rooms and attractive public areas – pricey for the standard, certainly, but it could hardly be more convenient. Buffet breakfast included. ❼

Cortés c/Santa Anna 25 ☎933 179 112, ℗934 126 608; ⓜCatalunya. Two-star hotel with its own bar-restaurant (breakfast included in the price). The modern, air-conditioned rooms don't have much to distinguish them – no balconies, for instance – but they're right for the price and location. The brightest and best are those at the rear, overlooking Santa Anna church. ❺

Duques de Bergara c/Bergara 11 ☎933 015 151, ⓦwww.hoteles-catalonia.es; ⓜCatalunya. This handsome late nineteen-teenth-century building, designed by Gaudi's mentor Emili Sala, has had a complete makeover. Rooms have a bright, contemporary air, with parquet floors, brown marble bathrooms and little sitting areas – upgrade to a junior suite and you get jet-black marble and a Jacuzzi bath, lounge area and huge TV. It's set in a small side street, but there are Catalunya views from some balconies, and a small first-floor outdoor pool and deck. A big buffet breakfast spread is €12. ❼

Ginebra Rambla de Catalunya 1, 3° ☎933 171 063, ℯhotelginebra@telefonica.net; ⓜCatalunya. Even on a budget, if you spend a bit more you get a bit more space – good-sized rooms with nice old furniture, bathrooms you can turn round in for a change, pot plants, cappuccino machine and small bar. All rooms come with TV and air conditioning, and some have impressive views of Pl. de Catalunya – be sure to ask for one of the four with a balcony. Winter discounts knock around ten percent off. ❹

Lausanne Avgda. Portal de l'Àngel 24, 1° ☎933 021 139; ⓜCatalunya/Urquinaona. They could make more of this lovely old building, but then the prices would be higher. As it is, you get plain rooms with tile floors and tacked-on shower cubicles, and some tiny singles pressed into service as doubles in busy periods. But you also get a quiet, rear *terrassa*, a period piece of a lounge with carved ceiling and Fifties armchairs, a safe location and English-speaking management. No credit cards. ❸

Nouvel c/Santa Anna 18–20 ☎933 018 274, ⓦwww.hotelnouvel.com; ⓜCatalunya. Dating from 1917, this three-star has kept its handsome period details while updating most of the rooms. They differ in size but come with brass or wooden bedsteads, high ceilings, air conditioning and compact bathrooms with brown marble detailing – one has a Jacuzzi bath. It's best at the back, where rooms have little sunny terraces, though four spacious corner rooms at the front have curvacious double balconies. Be warned – the street might be pedestrianized, but it's not noise-free. Breakfast included. No American Express. ❻

Santa Anna c/Santa Anna 23 ☎933 012 246; ⓜCatalunya. So clean it squeaks – as do the yappy dogs and cat that prowl the buffed corridors. Attractive little rooms (with and without private shower room) on two floors, many with a small balcony onto the street or the rear. Room 202 has a lovely private terrace, though the bathroom for this one is down the hall; singles are box-like but cheap. Not much English spoken, but it's such good value for the area it fills quickly. No credit cards. ❷

Around Pl. Urquinaona

Pensió 2000 c/Sant Pere Més Alt 6, 1° ☎933 107 466; Ⓜ️Urquinaona. As close to a family-style bed and breakfast as Barcelona gets – six huge rooms (some overlook the Palau de la Música Catalana, across the street) in a welcoming mansion apartment strewn with books, plants and pictures. A third person could easily share most rooms (€18 supplement), while a choice of breakfasts (€3) is served either in your room or on the internal patio. ❷

Ribagorza c/Trafalgar 39/Méndez Núñez 17, 1° ☎933 191 968, ☎933 191 247; Ⓜ️Urquinaona. On a street corner on the edge of the old town, with a mixed bag of rooms overseen by an enthusiastic owner. Most have mosaic-tile floors and sinks and, though the very cheapest are internal, others have balconies (some conservatory-style) and en-suite bathrooms. Communal bathrooms are large and clean, there's a hot-drinks machine, and a rather grand salon-lounge, which is sometimes used as a room when space is at a premium. ❷, en suite ❸

Urquinaona Ronda de Sant Pere 24 ☎932 681 336, ☎www.barcelonahotel.com/urquinaona. Decent-sized air-conditioned rooms in a convenient location. Ones at the front (with balconies) overlook the hugely busy Pl. Urquinaona, but soundproofing does a reasonable job. Special rates often mean this drops a price category. Internet access available; breakfast included in the price. ❺

Passeig de Gràcia and Dreta de l'Eixample

Ciudad Condal c/Mallorca 255, 2° ☎932 151 040; Ⓜ️Passeig de Gràcia. Plain rooms with high ceilings and tile floors, and generally comfortable enough, though you may want to look at one or two, as space is at a premium. All come with bath and TV – some have French windows onto balconies over the busy street, while those at the back give onto an indoor patio and overlook a pretty garden with orange trees. ❹, patio rooms ❺

Claris c/Pau Claris 150 ☎934 876 262, ☎www.derbyhotels.es; Ⓜ️Passeig de Gràcia. Very select, very palatial, from the incense-scented marble lobby complete with authentic Roman mosaics, to the hugely appealing rooms ranged around a soaring, water-washed atrium. And how many hotels have their own private antiquities museum? If there's a gripe, it's that there's not a lot of room space for your euro, but the staff couldn't be more accommodating, there's a rooftop terrace pool for those idle moments, a great bar and one of the best hotel restaurants in the city. Prices, needless to say, are on the ludicrous side, though they soften at weekends. ❾

Condes de Barcelona Pg. de Gràcia 73–75 ☎934 674 780, ☎www.condesdebarcelona .com; Ⓜ️Passeig de Gràcia. Straddling two sides of c/Mallorca, the *Condes* is fashioned from two former palaces – that on the north side has kept its interior marble-work and wrought-iron balconies, but there's little difference between the rooms themselves, which are all classily turned out in contemporary style, some with Jacuzzi and balcony, and some with views of Gaudí's La Pedrera. Best deal are those on the south-side, seventh-floor exterior, with fantastic private terraces but charging standard room rates. There's also a pretty roof terrace and plunge pool, bar and restaurant. ❽

Girona c/Girona 24, 1° ☎932 650 259, ☎www.hostalgirona.com; Ⓜ️Urquinaona. Has a positively baronial stairway and things are scarcely any less impressive inside the family-run building – corridors laid with rugs, polished wooden doors, paintings and restored furniture. A fair choice of rooms, too, either with full bathroom or just shower (plus some bathroom-less singles), internal or with balcony. ❷, en suite ❸

Goya c/de Pau Claris 74, 1° ☎933 022 565, ☎www.hostalgoya.com; Ⓜ️Urquinaona. Upgraded mansion building with a dozen older-style *hostal* rooms, not all en suite, and seven more on the "boutique hotel" floor below (formerly the owners' own apartment), which have been fitted with laminate flooring, air conditioning, stylish bed linen and modern bathrooms – the three largest (and most expensive) open directly onto a lovely rear terrace. There's a library corner with comfy sofas in the hotel part, an equally attractive common room in the *hostal*, and free coffee and tea available on both floors. hostal ❷, hotel ❹

Gran Hotel Havana Gran Via de les Corts Catalanes 647 ☎934 121 115,

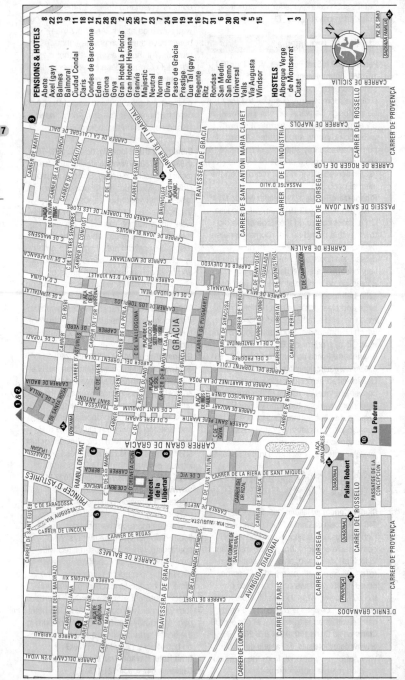

PENSIONS & HOTELS

Abete	8
Axel (gay)	22
Balmes	13
Balmoral	9
Ciudad Condal	11
Claris	18
Condes de Barcelona	12
Eden	28
Girona	29
Goya	2
Gran Hotel La Florida	25
Gran Hotel Havana	26
Granvia	17
Majestic	23
Neutral	7
Norma	24
Oliva	19
Paseo de Gràcia	10
Prestige	14
Que Tal (gay)	16
Regente	27
Ritz	31
Rondas	6
San Medin	30
San Remo	20
Universal	4
Valls	5
Via Augusta	15
Windsor	1

HOSTELS

Albergue Verge de Montserrat	1
Ciutat	3

EIXAMPLE & GRÀCIA ACCOMMODATION

Sagrada Família

PGE DE FONT

PLAÇA DE PABLO NERUDA

CARRER DE SARDENYA

PLAÇA DE LA SAGRADA FAMÍLIA

PGE DE MAIOL

CARRER DE SARDENYA

MONUMENTAL

CARRER DE MALLORCA

PGE DE GAIOLA

CARRER DE SICILIA

CARRER DEL CONSELL DE CENT

CARRER DE NÀPOLS

CARRER DE LA DIPUTACIO

CARRER DE ROGER DE FLOR

PGE DE TASSO

DRETA DE L'EIXAMPLE

PASSEIG DE SANT JOAN

CARRER D'ARAGO

CARRER DE BAILEN

PLAÇA DE TETUAN

TETUAN

CARRER DE CASP

CARRER DE AUSIAS MARC

AVINGUDA DIAGONAL

VERDAGUER

CARRER VALENCIA

PGE DE PLÀ

CARRER DE GIRONA

CARRER DEL BRUC

GIRONA

CARRER DE ROGER DE LLURIA

GRAN VIA DE LES CORTS CATALANES

RONDA DE SANT PERE

CARRER DE PAU CLARIS

CARRER DELS CAMP ELISIS

PASSEIG DE GRACIA

Museu del Perfum

PASSEIG DE GRACIA

CARRER DE PAU CLARIS

El Corte Inglés

RONDA DE SANT PERE

CARRER DE FONTANELLS

Fundació Antoni Tàpies

Casa Batlló

Casa Amatller

Casa Lleó Morera

PGE DE DOMINGO

RAMBLA DE CATALUNYA

CARRER DE LA DIPUTACIO

RONDA DE LA UNIVERSITAT

CARRER DE BERGARA

PLAÇA DE CATALUNYA

CATALUNYA

CATALUNYA

CATALUNYA

ESQUERRA DE L'EIXAMPLE

CARRER DE MALLORCA

VALENCIA

CARRER D'ARAGO

CARRER DE BALMES

CARRER DEL CONSELL DE CENT

CARRER

CARRER DE PELAI

CARRER DELS TALLERS

Universitat de Barcelona

PLAÇA DOCTOR LETAMENDI

RONDA DE LA UNIVERSITAT

PLAÇA DE LA UNIVERSITAT

UNIVERSITAT

CARRER DE VALLDONZELLA

CARRER DE MONTALEGRE

CARRER D'ARIBAU

0   200 m

165

ⓦwww.granhotelhavana.com; ⓂGirona. The nineteenth-century facade has been retained but everything else is sharply contemporary, from the tadpole-shaped atrium to the Italian marble bathrooms. Rooms are on the sober side, but there's a comfortable atrium bar from which to plan the next day's outing. ❼

Granvía Gran Via de les Corts Catalanes 642 ☏933 181 900, ⓦwww.nnhotels.es; ⓂCatalunya/Passeig de Gràcia. An attractive townhouse, built for a nineteenth-century banking family, with extremely swish public rooms exuding old-style comfort. You may be less lucky with your own room, as some of the accommodation is cramped, but there's a nice roof terrace. Prices are pretty reasonable, too, given that air conditioning, full bath and satellite TV come as standard; breakfast costs €8. ❺

Majestic Pg. de Gràcia 68 ☏934 881 717, ⓦwww.hotelmajestic.es; ⓂPasseig de Gràcia. Big, traditional hotel, refitted in muted colours to provide a tranquil base. *Objets* and limited-edition art adorn the public areas, and the rooms – bigger than many in this price bracket – have been pleasantly refurbished, but the absolute clincher is the rooftop pool and deck, with amazing views over the rooftops to the Sagrada Família. The high quoted prices can almost always be beaten (bringing spacious junior suites into the equation), and at weekends and in summer prices they fall by up to twenty percent. ❽

Oliva Pg. de Gràcia 32, 4° ☏934 881 789 or 934 880 162, ⓦwww.lasguias.com/hostaloliva; ⓂPasseig de Gràcia. Ride the antique elevator to the top floor for an Eixample bargain – marble floors, high ceilings and plenty of light in rooms that have been freshly decorated with a bit of zest. Rooms without private bathroom save you around €7 a night. If you want a balcony and a view, be warned that the noise permeates, even at these rarified levels. No English spoken; no credit cards. ❸

Paseo de Gràcia Pg. de Gràcia 102 ☏932 155 824, ☏932 153 724; ⓂDiagonal. Some might find this funereal, others will delight in its faded Fifties charm – the lounge, in particular, is an untouched relic of bygone days. Rooms, too, have yet to see a renovator, which means ageing tiling and furniture, but prices are pitched accordingly and the hotel is in a great location, handy for the

Eixample and Gràcia. Fortune favours those who get space on the upper floors, where some rooms have terraces and city views, but you can't book these in advance. Breakfast available (€3.25). ❹

Prestige Pg. de Gràcia 62 ☏932 724 180, ⓦwww.prestigepaseodegracia.com; ⓂPasseig de Gràcia. A sharp redesign of a Thirties Eixample building has added achingly fashionable minimalist rooms, an Oriental-style internal patio garden and the *Zeroom*, a lounge with wireless Internet facility and style library. It's almost a parody of itself, it's so cool, but the staff keep things real and are very helpful. Breakfast costs €15. ❼

Ritz Gran Via de les Corts Catalanes 668 ☏935 101 130, ⓦwww.ritzbcn.com; ⓂPasseig de Gràcia. Still possibly the most luxurious hotel in Barcelona, built in 1919 and giving the new designer hotels a run for their money in the comfort stakes. Formally attired staff jump to your every command, while your domain extends to opulent lounges, a terrace garden, bar, restaurant and health club. The suites are sensational, but for these – as for the deluxe rooms (there's no such thing as "standard" at the *Ritz*) – you're paying crazily inflated prices (from €380). ❾

Rondas c/Girona 4, 3° ☏932 325 102; ⓂUrquinaona. About as cheap as you'll find in the Eixample, the *Rondas* might not have a lot of space or many flourishes, but you'll get a friendly English-speaking welcome and a touch of domesticity – an old carved bed in one room, the share of a balcony onto the street in another. The museum piece of an elevator is a talking point in itself. Good for lone travellers, as there are four singles; otherwise six cramped doubles which come without facilities, with just a shower, or with shower and loo. No credit cards. ❷

San Remo c/del Bruc 20, 2° ☏933 021 989, ☏933 010 774; ⓂUrquinaona. The doubles aren't a bad size for the money and the small tiled bathrooms are pretty nice for this price range. There's double glazing, but even so you'll get more peace at the back – though the internal rooms aren't nearly as appealing as those with balconies. The seven rooms include one decently priced single. Not much English spoken. ❸

Universal c/Aragó 281, 2° ☏934 879 762, ☏934 874 028; ⓂPasseig de Gràcia. The English-speaking owner keeps things nice and tidy, and the prices (pegged the same year-round) are fair for what are dated but clean, carpeted rooms with private bath and TV. All but four have windows opening onto balconies overlooking the street – though it's quieter in the internal rooms. A small, plain lounge boasts an antique telephone exchange. ❸

Rambla de Catalunya and Esquerra de l'Eixample

Balmes c/Mallorca 216 ☎934 511 914, ⊛www.derbyhotels.es; Ⓜ Passeig de Gràcia. Agreeable boutique hotel with sharp-as-a-knife dining and bar facilities, classy rooms with parquet floors and leather sofas, and some duplexes available. A couple of ground-floor rooms have their own terrace overlooking the lush patio garden, complete with swimming pool and bar, and on your way in and out every day you get to browse the African art and sculpture in the lobby. ❽
Eden c/Balmes 55, 1° ☎934 526 620, ⊛www.hostaleden.net; Ⓜ Passeig de Gràcia. Eager-to-please, English-speaking staff and a wide choice of simply furnished rooms, but overpriced given its student-dorm atmosphere and occasional rough edges. Make sure you get a room facing the back patio for a quiet night, though you'll want to avoid the odd one that doesn't have a window. Plenty of facilities attract a backpacker crowd – TV/DVD lounge, free Internet access, 24hr reception, laundry and coffee machine – and discounts for longer stays negotiable. ❷, en suite ❸
Neutral Rambla de Catalunya 42 ☎934 876 390, ⊕934 876 848; Ⓜ Passeig de Gràcia. Fixtures and fittings are a bit on the tired side, but you can't fault the location or the price. It's on the first floor, so front rooms with avenue views will be noisy, but they're decent enough, with TV, shower or bath, available for two to four people. ❷
Regente Rambla de Catalunya 76 ☎934 875 989, ⊛www.hcchotels.es; Ⓜ Passeig de Gràcia. They've restored the *modernista* facade and kept the decorative internal panelling and stained glass; together with the rooftop pool, garden terrace and funky bar, that's some attraction. But even the hotel recommends an internal room to escape the street noise, and the trouble is they're none too light, so it's best to book a rear top-floor room with private green-baize terrace

and city views. These are the same price as other rooms but go quickly. Weekend rates typically knock around thirty percent off all rooms. ❼
Windsor Rambla de Catalunya 84 ☎932 151 198; Ⓜ Passeig de Gràcia. Genteel *hostal* with English-speaking management, set in a lovingly furnished building on the Eixample's nicest avenue. There are fifteen rooms, all with en-suite shower and toilet (and often booked days in advance), but you'll have to go out for breakfast. No credit cards. ❸

Gràcia

Abete c/Gran de Gràcia 67 ☎932 185 524; Ⓜ Fontana. Compact family-run hotel on the busy main street, whose simple, old-fashioned rooms all have showers; some have toilets too, otherwise you'll have to use the clean communal loos. It's a bit overpriced really, for what's basically just a bed for the night, but it is well located. ❸
Balmoral Via Augusta 5 ☎932 178 700, ⊛www.hotelbalmoral.com; Ⓜ Diagonal. On the southwestern fringes of Gràcia, this boxy modern four-star hotel contains smallish rooms with plenty of closet space and sleek marble bathrooms, while double glazing deals effectively with the traffic noise. It's not a bad deal at all compared to others of its rating, especially at weekends when there are special deals. ❻
Norma c/Gran de Gràcia 87, 2° ☎932 374 478; Ⓜ Fontana. The narrow, down-at-heel stairway leads to something better – half a dozen little rooms giving onto the internal patio (the quietest choice) or the street. A big corridor window lets in the light – the rooms off this have tile floors and trim bathrooms, and there's a friendly owner who may come down a few euros out of season. You're also really close to the market for breakfast with the locals. ❷
San Medín c/Gran de Gràcia 125 ☎932 173 068, ⊕934 154 410; Ⓜ Fontana. Better looking inside than out, this friendly and well-located pension has twelve rooms, some with shower. The affable owner is busily renovating, but he can't stop the traffic, so for a decent night's sleep you'll want to ask for an interior room. ❷, en suite ❸
Valls c/Laforja 82, 2° ☎932 096 967; Ⓜ Fontana. Just west of Gràcia (past c/d'Aribau), and kept spick-and-span by the family. If the nine rooms are a bit drab

(some internal, others overlooking the street), you do at least get a clean, quiet base for the night in a residential neighbourhood (5min from Via Augusta), an English-speaking welcome and an inclusive breakfast. ❸

Via Augusta Via Augusta 63 ☎932 179 250; Ⓜ**Fontana.** Decently priced two-star with rooms ranged across five floors. The marble lobby misleads, since in some rooms the tile floors and bathrooms are in need of a bit of TLC – a restoration job is slowly smartening the place up – and rooms at the front are potentially noisy, but there's a breakfast salon on the third floor (continental €4, buffet €8), and you're handily poised for the neighbourhood's sights and attractions. ❹

Tibidabo

Gran Hotel La Florida Carreterra Vallviderera a Tibidabo 83–93, 7km from the centre ☎932 593 000, ⓦwww.hotellaflorida.com. Describing itself as an "urban resort", the newly renovated *Gran Hotel* recreates the glory days of the Fifties, when it was at the centre of Barcelona high society. High on the hillside, its terraces and pool all have amazing views, while some rooms and suites have private garden or terrace and Jacuzzi. Also a restaurant, lobby lounge and poolside bar. You'll pay five-star rates for five-star service, starting at €310 a room (sea views from €390), though you might get a better rate than this on request. ❾

Youth hostels

There are lots of central hostels in Barcelona, though you should always call ahead to reserve a bed, as most of them are very popular. You won't save a huge amount of money over taking the cheapest available pension room, but hostel facilities are usually pretty good, most of them offering Internet access, kitchens, common/games rooms and laundry. If you don't have your own sleeping bag or sheet sleeping bag, most places can rent them to you. Rates everywhere tend to drop a few euros in the winter. Always use the lockers or safes provided. You only need an International Youth Hostel Federation (IYHF) card for a couple of the hostels, but you can join on check-in. The only tourist office to handle youth hostel bookings is the one at Barcelona Sants.

Barri Gòtic

Alberg Palau c/Palau 6 ☎934 125 080, ⓔalbergpalau@champinet.com; Ⓜ**Liceu.** A bit on the threadbare side, but a good location and reasonably quiet. Rooms with steel-frame bunks and lockers sleep four to eight people (forty beds in total); mixed and single-sex dorms available. Small kitchen/lounge, Internet access, and a 3am curfew. Price includes breakfast. No credit cards. Dorms €15, sheets €1.50

Itaca c/Ripoll 21 ☎933 019 751, ⓦwww.itacahostel.com; Ⓜ**Jaume I.** Bright and breezy converted house close to the cathedra,l with spacious dorm rooms (sleeping eight or twelve) with lockers and balconies. Dorms are mixed, though there is a six-bed women-only dorm and one double room (€44). No TV lounge, but a kitchen, coffee machine and choice of €2 breakfasts. Dorms €18, sheets and towels €1.20

Kabul Pl. Reial 17 ☎933 185 190, ⓦwww.kabul-hostel.com; Ⓜ**Liceu.** A budget travellers' haven in the heart of the old town – open 24hr, with a good noticeboard and weekly pub crawls to help you get acquainted. It's a safe hostel with lots of facilities, including a big, monastic-style common room/bar that overlooks the square, a kitchen, laundry and TV. Price includes breakfast. Dorms €16

El Raval

Barcelona Mar c/de Sant Pau 80 ☎933 248 530, ⓦwww.youthostal-barcelona.com; Ⓜ**Paral.lel/Drassanes.** Large, rather clinically furnished hostel with lots of beds, on the fringe of the Rambla de Raval, so slightly edgy surroundings around here at night. It's a secure place, with 24hr reception, lockers, air conditioning, TV room, laundry and Internet. Dorms – in six-, eight-, ten-, fourteen- or sixteen-bedded rooms –

are mixed, and beds are ship's-bunk-style; bring your own sleeping bag or rent sheets for €2.10. Price includes continental breakfast, and rates €4 or €5 drop out of summer. Dorms €23

Center Ramblas c/Hospital 63 ☎934 124 069, ⓦwww.center-ramblas.com; ⓂLiceu. *Very* popular 200-bed hostel, given its location 100m from the Ramblas, and well equipped, with lounge, bar, laundry, Internet access, travel library, luggage storage and more. Dorms – sleeping from three to ten – have flagged floors and individual lockers, and there's 24hr access. IYHF membership required (you can join on the spot). Price includes breakfast. No credit cards. Under-26s €15.50, over-26s €20

La Ribera

Gothic Point c/Vigatans 5 ☎932 687 808, ⓦwww.gothicpoint.com; ⓂJaume I. This stunning conversion provides over 130 beds in a great old-town location. A grand downstairs communal area shows off the building's dramatic proportions, and on the roof there's mini-golf. Rooms have fourteen bunks and attached bathrooms, and each bed gets its own bedside cabinet and reading light. Lockers, left-luggage and bike rental. Price includes breakfast and free Internet. Open 24hr. Dorms €21, out of season €18

Barceloneta

Sea Point Pl. del Mar 1–4 ☎932 247 075, ⓦwww.seapointhostel.com; ⓂBarceloneta. For Barcelona beachfront accommodation, you're looking at the five-star *Hotel Arts* – and this place. Neat little modern bunk rooms sleeping six or seven, with an integral shower-bathroom and big lockers in each one. No sea views yet, though a new extension might resolve this, but the attached *Raska* café, where you have breakfast, looks right out onto the boardwalk and palm trees. Price includes break-

fast and free Internet. Open 24hr. Dorms €21, out of season €18, lockers €1.20 a day

Gràcia

La Ciutat c/Ca l'Alegre de Dalt 66, corner with c/Martí ☎932 130 300, ⓔlaciutat@nnhoteles.es; ⓂAlfons X. Large student residence that welcomes individuals and groups – accommodation is either in plain four- or six-bed dorms, single rooms (€30 per person) or twins (€24 per person), each of which has wardrobe space and an attached toilet and sink, while showers are down the hall. The private rooms have TVs too. There's left-luggage and laundry facilities, a kitchen and TV room, and you're just 10min walk from Pl. Virreina, 15min from Pl. del Sol. Price includes breakfast and free Internet access. Reception open 8am–11pm; main door open 24hr. Dorms €17

Horta

Albergue Verge de Montserrat Pg. de la Mare de Déu del Coll 41–51 ☎932 105 151, ⓦwww.tujuca.com; ⓂVallcarca (follow Avgda. República d'Argentina, c/Viaducte de Vallcarca and then signs) or bus #28 from Pl. de Catalunya stops just across the street. Stunning converted mansion with tile-and-stained-glass interior, gardens, terrace and city views – a long way out, but close to Parc Güell. Multi-bedded dorms (sleeping four, six, eight and twelve), lockers and left luggage, laundry, lounge room and games, Internet access, with local restaurant just around the corner or meals provided. IYHF membership required; five-night maximum stay; reception open 8am–3pm & 4.30–11pm; main door closes at midnight, but opens every 30min thereafter. Price includes breakfast. Dorms €23, low season €19, sheets and towels €3

Eating

There is a great variety of food available in Barcelona and even low-budget travellers can do well for themselves, either by using the excellent markets and filling up on sandwiches and snacks, or eating cheaply from the set menu. Nearly all cafés and restaurants offer a three-course **menú del dia** (menu of the day) at lunchtime, with the cheapest starting at about €7, rising to €10/12 in fancier places. In many places, the price includes a drink, so this can be a real bargain. At night, the set menus aren't generally available, but eating out is still pretty good value and you'll be able to dine in a huge variety of restaurants for under €20 a head (though you can, of course, pay a lot more). Alternatively, you can do the rounds of the city's **tapas** bars, eating a succession of small tapas dishes or larger portions called *raciones.*

Good tapas bars and restaurants are easily found all over the city, though you'll probably do most of your eating where you do most of your sightseeing, in the old town, particularly in the **Barri Gòtic**. However, if you step no further than the Ramblas, or the streets around the cathedral, you are not going to experience the best of the city's cuisine — in the main tourist areas food and service can be indifferent and prices high. You need to be a bit more adventurous, and explore the back streets of **La Ribera**, **El Raval** and **Poble Sec**, where you'll find excellent restaurants, some little more than hole-in-the-wall cafés or traditional taverns, others surprisingly funky (and surprisingly expensive). In the **Eixample** prices tend to be higher all round, though you'll find plenty of bargains in cafés and restaurants aimed at lunching workers. **Gràcia**, further out, is a nice place to

Rough Guide star picks

Al fresco dining: *Agua* (p.191), *Bar Ra* (p.187), *Café de la Ribera* (p.184).

Artistic ambience: *Casa Calvet* (p.193), *Fonda España* (p.189), *Quatre Gats* (p.183).

Best cheap eats: *Bar Salvador* (p.184), *L'Económic* (p.184), *Mesón David* (p.187).

Catch of the day: *Arrel del Born* (p.186), *Els Pescadors* (p.192), *Mar de la Ribera* (p.184).

Chill-out cafés: *Café d'Estiu* (p.174), *Cerería* (p.174), *Salambo* (p.178).

Fusion sensations: *Oolong* (p.182), *Salero* (p.185), *Silenus* (p.189).

Money no object: *Comerç 24* (p.186),

East 47 (p.193), *Jean Luc Figueras* (p.197).

Only in Barcelona: *Espai Sucre* (p.186), *Flash, Flash* (p.196), *Orígens 99.9%* (p.178).

Romance in the air: *Café de l'Acadèmia* (p.183), *Octubre* (p.197), *Pla de la Garsa* (p.184).

Start the day right: *Bagel Shop* (p.174), *Kasparo* (p.175), *Laie Llibreria Café* (p.176).

Top tapas: *Bar Tomás* (p.180), *Mosquito* (p.178), *Quimet i Quimet* (p.179).

Traditional classics: *Can Culleretes* (p.182), *Caracoles* (p.183), *Set Portes* (p.186).

Unless you're staying somewhere with a decent buffet breakfast spread, you may as well pass up the overpriced coffee-and-croissant option in your hotel and join the locals in the bars, cafés and patisseries. A couple of euros should get you a hot drink and a brioche/croissant/sandwich just about anywhere – many advertised deals run until noon. *Ensaimadas* (pastry spirals) are a popular choice, and *xocolata amb xurros* (*chocolate con churros* – long, fried tubular doughnuts with thick drinking chocolate) is a good cold-weather starter. A slice of *truita (tortilla)* – or just about anything else – in a *flauta* (thin baguette) also makes an excellent breakfast. The traditional country breakfast is *pa amb tomàquet* (*pan con tomate*) – bread rubbed with tomato, olive oil and garlic, perhaps topped with some cured ham or sliced cheese. For toast, ask for *torrades* (*tostadas*).

spend the evening, with plenty of good mid-range restaurants. For the food of which Barcelona is really proud – elaborate *sarsuelas* (fish stews), paellas, *fideuàs* (noodles) and all kinds of fish and seafood – you're best off in **Port Vell** by the Palau de Mar, in the harbourside **Barceloneta** district or at the **Port Olímpic**.

Cafés and fast food

There are thousands of **cafés** in Barcelona – you're rarely more than a step away from a coffee fix or a quick sandwich. In terms of what you might be able to eat and drink, there's often little difference between a bar and a café, but the places detailed in this section have been chosen for their food or ambience. You might be able to get a full meal, but they are more geared towards breakfast, snacks and sightseeing stops. Many are classics of their kind – century-old cafés or unique neighbourhood haunts – while others specialize in certain food and drink, worth going out of your way for in either case. Most are open long hours – from 7am or 8am until midnight, or much later in some cases – so whether it's coffee first thing or a late-night nibble, you'll find somewhere to cater for you.

A quick primer will help you sort out what's what in the café world. A **forn** is a bakery, a **patisseria** a cake and pastry shop, both often with cafés attached. A **xocolateria** specializes in chocolate, including the drinking kind. In a **granja** or **orxateria**, more like milk bars than regular cafés, you'll be able to sample traditional delights like *orxata* (*horchata*, tiger-nut drink), ice cream and *granissat* (*granizado*), a crushed ice drink flavoured with orange, lemon or coffee.

Pizza, **burger**, **felafel/kebab** and **cappuccino** joints are ubiquitous, especially well represented on the Ramblas and on the main streets in the Eixample and including most of the major international players. Even *Starbuck's* has got a toehold, but if you need to drink your coffee in here you're hardly entering into the Catalan spirit. **Local and Spanish chains** include: *Pans & Company* and *Bocatta*, for hot and cold baguette-based sandwiches and salads; *Fresh and Ready* for deli, sandwich and juice offerings; *Il Caffe di Roma*, serving coffee and other hot drinks, pastries and ice creams; the classier *Aroma* cafés; and the warehouse-style *Café di Francesco* for coffee (plus added alcohol or cream combinations), thirty types of tea, and croissants.

Ramblas and the Barri Gòtic

Antiga Casa Figueres Ramblas 83 ☎933 016 027; Ⓜ Liceu. Pastries from the Escribà family business in a *modernista* pastry shop, with a few tables inside and out. Many people rate this as the best bakery in Barcelona. Mon–Sat 9am–3pm & 5–8.30pm.

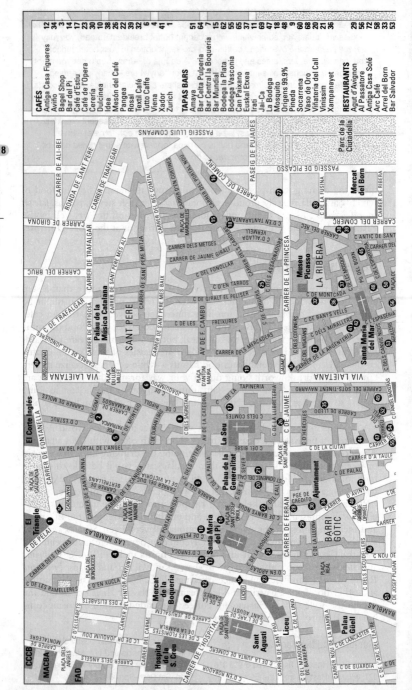

CAFÉS

Antiga Casa Figueres	12
Aviño	34
Bagel Shop	3
Bar del Pi	14
Café d'Estiu	17
Café de l'Opera	23
Cereria	30
Dulcinea	10
Idea	38
Mesón del Café	26
Pangea	22
Rosal	39
Textil Café	32
Tutto Caffe	6
Viena	4
Xador	41
Zurich	1

TAPAS BARS

Amaya	51
Bar Celta Pulperia	64
Bar Central la Boqueria	7
Bar Mundial	15
Bodega la Plata	62
Bodega Vasconia	55
Can Paixano	65
Euskal Etxea	37
Irati	11
Jai-Ca	69
La Bodega	47
Mosquito	18
Origens 99.9%	48
Pineda	9
Socarrena	60
Vaso de Oro	68
Vinateria del Call	20
Vinissim	21
Xampanyet	36

RESTAURANTS

Agut d'Avignon	29
Al Passatore	56
Antiga Casa Solé	72
Arc Café	58
Arrel del Born	33
Bar Salvador	53

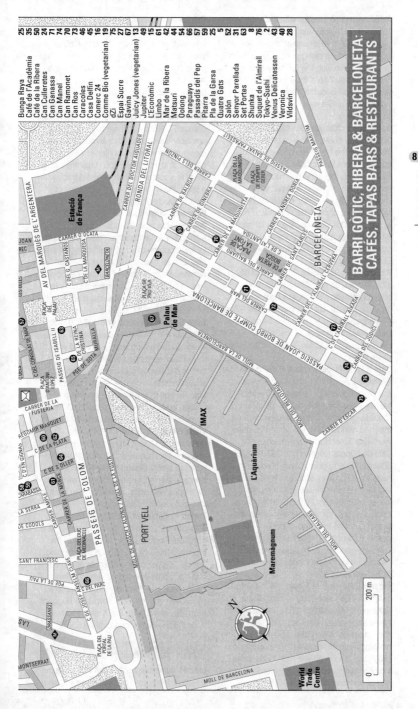

BARRI GÒTIC, RIBERA & BARCELONETA: CAFÉS, TAPAS BARS & RESTAURANTS

Bunga Raya	25
Café de l'Acadèmia	35
Café de la Ribera	50
Can Culleretes	24
Can Ganassa	71
Can Manel	74
Can Ramonet	70
Can Ros	73
Caracoles	46
Casa Delfín	45
Comerç 24	16
Comme Bio (vegetarian)	19
dZi	75
Espai Sucre	27
Gavina	67
Juicy Jones (vegetarian)	13
Jupiter	49
L'Econòmic	15
Limbo	61
Mar de la Ribera	42
Matsuri	44
Oolong	54
Paraguayo	66
Passadis del Pep	57
Pitarra	59
Pla de la Garsa	25
Quatre Gats	5
Salón	52
Senyor Parellada	31
Set Portes	63
Shunka	8
Suquet de l'Almirall	76
Tokyo-Sushi	2
Venus Delicatessen	43
Veronica	40
Vildsvin	28

Aviñó c/d'Avinyó, junction with Bxda. de Sant Miquel, no phone; Ⓜ**Jaume I.** Pleasant little old-town bar for a croissant and coffee. It operates a no-smoking policy, so it doesn't see eye to eye with the furiously fuming Barcelona youth, but it's a longtime Rough Guide favourite. Mon–Fri 7.30am–7pm, Sat 8am–1pm; closed two weeks in Aug.

Bagel Shop c/Canuda 25 ☏933 024 161; Ⓜ**Catalunya.** Funky yellow café which first introduced the bagel to Barcelona – there's cream cheese and smoked salmon, plus many others, including one rubbed with tomato, olive oil, garlic and salt for the local crowd. Bagel-and-coffee breakfast runs until noon (or choose pancakes and maple syrup), and there's a bagel-and-dip combo after 4pm, brunch on Sunday and devilish choc brownies. Mon–Sat 9.30am–9.30pm, Sun 11am–4pm.

Bar del Pi Pl. Sant Josep Oriol 1 ☏933 022 123; Ⓜ**Liceu.** Small old-town café-bar with a tiny upper gallery inside, but best known for its great terrace. Service can be slow – not that anyone's in a hurry in this prime people-watching spot. Mon–Sat 9am–11pm, Sun 10am–10pm; closed third week in Aug.

Café d'Estiu Pl. de Sant Iu 5–6 ☏933 103 014; Ⓜ**Jaume I.** A summer-only café housed on the delightful interior terrace of the Museu Marès. Relax with the newspapers during the day, or come for the candlelit evenings. It serves sandwiches, cakes and pastries. April–Oct Tues–Sun 10am–10pm.

Café de l'Opera Ramblas 74 ☏933 177 585; Ⓜ**Liceu.** If you're going to pay through the nose for a Ramblas seat, it may as well be at this famous old café-bar, which retains its late nineteenth-century decor as well as a bank of sought-after pavement tables. It's not a complete tourist-fest, though – locals pop in throughout the day and night for fine coffee, a good range of cakes, snacks and tapas, or a late-night *sangria de cava*. Daily 9am–3am.

Cererìa Bxda. de Sant Miquel 3–5 ☏933 058 110; Ⓜ**Jaume I.** Amicably hip café that attracts its fair share of goateed literary types and pseudo-intellectuals. Decor is thrift-store chic, with piles of old papers and magazines to while away the hours; food is breakfast- and veggie-friendly, with great-looking cakes and a changing roster of *platos del dia*. Daily 10am–10pm.

Dulcinea c/Petritxol 2 ☏932 311 756; Ⓜ**Liceu.** Traditional *granja* specializing in hot chocolate, slathered in cream if you like it that way, plus all manner of pastries, *mel i mato* (curd cheese with honey) and other treats. A dickie-bow-wearing waiter patrols the beamed and panelled room bearing a silver tray. Daily 9am–1pm & 5–9pm; closed Aug.

Mesón del Cafe c/Llibreteria 16 ☏933 150 754; Ⓜ**Jaume I.** Narrow, offbeat bar where you'll probably have to stand to sample the pastries and the excellent coffee – including a cappuccino laden with fresh cream – though there is a sort of cubbyhole at the back with a few tables. The bar attracts all sorts of local characters. Mon–Sat 7am–11pm.

Pangea c/Banys Nous, mob☏646 553 930; Ⓜ**Liceu.** Run by a Canadian guy with a mission to serve fantastic fruit smoothies and juices, accompanied by stuffed veggie pitas and salads. It's a virtual hole in the wall, reminiscent of a student lounge; new premises at c/d'Avinyo 18 promise a bit more space, but the same vibe and menu. Mon–Sat 11am–11pm, Sun 3–11pm.

Tutto Caffe Via Laietana 41 ☏933 020 843; Ⓜ**Jaume I.** They've exposed the old stone walls, added a long marble bar and little round marble-topped tables, and it's become a favoured breakfast/shopping stop. Choose from a variety of coffees and teas, tempting pastries, ice creams and *orxata*, and be prepared to stand. Daily 7am–midnight, except Sat 8am–12.30pm.

Viena Ramblas 115 ☏933 171 492; Ⓜ**Catalunya.** Mock turn-of-the-century decor, and good croissants and coffee for breakfast eaten at stools around the lively bar. What brings in the regulars are the sandwiches in all shapes and sizes, stuffed or grilled, eat in or takeaway. Daily 8am–2am.

Zurich Pl. Catalunya 1 ☏933 179 153; Ⓜ**Catalunya.** The most famous meet-and-greet café in town, right at the top of the Ramblas underneath El Triangle shopping centre. It's good for croissants and breakfast *bocadillos* and there's a huge terrace. Sit inside if you don't want to be bothered by endless rounds of buskers and beggars. Mon–Fri 8am–11pm, Sat & Sun 10am–11pm, June–Sept open until 1am.

La Ribera

Idea Pl. Comercial 2 ☏932 688 787; Ⓜ**Jaume I.** Relaxed little café-bookshop-cybercafé

Coffee and tea

Coffee – served in cafés, bars and some restaurants – is invariably espresso, slightly bitter and, unless you specify otherwise, served black – ask for a *café sol* (*café solo*) or simply *un café*. A slightly weaker large black coffee is called a *café americano*. A *tallat* (*cortado*) is a small strong black coffee with a dash of steamed milk; a larger cup with more hot milk is a *café amb llet* (*café con leche*). Black coffee is also frequently mixed with brandy, cognac or whisky, all such concoctions being called *cigaló* (*carajillo*); liqueur mixed with white coffee is a *trifásico*. Decaffeinated coffee (*descafeinat, descafeinado*) is available, usually in sachet form, though increasingly you can get the real thing – ask for it *de maquina*.

Tea comes in tea-bag form, without milk unless you ask for it, and is often weak and insipid. If you do ask for milk, chances are it'll be hot and UHT, so your tea isn't going to taste much like the real thing. Better are the infusions that you can get in most bars, like mint (*menta*), camomile (*camomila*) and lime (*tila*).

across from the old Mercat del Born, with a few tables in the shade outside, plus weekly classical music recitals and other events. Daily 8am–10pm.

Rosal Pg. del Born 27 no phone; ⓜJaume I. The *terrassa* at the end of the Born gets the sun all day, making it a popular meeting place, though it's also packed on summer nights. Menu specials here are couscous/curry combinations, and if you can raise a smile from the staff you're on a roll. Daily 9am–2am.

Textil Café c/de Montcada 12–14 ☎932 682 598; ⓜJaume I. Set inside the shady, cobbled medieval courtyard of the Museu Textil i d'Indumentaria, this is often packed when the Museu Picasso over the way is open but mellows out later on. Serves hummous, tzatziki, quiche, salads, chilli, lasagne and big sandwiches – and there are jazz nights on Wed (9.45pm; €3) with the Barcelona Swing Serenaders, for which you'll need to book ahead. Tues–Sun 10am–midnight.

Xador c/Argenteria 61–63 ☎933 193 648; ⓜJaume I. *Modernista*-styled *granja/xocolateria* just round the corner from Santa Maria del Mar – a nice place for a mid-morning hot chocolate and snack. Tues–Sun 8.30am–1am.

El Raval

Buenas Migas Pl. Bonsuccés 6 ☎933 183 708; ⓜCatalunya. *Foccaccia* slices and wedges of thick pizza, and fine cakes, puds and pastries, eaten in either the cosy rustic interior or on the traffic-free *terrassa*. If you're intent on an alfresco snack you may have to hover between here and the *Kasparo*,

just through the arcade, waiting for a free table. Wed & Sun 10am–11pm, Thurs–Sat 10am–midnight.

Granja M. Viader c/Xuclà 4–6 ☎933 183 486; ⓜLiceu. The oldest milk bar (*granja*) in town, tucked away down a narrow alley just off c/del Carmé, with a pavement plaque outside for services to the city. Sr. Viader was the proud inventor of "Cacaolat" (a popular chocolate drink), but you could also try the *mel i mató*, the *leche Mallorquia* (fresh milk with cinnamon and lemon rind) or a *suizo* (thick hot chocolate topped with fresh cream). Mon 5–8.45pm, Tues–Sat 9am–1.45pm & 5–8.45pm.

Fortuny c/Pintor Fortuny 31 ☎933 179 892; ⓜCatalunya. A funky and colourful backdrop for salads, guacamole, couscous, curries and other dishes of the day. Tues–Sun 10am–2am.

Kasparo Pl. Vicenç Martorell 4 ☎933 022 072; ⓜCatalunya. Sited in the arcaded corner of a quiet square off c/Bonsuccés, this tiny bar with its own *terrassa* is popular with locals who come to let their kids play in the adjacent playground. Sandwiches, tapas and assorted *platos del dia* on offer – things like hummous and bread, vegetable quiche, couscous or pasta – or muesli, Greek yoghurt, and toast and jam for early birds. Daily 9am–10pm; until midnight in summer.

Port Olímpic

Laie Marítim Pg. Marítim 35 ☎932 247 173; ⓜCiutadella-Vila Olímpica. This outpost of the *Laie* bookshop café, attached to the Poliesportiu Marítim sports centre (and next to the hospital), is a bit of a find amidst the chain bars and pricey restaurants. 2min from the beach, with a sunny *terrassa*, it's the spot for great coffee, tapas and sandwiches, or the salad bar and light meals at lunch. Mon–Sat 8am–9.30pm, Sun 8.30am–5pm.

Poble Nou

El Tío Ché Rambla Poble Nou 44–46 ☎933 091 872; Ⓜ Poble Nou, or bus #36 from Ⓜ Barceloneta. Famous old *orxateria* in a down-to-earth neighbourhood that's a bit off the beaten track – though you can stroll up easily enough from Bogatell beach (15min). Orange or lemon *granissat* and *orxata* come in various servings up to a litre, and there are also *torrons* (almond fudge), hot chocolate laden with cream, coffee, croissants and sandwiches – order and pay at the counter and grab an outdoor seat on the street corner. Daily 10am–midnight; reduced hours in winter.

Eixample

Café del Centre c/Girona 69 ☎934 881 101; Ⓜ Girona. Formerly a casino, later converted into a café, but retaining its *modernista* wood decor. It's a couple of blocks from the tourist sights, but a good stop for *pa amb tomàquet*, coffee, or lunchtime *platos del día*. Mon–Fri 7am–1am, Sat 7pm–1am.
Forn de Sant Jaume Rambla de Catalunya 50 ☎932 160 229; Ⓜ Passeig de Gràcia. Glittering windows piled high with goodies from this classic old *patisseria* and *bomboneria* – croissants, cakes and sweets, either to take away or eat at the busy little adjacent café. Mon–Sat 9am–9pm.
Laie Llibreria Café c/Pau Claris 85 ☎933 027 310; Ⓜ Urquinaona. Head up the stairs in front of the bookshop, past the light fittings in coffee cups, and your choice is the bar and mezzanine seating or the roomier salon at the back under bamboo matting. The buffet breakfast spread is popular, and there are set lunch and dinner deals, à la carte dining, Internet access, and magazines (*National Geographic* to *Marie Claire*) to browse. Mon–Fri 9am–1am, Sat 10am–1am.
Mauri Rambla de Catalunya 102 ☎932 151 020; Ⓜ Passeig de Gràcia. Art Nouveau deli specializing in cakes and pastries, with an attached café where you can try them all out. The brioche/croissant-plus-coffee deal (€1.50) runs until noon. Mon–Fri 8am–9pm, Sat 9am–9pm, Sun 9am–3pm.
Torino Pg. de Gràcia 59 ☎934 877 571; Ⓜ Passeig de Gràcia. Café modelled on a famous (now long gone) *modernista* hangout of the same name. Still serving good coffee and croissants, and with a sandwich bar for something more substantial, plus a summer street-side terrace. Daily 8am–11pm.
Valor Rambla de Catalunya 46 ☎934 876 246; Ⓜ Passeig de Gràcia. Ornate uptown chocolate specialist, serving the gentle folk since 1881. A warming hot choc and *xurros* sends you happily on your way on a chilly morning. Mon–Thurs 8.30am–1pm & 3.30–1pm, Fri–Sun 9am–midnight.

Gràcia

Bagel Shop Pl. Rius i Taulet 8 ☎932 176 101; Ⓜ Fontana. Stuffed bagels, muffins, pies and carrot cake – it's a good breakfast or snack stop, whether you eat in or get the goods to go and grab bench space in Gràcia's prettiest square. Mon & Wed–Fri 8am–10pm, Sat & Sun 10am–10pm; closed Tues.
Café del Sol Pl. del Sol 16 ☎934 155 663; Ⓜ Fontana. Hugely popular neighbourhood bar that sees action day and night. The seats outside provide a window onto the local comings and goings; otherwise you can cram in the bar until late. Daily 1pm–2.30am.
Mos Via Augusta 112 ☎932 371 313; FGC Plaça Molina. Self-service, designer style – graze the sleek counters, picking up a croissant or tuna turnover, or maybe one of the cooked dishes, pasta servings or seasonal salads, then repair upstairs, helping yourself to coffee from the *maquina* (regular or decaf). Finish off with a handmade chocolate, a house speciality; pay on your way out. Daily 7am–10pm.
Salambo c/Torrijos 51 ☎932 186 966; Ⓜ Joanic. Stylish neighbourhood drink-and-meet spot. The pre- and post-cinema crowd pops in for *cafetières* of coffee, sandwiches and meals, and there are lots of wines and *cava* by the glass. Upstairs, you can shoot pool. Daily noon–2.30am.

Tapas bars

Tapas are not a particularly Catalan phenomenon, and most **tapas bars** in the city are run by people from other parts of Spain, especially Galicia and the Basque country. That's not to say the tapas bars aren't any good – far from it – and jumping from bar to bar, with a bite to eat in each, is as good a way as any to fill up on some of the best food that the city has to offer. Done this way, your evening needn't cost more than a meal in a medium-priced restaurant – say €15–20 a head.

The oldest and most traditional tapas bars – or *tasques* – in the Barri Gòtic are down by the port, between the Columbus monument and the post office (ⓂDrassanes/Jaume I). Virtually anywhere here – along c/Ample, c/de la Mercè, c/d'en Gignas, c/del Regomir and their offshoots – is worth sampling, though make sure you know how much things are going to cost before you order. Most places have blackboards or price lists, but those that don't can turn out to be fairly steeply priced. Most tapas bars have their own specialities (including Basque tapas, or *pintxos,* bite-sized slices of baguette piled with various combinations of meat, cheese and fish held together with a cocktail stick – around €1.10 a go), so look at what the locals are eating before diving in. More Catalan in execution are the city's **llesqueries**. A *llesca* is a thick slice of country bread which is toasted, rubbed with garlic and tomato, and sprinkled with olive oil, and better known as *pa amb tomàquet* (bread with tomato). This is served in more upmarket bars, along with cured ham or cold cuts, cheeses or *escalivada* (roasted pepper, onion and aubergine).

Ramblas and the Barri Gòtic

Amaya Ramblas 20–24 ☎933 026 138; ⓂDrassanes. Restaurant on one side, smoke-filled tapas bar on the other, serving very good Basque seafood specialities at its stainless-steel bar – octopus, baby squid, clams, mussels, anchovies and prawns. You can wash the food down with a glass of cava. Daily 10am–12.30am.

Bar Celta Pulpería c/de la Mercè 16 ☎933 150 006; ⓂDrassanes. This no-nonsense Galician tapas bar specializes in octopus, fried *pimientos* (peppers) and heady regional wine. Eat at the U-shaped bar or at tables in the back room. It's best to ask prices as you go here – the food's good but the bill has a habit of mounting up, especially for out-of-towners. Mon–Sat 10am–1am.

Bar Central la Boqueria Mercat de la Boqueria, Ramblas, no phone; ⓂLiceu. The gleaming chrome stand-up bar in the central aisle is the venue for ultra-fresh *raciones* of market produce, served by blue-smocked staff who work at a fair lick. Breakfast, snack or lunch, it's all the same to them – salmon cutlets, sardines, calamari, razor clams, hake fillets, sausages, pork steaks, asparagus spears and the rest, plunked on the griddle and sprinkled with salt. It's the best show in the market, and is packed at lunchtime. Mon–Sat 6.30am–4pm.

Bodega c/del Regomir 11, no phone; ⓂJaume I. A great barn of a place with long wooden benches, where you're served jugs of wine as rough as a rat-catcher's glove – armed with which the student clientele play rowdy drinking games. Tues–Sun 1pm–2am; closed first two weeks of Aug.

Bodega la Plata c/de la Mercè 28 ☎933 151 009; ⓂDrassanes. Small and basic, open to the street, with a limited selection of food, and wine barrels piled up over the bar. Very popular with the locals and good value – the speciality here is sardines. Breakfast is an experience: take your own sandwich along and have a glass of wine. Daily 10am–4pm & 8–11pm.

Bodega Vasconia c/d'en Gignas 13, no phone; ⓂJaume I. Sawdust-and-tile bar where the TV is always on for the benefit of the idling locals, who look as if they've been coming here since 1941 (the date above the door). Slices of sausage, the good *boquerones* and a glass of Rioja are what you drop by for. Daily 10am–4pm & 8–11pm.

Irati c/Cardenal Casañas 17 ☏933 023 084; Ⓜ**Liceu.** Crowded brick-walled bar that has been around longer than most of the Basque-come-lately places – locals still think favourably of the *pintxos*, which run the gamut from country sausage to smoked salmon. There's a seasonally changing Basque menu in the restaurant if finger food isn't your thing. Tues–Sun noon–midnight; *pintxos* served noon–3pm & 7–11pm.

Pineda c/del Pi 16 ☏93 3024 393; Ⓜ**Liceu.** Old-fashioned grocery store with a tiny bar and a few tables at the back where the old guys hang out. Selections from the cured hams suspended over the counter are the thing to eat, with *pa amb tomaquet*; drink the powerful local wine. Mon–Sat 9am–3pm & 6–10pm.

Socarrena c/de la Mercè 21, no phone; Ⓜ**Drassanes.** There's often a party crowd in this Asturian bar, where you can sample strong goat's cheese, cured meats and excellent cider (*sidra*). Check out the waiter's contortionist, but traditional, pouring technique (over the back of his head), designed to aerate the cider – and water the floor. The strange alcoholic milk drink, *leche de pantera*, is available here, too. Daily 1.30–3pm & 6pm–3am.

Viñatería del Call c/Sant Domènec del Call 9 ☏933 026 092; Ⓜ**Jaume I.** A typical *llesquería*, serving *pa amb tomàquet* with cheese, ham, *escalivada*, fish, fried peppers and much more, plus a wide range of wines. Mon–Sat 6pm–1am.

Vinissim c/Sant Domènec del Call 12 ☏933 014 575; Ⓜ**Jaume I.** Good food (served as *raciones*) accompanied by fine wines available by the glass. Don't be afraid to ask for advice, as the staff will happily introduce you to lesser-known, but very good, Catalan wines. Set lunch available, too. Tues–Sun noon–4pm & 6pm–1am.

Sant Pere

Bar Mundial Pl. de Sant Agusti el Vell 1 ☏93 319 90 56; Ⓜ**Jaume I.** Simple seventy-year-old neighbourhood bar, famous for its seafood tapas and meals. The best bet is soup followed by a seafood platter and washed down with cold white wine. Mon & Wed–Sat 10am–11pm, Sun 10am–4pm; closed two weeks in mid-Aug.

Mosquito c/dels Carders 46 ☏932 687 569;

Ⓜ**Jaume 1.** Delicious tapas from all over Asia, including fragrant noodle salads, aubergine-and-coriander won tons and crispy spinach pakoras. Add friendly service, good music, relaxed atmosphere and reasonable prices, for a winning mixture. Wed–Sun 7pm–2am.

La Ribera

Can Paixano c/Reina Cristina 7 ☏933 100 839; Ⓜ**Barceloneta.** Unmarked stand-up bar (next to *Bazar Internacional*) where the drink of choice (all right, the only drink) is champagne. Don't go thinking sophistication – it might come in traditional champagne saucers (the sort of thing Dean Martin used to stack in a pyramid and then pour wine over), but this is a counter-only joint where there's fizz, tapas and tapas-in-sandwiches, and that's your lot. And who could want more? Mon–Sat 9am–10.30pm.

Euskal Etxea Placeta Montcada 1–3 ☏933 102 185; Ⓜ**Jaume I/Barceloneta.** A Basque restaurant and cultural centre specializing in *pintxos*, which are served around 12.30pm and 7.30pm. Fight for a place at the bar or join the crowds spilling onto the street. Tues–Sat 9am–11pm, Sun 12.30–4.30pm.

Orígens 99.9% c/Vidrieria 6–8 ☏933 107 531; Ⓜ**Jaume.** Proclaims itself to be a "Catalan gastronomic space", which – together with the name – means that everything you eat is Catalan, pure and simple. An old stone arch divides the spaces, one side a shop for Catalan wine and supplies, the other a tavern-bar for tasting-plate dishes of minted beans, baked aubergine, duck with turnips, rabbit and thyme, roast tuna, and the like. There are some outside tables but they never get the sun. Daily 12.30pm–1.30am.

Xampanyet c/de Montcada 22 ☏933 197 003; Ⓜ**Jaume I/Barceloneta.** Blue-tiled bar doing a roaring trade in sweet sparkling wine by the glass or bottle and local *sidra.* Salted anchovies are the house speciality, but (amongst other highlights) there's also marinaded tuna, spicy mussels, sun-dried tomatoes, sliced meats and cheese, and *pa amb tomàquet.* As is often the way, the drinks are cheap and the tapas turn out to be rather pricey, but there's always a good buzz about the

place. Tues–Sat noon–4pm &
6.30–11pm, Sun noon–4pm; closed Aug.

Barceloneta

Jai-Ca c/Ginebra 13 ☏932 683 265;
ⓂBarceloneta. There's often a bit of a scrum
in this traditional local bar, but you can usually get a view of the tapas list on the wall or
just check what your neighbour's having – a
bundle of *navajas* (razor clams), say, or some
plump anchovies. Meanwhile, the fryers in
the kitchen work overtime, turning out crisp
chipirones (baby squid) and little green peppers scattered with salt. Take your haul to a
tile-topped cane table, or outside onto the
tiny street-corner patio. Daily 10am–11pm.
Vaso de Oro c/Balboa 6 ☏933 193 098;
ⓂBarceloneta. If you can get in this corridor
of a bar you're doing well (Sunday lunch is
particularly busy), and there's no menu or
list, so order the *patatas bravas*, some thick
slices of fried sausage and a dollop of tuna
salad and you've touched all the bases. Tall
schooners of own-brewed beer come either
light or dark. Daily 9am–midnight.

Poble Sec

Quimet i Quimet c/Poeta Cabanyes 25 ☏934
423 142; ⓂParal.lel. The neighbourhood's
nicest tapas joint, with bottles stacked five
shelves high – there's a chalkboard menu of
twenty wines by the glass – and little plates
of food served from the minuscule counter.
Order a roast onion, a marinaded mushroom or two, stuffed cherry tomatoes,
grilled aubergine and anchovy-wrapped
olives – classy finger food for the discerning
nibbler. Tues–Sat noon–4pm & 7–11pm,
Sun noon–4pm.

Eixample

ba-ba-reeba Pg. de Gràcia 28 ☏933 014 302;
ⓂPasseig de Gràcia. A big range of tapas,
from all corners of Spain, spreads along a
20m bar in this slick, industrial-sized operation. It sees a lot of business and shopping
traffic, and caters for all needs from breakfast
to supper time and beyond. Daily
7.30am–1.30am.
Barrils c/d'Aribau 89 ☏934 531 091;
ⓂProvença. Hanging hams and barrels set
the tone inside, and the stuffed boar and
moose keep watch on punters tucking into
good, country-style tapas – cured meats a

speciality. A sheltered *terrassa* provides a
breath of fresh air. Daily 9am–2am; closed
Tues, and first two weeks in July.
Berriketa Gran Via de les Corts Catalanes 596
☏933 424 144; ⓂUniversitat. Basque-run
establishment with well-made and reasonably
priced *pintxos*, including *chistorra* (spicy
sausage) from Pamplona. *Txacolí* (Basque
white wine) is the stuff to drink with it. There's
a restaurant, too (1–4pm & 8.30pm–midnight),
with a €12 *menú del dia*. Daily 8am–1am.
Bodegueta Rambla Catalunya 100 ☏932 154 894;
ⓂDiagonal. Long-established basement
bodega with *cava* by the glass, a serious
range of other wines, and good ham, cheese,
anchovies and *pa amb tomàquet* to soak it all
up. The battered marble tables and old stools
are soon occupied – you may have to stand
to snack, or take a seat outside on the *rambla*.
Daily 8am–2am; closed mornings in Aug.
Casa Alfonso c/Roger de Llúria 6 ☏933 019
783; ⓂUrquinaona. It's about half-past 1930
in *Alfonso's* – bar and *xarcuteria* up front,
country-style wood-panelled dining room at
the rear. Tapas, of course, but also two-
person platters (like mixed cheeses or
smoked fish), slices straight from the
hanging ham, or selections from the grill,
served with garlic or *romesco* sauces.
Mon–Fri 8am–1am, Sat noon–1am.
Ciudad Condal Rambla de Catalunya 18 ☏933
181 997; ⓂPasseig de Gràcia. Describes itself
as a *cerveceria* (and indeed has twenty beers
available), but that's only half the story in this
cavernous city pit stop. Breakfast sees the
bar groan under the weight of a dozen types
of crispy baguette sandwich, piled high on
platters, supplemented by a cabinet of croissants and pastries, while the tapas selection
ranges far and wide, *patatas bravas* to
octopus. Daily 7.30am–1.30am.
Quasi Queviures Pg. de Gràcia 24 ☏933 174
512; ⓂPasseig de Gràcia. Mega grocery-cum-
brasserie, where you can choose from a
large range of tapas at the bar and then buy
your cheese or cold meats at the *xarcuteria*
counter. Buffet breakfast and well-priced
meals (say, tuna steak or lamb brochette)
served in the rear restaurant; it's pricier to sit
out at the pavement tables. Daily
7.45am–2am.

Gràcia

Roble c/Luis Antunez 7, corner c/de la Riera de
Sant Miquel ☏932 187 387; ⓂDiagonal.

Roomy L-shaped bar on a busy corner with locals popping in for a snack and a chat. Big tapas/*raciones* selection served promptly at your table (order at the bar; there's a list on the wall) or nudge your way up to the counter and peruse the day's specials. Mon–Sat 7am–midnight.

Sarrià

Bar Tomás c/Major de Sarrià 49 ℗932 031 077; FGC Sarrià. It requires a special trip to the 'burbs (12min on the train from Pl.

Catalunya FGC station) but it has to be done for a taste of the *patatas bravas* of the gods – a dish of fried potatoes with garlic mayo and *salsa picante* for €1.55. It's not all they serve in this utterly unassuming, white-Formica-table bar (the *tuna empandillas* are great, as are the *croquetas* and Catalan sausage), but it might as well be, as that's what the queues are for. They fry between noon and 3pm and 6pm and closing, so if it's *bravas* you want, note the hours. Daily except Wed 8am–10pm.

Restaurants

The most common restaurants in Barcelona are those serving local **Catalan** food, though more mainstream Spanish dishes are generally available too. The feature on p.185 provides a rundown of specialities, while for a **menu reader** turn to p.282. **Regional Spanish** and **colonial Spanish** cuisine is fairly well represented, too, from Basque and Galician to Cuban and Filipino, while traditionally the fancier local restaurants have tended towards a refined Catalan-French style of dining. This has been superseded recently by the two dominant trends in contemporary Spanish cooking, namely the food-as-chemistry approach pioneered by superchef Ferran Adrià (see p.186) and the more accessible tendency towards so-called "fusion" cuisine (basically Mediterranean flavours with exotic touches). Other specialist places to note are the city's *marisqueríes* (*marisquerias*), which concentrate on fish and seafood, and the traditional taverns where grilled chicken and meats are the house speciality. The range of **foreign and ethnic** restaurants is not as wide as in other European cities, with Italian, Chinese, Middle Eastern and Indian/Pakistani food providing the main choices, though the cuisines of Latin America, North Africa, Southeast Asia and Japan are also represented. **Vegetarians** have the run of many of the Italian or ethnic restaurants, as well as a dozen or so specialist vegan and vegetarian eating places (see feature opposite).

It's always cheapest to eat at lunchtime, when the **menú del dia** is on offer (usually Mon–Fri, unless otherwise stated in the reviews below). For €8 or €9 you'll have virtually the run of the city, though the same three-course meal at dinner in the same restaurant might cost three times as much. If your main criteria are price and quantity, you'll need to seek out one of the declining number of simple workers' dining rooms – often only open at lunchtime – or

Restaurant prices

The restaurant listings in this chapter are divided into price categories. As a rough guide, you'll get a three-course meal (per person) excluding drinks for:

Inexpensive Under €15
Moderate €15–30
Expensive €30–45
Very expensive Over €45

Do bear in mind that the lunchtime *menú del dia* usually allows you to eat for much less than the price category might lead you to expect (and often includes a drink); check the listings for details.

The restaurants listed below are the pick of the specifically vegetarian places in Barcelona, but you'll also be able to do pretty well for yourself in regular tapas bars and modern Catalan brasseries and restaurants. Some salads and vegetable dishes are strictly vegan – like *espinacs a la Catalana* (spinach, pine nuts and raisins) and *escalivada* (roasted aubergine, onions and peppers). Otherwise, there are plenty of Middle Eastern and Indian/Pakistani restaurants, where you can order veg curries or a falafel-stuffed pita, while pizza restaurants will serve you a vegetarian pizza without cheese – ask for *vegetal sense formatge* (*vegetal sin queso*).

Arco Iris c/Roger de Flor 216, Eixample ☎934 582 283; Ⓜ Verdaguer. Simple café serving a low-cost, four-course lunchtime veggie *menú del dia* for €8.20 (drinks extra). Typically, you'll start with a cream of vegetable soup or consommé, and finish with fresh fruit. Mon–Sat 1–4pm; closed Aug. Inexpensive.

L'Atzavara c/Muntaner 109, Eixample ☎934 545 925; Ⓜ Provença. Lunch-only spot for fresh-tasting vegetarian dining on proper tablecloths. It's a bit more gourmet than many similar places: you pay €8.10 and choose from half a dozen starters and soups, three mains (stuffed peppers, say, or a vegetarian *fideuà*) and four puds. Drinks are another €1 on top – an all-round bargain. Mon–Sat 1–4pm. Inexpensive.

Biocenter c/Pintor Fortuny 25, El Raval ☎933 014 583; Ⓜ Liceu. One of the longest-running Raval veggie places, *Biocenter* now serves its good-value meals in an agreeable restaurant-bar across the road from the original health-food store. The €7.75 *menú* starts serving at 1pm, with a trawl through the salad bar the best option for a first course, followed by market-fresh mains. Mon–Sat 9am–5pm. Inexpensive.

Comme-Bio Via Laietana 28, Sant Pere ☎933 198 968; Ⓜ Jaume I; branch at Gran Via de les Corts Catalanes 603, Eixample ☎933 010 376; Ⓜ Passeig de Gràcia. Restaurant, juice and sandwich bar within a big store selling organic fruit and vegetables, health foods and related items. The buffet lunch spread

(Mon–Sat 1–3.45pm, Sun 1.15–4pm; €8.45) is the big attraction, though there's also a restaurant menu, served a bit more formally. Mon–Sat 8am–11.30pm, Sun noon–11.30pm. Moderate.

Illa de Gràcia c/Sant Domènec 19, Gràcia ☎932 380 229; Ⓜ Diagonal. Decorative harmony reigns in this spacious, sleek vegetarian dining room, where the food is a cut above – think grilled tofu, stuffed aubergine gratin or wholewheat spaghetti *carbonara*. The veggie lasagne is a weekend special (when this place buzzes) and the tofu burger also comes highly recommended. Tues–Fri 1–4pm & 9pm–midnight, Sat & Sun 2pm–midnight; closed mid-Aug to mid-Sept. Inexpensive.

Juicy Jones c/Cardenal Casañas 7, Barri Gòtic ☎933 024 330; Ⓜ Liceu. Veggie-vegan restaurant/juice bar with a €7 *menú del día* that touches all corners of the world – cashew, carrot and coriander soup could be followed by pumpkin-stuffed gnocchi. The restaurant part of the operation inhabits a mural-and-graffiti-ridden cellar at the back – juices are squeezed and soy milkshakes whizzed at the front bar. Daily 10am–midnight. Inexpensive.

Sesamo c/Sant Antoni Abat 52, El Raval ☎934 416 411; Ⓜ Sant Antoni. Innovative vegetarian cooking that will please the most discerning palate. The recipe: fresh, organic ingredients and influences from all over the globe. The three-course *menú del dia* is €8. Mon & Wed–Sat 1pm–1am, Sun 7pm–1am.

eat in a bar or café, where meals often come in the form of a *plat combinat* (*plato combinado*) or "combined plate". There will be a shiny photograph of the dishes on offer – things like eggs, steak, calamari or chicken with fries and salad – usually served with bread and sometimes with a drink included, and you can expect to pay €4–6. Be warned that many cheaper restaurants and cafés might not provide a written menu, with the waiter merely reeling off the day's dishes at bewildering speed. To ask for a menu, request "*la carta*".

Opening hours for restaurants are generally 1pm to 4pm and 8.30pm to 11pm, though most locals don't eat lunch until 2pm and dinner at 9pm or 10pm. However, in tourist areas, and in entertainment zones like Maremàgnum and the Port Olímpic, restaurants tend to stay open all day and will serve on request. A lot of restaurants **close on Sundays or Mondays, on public holidays and throughout August** – check the listings for specific details but expect changes, since many places imaginatively interpret their own posted opening days and times.

If there's somewhere you'd particularly like to eat – certainly at the more fashionable end of the market – you should **reserve a table**. Some places are booked solid for days, or weeks, in advance. Finally, all restaurant menus should make it clear whether the seven percent **IVA** tax is included in the prices or not.

Ramblas and the Barri Gòtic

Inexpensive

Arc Café c/Carabassa 19 ☎ 933 025 204; ⓂDrassanes. One of the old town's best contemporary brasserie-bars, popular with students, travellers and arty types. The cuisine is a smorgasbord of Mediterranean flavours concocted by the two German owners. Breakfasts served until 1pm, otherwise a €7.50 *menú* and a seasonally changing à la carte choice. Mon–Thurs 9am–1am, Fri 9am–3am, Sat 11am–3am, Sun 11am–1am.

Jupiter c/Jupi 4 ☎ 932 683 650; ⓂJaume I. Inventive salads, sandwiches, pastas and crepes, plus Barcelona's best home-made cakes. It's very relaxed and cosy – you can also just huddle up on the sofa, sipping a glass of wine – but if you can't find a table here, try their other place around the corner, *La Luna de Jupiter*, Pl. dels Traginers 8. Tues–Fri 7pm–1am, Sat & Sun until 2am.

Venus Delicatessen c/Avinyó 25 ☎ 933 011 585; ⓂLiceu/Jaume I. A hip café, which gets crowded after 10pm – at other times, it's usually a relaxed spot to rest up awhile. The Med-bistro cuisine is good for vegetarians, with things like lasagne, couscous, moussaka and salads, and there's a weekday lunchtime *menú* for €8. Mon–Sat noon–midnight.

Moderate

Can Culleretes c/Quintana 5 ☎ 933 173 022; ⓂLiceu. Supposedly Barcelona's oldest restaurant (1786), serving good-value Catalan food in traditional surroundings that brings local families in droves, especially for Sunday lunch. There are lunch *menús* at €10.50 and

€13.50 (Tues–Fri only), with the pricier one also available in the evening, though à la carte prices are more than reasonable – only the house special, a seafood platter (raw, grilled and fried) at €21.50 a head (minimum two people), breaks budgets. Tues–Sat 1.30–4pm & 9–11pm, Sun 1.30–4pm.

Matsuri Pl. Regomir 1 ☎ 932 681 535; ⓂJaume I. Excellent Southeast Asian cuisine, including a very-good-value set menu at lunch. Service is friendly, and the wooden Indonesian-style furniture and terracotta colours make for a relaxed meal. Mon–Fri 1.30–3.30pm & 8–11.30pm, Sat 8–11.30pm.

Oolong c/d'en Gignas 25 ☎ 933 151 259; ⓂJaume I. Refined fusion food in an informal, quiet and elegant setting. The menu changes weekly, but Asian and South American flavours set the tone – things like Vietnamese shrimp rolls and chicken fajitas grab diners' taste buds. Daily 8pm–1am.

Paraguayo c/del Parc 1 ☎ 933 021 441; ⓂDrassanes. Specialities from Paraguay and Argentina; tender cuts of meat served on wooden boards, accompanied by potatoes roasted with oregano and butter, and the delicious *dulce de leche* for dessert. Plenty of pasta and salad dishes, too, including ravioli and gnocchi. Tues–Sun 1.30–4pm & 8.30pm–midnight.

Pitarra c/d'Avinyó 58 ☎ 933 011 647; ⓂDrassanes. A renowned Catalan restaurant in operation since 1890, lined with paintings and serving good, reasonably priced local food – from fish soup to jugged hare. About €20 a head, though more if you opt for *sarsuela* or the classier fish specials. Mon–Sat 1–4pm & 8.30–11pm.

Veronica c/d'Avinyo 30 ☎ 934 121 122; ⓂJaume I. Crispy pizzas (all bar one vegetarian) and

inventive salads – say *escalivada* on your
dough, and sunflower seeds, red cabbage,
onions and olives with mixed greens on the
side. Tables outside on funky Pl. George
Orwell catch the sun (and the square-
dwelling crusties) during the day; at night
there's a bit of a gay scene as the urban-chic
bar-restaurant comes into play. Daily
noon–1am; closed two weeks in Aug.
Vildsvin c/de Ferran 38 ☎933 179 407;
ⓂLiceu. A bit difficult to classify – "to drink,
to snack, to eat" runs the tagline – but its
clean interior Scandinavian lines and outdoor tables in a quiet covered passageway
are part of the attraction. It's a good breakfast stop (€3 buys a coffee, fruit juice and
flauta), while tapas lean towards the Nordic
(herring, German sausage, Bavarian pastry
rings, blinis), as do the reasonably priced
meals served down in the vaulted brick
cellar. This *has* to be the only place in town
serving smoked reindeer. Mon–Thurs & Sun
8.30am–3am, Fri & Sat 8.30am–2am.

Expensive

Agut d'Avignon c/Trinitat 3 ☎933 026 034;
ⓂLiceu. This old-fashioned, but highly rated
restaurant down an alley off c/d'Avinyó
serves up a varied mix of Catalan seasonal
produce and Continental-influenced dishes.
It's the Catalan classics that are worth investigating – goose with pears, duck with figs,
or chicken combined with prawns, with perhaps a garlic omelette or cream of oyster
soup to start. Daily 1–3.30pm & 9–11.30pm.
Café de l'Acadèmia c/Lledó 1 ☎933 198 253;
ⓂJaume I. Creative Catalan cooking in a
lovely stone-flagged old-town restaurant –
things like confit of *bacallà* with spinach

and pine kernels, or aubergine terrine with
goat's cheese, plus assorted grills, fresh
fish and rice dishes. The prices are very
reasonable and it's always busy, so reservations are essential (the luckiest diners get to
eat on the *terrassa*). Or come in the
morning for coffee and pastries. Meals
Mon–Fri 1.30–4pm & 8.45–11.30pm;
closed two weeks in Aug.
Caracoles c/Escudellers 14 ☎933 023 185;
ⓂLiceu/Drassanes. A cavernous Barcelona
landmark with spit-roast chickens turning
on grills outside, dining rooms on various
floors adorned with chandeliers and oils,
and an open kitchen straight out of Mervyn
Peake's *Gormenghast*. The restaurant
name means "snails", a house speciality,
and the chicken's good, too, but there's a
full Catalan/Spanish menu in a multitude of
languages. Service can be chaotic, to say
the least, and the best that can be said
about the whole affair sometimes is that it's
been an experience – you certainly won't
forget it. Daily 1pm–midnight.
Limbo c/de la Mercè 13 ☎933 107 699; ⓂLiceu.
Designer restaurant with an intimate feel, presenting an interesting fusion of modern and
traditional Catalan cuisine, like steak with blue
cheese and *mero* (perch) served in a
Thai-style curry. Tues–Thurs & Sun 9pm–midnight, Fri & Sat 9pm–1am.
Quatre Gats c/Montsió 3 ☎933 024 140;
ⓂCatalunya. The *modernista*-designed haunt
of Picasso and his contemporaries – the lofty
interior has rich furnishings and paintings,
and was the setting for Picasso's first public
exhibition. Now a pricey Catalan restaurant-
and-bar (lunchtime *menú* is €10) that some
find a bit disappointing, foodwise at least.
Mon–Sat 11am–2am, Sun 5pm–2am.
Salón c/L'Hostal d'en Sol 6–8 ☎933 152 159;
ⓂJaume I. Renovated old building with a
Gothic sort of feel, serving imaginative
dishes in a relaxed atmosphere. The menu
ranges far and wide from, say, rabbit with a
mole sauce and tacos to curried vegetables
with a yoghurt and coconut sauce. The
weekday lunchtime *menú* is €9.50; you can
stay late and drink at the bar, too. Mon–Sat
1.30–4.30pm & 8.30pm–midnight.
Shunka c/Sagristans 5 ☎934 124 991;
ⓂJaume I. The proof that Japanese food is
more than just sushi: mouth-watering
dishes (small portions) served to you by
highly professional staff who are willing to
explain how all these culinary marvels are

prepared. *Menú del dia* is €12. Tues–Sun 1.30–3.30pm & 8.30–11.30pm.

Tokyo-Sushi c/Comtal 20 ☎933 176 180; ⓂCatalunya. There are times when heavy-handed olive oil cookery just won't cut it, and that's when you want *Tokyo-Sushi*. Sit at the lacquerwood bar, or at the wooden tavern tables under paper globe lighting, and choose from a full Japanese menu. Best deal is undoubtedly the lunchtime €12 *menú*, which starts with salad and miso soup, follows up with a crisp tempura selection and then presents you with a small sushi/sashimi platter. Mon–Sat 1.30–4pm & 8–11pm; closed Aug.

Sant Pere

Inexpensive

L'Econòmic Pl. de Sant Agusti Vell 13 ☎933 196 494; ⓂJaume I. The beautifully old tiled dining room dates back to 1932, and makes the perfect surroundings for a hearty lunch, served up, as the name implies, for a very reasonable price – €7.60 for a three-course meal and wine. Well-cooked standards (grilled pork or chicken escalopes, a fish of the dish) alternative with finer fare – like a pasta salad with black olive paste and salmon. It's nearly always full, but you can wait outside under the arcades until a table is free. Mon–Fri 12.30–4.30pm; closed Aug.

Moderate

Bunga Raya c/Assaonadors 7 ☎933 193 169; ⓂJaume I. Bamboo-decorated Malaysian and Indonesian restaurant, where the food is highly spiced and filling, and the house set meal at €12 is a bumper spread. However, the service is sometimes a bit slow. Tues–Sun 8pm–midnight.

Pla de la Garsa c/Assaonadors 13 ☎933 152 413; ⓂJaume I. Seventeenth-century stone-and-beam house that's a relaxing place to sip wine, eat pâté, cheese and sliced meats, and enjoy the classical music. The *menú degustación* – for a selection of the choicest cuts and dishes – is €13 (€20 if you add drinks and dessert). Daily 8pm–2am.

La Ribera

Inexpensive

Bar Salvador c/dels Canvis Nous 8 ☎933 101 041; ⓂJaume I/Barceloneta. So cheap, so good – fillets of *mero* (perch) in egg batter,

grilled steak with potato wedges, huge plates of *escalivada*, chickpeas with sausage, cod fishcakes, or garlic chicken, are examples from a changing menu of six or seven starters, six or seven mains and a few classic puds. Everything is in the €3.30–4.30 range (apart from the wine, somehow even cheaper) which is why tables in the chatter-filled dining room are packed at lunch, but you shouldn't have to wait long. Lunch starts at 1.30pm – before that, it's filled crusty sandwiches and the odd hot dish for Catalan breakfast. Mon–Fri 9am–5pm.

Café de la Ribera Pl. de les Olles 6 ☎933 195 072; ⓂBarceloneta. Tables outside in the pretty square, by a couple of spreading trees and a house with a Gothic tower-window, are the main attraction – a prime spot in the sun for reasonably priced tapas and *platos*, including a creamy ground-beef-topped aubergine with rice, good *patatas bravas* and stuffed squid. Tues–Sat 11am–1am.

Casa Delfin Pg. del Born 36 ☎933 195 088; ⓂJaume I/Barceloneta. Old-school paper-tablecloth bar-restaurant that packs in the locals for a cheap-and-cheerful *menú del dia* with plenty of scope for dithering – up to ten fish and ten meat choices, from grills to stews, preceded by mountainous servings of stomach-fillers like *arroz a la cubana* (rice with tomato sauce and fried egg) and topped off by home-made desserts or fruit. Mon–Sat 8am–5pm; closed Aug.

Moderate

Al Passatore Pl. del Palau 8 ☎933 197 851; ⓂBarceloneta. Queues form here in good weather (and on Sunday) so get your name on the list if you want an outdoor table. The pizzas are immense, and there's pasta, risotto, meat and fish too (all reasonably priced) with gluggable house wine. Mon–Wed 1pm–12.30am, Thurs–Sun 1pm–1am.

Mar de la Ribera c/Sombrerers 7 ☎933 151 336; ⓂJaume I. A friendly little place around the back of Santa Maria del Mar serving the best Galician-style seafood at prices that encourage large, leisurely meals. Try any of the simple steaks and fillets – hake, salmon, tuna, sole, calamari – dressed with oil, garlic and chopped parsley, accompanied by tasty platters of grilled vegetables. Mixed fried fish and paella are also highly recommended, while the daily *menú del dia* (including a rice dish) goes for around €9. Mon 8–11.30pm, Tues–Sat 1–4pm & 8–11.30pm.

Catalan food and dishes

Traditional Catalan food is solid and nourishing, with heavy emphasis on meat, olive oil, garlic, fruit and salad. The cuisine is typified by a willingness to mix flavours, so savoury dishes cooked with nuts or fruit are common, as are salads using both cooked and raw ingredients.

Meat is usually either grilled and served with a few fried potatoes or salad, or – like ham – cured or dried and served as a starter, or in sandwiches. Grilled sausage served with a pool of stewed haricot beans is a classic menu item in traditional taverns. Stewed veal and other casseroles are common, while poultry is often mixed with seafood (chicken and prawns) or fruit (chicken/duck with prunes/pears) for tastes very definitely out of the Spanish mainstream. In the mountains (and in some good city restaurants) **game** is also available, especially partridge, hare, rabbit and boar.

Surprisingly, fresh **fish and seafood** is almost always expensive, since much of it is imported despite the local fishing industries up and down the Catalan coast. However, you'll be offered hake, tuna, squid or cuttlefish even in cheap restaurants, and the local anchovies are superb, available in most tapas bars. Cod is often salted and turns up in *esquiexada*, a summer salad of *bacallà* (salt cod), tomatoes, onions and olives. Fish stews are a speciality in certain restaurants, though the mainstays of seafood restaurants throughout the city are the rice- and noodle-based dishes. **Paella** comes originally from Valencia, but as that region was historically part of Catalunya, the dish has been enthusiastically adopted as Catalunya's own. More certainly Catalan is **fideuà**, thin noodles served with seafood in a flat pan – you stir in the fiery *all i olli* (garlic mayonnaise) provided. **Arròs negre** (black rice) is another local delicacy: rice cooked with squid in squid ink.

Vegetables rarely amount to more than a few French fries or boiled potatoes with the main dish, though uniquely Catalan vegetable dishes do appear on some menus, from Catalan spinach (tossed with raisins and pine nuts) to *samfaina*, a ratatouille-like stew. Spring is the season for **calçots**, huge spring onions, which are roasted whole and eaten with a spicy *romesco* dipping sauce. Autumn sees the arrival of **wild mushrooms**, mixed with rice, omelettes, salads or scrambled eggs. In winter, a dish of stewed beans or lentils is also a popular starter, almost certainly flavoured with bits of sausage, meat and fat. Or you can start your meal with a **salad** or a platter of sliced, cured meats and cheese.

The **best dessert** is often fresh **fruit**, especially in summer, when you can expect a choice of melon, watermelon, peach, apricot, pear and orange. There's always *crème caramel (flam* in Catalan) – fantastic when home-made – though *crema Catalana* is the local choice, more like a crème brûlée, with a caramelized sugar coating. Or you might be offered *música*, nuts and dried fruit served with a glass of sweet *moscatel* wine.

Check the **food glossary**, p.282, for help when faced with a restaurant menu; it gives all the basic food words and plenty of Catalan specialities, too. For details of **how to cook** Catalan food, see p.265.

Salero c/Rec 60 ☎933 198 022; Ⓜ Barceloneta. Mediterranean cuisine with subtle Asian touches, presenting delights like an aubergine curry with coconut or a *mee goreng* (fried noodle) of the day. It's a crisp, modern space – if white is your colour, you'll enjoy the experience – with a cool and relaxed atmosphere. Open from 9am Mon–Fri for cakes and sandwiches. Meals Mon–Fri 1–4pm & 9pm–midnight, Sat 9pm–midnight.

Senyor Parellada c/Argenteria 37 ☎933 105 094; Ⓜ Jaume I. Utterly gorgeous renovation of an eighteenth-century building has kept the arcaded interior and splashed the walls yellow. Food is Catalan through and through – *sepia* (cuttlefish) and *bacallà* (cod), duck with figs, a *papillote* of beans with herbs – served from a long menu that doesn't bother dividing starters from mains. No less than fourteen puds await those who struggle through. Daily 1–4pm & 8.30pm–midnight.

Expensive

Arrel del Born c/Fusina 5 ☎933 199 299; Ⓜ**Barceloneta.** Lovely, light-filled contemporary restaurant with a roomy warehouse-style interior, opposite the old Born market. Fish is the speciality here, exquisitely cooked, and if there's a rice dish on the menu you should choose it. The *menú del dia* is €15, weekends €21. Mon–Sat 1–4pm & 8.30pm–midnight, Sun 1–4pm.

Espai Sucre c/de la Princesa 53 ☎932 681 630; Ⓜ**Jaume I.** The "Sugar Space" takes the current fad for food deconstruction off at a tangent by serving pretty much just dessert – inspired creations by Jordi Butrón, who assembles flavours and textures with the skill of a magician. There's a three-course (€21) or five-course (€32) seasonally changing pudding menu, with a small selection of savoury "mains" to pad out the experience. Ask about the dessert demos, usually at 5pm before that night's dinner. Tues–Sat 9pm–midnight.

Set Portes Pg. d'Isabel II 14 ☎933 192 950 or 933 193 033; Ⓜ**Barceloneta.** A wood-panelled classic with the names of its famous clientele inscribed on plaques above the seats. The decor in the "Seven Doors" has barely changed in 150 years and, while very elegant, it's not exclusive – you should book ahead, though, as the queues can be horrendous. The rice dishes are famed – with seafood, vegetables or squid ink – as is the *fideuà* with shrimps. These are fairly reasonably priced (€11–16), but for a full meal you're looking at around €30 a head and up, plus drinks. Daily 1pm–1am.

Very expensive

Comerç 24 c/Comerç 24 ☎933 192 102; Ⓜ**Jaume I.** The extraordinary creations served here might be termed designer tapas, served in an eye-catching modern interior. Chef Carles Abellan presents "glocal" cooking (ie global + local); in other words, dishes from across the world, interpreted locally by a master of invention. For anyone unable to make it to *El Bulli* (see box), this might just be as good as it gets – and at about half the price. Tues–Sat 1.30–3.30pm & 8.30pm–12.30am.

Passadís del Pep Pl. del Palau 2 ☎933 101 021; Ⓜ**Barceloneta.** Hidden down a passageway on the square, with no sign and hardly visible from the street. There is no menu; instead you are offered wonderfully prepared shellfish, landed at local ports, and fish dishes that change every day, prepared with squeaky-fresh seasonal ingredients. Reservations essential; expect to pay around €70 a head. Tues–Sat 1.30–4pm & 9–11.30pm.

What's cooking?

The best chef in the world, by common consent, is Catalan. **Ferran Adrià**, a self-taught chef from Barcelona, presides over *El Bulli*, his triple-*Michelin*-starred restaurant just outside the town of Roses on the Costa Brava. Dinner here costs €150 a head, not including drinks, but it's barely worth worrying about the price because the tables are booked solid until the next millennium. It's strange, because what Adrià does is less like cooking and more like chemistry, spending the winter months each year when the restaurant is closed refining his techniques in his Barcelona "laboratory". He is the man responsible for breaking down dishes into their constituent ingredients and then playing with them – turning food into foam, distilling vegetable essence into gelatin blocks, injecting a seafood reduction into Rice Krispies, or adding herbs or cheese to ice cream. You're either going to think this is fantastic or plain ridiculous, but Adrià has spawned a generation of young regional Spanish chefs – Jordi Vilà, Paco Guzman, Andoni Luis Aduriz, Carles Abellan, Ramon Freixa, Xavier Pellicer – who are challenging contemporary tastes in an equally inventive fashion. This is hardly everyday dining, but if you're up to the challenge (and the prices), current new wave hot spots in Barcelona include **Abac** (c/del Rec 79–89, La Ribera ☎933 196 600), **Biblioteca** (c/Junta del Comerç 28, El Raval ☎934 126 261), **Comerç 24** (c/Comerç 24, La Ribera ☎933 192 102), **Espai Sucre** (c/de la Princesa 53, La Ribera ☎932 681 630), **El Racó d'en Freixa** (c/Sant Elies 22, Sant Gervasi ☎932 097 559) and **Santa Maria** (c/Comerç 17, La Ribera ☎933 151 227).

El Raval

Inexpensive

Fragua Rambla del Raval 15 ☎934 428 097; Ⓜ**Liceu/Paral.lel.** Classic old *bodega* with the smell of wood smoke in the air as the chefs go to work on the blackened range. Tables on the *rambla* are at a premium, especially at night, though this is a cosy winter's day kind of place, too. Food is standard Catalan – lots of chargrilling (vegetables as well as meat and fish), tapas and a short vegetarian menu (lasagne, spinach with bechamel sauce, spaghetti with garlic) – and the prices are low, even discounting the €6.95 *menú del dia* (€8.50 at night). Tues–Sun 1–4pm & 8pm–1am.

Mesón David c/de les Carretes 63 ☎934 415 934; Ⓜ**Paral.lel.** Down-to-earth Galician bar-restaurant that's a firm favourite with neighbourhood families who bring their kids before they can walk (or even eat). The €6 *menú* is a steal – maybe some lentil broth followed by a grilled, butterflied trout and home-made *flan* – though it's the octopus and the *combinado Gallego* ("ham, salami, ear") that has the locals purring. There's a bang on the clog-gong for anyone who tips. Daily except Wed 1–4pm & 8pm–midnight.

Pollo Rico c/de Sant Pau 31 ☎934 413 184; Ⓜ**Liceu.** It's been here forever and, while it's not to everyone's taste, if you're in the market for spit-roast chicken, fries and a beer or a glass of *cava*, served quick-smart at the bar, this is the place. The *menú del dia* is a real steal. Daily 10am–midnight.

Romesco c/Arc de Sant Augusti s/n ☎933 189 381; Ⓜ**Liceu.** Cheap-and-cheerful diner, where the *frijoles negros* (black beans) are the house speciality. If it's full, wait for a table at the bar. Mon–Sat 1pm–midnight.

Tres Bots c/de Sant Pau 42 ☎933 171 042; Ⓜ**Liceu.** An extensive list of Spanish and Catalan favourites served quickly and efficiently at tables at the back of a frills-free bar. The *menú del dia* (€5.95) can hardly be beaten for price, otherwise put together a nourishing meal – say, fish soup, grilled tuna, *flam* – for well under €10. Daily 7am–1am.

Moderate

ànima c/dels Angels 6 ☎933 424 912; Ⓜ**Liceu.** Funky joint with a modern interior and a young crowd, who come for the seasonally influenced fusion cooking – courgette flowers and mussels *tempura* followed by monkfish with a garlic and pistachio crust are typical summer dishes. It's a nice place for lunch (*menú del dia* €8), especially if you can get a table outside. Daily 1–4pm & 9pm–midnight.

Bar Ra Pl. de la Garduña ☎934 231 878; Ⓜ**Liceu.** Extremely hip restaurant-bar behind the Boqueria market, serving up eclectic world cuisine for lunch and dinner on a sunny patio. Breakfasts are good too, and it's a nice place to drop in for a drink outside meal times. Mon–Sat 9am–2am.

Can Lluís c/de la Cera 49 ☎934 411 187; Ⓜ**Sant Antoni.** Decorated with old cabaret posters (and a beckoning Groucho Marx on the counter), this simple Catalan tavern presents a long menu of traditional dishes, including *esqueixada* (a sort of salt-cod salad), squid sautéed with onions and cod baked with white beans. Special menus around the €20–25 mark offer a good range of dishes, though the weekday lunchtime *menú del dia* (€6, drinks extra) is a pretty cheap way to get acquainted with local tastes. Mon–Sat 1.30–4pm & 8.30–11.30pm.

Casa de la Rioja c/Peu de la Creu 8–10 ☎934 433 363; Ⓜ**Catalunya.** The Riojan Centre's contemporary-styled restaurant (wood-cladding and smoked-glass windows downstairs, ocean-liner-style upper dining room) introduces Barcelona to the regional food of La Rioja, like *empedrado* (a potato, pork, pimiento and onion broth) or grilled *jurel* (a white fish) smothered in anchovy paste. The lunchtime *menú del dia* (€8.50) is an absolute steal, with three courses, coffee and a bottle of, what else, Rioja. Or the bar is open beyond meal times (and late) for tapas – snails to veal, pepper and onion brochettes – and scrambled egg platters. Mon–Sat 1–4pm & 8–11pm; bar open from 9am and after 11pm.

Dostrece c/Carme 40 ☎933 017 306; Ⓜ**Liceu.** A changing menu of internationally inspired dishes served, in typical New Raval style, by sharp waiters in a cool bar-restaurant, with club downstairs. Good set menu at lunchtime, and on Sundays there's a Mexican brunch. Daily 1pm–3am.

Fil. Manila c/de les Ramelleres 3 ☎933 186 487; Ⓜ**Catalunya.** There's a token effort at bamboo cladding, but this resolute mom-and-pop Filipino

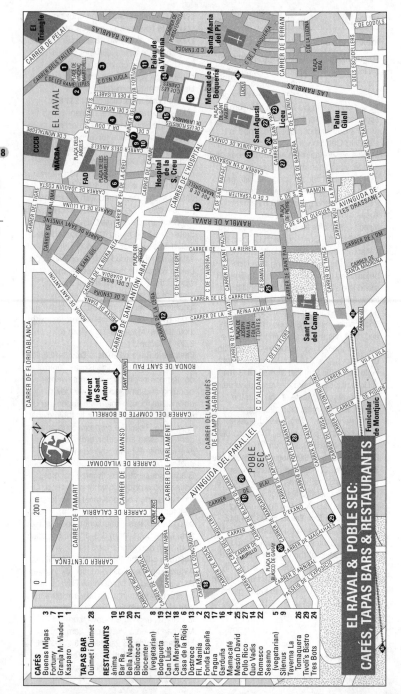

EL RAVAL & POBLE SEC: CAFÉS, TAPAS BARS & RESTAURANTS

CAFÉS
Buenas Migas 3
Fortuny 7
Granja M. Viader 11
Kasparo 1

TAPAS BAR
Quimet i Quimet 28

RESTAURANTS
ànima 10
Bar Ra 15
Bella Napoli 20
Biblioteca 21
Biocenter (vegetarian) 8
Bodegueta 19
Can Lluís 17
Can Margarit 18
Casa de la Rioja 6
Dostrece 13
Fil Manila 2
Fonda España 23
Fragua 16
Garduña 4
Mamacafé 25
Mesón David 27
Pollo Rico 14
Quo Vadis 22
Romesco 5
Sesamo (vegetarian) 9
Silenus 26
Taverna La Tomaquera 29
Tivoli's Bistro 24
Tres Bots

establishment is little more than an extension of the family kitchen – the radio or TV provides background, and the kids are fed alongside customers. Sizzling is what the menu does best, but there are warming soups, grilled fish in banana leaves, sautéed meat/fish with garlic sauce, barbecued pork ribs – all good hearty stuff. Daily 11am–4.30pm & 7.30pm–midnight; closed Tues.

Fonda España c/de Sant Pau 9–11 ☎933 181 758; Ⓜ**Liceu.** Eat in *modernista* splendour in the lavishly tiled dining room of a building designed by Domènech i Montaner. The decor is generally more memorable than the food, though the *menú del dia* is good value at €7.90 (a few euros more at night) – or you can take your custom across the hall to the *Salo Arnau* (less spectacularly decorated, though still with an amazing 5m-high sculpted fireplace), which has a *menú* that's €1 cheaper. Daily 1–4pm & 8.30pm–midnight.

Garduña c/Jerusalem 18 ☎933 024 323; Ⓜ**Liceu.** Tucked away at the back of the frenetic Boqueria market, this is a great place for lunch (when there's a €9 *menú del dia*; otherwise €12.50 at night) – basically, you're going to be offered the best of the day's produce at pretty reasonable prices and if you're lucky you'll get a window seat with market views. Mon–Sat 1–4pm & 8pm–midnight.

Mamacafé c/del Dr Joaquim Dou 10 ☎933 012 940; Ⓜ**Catalunya.** It looks like a spruced-up boiler room – aluminium ducts, concrete floor, bare colourwashed walls with a splash of art – but the modern Catalan food is pretty good and the atmosphere laidback. Mains cover everything from a house hamburger to salmon with Indonesian-style rice and, though prices are on the high side, ingredients are fresh and carefully judged. A good-value *menú del dia* is €8, and outside meal times (1–4pm & 9pm–midnight) it operates as a café. Mon–Sat 1pm–1am; Aug open evenings only.

Expensive

Biblioteca c/Junta del Comerç 28 ☎934 126 261; Ⓜ**Liceu.** The name's a nod to the library of cookbooks on display, and the menu has taken them to heart too – fish might be cooked Japanese- or Basque-style, clams paired with *jamòn*, lamb given the local treatment (with parsnip and

turnip), or venison pie served with a market-fresh purée of the day. This is one of the more agreeable of Barcelona's current dining hot spots – a €9 lunchtime *menú* provides a more simple experience. Tues–Sat 1–4pm & 9pm–midnight; closed two weeks in Aug.

Silenus c/dels Àngels 8 ☎933 022 680; Ⓜ**Liceu.** Very arty place near MACBA (it's not a menu, it's a "short treatise") presenting some unique dishes – squid with broad beans and *foie gras*, for example, or even fillets of that well-known Catalan marsupial, the kangaroo. The interior is very Barcelona (distressed walls, leather banquettes, white tablecloths laid on marble tables), yet prices remain reasonable, certainly for the quality and ambience, while if you come for lunch you can eat from the *menù del dia* for a shade over €10. Mon 1–4pm, Tues–Sat 1–4pm & 8.30–11.30pm.

Very expensive

Quo Vadis c/del Carme 7 ☎933 024 072; Ⓜ**Catalunya.** Very smart, very expensive and very formal. It's Catalan-French dining of the highest order, encompassing the refined (seabass with fennel) and the earthy (pig's trotters with turnip). A €27 *menù* includes a glass of *cava*, but otherwise you're looking at well over €40 – plus whatever you spend investigating the superb wine list. Mon–Sat 1.15–4pm & 8.30–11.30pm; closed Aug.

Poble Sec

Moderate

Bella Napoli c/Margarit 14 ☎934 425 056; Ⓜ**Paral.lel/Poble Sec.** Authentic Neapolitan pizzeria, right down to the cheery waiters and cheesy pop music, both Italian. The pizzas – the best in the city – come straight from the depths of a beehive-shaped oven, or there's a huge range of *antipasti*, pastas, *risotti* and veal *scaloppine*, with almost everything priced between €7 and €10. A regular Italian clientele tells you what a find this is. Tues–Sun 1.30–4.30pm & 8.30pm–12.30am.

Bodegueta c/de Blai 47 ☎934 420 846; Ⓜ**Poble Sec.** Catalan taverna with food like mother used to make – or her mum anyway, in the case of the selection of omelettes *a la yaya* (granny's omelettes). Otherwise, it's *torrades*, salads and grills in a good-natured, red-check-tablecloth-and-barrels kind of place. Tues–Sun 1–4pm & 8.30pm–midnight.

Can Margarit c/Concòrdia 21 ⓣ934 416 723; Ⓜ**Poble Sec.** This barn of a restaurant maintains a rustic feel, and is extremely popular with people wanting to celebrate (every now and again the lights will go off as a bottle of champagne lit by a sparkler is carried in). Help yourself to wine from the barrels at the entrance and eat from the simple Catalan menu – the rabbit with caramelized onions and herbs is an absolute must. Booking essential. Mon–Sat evenings only, two sittings at 9pm and 11.30pm; closed Aug.

Taverna La Tomaquera c/Margarit 58, no phone; Ⓜ**Paral.lel/Poble Sec.** Sit down in this chatter-filled tavern and the *pa amb tomàquet* arrives with a dish of olives and two quails' eggs – and there any delicacy ends as the sweaty chefs set to hacking steaks and chops from great sides and ribs of meat. The grilled chicken will be the best you've ever had, and the entrecôtes are enormous, while the locals limber up with pan-fried snails with *chorizo* and tomato, and add a side order of grilled artichokes for good measure. Tues–Sat 1.30–3.45pm & 8.30–10.45pm, Sun 1.30–3.45pm.

Tivoli's Bistro c/Magalhaes 35 ⓣ934 414 017; Ⓜ**Paral.lel/Poble Sec.** Tasty Thai cuisine, very reasonably priced, especially the *menú degustació* (€16), which incorporates three starters and four main dishes, including steamed fish and a pork red curry. The owners, a Catalan–Thai couple, also organize cooking classes. Tues–Fri 8.30pm–midnight, Sat 1.30–4pm & 8.30pm–midnight; closed mid-Aug to mid-Sept.

Port Vell and Barceloneta

Inexpensive

Can Ganassa Pl. de Barceloneta 4–6 ⓣ932 216 739; Ⓜ**Barceloneta.** Extensive range of tapas, snacks and *torradas* on Barceloneta's central square. It's a real all-dayer – card school over coffee, brandy and tortillas in the morning, a cheap and filling €6.90 *menú del dia* at lunchtime, and more expensive seafood dinners if you want. A bit rough-and-ready inside, where you can usually cut the smoke-filled air with a knife, but tables sprout in the square in summer. Daily except Wed 9am–11pm; closed Nov.

Moderate

Can Manel Pg. Joan de Borbó 60 ⓣ932 215 013; Ⓜ**Barceloneta.** An institution since 1870, which fills very quickly, inside and out, because the food is both good and reasonably priced – not always the case down here. Paella, *fideuà* and *arròs a banda* (minimum two people for each) are staples, but the grilled cuttlefish is great too; you'll push on into pricier territory if you plump for fresh grilled fish or *suquet* (casserole). There's a weekday lunchtime *menú* at €8.25, but there's usually not much fish or seafood choice on this. Daily 1–4pm & 8pm–midnight.

Can Ros c/Almirall Aixada 7 ⓣ932 215 049; Ⓜ**Barceloneta.** This is one of the best places to sample paella, *arròs negre* or a *fideuà* with clams and shrimp, all of which cost around €9. The tables are packed in close together, but it's a comfortable, no-hurry kind of place, which is just as well since it'll take an age to choose your meal – many decide to eat just from the fine list of tapas-style appetizers. Daily 1–5pm & 8pm–midnight; closed Wed.

dZi Pg. Joan de Borbó 76 ⓣ932 212 182; Ⓜ**Barceloneta.** It's pronounced "zhee", which is a Tibetan sacred stone, but the lovely fresh-tasting food is Southeast Asian, mainly Chinese, Malaysian and Japanese, either served in the small, serene dining room with its huge waterlily painting, or outside on the shady *terrassa*. Yu-shian pork with aubergine or Formosa-style shrimps with ginger are great bets – the most expensive dishes (€12) are huge langoustines, either grilled or drizzled in oyster sauce – with green-tea ice cream amongst the desserts. A weekday lunch *menú* costs €8.85. Daily 1–4pm & 8pm–midnight.

Expensive

Can Ramonet c/Maquinista 17 ⓣ933 193 064; Ⓜ**Barceloneta.** Reputedly the oldest restaurant in the port area, it has the added attraction of a *terrassa* on a square in the heart of Barceloneta. Full seafood meals can turn out pricey, but you can always compromise and hunker down in the front bar where the tapas is piled high on wooden barrels – the *pernil* (cured ham) is a house speciality. Daily 10am–4pm & 8pm–midnight; closed Sun dinner & Aug.

Gavina Pl. Pau Vila 1 ⓣ932 210 595; Ⓜ**Barceloneta.** Underneath the Palau de Mar arches, *La Gavina*'s huge, open-air terrace overlooks the yachts and up to the heights of Montjuïc – a great place to be on a hot day. Menu highlight is rice with lobster (€29), but if that's too rich for you there's also a whole range of less extravagant paellas, *fideuàs*, grilled fish and home-made desserts. Daily 1–4.30pm & 8–11.30pm.

Suquet de l'Almirall Pg. Joan de Borbó 65 ☎932 216 233; ⓂBarceloneta. Let the restaurant do the work for you by plumping for one of the set-menu deals that rattle through the highlights – the *menu ciego* (€27) gets you seven tapas samplers with *arròs* to follow, while the six-course *menú degustació* (€34) rounds things off with home-made chocolates. But you don't have to have the works – sweet peppers with anchovies, or a dish of steamed mussels, provide reason enough to linger in the shrub-fronted suntrap *terrassa*. Tues–Sat 1–4pm & 9–11pm, Sun 1–4pm.

Very expensive

Antiga Casa Solé c/Sant Carles 4 ☎932 215 012; ⓂBarceloneta. Founded in 1903, it was here that *sarsuela* (Catalan fish stew) was invented. Since then, the *Casa Solé* has been dishing up market-fresh fish and seafood, either in stews or casseroles (*suquets*) or simply grilled, sautéed or mixed with rice. It's a quiet, formal estab-lishment, set in a handsome building, but you'll be made very welcome. Count on a good €40 a head. Tues–Sat 1–4pm & 8–11pm, Sun 1–4pm.

Port Olímpic

Moderate

Agua Pg. Marítim 30 ☎932 251 272; ⓂCiutadella-Vila Olímpica. Depending on your mood (or the weather), you can choose the sleek, split-level dining room or seafront boardwalk garden. It's a contemporary Mediterranean menu – say, rice with quail, asparagus and mushroom, or grilled tuna *sofrito* (caramelized onions and tomato) – but the house hamburger figures too, alongside a short selection of tapas, pastas and salads. The prices are pretty fair, so it's usually busy. Daily 1.30–4pm & 8.30pm–midnight, Fri & Sat until 1am.

Expensive

Bestial c/Ramon Trias Fargas 2–4 ☎932 240 407; ⓂCiutadella-Vila Olímpica. Right under Frank Gehry's fish you'll find a pleasant terrace garden in front of the beach. Inside the stylish, minimalist interior you might have to share your table with other diners. The cooking's Mediterranean, mainly Italian, with dishes given an original twist. At the weekends

RESTAURANTS
Agua 7
Bestial 5
Cangrejo Loco 8
Lungomare 4
Escribà 2
Els Pescadors 3

CAFÉS
El Tio Che 1
Llaie Marítim 6

PORT OLÍMPIC:
CAFÉS & RESTAURANTS

you can stay on and drink until 3am. Daily
1.30–4pm & 8.30pm–midnight, Sat & Sun
until 1am.

Cangrejo Loco Moll de Gregal 29–30 ⊕932 210
533; ⓂCiutadella-Vila Olímpica. The large outdoor terrace or huge picture windows at the
"Crazy Crab" offer panoramas of the local
coast and marina. The fish and shellfish are
first-rate, with the catch changing daily, but a
mixed fried fish plate or broad beans with
prawns are typical starters. Paella can be
thoroughly recommended too, and the
service is spot-on. Daily 1pm–1am.

Lungomare c/Marina 16–18 ⊕932 210 428;
ⓂCiutadella-Vila Olímpica. Smart, but not intimidating, Italian restaurant at the foot of the
Mapfre tower, with great views over the
Olympic port. It's not so much spag bol and
rubbery calamari as home-made pasta with
fresh clams or roast monkfish with confit potatoes and black olive tapenade – so you're
looking at over €30 a head as well as at the
bobbing boats and harbour lights. Mon–Sat
1–4pm & 8.30pm–midnight, Sun 1–4pm.

Poble Nou

Moderate

Escribà Ronda del Litoral 42, Platja Bogatell
⊕93 221 07 29; ⓂCiutadella-Vila Olímpica, or
bus #36 from Port Vell. Glorified beach shack
– a *xiringuito* in the parlance – that's
enough off the beaten track (a 20min walk
along the prom from the Port Olímpic) to
mark you out as in the know. A tapas
tasting plate for two (€18) is popular, and
the paellas and *fideuàs* (€12) fly out of the
kitchen; daily fish specials are more like
€20, and there's a ten percent terrace surcharge, but what the hell: the food and
views are great. Tues–Sat 11am–1am, Sun
11am–4pm; restricted hours in winter.

Very expensive

Els Pescadors Pl. Prim 1 ⊕932 252 018;
ⓂPoble Nou. Considered something of a pilgrimage for fish-lovers, a meal at *Els
Pescadors* should certainly include a house
special *fideuà* or a Catalan classic like cod
with *samfaina* – though that's only just
scratching the surface of a wide-ranging
menu. If you don't go mad, you'll escape
for about €50. The restaurant is hidden
away in a pretty square with gnarled trees
in the back alleys of Rambla Poble Nou.
Daily 1–4pm & 8pm–midnight.

Eixample

Inexpensive

Flauta c/d'Aribau 23 ⊕933 237 038;
ⓂUniversitat. Bar at the front, dining room
at the back, this is a real local favourite for
the excellent-value €8.50 lunchtime *menú
del dia*, which shows a bit more adventure
than most in this price range. It's also a
good pit stop at any time for a stuffed *flauta*
– a thin, crispy baguette sandwich – or a
range of tapas. Mon–Sat 8am–1am.

Fresc Co c/València 263 ⊕934 881 049,
ⓂPasseig de Gràcia; branches at Ronda
Universitat 29 ⊕933 016 837; ⓂPasseig de
Gràcia; Avgda. Diagonal 449 ⊕934 106 106;
ⓂDiagonal. Packed-out self-service diners
with an enormous salad bar and selection
of pizzas, pastas and desserts. No atmosphere, apart from the general hubbub at
peak trough times, but you can pile your
plate high for €6.90 at lunch (Mon–Fri) or
€8.80 evenings and weekends. Daily
1–5pm & 8pm–1am.

Glop de la Rambla Rambla de Catalunya 65
⊕934 870 097, ⓂPasseig de Gràcia; Glop
Braseria c/de Casp 21 ⊕933 187 575,
ⓂCatalunya. Reliable downtown Catalan
tavern-style diners, with a similar menu to
their Gràcia parents (*torrades*, salads, grills)
but a tad more stylish and attracting a
grab-it-and-go city clientele. Daily 1–4pm &
8pm–1am.

Mussol c/Aragó 261 ⊕934 876 151, ⓂPasseig
de Gràcia; branch at c/de Casp 19 ⊕933 017
610, ⓂCatalunya/Passeig de Gràcia. Big rustic
diners of the type that's all the rage in the
city, known for their meat and vegetables *a
la brasa*, most of which run between €4
and €8. *Calçots* (big spring onions) are a
spring speciality; snails are on the menu all
year round. There are also *torrades*, home-
made puds, tapas – the usual Catalan
menu – and it opens early for sandwich-
and-croissant breakfasts for city workers.
Meals daily 1pm–1am.

Moderate

Al Diwan c/València 218 ⊕934 540 712;
ⓂUniversitat. Traditional Lebanese cuisine,
with all of the usual tabbouleh, hummous
and *kofta* dishes. The restaurant puts
together 8, 12 or 16 *platitos* (for 2, 3 or 4
people) for around €12 a head, which is a
better way to graze the menu, and things
liven up in the evening (Thurs, Fri & Sat)

with traditional belly-dancing. Mon–Fri 1–4pm & 8.30–11pm, Sat 8.30–11pm.

Muscleria c/Mallorca 290 ⊤934 589 844; ⓂVerdaguer. Barcelona's mussels specialist, with a score of sauces/toppings on pots and platters, accompanied by some of the best fries in the city, plus Asturian cider or Galician or Penedès wines. Sautéed clams, *pulpo*, fried *chipirones* or calamares are offered as starters, and there are a few salad-and-snack plates offered, but basically, if bivalves don't appeal, you're in the wrong place. And the black-and-terracotta basement is no place for a quiet tête-à-tête either. Mon–Fri 1–4pm & 8.30pm–midnight, Sat 8.30pm–1am.

Tramoia Rambla de Catalunya 15 ⊤934 123 634; ⓂCatalunya/Passeig de Gràcia. Fashionable multi-space eatery for anything from a coffee and croissant to a filling meal. Snack downstairs on tapas and *torrades* or head upstairs for Catalan brasserie food, including meat, fish and seasonal vegetables straight from the grill. It's a bit on the pricey side, but the staff are very accommodating, and it's a handy meeting point. Daily 7.30am–1.30am.

Xix Kebab c/Còrsega 193 ⊤933 218 210; ⓂHospital Clinic. Highly recommended Syrian restaurant serving couscous and less typical dishes in a pleasant but not over-done Middle Eastern setting. Mon–Sat 1.30–4pm & 9pm–midnight.

Expensive

O'Nabo de Lugo c/de Pau Claris 169 ⊤932 153 047; ⓂDiagonal. A la carte meals in this renowned Galician seafood restaurant can easily top €40, but the budget-conscious can snack on the excellent tapas or arrive at lunch when a mere €9 (only €7.60 if you eat in the bar) buys you the three-course *menú del dia*, drink included. Thick, meaty broth usually figures, and simple standards like *butifarra* and potatoes – for more choice (and for some fish), trade up to the €16.50 *menú especial*. The gruff waistcoated waiters tend to know the locals by name but show the same generosity to all, leaving the wine bottle on your table for refills. Mon–Sat 1–4pm & 8.30pm–midnight.

Thai Gardens c/Diputació 273 ⊤934 879 898; ⓂPasseig de Gràcia. Barcelona's favourite Thai restaurant. Enjoy an excellent lunch menu for under €12 (Mon–Fri only), or an all-out *menu degustació* for €25 – an English-language menu smoothes the way, offering things like a

creamy prawn and vegetable curry or fiery lamb strips cooked in Thai basil. Daily 1.30–4pm & 8.30–midnight, until 1am at weekends.

Tragaluz Ptge. de la Concepció 5 ⊤934 870 621; ⓂDiagonal. In-your-face, designer-space fashionable, with beautiful people by the score and a retractable roof, but the classy Mediterranean-with-knobs-on cooking doesn't disappoint. Cheaper eats come cour-tesy of the *Tragarapid* menu, where blinis or a club sandwich cater for those fresh off the *modernista* trail (La Pedrera is just across the way). Daily 1.30–4pm & 8.30pm–midnight, Thurs–Sat until 1pm.

Very expensive

Bice c/Consell de Cent 333 ⊤934 880 050; ⓂPasseig de Gràcia. Barcelona branch of the famous Milanese restaurant of the same name offers the best Italian cuisine in the city, changing with the seasons though always strong on *risotti*. Its two levels are sumptuously decorated with Tàpies originals and there is a summertime patio. Daily 1.30–3.30pm & 8.30pm–midnight.

Casa Calvet c/de Casp 48 ⊤934 124 012; ⓂUrquinaona. Dining in Gaudí's wonderfully decorated *Casa Calvet* is a glam night out. A seasonally changing, modern Catalan menu runs the gamut from simple (shrimp with home-made pasta and parmesan) to elaborate (duck livers with a balsamic vinegar reduction), and the desserts – some of which you have to order on arrival – are an artwork in themselves. Mon–Sat 1–3.30pm & 8.30–11.30pm.

East 47 *Hotel Claris*, c/Pau Claris 150 ⊤934 874 647; ⓂPasseig de Gràcia. The city's most hip hotel features an equally cutting-edge restaurant, serving creative Mediterranean cuisine under the gaze of a line of Warhol self-portraits. The beautifully presented, sea-sonally changing dishes mix flavours with seeming abandon – like salad leaves with crispy *yucca* (bamboo), or coffee-scented *bacallà* – while the fearsomely fashionable staff work hard at making you feel at home. Leave time for a drink in the cool bar down-stairs, too. Daily 1–4pm & 8–11.30pm.

Gràcia

Inexpensive

Ca l'Augusti c/Verdi 28 ⊤932 185 396; ⓂFontana. A popular local choice, with

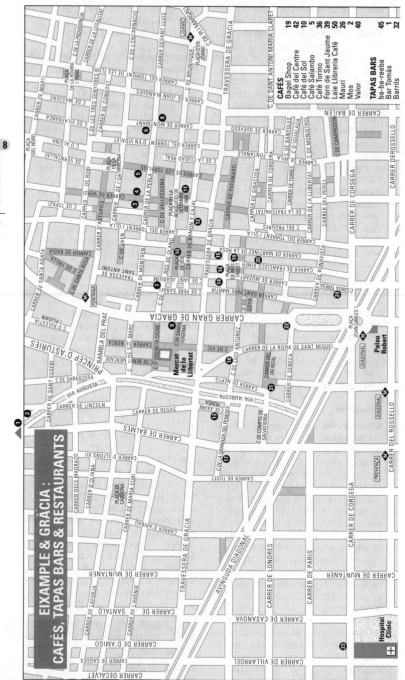

EIXAMPLE & GRÀCIA :
CAFÉS, TAPAS BARS & RESTAURANTS

CAFÉS	
Bagel Shop	19
Café del Centre	42
Café del Sol	10
Café Salambo	5
Café Torino	36
Forn de Sant Jaume	39
Laie Llibreria Café	50
Mauri	26
Mos	2
Valor	40

TAPAS BARS	
ba-ba-reeba	45
Bar Tomás	1
Barrils	32

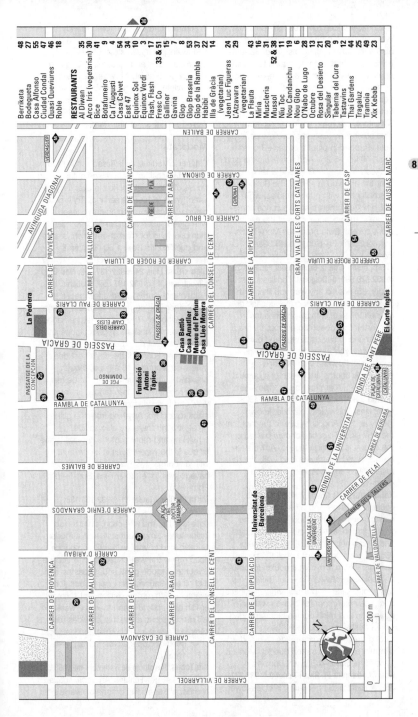

Berriketa	48
Bodegueta	27
Casa Alfonso	55
Ciudad Condal	47
Quasi Queviures	46
Roble	18

RESTAURANTS

Al Diwan	35
Arco Iris (vegetarian)	30
Bice	41
Botafumeiro	9
Ca l'Augusti	4
Casa Calvet	54
East 47	34
Equinox Sol	10
Equinox Verdi	3
Flash, Flash	17
Fresc Co	33 & 51
Galliner	7
Gavina	8
Glop	53
Glop Braseria	37
Glop de la Rambla	22
Habibi	14
Illa de Gràcia (vegetarian)	24
Jean Luc Figueras	29
L'Atzavara (vegetarian)	43
La Flauta	16
Miria	31
Muscleria	11
Mussol	52 & 38
Niu Toc	19
Nou Candanchu	6
Nou Glop	28
O'Nabo de Lugo	13
Octubre	21
Rosa del Desierto	20
Singular	9
Taberna del Cura	12
Tastavins	44
Thai Gardens	25
Tragaluz	49
Tramoia	23
Xix Kebab	

reasonably priced *torrades*, grilled meats, omelettes, and paella on Sunday. There's also a €7.50 lunchtime *menú del dia,* otherwise a couple of courses runs to €9 and upwards. Noon–4pm & 8.30pm–midnight; closed Tues dinner & all Wed.

Equinox Sol Pl. del Sol 14 ☎934 157 976; Equinox Verdi c/Verdi 21–23 ☎932 373 270; Ⓜ Fontana. Supreme falafels and *shawarma,* plus other delicious Lebanese dishes, available wrapped in pita for under €3 or as a "plat" (€4.50–5.25). Add some wicked (and wickedly cheap) *baklawa* and a tall glass of mint tea and you're all set. The Sol branch is smaller but with outside tables, while at *Equinox Verdi* there's always space somewhere in the various rooms of the exposed stone tavern. Both branches Mon–Thurs 6pm–2.30am, Fri–Sun noon–3.30am; closed Tues.

Flash, Flash c/de la Granada del Penedès 25 ☎932 370 990; Ⓜ Diagonal. Tortillas (most under €5) served any way you like, from plain and simple to elaborately stuffed or doused in salsa, with sweet ones for dessert. If that doesn't grab you, there's a small menu of salads, soups and burgers. Either way, you'll love the surroundings – very Austin Powers, with its white leatherette booths and monotone cutouts. Daily 1pm–1.30am, bar open 11am–2am.

Gavina c/Ros de Olano 17 ☎934 157 450; Ⓜ Fontana. This wacky pizzeria, known locally as "Els Angels" – due to the fact that the only sign is a series of *putti* pasted over the door – is a Gràcia legend. Arrive after 8pm and you will have a long wait, but no reservations are accepted. Tues–Sun noon–1am.

Habibi c/Gran de Gràcia 7 ☎932 179 545; Ⓜ Diagonal. Bright and breezy North African dining in a sky-blue interior with a corner water-garden, ten intimately placed tables and a summer *terrassa.* The *Plat Habibi* (€5.50) gives you a taste of all the house specials – from a minty tabbouleh to lamb and chicken *schawarma* – but there's plenty of choice for grazers and vegetarians alike; the *maghmour* (chickpeas with aubergine and mint) comes recommended. Add a fresh-squeezed juice (there's no alcohol served), a home-made *flam* and a mint tea and you're still on budget. Mon–Fri 1pm–1am, Sat 2–4.30pm & 8pm–1am.

Nou Candanchu Pl. Rius i Taulet 9 ☎932 377 362; Ⓜ Fontana. Sit beneath the clock tower

in summer and choose from the wide selection of local dishes – tapas and hot sandwiches but also steak and eggs, steamed clams and mussels, or cod and hake cooked plenty of ways. It's managed by an affable bunch of young guys, and there's lots of choice for €6–11, with a *menú del dia* at €6.65. Daily except Tues 7am–1am, Fri & Sat until 3am.

Moderate

Galliner c/Martínez de la Rosa 71 ☎932 185 327; Ⓜ Diagonal. Intimate restaurant in an old house offering cod cooked in over forty different ways (€10.70 a serving). Try it gratinated with creamed onion and cheese or with green sauce and clams, or you can plump instead for market-fresh fish, steaks and duck *confit.* Daily 1.30–3.30pm & 8pm–1am; closed Tues lunch & Sun dinner.

Glop c/Sant Lluís 24 ☎932 137 058; Nou Glop c/Montmany 49 ☎932 197 059; Ⓜ Joanic. Authentic tavernas within a few paces of each other. The original *El Glop* is a Rough Guide favourite – the rusticity (stone-flagged floors, beams, baskets of garlic) stops just the right side of parody and the €6.45 lunch *menú* is one of the city's best deals; otherwise around €15 a head, though cheaper if you're careful. In the large rear dining room, the kitchen ranges are open to view and busy waiters bear vast *torrada* slabs to and fro. Anything from the grill is great, though there are also salads, omelettes and more esoteric choices (snails or quail); the wine arrives in a *porrón* (a jug with a spout). At the weekend you may have to wait for a table. Tues–Sun 1–4pm & 8pm–1am.

Miria Pl. Rius i Taulet 11 ☎932 185 198; Ⓜ Diagonal. The sunny *terrassa* on the square is half the attraction, but it's nice inside too – simple but stylish, in a modern Catalan kind of way, with mellow sounds to accompany the well-priced food. A la carte favourites include great soups, pastas with a choice of sauces, designer salads (for example, with *romesco*-flavoured shrimps) or fish *en papillote* – and there's a weekend €7 *menú* (drinks extra) that provides three sample starters, main course and (amongst other treats) *turrón* ice cream. Daily 1–4pm & 7–11pm.

Níu Toc Pl. Revolució de Setembre de 1868 3 ☎932 137 461; Ⓜ Fontana. An *arròs, fideuà* and *bacallà* specialist on one of Gràcia's lesser-known squares. Outdoor tables fill quickly on hot days, while on Sundays neighbourhood families arrive to sample the special €20 *menú* that gives you a taste of the highlights – namely a cuttlefish and shrimp *fideuà*, followed by three *cazuelitas* (earthenware dishes) filled with differently styled cod. Daily 1–4pm & 8pm–midnight; closed Wed.

Octubre c/Julian Romea 18 ☎932 182 518; Ⓜ**Diagonal.** For romance and the food to go with it, it's hard to beat this warm, rustic little charmer. The Catalan menus are seasonal and somewhat unpredictable, but constants are the sensational desserts and the hard-to-beat prices – usually under €20 for three sparkling courses. Mon–Fri 1.30–3.30pm & 9–11pm, Sat 9–11pm; closed Aug.

Singular c/Francesc Giner 50 ☎932 375 098; Ⓜ**Diagonal.** Put together a meal from the list of dishes on the blackboard and you'll eat well for around €15. Come for supper before a night out in Gràcia's bars and clubs, like the rest of the young, lively clientele. Open 1–4pm & 9pm–midnight; closed Sat lunch & Sun.

Tastavins c/Ramon y Cajal 12 ☎932 136 031; Ⓜ**Fontana.** Small, select menu relying on top-drawer ingredients in a tavern where warm, personal service and a casual atmosphere set the tone. It's essentially traditional Catalan in flavour, though tuna in soy sauce and honey with won tons is an example of how far the kitchen ranges on occasion. The *menù del dia* is a good-value €8. Tues–Sat 1.30–3.30pm & 9pm–12.30am, Sun 1–4pm.

Expensive

Rosa del Desierto Pl. Narciso Oller 7 ☎932 374 590; Ⓜ**Diagonal.** Funky North African restaurant which puts its best efforts into the various couscous options – a "royale"

(€15.25) throws a bit of everything into the mix, though the veggie version is a few euros cheaper. Brochettes and other grills, plus a decent vegetarian choice, round off the menu. Tues–Sat 1–4pm & 9–11.30pm, Sun 1–4pm.

Taberna del Cura c/Gran de Gràcia 83 ☎932 181 799; Ⓜ**Fontana.** The more reasonably priced adjunct to the *Botafumeiro* next door, serving quality tapas (wild asparagus, a plate of juicy anchovies, the house snails) and grills in tavern-style surroundings. Prices soon edge up if you're going to tackle a fillet steak or shoulder of lamb, but there's a good-value lunchtime *menú*, which might see you served shellfish soup followed by fillet of salmon in a *cava* sauce. From the takeaway counter, order up spit-roast rabbit or chicken, country sausage, *tortilla* and *escalivada* at knock-down prices. Daily 1pm–1am.

Very expensive

Botafumeiro c/Gran de Gràcia 81 ☎932 184 230; Ⓜ**Fontana.** Justly famous for both its food and restrained and sophisticated atmosphere, this is perhaps Barcelona's best Galician seafood restaurant. Groaning glass cabinets full of fish and shellfish usher you in through the front door, and the huge menu – *arròs negro* and paellas included – should appeal to just about everyone, but if you want to let the restaurant decide, the *menú degustació* covers every option with exquisite class. Daily 1pm–1am, closed part Aug.

Jean Luc Figueras c/Santa Teresa 10 ☎934 152 877; Ⓜ**Diagonal.** Franco-Catalan cooking of the highest calibre, at the highest prices – reckon on at least €80 a head. It's a very sophisticated place, with a seasonally changing menu, which absolutely guarantees to delight. Mon–Fri 1.30–3.30pm & 8.30–11.30pm, Sat 8.30–11.30pm; closed Aug.

Drinking and nightlife

Whatever you're looking for from a night out, you'll find it in Barcelona, somewhere – bohemian boozer, underground club, cocktail bar, summer dance palace, techno temple, Irish pub or designer bar, you name it. If all you want is a drink, then any café or bar can oblige. We've already covered some of the finest cafés in the previous chapter, *Eating*, and undoubtedly one of the city's greatest pleasures is to pull up a pavement seat in the Barri Gòtic or in Gràcia and watch the world go by. But the bar scene proper operates at a different pace, and with a different set of rules.

Although there's often little discernible difference between a regular bar and a café, there's also a whole range of specialist **bars** in Barcelona – bodegas (specializing in wine), "pubs" and *cervecerías* (beer), *xampanyerías* (champagne and *cava*) and *coctelerías* (cocktails) – with the emphasis firmly on drinking rather than eating (though food is usually available). Best known of the city's nightlife haunts are its hip **designer bars**, while there's a stylish **club scene** that goes from strength to strength, fuelled by a potent mix of resident and guest DJs.

The lists below of bars and clubs provide a starting point for a decent night out in Barcelona, but you need to be aware that the scene changes rapidly. For full **listings**, get hold of a copy of the weekly *Guia del Ocio* from newsstands (out every Thursday), which covers current openings, hours and club nights in its "Tarde y Noche" section; it's in Spanish but easily decipherable. Bars, cafés, boutiques and music stores carry flyers, and you'll also be able to pick up an array of (sometimes short-lived) free magazines containing bar and club news and reviews. For the lowdown on **gay and lesbian** nightlife in Barcelona, see Chapter 12.

It's worth noting, that – unlike restaurants – most bars and clubs stay open throughout August.

Bars

Generally, the bars in the old town are a mixture of traditional tourist haunts, local drinking places or fashionista hangouts. **La Ribera** is still one of the hottest destinations, with Passeig del Born (the square at the end of c/de Montcada behind Santa María del Mar) the main focus. In the **Barri Gòtic**, it's the streets around c/d'Avinyó and c/Escudellers that have their share of the action. Over in the **Raval**, the most fashionable places are found in the upper part of the neighbourhood near MACBA, though you can still find tradition (and sleaze) further south, closer to the port, in the surviving bars of the old Barri Xines. The **Port Olímpic** and the **Port Vell** Maremàgnum complex are more mainstream summer-night playgrounds for locals and tourists alike. There are scores of bars in both these areas, all either themed or fairly mundane, but with the advantage that you can simply hop from one to another if you don't like your first choice. The more stylish designer bars (*bars modernos*) or DJ-led music bars (*bars musicals*) tend to be concentrated mainly in the **Eixample** and the streets to the west of **Gràcia**, particularly around **Plaça Molina** (and on c/Santaló and c/Marià Cubí) in **Sant Gervasi**. The "in" places here change rapidly, with new ones opening up all the time – the decor is often astounding, the drinks are always expensive.

Local bars are licensed to stay open usually till 11pm, although some keep going till 3am. Music bars usually go till 2am or 3am, after which you'll have to resort to a club.

Barri Gòtic

Antiquari c/Veguer 13 t933 100 435;
Ⓜ**Jaume I**. A former antique shop, this late-opening old-town bar attracts a decent mix of locals. There's terrace seating in Pl. del Rei, but you can end up waiting ages for your drinks here. Live music at the weekends. Daily 5pm–2am.
Ascensor c/Bellafila 3 ☎933 185 347;
Ⓜ**Jaume I**. Old lift doors and control panel signal the entrance to this popular local bar. It's not at all touristy, and has a comfortable feel – great for a late-night drink and a natter. Daily 6pm–3am.
Bahía c/Escudellers 46 ☎933 185 473;
Ⓜ**Drassanes**. Slightly scruffy bar on the grungy Pl. George Orwell, but a definite hit with local youth, who spill onto the summer *terrassa*. Daily noon–3am.
Bosc de les Fades Ptge. de la Banca 5
☎933 172 649, ⓦ www.museocerabcn.com;
Ⓜ**Drassanes**. Tucked away in an alley off the Ramblas, beside the entrance to the wax museum, the "Forest of the Fairies" is decorated with gnarled plaster tree trunks and populated by plastic gnomes. Couples cuddle in the dark recesses or listen to the frequent jazz and contemporary music sessions.
Mon–Thurs & Sun 10.30am–1am, Fri & Sat 10.30am–3am.
Glaciar Pl. Reial 3 ☎933 021 163;
Ⓜ**Liceu**. Traditional Barcelona meeting point, and the first and best of the bar-*terrassas* on Pl. Reial. Packed out at weekends. Mon–Thurs 4pm–2am, Fri & Sat 4pm–3am, Sun 9am–2am.

Leticia c/de Codols 21 ☎933 020 074;
Ⓜ**Drassanes**. Cosy bar with mellow sounds and a laidback clientele – the sofa at the back is the seat in demand. Monthly art exhibitions add some colour. Sandwiches, salads and cakes are served until late. Daily except Tues 7pm–3am.
Margarita Blue c/Josep Anselm Clavé 6
☎933 177 176, ⓦ www.margaritablue.com;
Ⓜ**Drassanes**. A bustling place with gigs or DJs a couple of times a week, attracting a young, trouser-swinging crowd. Have a seat at the lengthy bar and sip a cocktail or grab a table for a Tex-Mex meal, though both are pretty average quality – best advice is to go for the atmosphere and forget about the food. *Rita Blue*, Pl. Sant Agusti, the sister joint in the Raval, has a similar scene but a nicer location.
Mon–Wed 11am–2am, Thurs–Sun 7pm–3am.
El Paraigua c/l'Ensenyança 2 ☎933 021 131;
Ⓜ**Jaume I**. Impressive *modernista* interior – formerly an umbrella shop on the Ramblas – just the place for early evening drinks, cocktails and a burst of classical music. Some nights feature poetry readings and other literary events. Mon–Fri 6.30pm–2am, Sat 6.30pm–3am.
Parnasse c/Gignás 21 ☎933 101 247;
Ⓜ**Jaume I**. Weirdly hip bar where you come to listen to jazz, and to drink the modestly priced single-malt whiskies or the legendary absinthe *à la française* (with sugar and water on the side). Live jazz combos appear on some nights, while Miles invariably makes a recorded appearance.
Tues–Sat 8pm–3am.

English pubs and Irish bars

When only a pint of Guinness will do, or there's a big match on at home, you'll need the services of one of Barcelona's growing number of "pubs". There's little to choose between them, and not much reason to frequent them otherwise, though most also have live folk/rock acts on various nights of the week. Hours are as for bars, ie until 2am most nights, 3am at weekends.

Black Horse Avgda. Allada Vermell 16, La Ribera ☎932 683 338; ⓂJaume I.

Clansman c/Vigatans 13, La Ribera ☎933 197 169; ⓂJaume I.

Kennedy Irish Sailing Club Moll de Mestral, Port Olímpic ☎932 210 039; ⓂCiutadella-Vila Olímpica.

Michael Collins Pl. Sagrada Família

4, Eixample ☎934 591 964; ⓂSagrada Família.

Molly Malone c/de Ferran 7, Barri Gòtic ☎933 424 026; ⓂLiceu.

The Philharmonic c/de Mallorca 204, Eixample ☎934 511 153; ⓂDiagonal.

The Shamrock c/dels Tallers 72, El Raval ☎934 124 636; ⓂCatalunya.

Peña Espanyol Ptge. de Madoz, no phone; ⓂLiceu. Fans of Barcelona's "other" football club, l'Espanyol, gather here and even if you're not into sport this is undoubtedly the best bar in Pl. Reial, with stunning views over the square. Look for the sign on the first door around the left-hand corner from the *Quinze Nits* restaurant, ring the bell and go up to the first floor. Everybody is welcome. Daily 3pm–2am.

Pile 43 c/Aglá 4 ☎933 173 902; ⓂLiceu. Easy-listening cocktail joint that's a homage to the Sixties and Seventies, and pretty unique in its way, since all the fixtures and fittings are for sale. Mon–Thurs 1.30–4.30pm & 7pm–2am, Fri & Sat 1.30–4.30pm & 7pm–3am.

Pipa Club Pl. Reial 3 ☎933 024 732, ⓦwww.bpipaclub.com; ⓂLiceu. Very popular place that looks a bit like a Victorian English pub, with its various wood-panelled rooms. Historically a pipe-smoker's haunt, it's a jazzy, late-night kind of place – ring the bell for admission and make your way up the stairs. Daily 11pm–3am.

Schilling c/de Ferran 23 ☎933 176 787; ⓂLiceu. Fashionable café-bar, with high ceilings and wood and plate-glass interior. Quietest in the morning, and packed out with a mixed, chilled crowd later on. Mon–Sat 10am–2.30am, Sun noon–2.30am.

So-da c/d'Avinyó 24 ☎934 122 776; ⓂLiceu. In the daytime this place is a style-setting clothes shop, at night the designer rags are locked away into cupboards and the place turns into a wicked bar, with comfy armchairs, tasty cocktails and electronic tunes. DJ at the weekend. Daily 9pm–2.30am.

Travel Bar c/Boqueria 27 ☎933 425 252, ⓦwww.travelbar.com; ⓂLiceu. Backpacking Catalans have brought their experiences home to provide a bar where travellers can hang out and meet like-minded souls, sign up for walking/biking/drinking tours, check their email, practise their Spanish and generally chill out. Mon–Thurs & Sun 9am–2am, Fri & Sat 9am–3am.

Zoo c/Escudellers 33 ☎933 027 728; ⓂLiceu. Animals provide the central theme, the subject of the decoration and the inspiration for the names of the sandwiches and salads. There's an eating space at the back (try the wraps) and a wide music selection, from world to electronic. Daily 7pm–2am.

El Raval

Almirall c/de Joaquin Costa 33, no phone; ⓂUniversitat. Dating from 1860, Barcelona's oldest bar – check out the stunning *modernista* counter – is a venerated leftist hangout, not to mention a great place to kick off an evening of more intense bar-hopping. There's live music some nights. Daily 7pm–3am.

Benidorm c/de Joaquin Costa 39 ☎933 178 052; ⓂUniversitat. Lively bar where different DJs offer the best of different genres, though hip hop and funk predominate. It's just a little bit cheesy and none the worse for that. Daily 7pm–2.30am.

Boadas c/dels Tallers 1 ☎933 188 826; ⓂCatalunya. Shaking and stirring since 1933, this genuine Barcelona cocktail bar has been praised by the likes of Sophia Loren, while other famous visitors have also left mementoes. There's no list, so if you can't decide, go for the cocktail of the day. Mon–Thurs noon–2am, Fri & Sat noon–3am.

La Confitería c/de Sant Pau 128 ☏ 934 430 458; ⓂParal.lel. This old *modernista* bakery and sweet shop –carved wood bar, murals, beautiful chandeliers – is now a popular meeting point, with a friendly, relaxed atmosphere. Daily 6pm–3am.

Kabara c/Junta de Comerc 20 ☏ mob 606 142 478; ⓂLiceu. Multicultural space, both food and music-wise, with gigs most nights (singers, open-mike sessions, reggae bands) and a relaxed atmosphere in the bar and chillout areas. Mon–Thurs & Sun 7.30pm–2am, Fri & Sat 7.30pm–3am; closed Aug.

Kentucky c/Arc del Teatre 11 ☏ 933 182 878; ⓂDrassanes. Deep in the heart of the old Barri Xines, this is a kitschy dive where off-the-wall locals and wide-eyed foreigners mingle. Making your way through the narrow aisle might take you a while, but it's quite an experience. Tues–Thurs 10pm–3am, Fri & Sat 10pm–5am.

London Bar c/Nou de la Rambla 34 ☏ 933 186 251; ⓂLiceu. Opened in 1910, this well-known *modernista* bar attracts a mostly tourist clientele these days, but it's still worth looking in at least once. It puts on live jazz, swing, blues or tango most nights. Tues–Sun 7pm–4am.

Marsella c/de Sant Pau 65 ☏ 934 427 263; ⓂLiceu. Authentic, atmospheric, Thirties bar where absinthe is the drink of choice. It's frequented by a spirited mix of local characters and young trendies, who come for the occasional gigs and other performances. Mon–Sat 10pm–3am.

Mendizábal c/Junta de Comerç 2, no phone; ⓂLiceu. Don't look for a bar – there isn't one. This stand-up counter opposite the Hospital de la Santa Creu dispenses beers, juices and shakes to passing punters. The lucky ones grab a table over the road in the little square. Daily 8am–1am.

Muebles Navarro c/Riera Alta 4–6 ☏ 607 188 096; ⓂSant Antoni. Café-bar that occupies various rooms in a converted furniture store, hence the name, "Navarro Furniture". A friendly, comfortable place to have a drink, it also does tasty sandwiches and excellent home-made cheesecake. Tues–Thurs & Sun 6pm–midnight, Fri & Sat 6pm–3am.

Pastis c/Santa Mònica 4 ☏ 933 187 980; ⓂDrassanes. Tiny, dark bar awash with artistic and theatrical memorabilia, and soothed by wheezy French music. Tues night is tango night. Daily 7.30pm–2.30am.

Tres Delicias Rambla del Raval 47 ☏ 934 415 714; ⓂLiceu. Cute and cosy, with lots of character and a relaxed atmosphere. Temporary exhibitions inside, and a summer terrace out. Daily 6pm–2am.

La Ribera

Berimbau Pg. del Born 17 ☏ 933 195 378; ⓂJaume I/Barceloneta. The oldest Brazilian bar in town, still a good place for authentic sounds and cocktails. Daily 6pm–2.30am.

Borneo c/Rec 49 ☏ 932 682 389; ⓂJaume I. Downmarket hipness in this popular drinking hole, just off the main drag of the Born. It's a relaxed place to start or finish the night. Tues–Sat 8pm–3am.

Café del Born Pl. Comercial 10 ☏ 932 683 272; ⓂJaume I. Relaxed gay-friendly bar with pavement tables in summer, making it a popular meeting place. Come for breakfast and relax with the papers, or turn up later when it livens up a bit. Live music some nights. Mon–Thurs & Sun 9am–1am, Fri & Sat 9am–3.30am.

Espai Barroc c/de Montcada 8 ☏ 933 100 673; ⓂJaume I. Expensive and slightly snooty, the renovated interior of the fifteenth-century Palau Dalmasses looks like it may have served as a Peter Greenaway film set. Sip champagne or cognac or, once a week, enjoy live Baroque and chamber music (Thurs at 11pm, €18, drink included). Tues–Sat 8pm–2am, Sun 6–10pm.

Gimlet c/del Rec 24 ☏ 933 101 027; ⓂJaume I. Old-style cocktail bar with an impressive array of drinks – one for the drinks connoisseurs who seek the perfect tipple. Daily 7pm–3am.

Hivernacle Pg. de Picasso, Parc de la Ciutadella ☏ 932 954 017; ⓂArc de Triomf. Quiet, relaxing *terrassa* set amongst the palm trees inside the nineteenth-century glass conservatory. A genteel stop for drinks, fancy tapas or fine Catalan dining, with live music and jazz nights a couple of times a week. Daily 10am–1am.

Miramelindo Pg. del Born 15 ☏ 933 103 727; ⓂJaume I/Barceloneta. Jazz, Brazilian cocktails and snacks in a dark, barrel-vaulted bar with colonial-style accoutrements. Mon–Thurs & Sun 8pm–2.30am, Fri & Sat 8pm–3.30am.

Alcoholic drinks

The **beer** (*cervesa* in Catalan, *cerveza* in Spanish) in Barcelona is lager, with the two main brands you'll see everywhere being Damm's Estrella and San Miguel. Voll Damm is a stronger lager, Bock Damm a darker one, or you might also see draught *cervesa negra*, a black fizzy lager with a bitter taste. Beer generally comes in 300ml bottles, while, on draught, a *caña* is a small glass, a *caña grande* or a *jarra* a larger one, and a *tubo* a tall, cylindrical glass.

Wine (*vino*, *vi*), either red (*tinto*, *negre*), white (*blanco*, *blanc*) or rosé (*rosado*, *rosat*), is the invariable accompaniment to every meal. In bars, cafés and budget restaurants, it's whatever comes out of the barrel, or the house bottled special (ask for *vino/vi de la casa*). If you want to try this year's local wine, ask for *vi novell*. Catalan wine is mostly excellent, the wine-making industry centred on the Alt Penedès and Priorat regions, and with other local production coming from Empordà and around Lleida. The champagne-like *cava* from Sant Sadurní d'Anoia (see p.135) is definitely worth sampling. You'll also see a lot of standard Spanish wines, most notably Rioja, while the Galician and Basque bars and restaurants in the city serve wines from their own regions. The classic Andalucian wine, **sherry** – *vino de Jerez* – is served chilled or at *bodega* temperature, a perfect drink to wash down tapas. The main distinctions are between *fino* or *Jerez seco* (dry sherry), *amontillado* (medium) and *oloroso* or *Jerez dulce* (sweet), and these are the terms you should use to order.

In mid-afternoon – or even at breakfast – many Catalans take a *copa* of **liqueur** with their coffee (for that matter, many of them drink wine and beer at breakfast, too). The best – certainly to put in your coffee – is **brandy** (*coñac*), mostly from the south and often deceptively smooth. If you want a brandy from Catalunya, look for Torres or Mascaró. For other spirits, always specify *nacional* if you want to avoid getting an expensive foreign brand. Current drink of choice for the cool crowd is **absinthe**, served in a variety of old-town bars.

Mudanzas c/Vidrería 15 ℡933 191 137; Ⓜ Barceloneta. Very popular café-bar, converted from a former shop. Locals like the relaxed, graceful feel, while those in the know come for the wide selection of rums from around the world. Daily 10pm–3am.

Nus c/Mirallers 5 ℡933 195 355; Ⓜ Jaume I. Chic bar with split-level drinking, good music and the local, arty haircuts as clientele. It's a bit tricky to find, in a backstreet behind Santa María del Mar, but worth the search. Daily except Wed 7pm–2.30am.

Pas del Born c/Calders 8 ℡933 195 073; Ⓜ Barceloneta. A wacky haunt of musicians, artists and acrobats. Often hosts frenetic flamenco shows, as well as circus trapeze acts at the weekend. Mon–Thurs 7pm–2am, Fri & Sat 7pm–3am.

La Rosa de Foc c/del Rec 69 ℡933 195 171; Ⓜ Jaume I. Multicultural space presenting exhibitions and twice-weekly live music, plus book launches, poetry readings and similar events. The spacious bar has a very relaxing atmosphere. Daily 6pm–2.30am.

Suborn c/de Ribera 18 ℡933 101 110; Ⓜ Barceloneta. A tapas and light meals place in the early evening (the *terrassa* overlooks Parc de la Ciutadella), which transforms itself into a music bar as the night wears on. A rotation of DJs spin just about everything while you dine on imaginative Mediterranean cuisine, or simply enjoy a drink. Tues–Sun 9.30pm–3am.

Vinya del Senyor Pl. Santa Maria 5 ℡933 103 379; Ⓜ Jaume I. Nook-and-cranny wine bar with tables right outside the lovely church of Santa Maria del Mar. The wine list runs to novel length – a score of them available by the glass – and there are *platillos* of oysters, smoked salmon and the like to wash it all down. Mon–Thurs noon–1am, Fri & Sat noon–2am, Sun noon–midnight.

Port Vell

Luz de Gas in front of Palau de Mar ℡932 097 711; Ⓜ Barceloneta. Sip a drink on the moored boat for some great marina and harbour views. It's especially nice at night. March–Oct daily noon–3am.

Mojito Bar Maremàgnum ☎933 528 746; Ⓜ**Drassanes**. Typically Maremàgnum in style is this themed Caribbean playhouse, with tropical decor, cocktails and free daily salsa classes. The *salsoteca* packs them in on Fri and Sat nights, and there's live music with the Cuban big band on Sun. Daily 5pm–5am.

Port Olímpic

Café Café Moll de Mestral 30 ☎932 210 019; Ⓜ**Ciutadella-Vila Olímpica**. One of dozens of choices around the marina, this is one of the few that scores as a specific target, more relaxed than the others and serving lots more besides coffee. Mon–Thurs & Sun 3pm–3am, Fri & Sat 3pm–5am.

Poble Sec

Barcelona Rouge c/Poeta Cabanyes 21 ☎934 424 985; Ⓜ**Paral.lel**. It's red all right – couldn't be more red, in fact, inside this laidback cocktail emporium playing downtempo jazz, trip hop and other dreamy beats. Tues–Sat 11pm–3am.

Tinta Roja c/Creu dels Molers 17 ☎934 433 243; Ⓜ**Poble Sec**. Cosy bar at the front, and stage at the back that hosts an unbelievably kitsch tango show on Sat nights. Try not to titter into your *cervesa* too loudly or the tango lovers in the audience might take offence. Tues & Thurs–Sun 5pm–1am, Fri & Sat 5pm–3am.

Eixample

Arquer Gran Via de les Corts Catalanes 454 ☎934 239 908; Ⓜ**Rocafort**. Bar with – believe it or not – an archery range where you can have a go under the careful supervision of someone more sober than you. Tues–Sun 9pm–3am.

Dry Martini c/Aribau 166 ☎932 175 072; Ⓜ**Diagonal/Provença**. Legendary Barcelona cocktail bar, the rich dark wood and brass-highlighted interior exuding confident luxury. Business types dominate in the early evening, while a younger set moves in on weekend nights. Mon–Thurs 1pm–2.30am, Fri & Sat 1pm–3am, Sun 6.30pm–2.30am.

Fira c/Provença 171 ☎617 776 589; Ⓜ**Provença**. One of the city's most bizarre bars, complete with turn-of-the-century fairground rides, and decorated with circus paraphernalia. Popcorn and drinks (including *cava* by the glass) either served

at the bar fashioned from a circus awning, or sitting in dodgem cars. Tues–Thurs & Sun 11pm–3am, Fri & Sat 11pm–5am.

Les Gens Que J'Aime c/Valencia 286 ☎932 156 879; Ⓜ**Passeig de Gràcia**. Intimate brothel-like interior of red velvet, dimmed lights and atmospheric music. As a refuge from the club scene, it's very pleasant for a relaxing drink. Daily 7pm–2.30am.

Quilombo c/d'Aribau 149 ☎934 395 406; Ⓜ**Passeig de Gràcia**. Unpretentious music bar with live guitarists, South American bands and a clientele that joins in enthusiastically. Mon–Thurs & Sun 9pm–3am, Fri & Sat 7.30pm–3.30am.

Sante Café c/d'Urgell 171 ☎933 237 832; Ⓜ**Hospital Clinic**. One of the better contemporary bars in the Eixample, a minimalist sort of place that does the café thing during the day and the chill-groove thing at night, with DJs at the weekend. Mon–Fri 8am–3pm, Sat & Sun 5pm–3am; closed Aug.

Velòdrom c/Muntaner 213 ☎934 305 198; Ⓜ**Diagonal**. Old-style bar and pool hall whose Art Deco interior dates to before the Civil War. Mon–Sat 6pm–1.30am; closed Aug.

Zsa Zsa c/Rosselló 156 ☎934 538 566; Ⓜ**Hospital Clinic**. A designer bar showing off its fashionable wallhangings, and dishing out loud music and pricey cocktails to the well-dressed uptown set. Mon–Sat 10pm–3am.

Drinks with Gaudí

A summer's night, some cool rhythms, champagne, and a setting on the roof terrace of one of Gaudí's most extraordinary buildings – what could be more agreeable? The weekend event known as **La Pedrera de Nit** provides all of this, though you'll need to make reservations well in advance. See p.101 for all the details.

Gràcia

Bolsa c/Tuset 17 ☎932 022 635; Ⓜ**Diagonal**. Music bar where the prices go up and down according to demand, *la bolsa* being the Spanish for "stock exchange". Daily 8.30pm–3am.

Casa Quimet Rambla del Prat 9 ☎932 175 327; ⓜFontana. At the "guitar bar" you have to supply the music yourself: pick out your favourite from the collection and try your luck. The place is crammed with old photographs and trinkets. Tues–Sun 6.30pm–2am; closed Aug.

Gusto c/Francisco Giner 24 no phone; ⓜDiagonal. Alternative hangout where a DJ plays happening stuff to a pre-club crowd. Wed–Sat 11pm–3am.

Canigó Pl. de la Revolucio 10 no phone; ⓜFontana. Family-run neighbourhood bar now entering its third generation. It's not much to look at, but it's a friendly spot, packed out at weekends with a young, hip and largely local crowd, meeting to chew the fat. Tues–Sun 11am–midnight.

Cerveseria Artesana c/Sant Agustí 14 ☎932 379 594; ⓜDiagonal. The recipes at this Catalan attempt at a brewpub may need a bit of refinement, but fortunately a good range of imported English beer is also available. Wed–Sun 6pm–2.30am.

Mi Bar c/Guilleries 6, no phone; ⓜFontana. Favourite neighbourhood bar for Gràcia's alternative music set. The DJ spins a mix of everything from punk to flamenco. Tues–Sun 11pm–3am.

Mond Bar Pl. del Sol 21 ☎932 720 910; ⓜDiagonal/Fontana. Every night a different DJ plays the newest beats in the bar where "pop will make us free". Acts as an apéritif for the *Mond Club* (see p.207). Daily 8.30pm–3am.

Sabor Cubano c/Francesc Giner 32 ☎932 173 541; ⓜFontana. Great Cuban music and cocktails. Mon–Sat 10pm–3am.

Virreina Pl. de la Virreina 1 ☎932 379 880; ⓜFontana. Popular local bar with seats outside in one of Gràcia's loveliest squares. A great place to enjoy hard-to-find Trappist beers from Belgium. Mon–Thurs & Sun 10am–1am, Fri & Sat 10am–2am.

Plaça Molina/Sant Gervasi

Gimlet c/Santaló 46 ☎932 015 306; FGC Muntaner. Especially popular in summertime, when the tables outside are packed with the local beautiful people, who come here for snacks and cocktails. Daily 7.30pm–2.30am.

Mas i Mas c/Marià Cubí 199 ☎932 094 502, ⓦwww.masimas.com; FGC Muntaner. One of the bars that started it all and, in their own words, "a cross between a cocktail bar and a dancehall". The music policy is blues, acid jazz, hip hop, house and funk, and the crowd young and equally funky. Mon–Thurs & Sun 7pm–2.30am, Fri & Sat 7pm–3am.

Tres Torres Via Augusta 300 ☎932 051 608; FGC Sarrià. Large *terrassa* set in the beautiful grounds of an old house, which gets very crowded in summer. Mon–Sat 7pm–3am.

Universal c/Marià Cubí 182 ☎932 013 596; FGC Muntaner. A classic designer bar that's been at the cutting edge of Barcelona style since 1985 – and there are still queues. Be warned: they operate a strict door policy here and if your face doesn't fit you won't get in. Mon–Sat 11pm–4.30am.

Zig Zag c/de Plató 13 ☎932 016 207; FGC Muntaner. This long-established place has all the minimalist designer accoutrements – chrome and video – but more varied music (predominantly acid jazz, funk and hip hop) than usual, and a young, rich clientele. Thurs–Sat 11pm–3am.

Les Corts

Carpe Diem Avgda. Dr Gregorio Marañón 17 ☎933 340 258; ⓜPalau Reial. Near the university campus and Camp Nou stadium, *Carpe Diem* is a huge tent containing various bars, restaurants and dance floors. Open all year, but best and busiest in summer. Daily 6pm–5am.

Tibidabo

Danzatoria Avgda. Tibidabo 61 ☎932 116 261, ⓦwww.danzatoria.com; FGC Avgda. del Tibidabo & Tramvia Blau/taxi. Aerial views and swish drinks in a former mansion, set high above the city. Four rooms and music styles, ten bars and – best of all – a fantastic garden, which makes this very pleasant for summer nights. Wed–Sun 11pm–3am.

Mirablau Pl. del Dr Andrea, Avgda. Tibidabo ☎934 185 879; FGC Avgda. del Tibidabo & Tramvia Blau/taxi. Unbelievable city views from a chic, expensive bar that fills to bursting at times. Daily 11am–5am.

Clubs

The main city-centre **neighbourhoods** for clubbing are the Barri Gòtic, Raval, Eixample and Gràcia, though it's actually the peripheral areas where you'll find the bulk of the big-name warehouse and designer venues. Poble Nou, Poble Sec and Les Corts might not attract you during the day, but they'll be high on the list of any seasoned clubber, as will the otherwise tourist fantasy village of Poble Espanyol in Montjuïc.

Be warned that clubbing in Barcelona is extremely expensive, and that in the most exclusive places a beer is going to cost you roughly ten times what it costs in the bar next door. **Admission prices** are difficult to predict: some places are free before a certain time, others charge a few token euros' entry, a few only charge if there's live music, while in several entry depends on what you look like rather than how much is in your pocket. Those that do charge tend to fall into the €10–18 range, though this usually includes your first beer or soft drink (look for the word *consumició*). If there is free entry, don't be surprised to find that there's a minimum drinks charge of anything up to €10 – you'll be given a card as you go in, which is punched at the bar.

Note that the distinction between a music-bar and a club is between a closing time of 2am or 3am and at least 5am. Many of those listed below stay open until 6am or 7am at weekends – fair enough, as they've usually barely got started by 3am.

Barri Gòtic

Café Royale c/Nou de Zurbano 3 ☎934 121 433; Ⓜ**Liceu**. Glamorous lounge bar and club where all the beautiful people get together to show off their best moves to the Latin jazz, soul and funky tunes. Arrive after midnight and you'll have to join the queue. Daily 7pm–3am.

Dot c/Nou de Sant Francesc 7 ☎933 016 897, Ⓦwww.dotlightclub.com; Ⓜ**Drassanes**. Tiny bar, tiny dance floor, with music policy changing nightly – electronica, deep beats, Brazilian, funk – but always a backdrop movie for company. Mon–Thurs & Sun 11pm–2.30am, Fri & Sat 11pm–3am.

Fonfone c/dels Escudellers 24 ☎933 171 424, Ⓦwww.fonfone.com; Ⓜ**Drassanes**. Beautifully designed bar attracting a young crowd into fast, hard music, though it changes mood with satin soul and best-of-Eighties nights. Daily 10pm–3am.

Karma Pl. Reial 10 ☎933 025 680; Ⓜ**Liceu**. A studenty basement place that can get claustrophobic at times. Sounds are Indie, Britpop and US college, while a lively local crowd mills around the square outside. Tues–Sun 11.30pm–5am.

Macarena c/Nou de Sant Francesc 5 no phone; Ⓜ**Drassanes**. Once a place where flamenco tunes were offered up to La Macarena, the Virgin of Seville. Now it's a heaving, funky, electronic temple with a tolerant crowd – they have to be, as there's not much space. Entry usually free. Mon–Sat 11pm–4am.

El Raval

Concha c/Guardia 14 ☎933 024 118; Ⓜ**Drassanes**. The Arab–flamenco fusion throws up a great atmosphere, worth braving the slightly dodgy area for. Drag performances on Fri and Sat at midnight are the big draw, with uninhibited dancing to flamenco and *rai* afterwards. Daily 4pm–3am.

Dos Trece c/del Carme 40 ☎933 017 306, Ⓦwww.dostrece.net; Ⓜ**Liceu**. Small club under the restaurant where musicians and DJs take care of the ambience. Every night is different, though the crowd is always young and groovy. Daily 11.30pm–4am.

Moog c/Arc del Teatre 3 ☎933 017 282, Ⓦwww.masimas.com; Ⓜ**Drassanes**. Influential club playing techno, electro, drum 'n' bass, house, funk and soul to a cool crowd. Daily 11.30pm–5am.

Paloma c/Tigre 27 ☎933 016 897; Ⓜ**Universitat**. Fabulous *modernista* ballroom where old and young alike are put through their rumba and cha-cha-cha steps from 6pm to 9.30pm. Then, after 11.30pm, dancers climb onto the stage, and DJs take their positions. Mainly electronic, though

Saturday's Eighties night is a blast and there's a once-a-month punk party. Go early, because it tends to get very crowded. Thurs–Sat 6pm–5am.

Salsitas **c/Nou de la Rambla 22 ⓣ933 180 840; ⓂLiceu.** A peculiar place of dubious taste, where cocktails and dinner segue into funky club sounds after midnight. Tues–Sun 8pm–3am.

La Ribera

Astin **c/Abaixadors 9 ⓣ933 010 090, ⓦwww.nitsa.com/astin; ⓂJaume I.** Thumping bar-club for cutting-edge pop, house, techno and other beats. Live bands and guest DJs feature regularly. Thurs–Sat 10pm–3am.

Port Vell

Insólit **Local 111, Maremàgnum ⓣ932 258 178; ⓂDrassanes.** A multi-space venue which doubles as restaurant and Internet café during the week, only to turn into a big dance floor after midnight, where a mixed crowd dances to club sounds. Club Mon–Thurs & Sun midnight–5am, Fri & Sat midnight–6am.

Poble Nou

The Loft **c/Pamplona 88 ⓣ933 208 200, ⓦwww.theloftclub.com; ⓂBogatell/Marina.** Two dance floors located in an old warehouse, around the corner from *Razzmatazz* (see below), where resident and international DJs offer up a wide range of beats, from house to Spanish pop. It's cheaper, or can be free, before 2am, but no one really turns up that early. Fri & Sat 1–6am.

Oven **c/Ramon Turró 126 ⓣ932 210 602, ⓦwww.oven.ws; ⓂPoble Nou.** Fabulously designed restaurant/bar/club occupying former factory premises. Lounge room at the front, restaurant at the back with a stunning open kitchen, and live music a couple of nights a week. After midnight the place turns into a club, with DJs until 3am. Restaurant open Mon–Fri lunch & dinner (from 1.30pm), Sat dinner only (from 6pm); club Mon–Sat midnight–3am.

Razz Club, Razzmatazz **c/dels Almogavers 122 ⓣ933 208 200, ⓦwww.salarazzmatazz.com; ⓂBogatell/Marina.** This is the reincarnation of the legendary Barcelona club *Zeleste*, a huge former warehouse hosting gigs at weekends, after which the *Razz Club* takes over – "three clubs in one" spinning Indie, rock, pop, electro, Sixties and more. Fri & Sat 11pm–5am.

Montjuïc

Discothèque **Avgda. Marquès de Comillas, Poble Espanyol ⓣ934 231 285, ⓦwww.nightsungroup.com, ⓦwww.discothequebcn.com; ⓂEspanya.** The winter destination for dedicated hedonists. Almost two thousand cram in here for house, garage, big-name DJs and a whole lot of style on the main dance floor, plus a Fifties-syle chillout lounge. Oct–May Fri & Sat midnight–7am.

La Terrazza **Avgda. Marquès de Comillas, Poble Espanyol ⓣ934 231 285, ⓦwww.nightsungroup.com; ⓂEspanya.** Open-air summer club that's *the* place to be. Nonstop dance, house and techno, though don't get there until at least 4am, and be prepared for the style police. May–Oct Thurs–Sun midnight–6am.

Torres de Ávila **Avgda. Marqués de Comillas, Poble Espanyol ⓣ934 249 309; ⓂEspanya.** The creation of designers Mariscal and Arribas, located inside the mock-twelfth-century gateway in the "Spanish Village". It's a stunning fantasy, with a fabulous panoramic terrace. Thurs–Sat midnight–6am.

Poble Sec

Mau Mau **c/Fontrodona 33 ⓣ606 860 617; ⓂParal.lel.** Great underground club and chillout space with comfy sofas, a nightly menu of film and video projections playing on all the walls, and a roster of guest DJs playing deep, soulful grooves. Strictly speaking it's a private club, but membership is only €5 and they may let you check it out for a night if you're lucky. Thurs 11pm–2.30am, Fri & Sat 11pm–3.30am, Sun 6.30–11.30pm.

Nitsa **Club Sala Apolo, c/Nou de la Rambla 113 ⓣ933 010 090, ⓦwww.nitsa.com; ⓂParal.lel.** One of the city's buzziest nights out sees this former ballroom, now concert venue, host guest DJs at the weekends playing pumping house, techno and electronica. Also a quieter chillout area. Fri & Sat 12.30pm–6.30am.

Eixample

Antilla Barcelona **c/Aragó 141–143 ⓣ934 514 564, ⓦwww.antillasalsa.com; ⓂHospital Clinic.** Caribbean tunes galore: rumba, son, salsa, merengue, mambo, you name it. There are live bands, killer cocktails, and dance classes Mon–Thurs at 10.30pm. Daily 10.30pm–5am, weekends until 6am.

City Hall Rambla de Catalunya 2–4 ☎933 172 177; Ⓜ Catalunya. Weekend house and techno temple that's become pretty popular of late. A funky place with different dance floors, and a mixed crowd enjoying visiting DJs, party nights and vocal slots. Thurs–Sat 1–5am.

Costa Breve c/d'Aribau 230 ☎934 142 778; Ⓜ Diagonal. Late-night funk, pop, dance and soul "discoteca" that attracts an uptown crowd ready for a bit of serious boogieing. Thurs–Sat midnight–6am.

Risco c/Balmes ☎934 231 285, Ⓦ www .nightsungroup.com; Ⓜ Hospital Clinic. The Discothèque/Terrazza crowd (see "Montjuïc", opposite) do their pre-clubbing here. Mainly house and techno, though everyone gets out their Eighties gear on Sun for "Bloody Mary". Wed–Sun 11pm–3am.

Velvet c/Balmes 161 ☎932 176 714; Ⓜ Diagonal. The creation of designer Alfredo Arribas, inspired by the velveteen excesses of film-maker David Lynch. Daily 10.30pm–4.30am.

Gràcia

KGB c/Alegre de Dalt 55 ☎932 105 906; Ⓜ Joanic. This warehouse bar-club was designed in 1984 by Alfredo Vidal with a "spy" theme and has traditionally been a well-known after-hours techno club. These days it's more lively after gigs. Daily 10pm–5am.

Mond Club Sala Cibeles, c/Corsega 363 ☎933 177 994, Ⓦ www.mondclub.com; Ⓜ Diagonal. Old ballroom converted into stylish Friday-night club, with a bit of everything thrown into the mix – punk, glam, electronica and guest DJs. Fri 12.30am–6am.

Otto Zutz c/de Lincoln 15 ☎932 380 722, Ⓦ www.grupo-ottozutz.com; FGC Gràcia. Still one of the most fashionable places in the city, this three-storey former textile factory has a dance floor, three bars, VIP lounge and a shed-load of pretensions. With the right clothes and face, you're in (you may or may not have to pay, depending on how impressive you are, the day of the week, etc); the serious dancing is 2–5.30am. Tues–Sat midnight–6am.

Les Corts

Bikini c/Deu i Mata 105, off Avgda. Diagonal ☎933 220 005, Ⓦ www.bikinibcn.com; Ⓜ Les Corts/María Cristina. This traditional landmark of Barcelona nightlife (behind the L'Illa shopping centre) offers regular gigs and a night of clubbing variety – Espai BKN for pop, rock and dance, Latin fusion in Arutanga and the cocktail sounds of Dry Bikini. Tues–Sat midnight–5am.

Live music

Barcelona hosts a wide range of gigs, concerts and shows throughout the year. The main clubs, concert halls and venues are listed below, but for up-to-date programmes and schedules buy a copy of the weekly *Guía del Ocio* or consult ⓦ www.guiadelociobcn.com. For advance information and tickets for all Ajuntament-sponsored concerts, visit the **Palau de la Virreina**, Ramblas 99 (☏ 933 017 775, ⓦ www.bcn.es/cultura; Mon–Sat 10am–8pm, Sun 11am–3pm; Ⓜ Liceu).

You can **buy concert tickets** with a credit card using the **ServiCaixa** (☏ 902 332 211, ⓦ www.servicaixa.com) automatic dispensing machines in branches of La Caixa. It's also possible to order tickets by phone or online through *ServiCaixa* or **Tel-Entrada** (☏ 902 101 212, ⓦ www.telentrada.com). In addition, there's a concert ticket desk in the FNAC store, El Triangle, Plaça Catalunya (Ⓜ Catalunya), while the music shops along c/dels Tallers (just off the Ramblas; Ⓜ Catalunya) carry tickets too.

The various specialist music festivals are covered in the relevant sections below, but a number of other festivals present a wide range of concerts, none bigger than the Generalitat's summer-long **Grec** season, focused on the open-air Teatre Grec on Montjuïc. The other big event is **Sónar** (ⓦ www.sonar.es), the wild, three-day electronic music and multimedia art festival held every June. Also in June is the **Festa de la Musica** (ⓦ www.fusic.org/fm), on the 21st, which sees scores of concerts taking place in squares, parks, civic centres and museums across the city. All year round, the **Gràcia Territori Sonor** collective (ⓦ www.gracia-territori.com) sponsors a permanent experimental music festival, **LEM**, putting on free or cheap concerts in the bars, cafés and galleries of Gràcia, featuring local and international guests. For details of all other festivals, many featuring gigs and concerts, see the festival calendar in Chapter 13.

Classical music and opera

Most of Barcelona's classical music concerts take place in Domènech i Montaner's **Palau de la Música Catalana** (for more on which, see p.64) or at the purpose-built, contemporary **L'Auditori**, while opera is performed at its traditional home, the **Gran Teatre del Liceu** on the Ramblas (see p.47). However, these are just the showboat venues and a large number of other concert halls around the city put on regular programmes of music. Many of the city's churches, including the cathedral and Santa Maria del Mar, host concerts and recitals, while other interesting venues to watch out for include the Barri Gòtic's historic Saló del Tinell, El Triangle (the shopping centre) at Plaça de

Catalunya, Caixa Forum (see p.216), the Fundació Joan Miró and CCCB (particularly for contemporary music), and Teatre Mercat de les Flors. The two great figures of classical music in Catalunya are, of course, the opera stars José Carreras, known locally as Josep, and Montserrat Caballé, considered to be one of the finest postwar sopranos.

Apart from the Grec summer season (June – Aug), notable **festivals** include the Festival de Música Antiga (May), which brings medieval and Baroque groups from around the world. Paying concerts are held in larger venues, but free shows can be seen outdoors in old town squares. L'Auditori is the main venue for the Festival de Músiques Contemporànies (usually Oct/Nov), while there are free concerts in Barcelona's parks each summer, the so-called Clàssics als Parcs.

L'Auditori c/Lepant 150, Eixample ☎932 479 300, ⊛www.auditori.org; ⓂMarina/Monumental. Concerts by the Orquestra Simfònica de Barcelona i Nacional de Catalunya or OBC (⊛www.obc.es), whose season runs Sept – May, plus many other concerts and recitals. Under-26s with ID get fifty percent discount on all tickets, 1hr before performance. The "Bus de les Arts" runs back to Pl. de Catalunya after concerts. Box office open Mon–Sat noon–9pm.

La Casa Elizalde c/València 302, Eixample ☎934 880 590; ⓂPasseig de Gràcia. Regular small-scale classical concerts, usually with low-cost or free entry.

Gran Teatre de Liceu Ramblas 51–59 ☎934 859 900, ⊛www.liceubarcelona.com; ⓂLiceu. Full programme of opera and recitals, plus late-night concerts (sessions golfes). Check the website and make bookings well in advance. Box office open Mon–Fri 2–8.30pm, Sat 1hr before performance.

Palau de la Música Catalana c/Sant Francesc de Paula 2, off c/Sant Pere Més Alt ☎932 957 200, ⊛www.palaumusica.org; ⓂUrquinaona. Home of the Orfeó Català choral group, and venue for concerts by the Orquestra Ciutat de Barcelona among others. Concert season runs Oct–June. Box office open Mon–Sat 10am–9pm.

Flamenco

Although its home is indisputably Andalucia, the large *andaluz* population in Catalunya means it's fairly easy to find authentic flamenco. The main flamenco centres are all in suburbs and satellite towns – Cornellà, Hospitalet, Badalona – where the *andaluz* population is mainly found, but there are a few central clubs that are worth checking out. Annual **festivals** include the Feria de Abril (April), just outside Barcelona, hosting the best of Catalan flamenco; the three-day Festival de Flamenco (June), which attracts the biggest names from Andalucia; and the flamenco competition for local talent during the summer Grec festival.

Soniquete c/Milans 5, Barri Gòtic ☎639 382 354; ⓂDrassanes. Candlelit flamenco bar, one of the very few informal places in town to hear and see the real thing. No cover. Thurs–Sun 9pm–3am.

El Tablao de Carmen Poble Espanyol, Montjuïc ☎933 256 895; ⓂEspanya. Long-standing flamenco show in the Poble Espanyol, featuring a variety of styles and performers. Prices start at €28 for the show and a drink, rising to €53 and upwards for the show plus dinner. Advance reservations required. Tues–Sun from 9.30pm.

Tarantos Pl. Reial 17, Barri Gòtic ☎933 191 789, ⊛www.masimas.com; ⓂLiceu. Barcelona's oldest tablao flamenco, with daily performances at 10pm (from around €25), followed by Latin and world music sounds until 5am with the resident DJ.

Folk, roots and world

Celtic music is currently very popular in Barcelona and a glut of Irish-style pubs (see p.200) offer live music of varying standards. World acts play a variety of venues (including some listed below in "Rock and pop"), though Caixa Forum (see p.216) has a particularly strong programme.

Centre Artesà Tradicionàrius (CAT) Trav. de Sant Antoni 6–8, Gràcia ☎932 184 485 Ⓦwww.tradicionarius.com; ⓂFontana. Folk recitals by Catalan and visiting performers, usually on Fri around 10pm (though the bar is open nightly). Sponsors an annual international folk and traditional dance festival between Jan and April.
The Clansman c/Vigatans 13, La Ribera ☎933

197 169; ⓂJaume 1. Scottish pub hosting Celtic music every Fri & Sun. Daily 5pm–3am.
Irish Winds Maremàgnum, Local 202, Port Vell ☎932 258 187; ⓂDrassanes. A pretty good place to catch Irish/Celtic folk, with live music in the pub around 11pm most nights. Mon–Thurs & Sun 12.30pm–4am, Fri & Sat 12.30pm–5am.

Catalan popular music

Folk music, as it might be understood in the rest of Europe or North America, never had much of a chance to develop in Spain. In the Seventies, when the end of Francoism began to look conceivable, political songs were all-important. They didn't leave much room for folk music to take shape, and the only reliable Catalan names are Els Trobadors, a long-standing duo who adapt medieval songs and Catalan poems, and La Murga and Tradivarius. Where Catalunya is particularly strong is in its **singer-songwriters**, many of whom have flourished since the return to democracy. Names to look out for include: Joan Manuel Serrat, one of Spain's big record sellers; Lluís Llach, who defiantly sang only in Catalan during Franco's time; Pau Ribas, another *Catalanista* folk singer who made his mark during and after the dictatorship; and Maria del Mar Bonet, who reworks traditional folk songs from her birthplace Mallorca and beyond.

You may well hear the strains of **rumba catalana**, too, a local version of *andaluz* rumba, with gypsy origins. Flamenco, also a southern tradition, is strongly represented in Barcelona, mainly because of the number of *andaluz* immigrants in the city. Perhaps most famous, though – certainly as far as visitors are concerned – is the traditional music accompanying the nineteenth-century Catalan national dance, the **sardana**; you'll find more details about where to see the dance and listen to the music on p.213.

Some of the more established Catalan **rock and pop** bands are Sopa de Cabra, Lax 'n Busto, Els Pets and Jarabe de Palo, and hip-hop merchants 7 Notas 7 Colores. The biggest and most interesting figure in Barcelona **roots music** is Manu Chao, who blends musical styles and languages in engaging counterculture tunes. His influence has rubbed off on other current hot bands, like the ska-tinged acoustic roots outfit Dusminguet, the Latin American dub and reggae of GoLem System, or Ojos de Brujo ("Eyes of the Wizard"), who present a fusion reinvention of flamenco and Catalan rumba.

There's also been a recent boom in electronic **musica experimental**, notably by surrealistic "musical guerrilla" Joan Crek, and the collective Gràcia Territori Sonor. Finally, because of relatively large expatriate populations, Barcelona is also a good place to hear **Latin American** (particularly Cuban) and **African** music – keep an eye out for posters and check the local press.

Jazz, Latin and blues

There are a few good jazz clubs in Barcelona, while other gigs are held during the summer-long Grec season, and occasionally at some of the clubs listed under "Rock and pop". The big annual event is the **Festival de Jazz** in November/December (ⓦwww.the-project.net), which highlights visiting big-name solo artists and bands in the clubs and hosts street concerts. There's also the jazz/Latin-tinged **Festival de Gitarra** (March/April), with a series of high-profile concerts in venues across town.

La Boite Avgda. Diagonal 477, Eixample ☎933 191 789, ⓦwww.masimas.com; ⓜDiagonal. Regular jazz and blues sessions, plus funk, soul and salsa, with gigs Mon–Sat from around midnight. Tickets €9, rising to €22 for big names.

Circulo Maldà c/del Pi 5, Barri Gòtic ☎934 124 386; ⓜLiceu. A stylish and relaxing music venue, hidden away up the staircase on the second floor. Daily performances (which usually start around 10pm) of jazz, flamenco, cabaret, etc.

La Cova del Drac c/Vallmajor 33, Gràcia ☎933 191 789, ⓦwww.masimas.com; FGC Muntaner. One of Barcelona's best jazz clubs serves up live music Tues–Sat from 11pm. Cover charge €9–20 depending on the act. Closed Aug.

Game-B c/Atlantida 57, Pl. del Mercat, Barceloneta ☎620 564 848, ⓦwww.somor-rostro.net; ⓜBarceloneta. Cosy music venue, playing the best of Cuban bolero, jazz, cha-cha-cha and rumba every Sat, and with a live flamenco show on Sun.

Harlem Jazz Club c/Comtessa de Sobradiel 8, Barri Gòtic ☎933 100 755; ⓜJaume I. Small, usually jam-packed venue for mixed jazz styles, from African and gypsy to flamenco and fusion; live music nightly at 10.30pm and midnight (weekends 11.30pm & 1am); it's best to get advance tickets for the second spot. Cover charge up to €5. Closed Aug.

Jamboree Pl. Reial 17, Barri Gòtic ☎933 191 789, ⓦwww.masimas.com; ⓜLiceu. Jazz gigs nightly at 11pm and 12.30am, and then you stay on for the club, playing funk, swing, hip hop and R&B. Admission €6–9.

Rock and pop

Major rock and pop bands include Barcelona on their tours, playing at a variety of sports stadium venues including those at Montjuïc, Camp Nou or the Velòdrom d'Horta. Many bands are also booked to appear at the city's bigger clubs, like *Bikini*, *KGB* and *Otto Zutz* (all listed in the previous chapter), and tickets usually run from €30 to €50, depending on the act. However, there are also some specialist venues in town, while lots of the city's smaller clubs and bars regularly feature band too. Some of the more reliable venues are listed below, to which entrance is usually reasonably priced (€5–20) and often includes a complimentary drink.

Jazz Sí Club c/Requesens 2, El Raval ☎933 290 020, ⓦwww.tallerdemusics.com; ⓜSant Antoni. Extremely small club and bar, hosting some very good, inexpensive gigs. Every night from 9pm there's different music: rock, blues and jam sessions, plus jazz, son cubano and flamenco.

Luz de Gas c/Muntaner 246, Eixample ☎932 097 711, ⓦwww.luzdegas.com; ⓜDiagonal. Smart venue popular with a slightly older crowd, with live music (local rock, blues, soul, jazz and covers) every night around midnight. Foreign acts appear regularly, too, mainly jazz-blues types but also old soul acts and up-and-coming rockers.

Razzmatazz c/dels Almogavers 122 ☎933 208 200, ⓦwww.salarazzmatazz.com; ⓜBogatell/Marina. Former warehouse hosting the biggest in-town rock gigs (Fri & Sat). Razz Club (indie, pop, rock, electro and retro) takes over after 1am.

Sala Apolo c/Nou de la Rambla 113 ☎934 414 001, ⓦwww.nitsa.com; ⓜParal.lel. Regular live gigs with the occasional big name in an old-time ballroom setting. The techno/electronica Nitsa Club kicks off at weekends

after midnight (until 5am).
Sidecar c/Heures 4–6, Pl. Reial, Barri Gòtic
☎933 021 586; ⓂLiceu. Hip bar –

pronounced "See-day-car" – with a pool table, downstairs concert space and nightly gigs and DJs. Daily 10pm–3am.

Arts, film and culture

As you would expect from a city of this size, Barcelona has a full artistic and cultural life. Film and theatre are particularly well represented, and if you don't speak Catalan or Spanish there's no need to miss out. Many cinemas show films in their original language, while Catalan performers have always steered away from the classics and gone for the innovative, so the city boasts a long tradition of street and performance art. Barcelona excels in the visual arts, too – from traditional exhibitions of paintings to contemporary photography or installation works – and scores of arts centres and galleries put on varied shows throughout the year.

As ever, a useful first stop for tickets and information is the **Palau de la Virreina**, Ramblas 99 (Mon–Sat 10am–8pm, Sun 11am–3pm; ☎933 017 775, ⓦwww.bcn.es/cultura; ⓜLiceu). **ServiCaixa** (☎902 332 211, ⓦwww.servicaixa.com) and **Tel-Entrada** (☎902 101 212, ⓦwww.telentrada .com) are the main advance booking agencies for theatre, cinema and exhibition tickets. For art and culture **listings**, best first stop is always *Guía del Ocio* (ⓦwww.guiadelociobcn.com), online or from any newspaper stand, though there are similar listings in *El País* newspaper (particularly Fri & Sat), and also a free monthly guide in English published by the Ajuntament, available from tourist offices and the Palau de la Virreina.

Dance

Barcelona is very much a contemporary dance city, with regional and international performers and companies appearing regularly either at the Generalitat's dedicated dance space (see overleaf) or at theatre venues like the Institut del Teatre, Mercat de les Flors and Teatre Lliure. There's no resident ballet company. On the whole, however, tourists tend to hone in on two other dance forms, namely **flamenco** – on offer in several Barcelona clubs (see previous chapter) – and the **sardana**, Catalunya's national folk dance. Mocked in the rest of Spain, the Catalans claim theirs is a very democratic dance. Participants (there's no limit on numbers) all hold hands in a circle, each puts something in the middle as a sign of community and sharing, and, since it is not over-energetic (hence the jibes), old and young can join in equally. The accompanying instrumental group is called a *cobla*, and it includes the *flabiol* (a type of long flute), the *tambori* (drum), and tenor and soprano oboes. **Performances** take place in front of the cathedral (Feb–July & Sept–Nov Sat 6.30pm & Sun noon; ⓜJaume I); in Plaça Sant Jaume (Sun 6.30pm; ⓜJaume I); in Parc de l'Espanya Industrial (April–Sept Fri 7.30pm; ⓜSants Estació); and in Parc Joan Miró (Oct–April every other Sun at noon; ⓜTarragona).

Dance venue

L'Espai de Dansa i Música Trav. de Gràcia 63, Gràcia ☎934 143 133; ⓜDiagonal.

Contemporary dance performances, bolstered by a variety of contemporary soloists and music groups. Box office open Mon–Sat 6.30–10pm, Sun 5–9pm.

Film

All the latest films reach Barcelona fairly quickly, though at most of the larger cinemas and multiplexes (including the Maremàgnum screens at Port Vell) they're usually shown dubbed into Spanish or Catalan. However, several cinemas do show mostly **original-language** (*versión original* or "V.O.") foreign films; the best are listed below. Tickets cost around €6, and most cinemas have one night (usually Mon or Wed) – *el día del espectador* – when entry is **discounted**, usually to around €4. Many cinemas also feature **late-night** screenings (*madrugadas*) on Friday and Saturday nights, which begin at 12.30 or 1am.

The city hosts several small **film festivals** throughout the year, including an international festival of independent short films, plus festivals devoted specifically to women's film, gay and lesbian film, and African film. The Generalitat's Filmoteca (see below) is often the venue for festival screenings; current details available from the Palau de la Virreina or ⓦwww.bcn.es. The prestigious **Festival Internacional de Cinema de Catalunya** (ⓦwww.sitges.com/cinema), traditionally strong in sci-fi and horror, is held in nearby Sitges in October/November.

Cinemas

Casablanca Pg. de Gràcia 115, Eixample ☎932 184 345; ⓜDiagonal. Two screens, and late-night film on Fri & Sat. Discount night Mon.

Filmoteca Avgda. de Sarrià 33, Eixample ☎934 107 590, ⓦhttp://cultura.gencat.es/filmo; ⓜHospital Clinic. Run by the Generalitat, the *Filmoteca* has an excellent programme, showing three or four different films (often foreign, and usually in V.O.) every night; €2.70 per film, or buy a discounted pass allowing entry to ten films.

Icaria-Yelmo c/de Salvador Espriu 61, Vila Olímpica ☎932 217 585; ⓜCiutadella-Vila Olímpica. No fewer than fifteen screens showing V.O. movies at a comfortable multiplex. Late-night screenings on Fri and Sat; discount night Mon.

Maldá c/Pi 5, Les Galeries Maldá, Barri Gòtic ☎933 178 529; ⓜLiceu. Repertory cinema featuring two different shows per day (usually English V.O.) on a weekly rotation. Late-night sessions on Fri & Sat, matinees Sat & Sun; reduced price Wed.

Méliès c/Villaroel 102, Eixample ☎934 510 051; ⓜUrgell. A repertory cinema specializing in V.O. showings, with three to five different films daily in its two *salas*. Discount night Mon.

Renoir-Les Corts c/Eugeni d'Ors 12, Les Corts ☎934 905 510; ⓜLes Corts. Six screens showing V.O. films. Late-night sessions on Fri & Sat; discount night Mon.

Verdi c/Verdi 32, and **Verdi Park**, c/Torrijos 49, Gràcia ☎932 387 990; ⓜFontana. Sister cinemas in adjacent streets showing quality V.O. movies. Late-night films at *Verdi* on Fri & Sat; discount night at both on Mon.

Theatre and cabaret

The **Teatre Nacional** (National Theatre) was specifically conceived as a venue to promote Catalan productions, and features a repertory programme of translated classics (such as Shakespeare in Catalan), original works and productions by guest companies from elsewhere in Europe. The other big local theatrical project is the **Ciutat del Teatre** (Theatre City) on Montjuïc, which incorporates the

Catalan theatre companies

Els Comediants (🌐www.comediants.com) – a travelling collective of actors, musicians and artists, established in 1971 – use any open space as a stage to celebrate "the festive spirit of human existence".

La Cubana (🌐www.lacubana.es) is a highly original company that started life as a street theatre group, though has since moved into TV and theatre proper. It still hits the streets occasionally, taking on the role of market traders in the Boqueria or cleaning cars in the street in full evening dress.

Dagoll Dagom (🌐www.dagolldagom.com) specializes in hugely theatrical, over-the-top musicals.

La Fura del Baus ("Vermin of the Sewer"; 🌐www.lafura.com) are performance artists who aim to shock and lend a new meaning to audience participation. They've subsequently taken on opera, cabaret, film and installations, lending each a wild, challenging perspective.

Els Joglars (🌐www.elsjoglars.com) present political theatre, and are particularly critical of the church and government, who come in for regular satirical attacks.

Teatre Nu ("Naked Theatre"; 🌐www.teatrenu.com) was founded in 1991 by young Catalan actors who wanted to bring theatre back to its essence and "provoke social, moral and ideological dialectic between the audience and public".

El Tricicle (🌐www.tricicle.com) – a very successful three-man mime, circus and theatre group – has branched off into film and television, but always places its humour "somewhere between reality and the absurd".

fringe-style Mercat de les Flors, a second stage for Gràcia's Teatre Lliure and the Insitut del Teatre theatre and dance school. The centre for commercial theatre is Avinguda Paral.lel and the nearby streets. Some theatres draw on the city's strong **cabaret** tradition – more music-hall entertainment than stand-up comedy, and thus a little more accessible to non-Catalan/Spanish speakers. For **children's theatre**, see p.238. **Tickets** are available from the box offices or the usual agency outlets (see p.213), but for advance tickets for the Mercat de les Flors productions you have to go to the Palau de la Virreina (Ramblas 99), or try at the theatre itself one hour before the performance. A free monthly magazine **Teatre BCN** (🌐www.teatrebcn.com) carries listings and reviews (in Catalan).

Theatre venues

Artenbrut c/Perill 9–11, Gràcia ☎934 579 705; Ⓜ Diagonal. Small theatre hosting independent companies, often with late-night performances and theatre for children at the weekend.

Insitut del Teatre Pl. Margarida Xirgu, Poble Sec ☎932 273 900, 🌐www.diba.es/iteatre; Ⓜ Poble Sec. Regular performances at the school for dramatic arts and dance.

Mercat de les Flors c/de Lleida 59, Poble Sec ☎934 261 875, 🌐www.mercatflors.com; Ⓜ Poble Sec. Hosts visiting fringe theatre and dance companies in a splendid nineteenth-century building.

Teatre Lliure Pl. Margarida Xirgu, Poble Sec ☎932 289 747, Ⓜ Poble Sec; and c/Montseny 47, Gràcia ☎932 189 251, Ⓜ Fontana; 🌐www.teatrelliure.com. The "Free Theatre" – a progressive Catalan company – performs its own work and hosts visiting dance companies, concerts and recitals on two stages: in its Ciutat de Teatre location as well as its original home in Gràcia.

Teatre Nacional de Catalunya (TNC) Pl. de les Arts 1, Glòries ☎933 065 700, 🌐www.tnc.es; Ⓜ Glòries. Intended to foster Catalan works, this theatre – built as a modern emulation of an ancient Greek temple – features Spanish, Catalan and European companies.

Teatre Poliorama Ramblas 115 ☎934 413 979, 🌐www.teatrepoliorama.com; Ⓜ Catalunya. Specializes in modern drama (Catalan and translation) and musicals, often utilizing the talents of offbeat companies like El Tricicle and Dagoll Dagom (see box, p.215).

Teatre Romea c/Hospital 51, El Raval ☎933 015 504; Ⓜ️Liceu. The Centre Dramàtic de la Generalitat de Catalunya, based here, has an emphasis on Catalan-language productions (but puts on occasional English-language productions with simultaneous Catalan translation).

El Cangrejo c/Montserrat 9, El Raval ☎933 012 978; Ⓜ️Drassanes. This infamous bar hosts outrageous transvestite cabarets on Fri and Sat nights at midnight and 3.30am – come early to get a seat. Free, but your first drink will cost you €10.

Llantiol c/Riereta 7, El Raval ☎933 299 009, ⓦwww.llantiol.com; Ⓜ️Paral.lel. Cabaret café-bar featuring curious bits of mime, song, clowns, magic and dance. Shows normally begin at 9pm and 11pm. Closed Mon.

Visual arts

Barcelona has dozens of private art galleries and exhibition halls, in addition to the temporary displays on show in its major art centres, museums and galleries. If you've no fixed idea of what you want to see, there are several areas throughout the city where private, commercial galleries cluster together: in the **Barri Gòtic**, rewarding streets are c/de Montcada and Passeig del Born near the Museu Picasso, and c/Petritxol near the cathedral; in **El Raval** c/Àngels and c/Doctor Dou near the MACBA; in the **Eixample** Passeig de Gràcia, c/Consell de Cent and Rambla Catalunya. Note that most galleries are closed on Sundays, Mondays and in August. The Associació Art Barcelona (ⓦwww.artbarcelona.es) has gallery listings and exhibition news. In spring **photography** fans should look out for the Primavera Fotogràfica, when photography exhibitions are held at various venues around the city.

Art and cultural centres

Caixa Forum Avgda. del Marquès de Comillas 6–8 ☎934 768 600, ⓦwww.fundacio.lacaixa.es; Ⓜ️Espanya. Contemporary art.
Capella de l'Antic Hospital de la Santa Creu c/de l'Hospital 56, El Raval ☎934 427 171; Ⓜ️Liceu. Work by young Barcelona artists.
CCCB c/Montalegre 5, El Raval ☎933 064 100, ⓦwww.cccb.org; Ⓜ️Catalunya/Universitat. Contemporary art.
Centre d'Art Santa Mònica Ramblas 7, Barri Gòtic ☎933 162 810; Ⓜ️Drassanes. Contemporary Catalan art and photography.
Centre Civic Casa Elizalde c/València 302, Eixample ☎934 880 590; Ⓜ️Passeig de Gràcia. Wide range of shows.
FAD Pl. dels Àngels, El Raval ☎934 437 520, ⓦwww.fadweb.com; Ⓜ️Catalunya/Universitat. Industrial and graphic art, design, craft, architecture.
Fundació Foto Colectiana c/Julian Romea 6, Gràcia ☎932 171 626, ⓦwww.colectiana.es;

Ⓜ️Fontana. Spanish and Portuguese photography since 1950.
MACBA Pl. dels Àngels, El Raval ☎934 120 810, ⓦwww.macba.es;
Ⓜ️Catalunya/Universitat. Contemporary art.
Palau Robert Pg. de Gràcia 107, Eixample ☎932 384 000, ⓦwww.gencat.net/probert; Ⓜ️Diagonal. Wide range of shows, all with a Catalan connection.
Palau de la Virreina Ramblas 99, Barri Gòtic ☎933 017 775, ⓦwww.bcn.es/cultura; Ⓜ️Liceu. Traditional and contemporary art.
Sala d'Art Jove de la Generalitat c/Calabria 147, Eixample ☎934 838 413; Ⓜ️Rocafort. The Generalitat's youth art space.
Sala Montcada c/de Montcada, La Ribera ☎902 223 040,
ⓦwww.fundacio.lacaixa.es/salamontcada; Ⓜ️Jaume I. Modern art shows.

Commercial galleries

FNAC Triangle Pl. de Catalunya 4, Eixample ☎933 441 800, ⓦwww.fnac.es; Ⓜ️Catalunya.

Wide range of exhibitions and shows.

Galleria Joan Prats Rambla de Catalunya 54, Eixample ☎932 160 290, ⓦwww .galeriajoanprats.com; ⓂPasseig de Gràcia. Contemporary Catalan artists.

H2O c/Verdi 152, Gràcia ☎934 151 801; ⓂFontana. Design, photography, contemporary art.

Kowasa c/de Mallorca 235, Eixample ☎934 873 588, ⓦwww.kowasa.com; ⓂProvença.

Traditional and contemporary photography and photographic art.

Metrònom-Fundació Rafael Tous c/Fusina 9, La Ribera ☎932 684 299; ⓂJaume I. Contemporary art, photography and multimedia exhibits.

Sala Pares c/Petritxol 5–8, Barri Gòtic ☎933 187 020, ⓦwww.salapares.com; ⓂLiceu. Hosted Picasso's first show, now a showroom for modern and traditional art.

Gay and lesbian Barcelona

There's a vibrant gay and lesbian scene in Barcelona, backed up by an established organizational infrastructure and a generally supportive city council. Information about the scene in the city is pretty easy to come by, while locals and tourists alike are well aware of the lure of Sitges, forty minutes south by train and mainland Spain's biggest gay resort.

The expression for the gay scene in Spanish is *el ambiente*, which simply means "the atmosphere" – it's the name of the useful section in the weekly listings magazine *Guía del Ocio*, which lists gay and lesbian bars, clubs, restaurants and other services. Another useful expression is the question *Entiende?*, literally meaning "Does he/she understand?", but effectively meaning "Is he/she gay?"

We've picked out the best of bars, clubs, restaurants and hotels aimed specifically at a gay and lesbian clientele. They're scattered across the city, though there's a particular concentration of bars, restaurants and clubs in the so-called **Gaixample**, the "Gay Eixample", an area of a few square blocks just northwest of the main university in the Esquerra de l'Eixample. Bear in mind that you'll also be welcome at plenty of other nominally straight Barcelona dance bars and clubs – for full listings, see Chapter 9.

For up-to-date **information** and other advice on the scene, you can contact any of the organizations listed below, or call the **lesbian and gay city telephone hotline** on ☎900 601 601 (Mon–Fri 6–10pm only), which is run by the Ajuntament. *Guia del Ocio* (out every Thurs) can put you on the right track for bars and clubs, though there's also a good free **magazine** called *Nois*, which carries an up-to-date review of the scene. For full listings and other links, the web portal ⓦwww.gaybarcelona.net is extremely useful too.

Biggest **event** of the year is Carnaval in Sitges (see p.127), while there are international gay and lesbian film festivals in July and October. The city's annual lesbian and gay **pride march** is on the nearest Saturday to June 28, starting at Plaça Universitat.

Useful contacts

Ca la Dona c/de Casp 38, Eixample ☎934 127 161, ⓦwww.caladona.pangea.org; ⓜUrquinaona. A women's centre with library and bar, used for meetings of over twenty feminist and lesbian organizations; informa-tion available to callers.

Casal Lambda c/Verdaguer i Callis 10 ☎933 195 550, ⓦwww.lambdaweb.org; ⓜUrquinaona. A gay and lesbian group with a wide range of social, cultural and educational events.

Front d'Alliberament Gai de Barcelona (FAGB) c/Verdi 88, Gràcia ☎932 172 669;

Ⓜ**Fontana.** Association for gay men, with a library, meetings and video shows, and a gay youth group at the same address.

Shops and services

Antinous c/Josep Anselm Clavé 6, Barri Gòtic ☏933 019 070; Ⓜ**Drassanes.** Gay bookshop with useful contacts and information board – also has a café at the back.
Cómplices c/Cervantes 2, Barri Gòtic ☏934 127 283; Ⓜ**Liceu.** Gay and lesbian bookshop.
Sestienda c/Rauric 11, Barri Gòtic ☏933 188 676; Ⓜ**Liceu.** Sex shop where you can pick up a map of gay Barcelona, detailing bars, clubs, hotels and restaurants.

Accommodation

See p.153 for an explanation of the price codes.
Hotel Axel c/d'Aribau 33, Eixample ☏933 239 393, ⓦwww.hotelaxel.com; Ⓜ**Passeig de Gràcia/Universitat.** A snazzy hotel set in the Gaixample, with stylishly appointed rooms in which designer fabrics, complimentary beauty products, flat-screen TVs, movies on demand and Internet hook-ups come as standard. Relaxation is taken care of in the library corner, chillout area, terrace pool and sauna, or there's a fitness centre and massage treatments available. ❼
Hotel California c/Rauric 14, Barri Gòtic ☏933 177 766, ⓦwww.seker.es/hotel_california; Ⓜ**Liceu.** Tucked down a side street that crosses c/de Ferran, this friendly hotel has nicely colour-coordinated rooms with TV, air conditioning and full bathrooms, breakfast included in the price. There are some internal rooms, and all are double-glazed, but even so, you never quite escape the weekend noise in this part of town. And, in case you were wondering, you can check out any time you like (24hr reception), but you *are* allowed to leave. ❻
Hostal Que Tal c/Mallorca 290, Eixample ☏934 592 366, ⓦwww.quetalbarcelona.com; Ⓜ**Passeig de Gràcia/Verdaguer.** Pretty rooms, with and without private bath, in a good uptown location. It's a nice, if modest, choice, with an attractive courtyard patio. No credit cards. ❸, en suite ❹

Cafés and bars

Aire Sala Diana c/Valencia 236, Eixample ☏934 515 812; Ⓜ**Passeig de Gràcia.** The hottest, most stylish lesbian bar in town is a surprisingly relaxed place for a drink and a dance to pop, house and retro sounds. Gay men welcome too. Thurs–Sat 11.30pm–3am, Sun 6–10pm.
Café Dietrich c/Consell de Cent 255, Eixample ☏934 517 707; Ⓜ**Universitat.** This well-known music bar serves food until mid-night, with drag shows punctuating the DJ sets. Daily 6pm–2.30am.
Ironic Café c/Consell de Cent 245, Eixample no phone; Ⓜ**Urgell/Universitat.** High-concept cocktail bar with smooth sounds and tem-porary art shows – Sun night is Spanish music night. 7pm–2.30am.
Oui Café c/Consell de Cent 247, Eixample ☏934 514 570; Ⓜ**Urgell/Universitat.** A meet-and-greet destination, with a popular summer *terrassa*. Mon–Thurs & Sun 5pm–2am, Fri & Sat 5pm–3am.

Restaurants

Barcelona has several gay/lesbian-friendly or gay/lesbian-run restaurants, where you'll be assured of a warm welcome and sympathetic atmosphere. **Miranda** (c/Casanova 30, Eixample ☏934 535 249; Ⓜ**Universitat; reservations advised) probably has the highest profile, serving around-the-world bistro dishes (around €20 à la carte) to the accompaniment of singing drag queens, trapeze acts and contortionists. **La Diva** (c/Diputacio 172, Eixample ☏934 546 398, ⓦwww.ladivagay.com; Ⓜ**Urgell; weekend reservations advised) also offers dinner throughout the week, with a live show from Thursday to Sunday. More relaxed, moderately priced Mediterranean-style eateries include **Castro** (c/Casanova 85, Eixample ☏933 236 784; Ⓜ**Universitat; closed Sun) and **Roma** (c/Alfons XII 4, Sant Gervasi ☏932 013 513; FGC Plaça Molina), while for Cuban-style dishes there's **El Cubanito**, c/Casanova 70, Eixample ☏934 543 188; Ⓜ**Urgell; closed Mon).

Punto BCN c/Muntaner 63–65, Eixample ☎934 536 123; Ⓜ️Universitat. A Gaixample classic that attracts an uptown crowd for drinks, chat and music – it's a popular trysting place. Happy hour on Wed, while Fri night is party night. Daily 6pm–2am.

La Rosa c/Brusi 60, Sant Gervasi ☎934 146 166; FGC Pl. Molina. Long-standing scene bar with a mainly lesbian crowd, who pack in after 2am. Fri & Sat 11pm–4am.

Zeltas c/Casanova 75 ☎934 541 902, ⓦwww.zeltas.net; Ⓜ️Urgell. Pumped-up house music bar for the pre-club crowd. Wed–Sun 11pm–3am.

Clubs

Arena Madre c/Balmes 32, Eixample ☎934 878 342, ⓦwww.arenadisco.com; Ⓜ️Passeig de Gràcia. The "mother" club sits at the helm of the Arena empire, all in the same block, which includes the high disco antics of *Arena Classic* (c/de la Diputació 233; Fri & Sat 12.30–5am), and more of the same plus house and garage at the more mixed *Arena VIP* (Grand Via de les Corts Catalanes 593; Fri & Sat 12.30–6am). *Arena Madre* open Tues–Sat 12.30–5am, Sun 7pm–5am.

Metro c/Sepúlveda 158, Eixample ☎933 235 227, ⓦwww.metrodiscobcn.com; Ⓜ️Universitat/Urgell. A gay institution in Barcelona, with cabaret nights and other events midweek. Extremely crowded at weekends in its two rooms playing either current dance and techno or retro disco. Mon–Thurs & Sun midnight–5am, Fri & Sat midnight–6am.

Salvation Ronda de Sant Pere 19–21 ☎933 180 686, ⓦwww.matineegroup.com; Ⓜ️Urquinaona. Huge Ibiza-scene gay club playing the best in European house, and promoting all sorts of parties, events and performances. Fri–Sun midnight–5am.

Satanassa c/d'Aribau 27, Eixample; Ⓜ️Universitat. Attracts a friendly, funky, gay and straight crowd. There's no admission charge, and it gets very busy at the weekends. Daily 10pm–5am.

Festivals and holidays

A lmost any month you choose to visit to Barcelona you'll coincide with a festival or holiday, and it's hard to beat the experience of arriving to discover the streets decked out with flags and streamers, bands playing and the entire population out celebrating. Traditionally, each neighbourhood celebrates with its own *festa*, though the major ones – like Gràcia's **Festa Major** and the **Mercè** – have become city institutions. Each is different, but there is always music, dancing, traditional costume, fireworks and an immense spirit of enjoyment. The religious calendar has its annual highlights too, with Carnaval, Easter and Christmas a big time for parades, events and festivities across the city. Meanwhile, biggest and best of the annual arts events are the Generalitat's summer Grec season and the ever-expanding Sónar festival of electronic music. But there are plenty of other times when Barcelona lets its hair down, from specific music or arts festivals to saints' days or trade fairs.

We've rounded up the best of the annual festivals, holidays and events in a **month-by-month calendar**, though we can't pretend that this is an exhaustive list. Tourist offices have more information about what's going on at any given time; or call into the **Palau de la Virreina**, Ramblas 99, or check out the Ajuntament's useful **website** (@www.bcn.es). It's worth noting that, during the biggest and most popular festivals of all kinds, you'll find it difficult to find a bed, so if you're planning to coincide with something specific book your accommodation well in advance. Incidentally, not all **public holidays** coincide

Celebrating Catalan-style

The main event in a traditional Catalan festival is usually a **parade**, either promenading behind a revered holy image (as at Easter) or a more celebratory costumed affair that's the centrepiece of a neighbourhood festival. It's at the latter that you'll come across the **gegants**, grotesque giant figures with papier-mâché heads, up to 5m high, which run down the streets terrorizing children. **Capgrossos** ("bigheads") are their smaller companions. Also typically Catalan is the **correfoc** ("fire-running"), where brigades of drummers, dragons and devils with spark-shooting flares fitted to pitchforks cavort in the streets. Perhaps most peculiar of all are the **castellers**, the red-shirted human tower-builders who draw crowds at every traditional festival, piling person upon person, feet on shoulders, to see who can construct the highest, most aesthetically pleasing tower (ten human storeys is the record). There are some extraordinary photographs of this posted at @www.castellersdebarcelona.org.

with a festival, but many do – there's a complete list on p.36. In addition, saints' day festivals – indeed all Catalan celebrations – can vary in date, often being observed over the weekend closest to the dates given.

January

Cap d'Any (New Year's Eve): street and club parties, and mass gatherings in Pl. de Catalunya and other main squares. You're supposed to eat 12 grapes in the last 12 seconds of the year for 12 months of good luck. Next day, 1 Jan, is a public holiday.
Cavalcada de Reis (afternoon of Jan 5): this is when the Three Kings (who distribute Christmas gifts to Spanish children) arrive by sea at the port and ride into town, throwing sweets as they go. The parade begins at the port at about 5pm on the 5th; the next day is a public holiday.
Festival dels Tres Tombs (Jan 17): costumed horseback parade through the Sant Antoni neighbourhood, with local saint's day festivities to follow.

February

Festes de Santa Eulàlia (Feb 12, ⓦwww.bcn.es/santa-eulalia): the signal for a week's worth of music, dances, children's processions, *castellers* and fireworks in honour of one of Barcelona's patron saints.
Carnaval/Carnestoltes (the week before Lent, sometimes in March): costumed parades, dances, concerts and other traditional events in every city neighbourhood. However, it's Sitges, p.127 which has the best Catalan celebrations.

March/April

Festes de Sant Medir de Gràcia (1st week in March): horse-and-carriage parade around Pl. Rius i Taulet in Gràcia, before heading to the Sant Medir hermitage in the Collserola hills. Later, the procession returns to Gràcia, where sweets are thrown to children along c/Gran de Gràcia.
Setmana Santa (Easter, Holy Week): religious celebrations and services at churches throughout the city. Special services are on Thurs and Fri in Holy Week at 7–8pm, Sat at 10pm; there's a procession from the church of Sant Agustí on c/de l'Hospital (El Raval) to La Seu, starting at 4pm on Good Friday. Public holidays on Good Friday and Easter Monday.

Dia de Sant Jordi (St George's Day, April 23): celebrating Catalunya's patron saint and coinciding with the International Day of the Book, with book and flower stalls down the Ramblas, on Pg. de Gràcia and in Pl. de Sant Jaume. Men are traditionally presented with a book by their sweethearts, who are in turn presented with a rose (although, in recent years, modernization has demanded books for women as well).
Feria de Abril: The region's biggest Andalucian festival, with citywide events promoting ten days of food and flamenco.

May

Dia del Treball (May 1): May Day/Labour Day is a public holiday, with union parades.
Saló Internacional del Còmic (2nd week, ⓦwww.ficomic.com): the Internal Comic Fair takes place over three days in França station – stalls, drawing workshops, children's activities.
Dia de San Ponç (May 11): saint's day, celebrated by a market running along c/de l'Hospital in the Raval, with fresh herbs, flowers, cakes, aromatic oils and sweets.
Festival de Música Antiga (usually first two weeks): medieval and Baroque groups from around the world, with paying concerts in larger venues, but free shows outdoors in old town squares.
Barcelona Poesia (usually 2nd week, ⓦwww.bcn.es/barcelonapoesia): week-long international poetry festival with readings and recitals (mainly Catalan/Spanish) in venues all over the city, though with international guests too.
Festa de la Diversitat (mid-month, ⓦwww.sosracisme.org): three-day festival celebrating ethnic diversity by way of free concerts, marching bands, food stalls, children's activities and more.

June/July

Marató de l'Espectacle (Entertainment Marathon; ⓦwww.marato.com): a nonstop, two-day festival of local theatre, dance, cabaret, music and children's shows, which takes place at the Mercat de les Flors theatre.

Festival de Flamenco: attracts the biggest names from Andalucia for indoor and outdoor concerts across the city.

Verbena/Dia de Sant Joan (June 23/24): The "eve" and "day" of St John herald probably the wildest celebrations in the city, with a "night of fire" of bonfires and fireworks (particularly on Montjuïc), drinking and dancing, and watching the sun come up on the beach. *Coca de Sant Joan*, a sweet flatbread, and *cava* are the traditional accompaniments to the merriment. The day itself (June 24) is a public holiday.

Sónar (ⓦ www.sonar.es): Europe's biggest and most cutting-edge electronic music and multimedia art festival; three days of brilliant noise and spectacle.

Festival del Grec (ⓦ www.bcn.es/grec): starting in the last week of June (and running throughout July and into Aug), this performing arts festival incorporates theatre, music and dance, some of it free, much of it performed at Montjuïc's Teatre Grec. Information and booking at the Palau de la Virreina.

August

Festa Major de Gràcia (mid-Aug, ⓦ www .festamajordegracia.org): a fine example of what was once a local festival in the erstwhile village of Gràcia, with music, dancing, decorations, fireworks and human castles in the streets and squares.

Festa Major de Sants (last week, ⓦ www.bcn.es/sants-montjuic/fmsants): a week's worth of traditional festivities in an untouristed neighbourhood, in the streets behind Barcelona Sants station.

September

Moda Barcelona (2nd week, ⓦ www .moda-barcelona.com): Barcelona Fashion Week is the year's big couture event, with catwalk shows and exhibitions, including Gaudí Hombre (for men) and Gaudí Mujer (women).

La Diada (Sept 11): Catalan national day, commemorating the eighteenth-century defeat at the hands of the Bourbons. It's a public holiday in Barcelona, and special events include the city's more radical Catalan regionalists throwing bricks through burger-bar windows, fighting with the police and showing their patriotism by spraying graffiti on every available space.

Festa de la Mercè (Sept 24, ⓦ www.bcn.es/merce): the city's main festival, dedicated to another of Barcelona's patron saints, the Virgin of Mercè, and celebrated for three or four days around this date (the 24th is a public holiday). There are live bands outside the cathedral and in central squares, plus shows and events in Pl. de Catalunya, the *Ball de Gegants*, a dance of costumed giants down the street from Drassanes to Ciutadella, a huge *correfoc*, the *Piro Musical*, a breathtaking firework display choreographed to music, and *castellers* teams competing to form amazing human towers.

Festa Major de Sant Miquel/Barceloneta (last week): traditional festivities on the waterfront as Barceloneta celebrates its saint's day with fireworks, parades, *castellers*, music and dancing.

October/November

Festival de Jazz (ⓦ www.the-project.net): the annual jazz festival attracts big-name solo artists and bands to the clubs, as well as smaller-scale street concerts.

Tots Sants (All Saints' Day, Nov 1): when the Spanish remember their dead, with cemetery visits and special meals, it's traditional to eat roast chestnuts (*castanyas*), sold by street vendors, sweet potatoes and *panellets* (almond-based sweets). It's also a public holiday.

December

Fira de Santa Llúcia (Dec 1–22): for more than 200 years the Christmas season has seen a special market and crafts fair outside the cathedral.

Nadal/Sant Esteve (Dec 25/26): Christmas Day and St Stephen's Day are both public holidays, which Catalans tend to spend at home – the traditional gift-giving is on Twelfth Night (Jan 6).

Sports and outdoor activities

arcelona is well placed for access to the sea and mountains, which is one of the reasons it was picked for the 1992 Olympics. A spin-off from the games was an increased provision of top-quality sports and leisure facilities throughout Catalunya. However, while there are scores of sports centres and swimming pools in the city, there aren't actually that many that will appeal to tourists or casual visitors. Most people are content to hit the beach (pp.78, 125–127 and 140) or take off for a hike or jog in the surrounding hills of the Parc de la Collserola (p.121).

Attending the big match, whatever that might be, is a different matter. **Tickets** for all major sporting events can be bought from the usual agencies, **ServiCaixa** (☎902 332 211, ⓦwww.servicaixa.com) or **Tel-Entrada** (☎902 101 212, ⓦwww.telentrada.com). The main source of information about municipal sports facilities is the Ajuntament's **Servei d'informació Esportiva** (☎934 023 000 or 010), which has a drop-in office (Direcció d'Esports) on Montjuïc at Avgda. de l'Estadi 30–40 (ⓂEspanya), at the side of the Bernat Picornell swimming pool.

American football

The **Barcelona Dragons** – 1997 World Bowl champions – play in the Estadi Olímpic, Montjuïc, against other teams in the NFL Europe League (ⓦwww.nfleurope.com). The season is from April to June, with games on Saturdays at 5.30pm. Tickets cost from €10.50 to €42.50, available from the stadium, agencies or on ☎934 254 949 (ⓦwww.dragones.es).

Basketball

Second only to football in popularity, basketball has been played in Barcelona since the Twenties. Games are usually played September to June at weekends – you'll often catch the tail-end of one on TV in a bar – with most interest in the city's two main teams. **Club Joventat de Badalona**, founded in 1930, were European champions in 1994, while **FC Barcelona** (an offshoot of the football club as early as 1926) finished runners-up five times before finally becoming European champions in 2003. Tickets to games are fairly inexpensive (up to €25), and it's easiest to go and watch FC Barcelona, as Badalona is out in the sticks. See "Football" overleaf for stadium and contact details.

Cycling

Cycling as transport is something of a novel concept for Barcelonans, though to be fair the city authorities are doing their best by rapidly laying out rights of way along many of the most heavily trafficked streets. However, the population at large has yet to adapt, as the **cycle paths** are often ignored by cars or clogged with pedestrians, indignantly reluctant to give way to two-wheelers. Currently, there are around 100km of cycle paths throughout the city, with plans to double the network over the next few years. In particular, by 2005, a sixty-kilometre "green ring" cycle path will enclose the entire metropolitan area, running along the banks of the River Besòs to the east and on existing trails in the Parc de la Collserola before looping around through Montjuïc and along the seafront.

The best way to see the city by bike – certainly as a first-time visitor – is to take a **bike tour** (see Basics, p.28); bikes and equipment will be provided. If you would rather go on your own, you can **rent a bike** from one of the outlets listed in the Directory on p.241 – some of those also offer tours and guidance. A map detailing current cycle paths is available from the tourist office. The nicest place to get off the road is in the Parc de la Collserola, where there are already bike trails for varying abilities through the woods and hills. Montjuïc, around the castle, is another popular place for mountain-biking. Bikes are allowed on the metro, on FGC trains, and on the Montjuïc and Vallvidrera funiculars.

The city also hosts a variety of annual **cycling events**. The Semana Catalana (Ⓦ www.semanacatalana.com) at the end of March is the big regional race, while the Tour of Spain (*Vuelta Espana*) also usually passes through Catalunya. In Barcelona itself, May sees the Bicycle Fiesta, with a week's worth of rides and events, while September is another big month, with races during the Mercè festival and a day during the city's "Mobility Week" dedicated to cycling. In October, there's an annual international cycle race to Montjuïc. Best place to find out more is the main tourist office in Plaça de Catalunya, or call the city information line on ℡010.

14

LISTINGS | Sports and outdoor activities

225

Useful contact

Amics de la Bicic/Demostenes 19 ℡933 394 060, Ⓦ www.amicsdelabici.org; Ⓜ Plaça de Sants. The "Friends of the Bike" organize a full range of events and activities, from rides to bike mechanic courses.

Football

In Barcelona, football is a genuine obsession, with support for the local giants, FC (Futbol Club) **Barcelona**, raised to an art form. The team plays at the splendid Camp Nou stadium in the north of the city and, even if you don't coincide with a game, the stadium's football museum alone is worth the trip. All the details are on p.116. The other local team – though not to be compared – is RCD (Reial Club Deportiu) **Espanyol**, whose games are played at the Olympic stadium in Montjuïc.

The season runs from late August until May, with games usually played on Sundays (though sometimes on other days). You'll have little problem getting a **ticket** to see an Espanyol game: either just turn up on the day, or buy tickets up to three days in advance from the stadium ticket office. It's also fairly straightforward to get tickets for FC Barcelona. The Camp Nou seats 98,000, which means it's only really full for big games against Real Madrid, or regional rivals like Valencia and Bilbao, or for major European ties. For all other games, some tickets are put on general sale a week before each match (and may be available at ticket booths on the day), or try ServiCaixa. Touts and season-ticket holders at the ground also offer spare tickets for most matches. The cheapest seats at both grounds start at €20, though for a typical league game at Barcelona you're more likely to end up paying €30–40 (and be seated *very* high up).

Team contacts

FC Barcelona Camp Nou, Avgda. Arístides Maillol ☏ 934 963 600, ⓦ www.fcbarcelona .com; Ⓜ Collblanc/Maria Cristina.

RCD Espanyol Estadi Olímpic, Pg. Olímpic 17–19 ☏ 932 927 700, ⓦ www.rcdespanyol .com; Ⓜ Espanya, then free shuttle bus from Pl. d'Espanya on match days.

Horse riding

The municipal riding school on Montjuïc offers lessons and courses for adults (beginners especially welcome), children and disabled people, or you can just have a taster with an hour-long riding session for around €15.

Riding school

Escola Municipal d'Hípica La Foixarda Avgda. Montanyans 1, Montjuïc ☏ 934 261 066;

Ⓜ Espanya, then bus #50. Office open Mon–Fri 4.30–9.30pm.

Ice-skating

There are a couple of ice rinks in the city, including one at FC Barcelona's Camp Nou stadium. At the Roger de Flor rink there's a bar from where you can watch the action. It's a good idea to have someone check hours and restrictions before you go, as weekends and holidays especially can see the rinks inundated with children.

Ice rinks

Pavelló Pista Gel Camp Nou, c/Arístides

Maillol 12 ☏ 934 963 600; Ⓜ Collblanc/Maria Cristina. Public hours Mon 10am–2pm & 4–6pm, Tues–Thurs 10am–2pm &

4–7.30pm, Fri 10am–2pm & 4–8pm, Sat & Sun 10am–1.45pm & 4.30–8.45pm. Admission €8, including skate rental. **Skating Pista de Gel** c/Roger de Flor 168, **Eixample** ☎932 452 800, ⓦwww.skatingbcn.com; ⓂTetuan. Public

hours Mon 5–10pm, Tues–Thurs 10.30am–1.30pm & 5–10pm, Fri 10.30am–1.30pm & 5pm–midnight, Sat 10.30am–2pm & 5pm–midnight, Sun 10.30am–2pm & 5–10pm. Admission €9.50, including skate rental.

Roller skating/blading

There are a couple of places where you can rent skates and blades, and an increasing number of locations where you can hang out in like-minded company. The Passeig Marítim and Port Olímpic area (ⓂCiutadella-Vila Olímpica) see heavy traffic, skaters and pedestrians alike, while other popular runs include Arc de Triomf (ⓂArc de Triomf), Parc Joan Miró (ⓂTarragona), Barceloneta, next to the Palau del Mar (ⓂBarceloneta), and Plaça de les Glòries (ⓂGlòries).

Skate/blade rental

Decathlon Pl. Vila de Madrid 1–3, Barri Gòtic ☎933 426 161; ⓂCatalunya. Big sports store with rental outlet.
Scenic c/de la Marina 22, Vila Olímpica

☎932 211 666; ⓂCiutadella-Vila Olímpica. This bike rental shop also rents skates and blades, from €5 an hour. You can ask here about organized group skates, which usually depart from the shop once a week.

Running and jogging

The Passeig Marítim (ⓂCiutadella-Vila Olímpica) is the best place for a seafront run – there's a five-kilometre promenade from Barceloneta all the way to the River Besòs. To get off the beaten track, you'll need to head for the heights of Montjuïc or the Parc de la Collserola.

The **Barcelona Marathon** is in March; information on ☎932 680 114. There's also a half-marathon and road races during the September Mercè festival, and an annual twelve-kilometre run (June) organized by El Corte Inglés, which attracts thousands onto the streets.

Sports centres

Every city neighbourhood has a sports centre, most with swimming pools but also offering a variety of other sports, games and activities. Schedules and prices vary, so it's best to contact the centres directly for any sport you might be interested in. Most have a general daily admission fee (around €12–15) if all you want is a swim and use of the gym. A couple of the more useful centres are listed below, but for a full rundown call ☎010 or consult the sports section database on ⓦwww.bcn.es.

Poliesportiu Marítim Pg. Marítim 33, Vila Olímpica ☎932 240 440, ⓦwww.claror.org; ⓂCiutadella-Vila Olímpica. Large complex by the Port Olímpic with a pool, gym and sauna, plus a wide range of organized

activities and games, from aerobics, dance and yoga to indoor biking, beach tennis and hydrotherapy. Open Mon–Fri 7am–midnight, Sat 8am–9pm, Sun 8am–5pm.

Poliesportiu Municpal Frontó Colom
Ramblas 18, Barri Gòtic ☎ 933 024 025;
Ⓜ**Drassanes**. Centrally situated sports
centre with pool and gym, where you can
see traditional Spanish *frontón* (handball)
and possibly a glimpse of the Basque *jai
alai*, a type of handball played with scoop-
shaped rackets, and reputedly the fastest
sport in the world. Mon–Fri 7.30am–10pm,
Sat 9am–8pm, Sun 9am–2pm.

Swimming

The city **beaches** are fine for a stroll across the sand and an ice cream, but the
water's none too welcoming and you'd do best to save your swimming for the
region's coastal beaches (Sitges is the best) or one of Barcelona's many municipal **pools**. There are scores of them, but we've picked out three of the best
below. You may need to show your passport before being allowed in, and you'll
need to wear a swimming cap. If you're hardy enough, the annual Christmas
swimming cup involves diving into the port on December 25 and racing other
like-minded fools.

Swimming pools

**Club Natació Atlètic Barceloneta Pl. del
Mar, Barceloneta** ☎ 932 210 010,
Ⓦwww.cnab.org; ⓂCiutadella-Vila Olímpica.
One indoor pool, one outdoor, plus bar,
restaurant and gym facilities. Public hours
Mon–Fri 6.30am–11pm, Sat 7am–11pm,
Sun 8am–5pm (until 8pm mid-May to
Sept). Daily admission for non-members
is around €7.
**Piscina Municipal de Montjuïc Avgda.
Miramar 31, Montjuïc** ☎ 934 430 046; **Funicular
de Montjuïc**. The city's most beautiful outdoor pool, high on Montjuïc. Only open
end July to mid-September, daily
11am–6pm. Admission is €4, but if you
present a metro/bus ticket you'll get €1
discount.
**Piscines Bernat Picornell Avgda. de l'Estadi
30–40, Montjuïc** ☎ 934 234 041, Ⓦwww
.picornell.com; ⓂEspanya, then bus #50.
Remodelled and expanded for the
Olympics, the indoor pools are open all
year, while the outdoor pools are open to
the public in summer. Public hours Mon–Fri
7am–midnight, Sat 7am–9pm, Sun
7.30am–4pm. Admission €8.

Tennis

The main municipal tennis centre at Vall d'Hebron is the best place to play.
Unlike many clubs in the city, you can rent courts by the hour without being a
member. There are asphalt and clay courts, costing around €15 an hour, plus a
pool, gym and café. Rackets are available for rent. Other municipal tennis
courts are listed on Ⓦwww.bcn.es, while for private clubs consult the website
of the Federació Catalana de Tennis (Ⓦwww.fctennis). One of these, the Reial
Club de Tennis Barcelona-1899, hosts the **Barcelona Open** every April.

Tennis courts

Centro Municipal de Tennis Pg. Vall d'Hebron
178–196, Vall d'Hebron ☎ 934 276 500;
ⓂMontbau. Public hours Mon–Fri
8am–11pm, weekends 8am–9pm.

Watersports

Courses and instruction in catamaran/laser sailing, kayaking and windsurfing,
from two hours to two days, are available from the Port Olímpic's sailing club,

Centre Municipal de Vela. At Base Nàutica, by Mar Bella beach, you can rent boats, windsurfers and snorkelling equipment, and there's a popular bar here as well. Prices at either vary considerably, but you can expect to pay around €30 for a couple of hours' windsurfing or €180 for a two-day elementary sailing course.

Watersports centres

Base Nàutica de la Mar Bella Avgda. Litoral ⊕ 932 210 432, ⊛ www.basenautica.org; Ⓜ Ciutadella-Vila Olímpica, then bus #41. Office open daily 9.30am–9pm.

Centre Municipal de Vela Moll de Gregal, Port Olímpic ⊕ 932 257 940, ⊛ www.vela -barcelona .com; Ⓜ Ciutadella-Vila Olímpica. Office open Mon–Fri 9am–9pm, Sat & Sun 9am–8pm.

Shopping

While for sheer size and scope Barcelona cannot compete with Paris or the world's other fashion capitals, it is one of the world's most stylish cities – architecture, fashion and decoration are thoroughly permeated by Catalan *disseny* (design). All of this, naturally, makes for great shopping, from designer clothes and accessories to crafts and household accompaniments. Moreover, Barcelona is an undeniably pleasant place to shop: the wide boulevards of the Eixample, and the pedestrianized streets in the Barri Gòtic and La Ribera, both encourage lengthy browsing.

Many visitors will find the city to be relatively cheap for a lot of items, and even more so if you coincide with the **annual sales** (*rebaixes, rebajas*) that follow the main fashion seasons – mid-January until the end of February, and throughout July and August. Non-EU residents can get a VAT refund on each purchase over the value of €90; look for the "Tax-Free Shopping" logo in stores.

Shop **opening hours** are typically Monday to Saturday 10am to 1.30/2pm and 4.30 to 7.30/8pm, though all the bigger shops, various markets, department stores and shopping centres stay open over lunchtime. Some department stores and shopping malls stay open until 10pm, while smaller shops close on Saturday afternoons or may vary their hours in other ways. All the stores below are open in August unless otherwise stated. Barcelona's daily food **markets**, all in covered halls, are open from Monday to Saturday, 8am to 3pm and 5pm till 8pm, though the most famous, La Boqueria on the Ramblas, opens right through the day.

Where to shop

The best general **shopping areas** in the Barri Gòtic are the old streets off the upper part of the Ramblas, like c/Portaferrissa, c/del Pi, Avinguda Portal de l'Àngel and Baixada de la Llibreteria. In the Eixample, you start with the area immediately around Plaça de Catalunya, and then move along Passeig de Gràcia and Rambla de Catalunya, before heading further north along streets like c/Muntaner, Avinguda Diagonal and Via Augusta. It's in this last area that the big international designer names such as Calvin Klein and Versace are to be found. New **designers** can be found in the streets of La Ribera, around Passeig del Born (c/Flassaders, c/Rec, c/Calders, c/Espartería, c/Vidrería, c/Bonaire) where recently a series of funky shops has opened up. For **secondhand and vintage clothing**, stores line the whole of c/de la Riera Baixa (El Raval), with others nearby on c/del Carme and c/de l'Hospital, and on Saturdays there's a street market here. For **antiques** – books, furniture, paintings and artefacts – the main Barri Gòtic streets are c/de la Palla (starts at Plaça Nova, by La Seu), c/Banys Nous and Baixada Santa Eulàlia, best combined with the antique market on Thursdays in front of the cathedral. Independent **music** and CD stores are concentrated on c/dels Tallers (El Raval), just off the top of the Ramblas.

Barcelona souvenirs

If you're looking for original gift ideas, some of the best hunting can be found in the shops of any of the city's museums, where you'll find reasonably priced and unique examples of Catalan *disseny*, and other original items ranging from postcards to replica works of art. Other good souvenirs include:

* ceramics, widely sold in the streets around La Seu.
* anything from the city's delicatessens, like cooked Catalan meats and sausages, artisan cheeses, *turrón* (almond fudge), *mojama* (smoked tuna) and dried wild mushrooms.
* a *porrón* (the long-spouted glass drinking jar).
* CDs and tapes of Catalan rock and pop, *sardana* music, Spanish rock or flamenco.
* unique pieces from some of the workshops around the Born (La Ribera).

Antiques

Antigua Cerería de Luis Codina c/Bisbe 2, Barri Gòtic; Ⓜ Jaume I. Candles and religious artefacts.

L'Arca del Avia c/Banys Nous 20, Barri Gòtic; Ⓜ Liceu. Catalan brides used to fill up their nuptial trunk (*arca*) with embroidered bed linen and lace. Period (eighteenth-, nineteenth- and early-twentieth century) costumes can be hired or purchased as well – Kate Winslet's *Titanic* costume came from here.

El Bulevard dels Antiquarius Pg. de Gràcia 55–57, Eixample; Ⓜ Passeig de Gràcia. Over seventy shops full of (overpriced) antiques of all kinds.

En La Prensa de Aquel Día c/Tigre 20, El Raval; Ⓜ Universitat. Old newspapers from the early 1900s onwards for sale.

Fernando Selvaggio c/Freneria 12, Barri Gòtic; Ⓜ Jaume I. Antique books, postcards, maps and drawings.

Las Tres Ranas c/Nou de Sant Francesc 17, Barri Gòtic; Ⓜ Drassanes. Beautifully restored furniture and period objects combined with some of their own designs. The unusual facade might remind you of the Addams' family's house.

Urbana c/Còrsega 258, Eixample; Ⓜ Diagonal. Shop selling restored mirrors, fireplaces and other fittings rescued from demolition. The other branch, at c/Sèneca 13, Gràcia, (Ⓜ Diagonal), does the same with old furniture.

Arts and crafts

Art Escudellers c/Escudellers 23–25, Barri Gòtic; Ⓜ Liceu. An enormous shop selling ceramics from different regions of Spain. Not cheap, but a good selection.

Baraka c/dels Canvis Vells 2, La Ribera; Ⓜ Barceloneta. All things Morroccan – *objets*, gifts, books and music.

La Caixa de Fang c/Freneria 1, Barri Gòtic; Ⓜ Jaume I. This has very good-value ceramics and recycled glass. It's off Bxda. Llibreteria, behind the cathedral.

Centre Català d'Artesania Pg. de Gràcia 55, Eixample; Ⓜ Passeig de Gràcia. Government-run Catalan Crafts Centre, with a shop full of handicrafts plus exhibitions of regional arts and crafts.

Cereria Subirà Bxda. Llibreteria 7, Barri Gòtic; Ⓜ Jaume I. Barcelona's oldest shop (since 1760), with a beautiful original interior, selling hand-crafted candles with original designs.

Espai Vidre c/dels Angels 8, El Raval; Ⓜ Liceu. Famous gallery selling artistic items of glass and crystal by different designers.

Grafiques El Tinell c/Freneria 3, Barri Gòtic; Ⓜ Jaume I. Expensive, handmade decorated paper and books with interesting designs.

Incas c/de la Boqueria 21, Barri Gòtic; Ⓜ Liceu. Local Andean outlet with Ecuadorian, Bolivian and Peruvian crafts.

Kitsch Pl. de Montcada 10, La Ribera; Ⓜ Jaume I. Known for its papier-mâché models – matadors, flamenco dances, pierrots and other characters – which are all unique. Also handmade paper fans.

Papirum Bxda. Llibreteria 2, Barri Gòtic; Ⓜ Jaume I. Superb hand-painted paper.

1748 Pl. de Montcada 2, La Ribera; Ⓜ Jaume I. Good (if touristy) ceramic shop with one of the widest selections in the old town.

2 Bis c/Bisbe 2 bis, Barri Gòtic; Ⓜ Jaume I. Expensive, but interesting, ceramics, glassware, masks and mobiles.

Craft workshops: a tour of the Born

Crafts have always been central to Barcelona's industry, with a history dating back to the Middle Ages. To learn and exercise a certain craft, you had to be a member of a guild, while many of the street names in the Born (ⓂJaume I/Barceloneta), particularly, refer to the crafts once practised there; eg c/de la Argenteria, silversmith's street, c/Mirallers, the street where they used to make mirrors, or c/Sombrerers, where hats (*sombreros*) were made. In recent years, the Born has once again become a craft centre as empty buildings and warehouses have been opened up as workshops. Some artists work behind closed doors, while others have a space at the front where they sell their limited series or unique pieces.

The **workshops** are concentrated in the streets around the Museu Picasso, particularly on c/Cotoners, c/Esquirol, c/Barra de Ferro, c/Mirallers, c/Banys Vells and c/Flassaders. A good way to see them is to coincide with the **Tallers Oberts** (or open workshops), on the last weekend of May and first weekend in June. Information can be obtained from Foment de les Arts Decoratives (FAD), Pl. dels Àngels 5–6 (☎934 437 520, ☻www.fadweb.com). For a self-guided itinerary around the **textile galleries and workshops** of the Born, consult ☻www.itineraritextil.com, or contact My Favourite Things (see p.29 for details), whose **workshop tour** ("Creative talent in Barcelona") introduces you directly to selected artists, who demonstrate their crafts (with the option to buy).

Books

General

BCN c/Roger de Llúria 118, Eixample; ⓂDiagonal. Good selection of novels and English-language teaching books.
Casa del Llibre Pg. de Gràcia 62, Eixample; ⓂPasseig de Gràcia. Barcelona's biggest book emporium, strong on literature and humanities with lots of English titles.
Crisol Rambla de Catalunya 81, Eixample; ⓂPasseig de Gràcia. Magazines, books, DVDs and music – open until 1am.
Elephant c/Creu dels Molers 12, Poble Sec; ⓂPoble Sec. Only stocks English-language books, with cheap prices for current novels, classics, children's books and secondhand. Small café at the back serves English tea, home-made brownies, cakes and cookies.
Happy Books c/Pelai 32, and Pg. de Gràcia 77, Eixample; ⓂUniversitat/Catalunya. Good travel and dictionary sections as well as some other English-language titles. Generally the best prices and some very good sales.
Laie c/Pau Claris 85, Eixample; ⓂPasseig de Gràcia. Excellent selection of humanities and literature and lots of English-language titles. Café/restaurant upstairs.

Art, design and photography

Kowasa c/de Mallorca 235, Eixample; ⓂProvença. The city's best bookstore for photography and photographic art.
Museu Nacional d'Art de Catalunya Palau Nacional, Montjuïc; ⓂEspanya. The gallery shop has the city's best selection of books on Catalan art, architecture, design and style.
Ras c/Doctor Joaquim Dou 10, El Raval; ⓂLiceu. Specializes in books and magazines on graphic design, architecture and photography. Temporary exhibitions at the back.

Travel, guides and maps

Altair Gran Via de les Corts Catalanes 616, Eixample; ⓂUniversitat. Travel books, guides, maps and world music.
Guia-Llibreria de Viatges Trav. de Gràcia 146, Gràcia; ⓂDiagonal. Small bookshop specializing in travel books, maps and guides. Closed Aug.
Llibreria Quera c/Petritxol 2, Barri Gòtic; ⓂLiceu. Maps and trekking guides in a cramped little store. Closed Sat in Aug.

Clothes, shoes and accessories

Designer fashion

Adolfo Domínguez Pg. de Gràcia 32 & 89, Eixample; ⓂPasseig de Gràcia. Superior men's and women's designs from the well-known *gallego* designer.

Agua del Carmec/Bonaire 5, La Ribera; Ⓜ Jaume 1. Original designs by Rona, limited series, kitschy but stylish.

Antonio Miróc/Consell de Cent 348, Eixample; Ⓜ Passeig de Grácia; plus **Groc**Rambla de Catalunya 100, Eixample, Ⓜ Diagonal; and c/Muntaner 385, Eixample, Ⓜ Passeig de Grácia. The showcases for Barcelona's most innovative designer, Antonio Miró, especially good for men's suits, with Miró clothes and shoes for men and women plus other labels at the *Groc* outlets.

Armand Basi Pg. de Grácia 49, Eixample; Ⓜ Passeig de Grácia. Men and women's clothes, jackets and accessories from the hot Spanish designer.

Cuca Ferac/Cremat Gran 9, La Ribera; Ⓜ Jaume I. Very original children's clothing, a combination of new and vintage – in the alleyway next to the Picasso Museum.

Custo Barcelona Pl. de les Olles 7, La Ribera, Ⓜ Barceloneta; and c/Ferran 40, Barri Gòtic, Ⓜ Liceu. Hugely colourful designer T-shirts, tops and sweaters of all kinds for men and women; denim too.

Futurac/Escudellers 56, Barri Gòtic; Ⓜ Liceu. Argentinean designer producing clothes from interesting, colourful fabrics.

Giménez & Zuazoc/Elisabets 20, El Raval, Ⓜ Catalunya; and c/del Rec 42, La Ribera, Ⓜ Jaume I. Cutting-edge women's fashion, funky and informal.

Gonzalo Comella Pg. de Grácia 6, Eixample; Ⓜ Passeig de Grácia. Classic clothes since 1924 for men and women.

JaninaRambla de Catalunya 94, Eixample, Ⓜ Diagonal; and Avgda. Paul Casals 8, FGC Muntaner. Barcelona's premier lingerie designer. Also swimsuits.

Jean-Pierre Bua Avgda. Diagonal 469, Eixample; Ⓜ Diagonal. The city's temple for fashion victims: a postmodern shrine for Yamamoto, Gaultier, Miyake, Westwood, Miró and other international stars.

Merxe Hernándezc/Rec 32, La Ribera; Ⓜ Jaume I. Innovative designs: colourful and frilly.

Naifac/Doctor Joaquim Dou 11, El Raval, Ⓜ Liceu; and c/Rec 22, La Ribera, Ⓜ Jaume 1. Original, colourful, informal, very reasonably priced women's clothing.

Natalie Capell, Atelier de Modac/Banys Vells 4, La Ribera; Ⓜ Jaume I. Her own very elegant designs, in Twenties and Thirties style.

High-street fashion

MangoAvgda. Portal de l'Ángel 7, Barri Gòtic,
Ⓜ Catalunya; Pg. de Grácia 65, Eixample, Ⓜ Diagonal; La Maquinista, Ⓜ Sant Andreu; l'Illa, Ⓜ María Cristina; plus others. Now available worldwide, Barcelona is where Mango began (and the prices here are cheaper than in North America and other European countries).

ZaraAvgda. Portal de l'Ángel 7, Barri Gòtic, Ⓜ Catalunya; Avgda. Diagonal 584, Eixample, Ⓜ Diagonal; c/Pelai 58, Eixample, Ⓜ Universitat; Rambla de Catalunya 67, Eixample, Ⓜ Passeig de Grácia; La Maquinista, Ⓜ Sant Andreu; plus others. Trendy but cheap seasonal fashion from the Spanish chain with shops in over forty countries. Their *Bershka* outlets (on c/Pelai and Avgda. Portal del l'Angel; Ⓜ Catalunya) sell funky stuff for teenagers.

Jewellery and accessories

Atalanta Manufactura Pg. del Born 10, La Ribera; Ⓜ Jaume I. Naturally dyed and painted silk and linen – lovely scarves and wallhangings.

Forum Ferlandinac/Ferlandina 31, El Raval; Ⓜ Universitat. Inventive, contemporary jewellery using a variety of design mediums.

Joaquín Beraoc/Rosselló 277, Eixample; Ⓜ Diagonal. Avant-garde jewellery in a stunningly designed shop.

Obach Sombreriac/del Call 2, Barri Gòtic; Ⓜ Liceu. An excellent selection of hats and caps of all types, from berets to stetsons.

Rafa Teja Atelierc/Santa Maria 18, La Ribera; Ⓜ Jaume I. Gorgeous silk scarves, mohair wraps and Chinese-style silk jackets and dresses.

Leather

LoewePg. de Grácia 35, Eixample, Ⓜ Passeig de Grácia; Avgda. Diagonal 570, Eixample, Ⓜ Diagonal. Superb leather jackets, coats, gloves and other accessories at heart-stopping prices.

Secondhand, vintage and discount outlets

Argotc/de l'Hospital 107, El Raval; Ⓜ Liceu. Small, secondhand clothes shop where good bargains occasionally turn up.

Contribucionsc/Riera de Sant Miquel 30, Grácia; Ⓜ Diagonal. Discount outlet for Spanish and Italian designer labels.

Lailoc/Riera Baixa 20, El Raval; Ⓜ Liceu. Secondhand and vintage clothes shop that's usually worth a look, with a massively wide-ranging stock. Theatre costumes for rent at the back.

Recicle Recicle c/Riera Baixa 13, El Raval; ⓂLiceu. Secondhand and vintage fashion, from the Fifties onwards, with a rapid turnover.

Stock land c/Comtal 22, Barri Gòtic; ⓂUrquinaona. Bargain-hunter's dream. Top-name haute couture at thirty- to sixty-percent discounts.

Shoes

Calçats Solé c/Ample 7, Barri Gòtic; ⓂDrassanes. Handmade shoes and sandals from different regions of Spain at reasonable prices.

Camper El Triangle, Pl. de Catalunya, ⓂCatalunya; also in Eixample at c/Muntaner 248, ⓂDiagonal; c/València 249, ⓂPasseig de Gràcia; and Avgda. Pau Casals 5, ⓂDiagonal. Spain's most stylish, value-for-money shoe-shop chain, with the handiest outlet inside Plaça de Catalunya's Triangle.

La Manual Alpargatera c/d'Avinyó 7, Barri Gòtic; ⓂLiceu. Workshop making and selling *alpargatas* (espadrilles) to order, as well as other straw and rope work.

Muxaert c/Rosselló 230, Eixample, ⓂDiagonal; and Rambla de Catalunya 47, Eixample, ⓂCatalunya. Barcelona's top-class shoe designer, pricey gems for men and women.

Rouge Poison c/Flassaders 34, La Ribera; ⓂJaume I. Beautifully designed shop, with expensive handmade shoes by Rupert Sanderson and Jean-Baptiste Rautureau.

Department stores and shopping malls

Bulevard Rosa Pg. de Gràcia 55, Eixample; ⓂPasseig de Gràcia. Barcelona's first shopping arcade, with over one hundred shops, specializing in chic designer gear. Mon–Sat 10.30am–8.30pm.

Tomb Bus

The Tomb Bus shopping line service connects Pl. de Catalunya with the Diagonal (Pl. Pius XII), an easy way to reach the uptown L'Illa and El Corte Inglès shopping centres. Departures are every 7min (Mon–Fri 7am–9.38pm, Sat 9.10am–9.20pm); tickets (available on the bus) are €1.25 one way, €5 for one day's unlimited travel, or €8 for seven trips.

Centre Comercial Barcelona Glòries Pl. de les Glòries Catalanes 1, Eixample; ⓂGlòries. Big mall with all the national high-street names as well as bars, restaurants and a cinema complex. Mon–Sat 9.30am–1pm.

El Corte Inglés Pl. de Catalunya 14, ⓂCatalunya; Avgda. del Portal de l'Angel 19–21, Barri Gòtic, ⓂCatalunya; Avgda. Diagonal 471 & 617, Eixample, ⓂMaría Cristina. The city's biggest department store has several branches – for music, books, computers and sports gear, head for the Portal de l'Angel branch; visit the Pl. de Catalunya branch for its top-floor café. Mon–Sat 10am–9.30pm.

Les Galeries Maldà c/Portaferrissa 22, Barri Gòtic; ⓂLiceu. An old-town arcade full of boutiques with local and international labels. Mon–Sat 10am–8pm.

L'Illa Avgda. Diagonal 555–559, Eixample; ⓂMaría Cristina. Uptown shopping mall with national and international shops, including a FNAC, which is good for music and books. Mon–Sat 10am–10pm.

La Maquinista Pg. de Potosí, Sant Andreu; ⓂSant Andreu. Huge shopping centre in a restored locomotive factory with over 200 shops (including Mango, Zara, Bershka Cortefiel, Miró), a multiplex cinema and bowling alley. Mon–Sat 10am–10pm.

Maremàgnum Moll d'Espanya, Port Vell; ⓂDrassanes. Souvenir, leisure and sports-wear shops – including an official FC Barcelona store – alongside restaurants, fast-food joints and a multiscreen cinema. Daily 11am–11pm.

El Mercadillo c/Portaferrissa 17, Barri Gòtic; ⓂLiceu. Double-decker complex of shops selling skate-, club- and beachwear and shoes – look out for the camel marking the entrance. There's a bar upstairs with a nice patio garden. Mon–Sat 11am–9pm.

El Triangle Pl. de Catalunya 4, Eixample; ⓂCatalunya. Shopping centre dominated by the flagship FNAC store, which specializes in books (good travel and English selections), music CDs and computer software. Also a Habitat, Sephora for cosmetics, various clothes shops, plus magazines and café on the ground floor. Mon–Sat 10am–10pm.

Design, decorative art and household goods

BD Edicions de Diseño c/Mallorca 291, Eixample; ⓂDiagonal. The building is by

Domènech i Montaner, the interior filled with the very latest in furniture and household design. Also reproductions of Gaudí, Dalí, Eames, etc.

Daaz c/Flassaders 27–29, La Ribera; ⓂJaume I. Pascal Frot designs furniture and lamps and is also responsible for the interior of various shops in Barcelona (eg the shoe shop opposite). Temporary exhibitions as well.

D.Barcelona Avgda. Diagonal 367, Eixample; ⓂDiagonal. Contemporary, imaginative personal and household items.

Dom Pg. de Gràcia 76, Eixample, ⓂPasseig de Gràcia; and c/d'Avinyo 7, Barri Gòtic, ⓂLiceu. Original, amusing household and personal items (alarm clocks to olive-oil dispensers, knives and forks to bouncy chairs) at accessible prices.

Ganivetería Roca Pl. del Pi 3, Barri Gòtic; ⓂLiceu. Nice old shop, dating from 1911, selling a big range of knives, cutlery, corkscrews and other household goods – including a fine array of gentlemen's shaving gear.

Gotham c/Cervantes 7, Barri Gòtic; ⓂJaume 1. Small shop selling Fifties, Sixties and Seventies furniture, lighting and accessories.

Pilma Avgda. Diagonal 403, Eixample; ⓂDiagonal. Expensive and stylish household design and furniture.

Vinçon Pg. de Gràcia 96, Eixample; ⓂPasseig de Gràcia. Stylish and original household items, pioneered by Fernando Amat – known as the "Spanish Terence Conran". It's a fantastic building (with an impressive *modernista* fireplace upstairs), never mind what's on sale, and there are temporary art and design exhibitions.

Food

Daily food markets

Mercat de la Barceloneta Pl. de la Font, Barceloneta; ⓂBarceloneta.

Mercat de la Concepció c/Valencia, Eixample; ⓂPasseig de Gràcia.

Mercat de la Llibertat Pl. de la Llibertat, Gràcia; ⓂFontana.

Mercat Sant Antoni Ronda de Sant Pau/Ronda de Sant Antoni, Eixample; ⓂSant Antoni.

Mercat Sant Josep/La Boqueria Ramblas; ⓂLiceu.

Mercat Santa Catarina Avgda. Francesc Cambó 16, Sant Pere; ⓂJaume I.

Specialist food stores

La Casa del Bacalao c/del Comtal 8, Barri Gòtic; ⓂCatalunya. For a shop selling nothing but salt cod (sealed to take home, if you decide to buy), the window is as pretty as a picture.

Casa Gispert c/Sombrerers 23, La Ribera; ⓂJaume I. Roasters of nuts, coffee and spices for over 150 years – a truly delectable store.

Colmado Quilez Rambla de Catalunya 63, Eixample; ⓂPasseig de Gràcia. Classic Catalan grocery, piled high with tins, preserves, wines and chocolates, plus a groaning *xarcuteria* counter.

Fleca Balmes c/Balmes 156, Eixample; ⓂPasseig de Gràcia. Extraordinary range of plaited and shaped breads from one of the oldest bakeries in the city – look for the sign of the long baguette.

Formatgeria La Seu c/Daguería 16, Barri Gòtic; ⓂJaume I. The best farmhouse cheeses from all over Spain. Catherine, who's Scottish, will introduce you into the world of cheese with Saturday cheese tastings.

Origens 99,9% c/Vidrería 6–8, La Ribera; ⓂJaume I. Catalan delicatessen extraordinaire: pâtés, special sauces, olive oils, *turron* and more.

Tot Formatge Pg. del Born 13, La Ribera; ⓂJaume I. A stupendous array of cheeses from Spain and elsewhere in Europe.

Troika c/de la Unio, El Raval; ⓂLiceu. A definite first for Barcelona – a Russian deli, with everything from huge jars of pickles to flavoured vodka.

Markets

Antiques Avgda. de la Catedral, Barri Gòtic; ⓂJaume I. Every Thurs (not Aug) from 9am. Better for bargains is the market on the Port Vell harbourside (ⓂBarceloneta) at weekends from 11am.

Art Pl. Sant Josep Oriol, Barri Gòtic; ⓂLiceu. Every weekend from 10am: still lives to kistch harbour views.

Christmas Avgda. de la Catedral, and surrounding streets, Barri Gòtic; ⓂJaume I. The *Fira de Santa Llúcia*, daily Dec 1–22, 10am–9pm.

Coins, books and postcards Mercat Sant Antoni, Ronda de Sant Pau/Ronda de Sant Antoni, Eixample; ⓂSant Antoni. Every Sun

from 9am to 2pm. Finish off with a *vermouth negre* in the *Tres Tombs* bar.
Coins and stamps Pl. Reial, Barri Gòtic; ⓂLiceu. Every Sun 10am to 2pm.
Farmers' market Pl. del Pi, Barri Gòtic; ⓂLiceu. First and third Fri and Sat of the month – honey, cheese, cakes and other produce; also during the Festa de la Mercè in Sept, and the Festa de Sant Ponç in c/de l'Hospital on May 11.
Flea market Els Encants, northwest side of Pl. de les Glòries Catalanes, Eixample; ⓂGlòries. Every Mon, Wed, Fri & Sat 8am–1.30pm, for clothes, jewellery, junk and furniture. An absolute must for flea-market addicts.
Flowers and birds Ramblas; ⓂLiceu. Stalls present daily; flowers also in abundance at Mercat de la Concepció.

good place to pick up concert tickets.
Etnomusic c/del Bonsuccés 6, El Raval; ⓂCatalunya. World music specialist, especially good for all types of South American music.
Music World-4 c/Tallers 1, El Raval; ⓂCatalunya. Specializes in rock and pop as well as tickets for live shows.
Planet Music c/Mallorca 214, Eixample; ⓂPasseig de Gràcia. Big selection, particularly good on flamenco, classical and world music.
Revolver c/Tallers 11 & 13, El Raval; ⓂCatalunya. Barcelona's most famous specialist store for rock and pop music. Has vinyl, CDs and tapes, both new and secondhand, and is one of the main ticket outlets in Barcelona.

Museums, galleries and attractions

L'Aquàrium Moll d'Espanya, Port Vell; ⓂDrassanes/Barceloneta. A fish-related extravaganza, from the mundane (T-shirts, stationery, posters, games, toiletries) to cult must-haves (Mariscal-designed bathroom transfers).
Les Muses el Palau c/Sant Pere Més Alt 1, Sant Pere; ⓂUrquinaona. Shop associated with the Palau de la Música Catalana, just across the square – *modernista*-styled porcelain, jewellery and crystal plus art supplies, artistic reproductions and choral music CDs.
Museu d'Art Contemporani de Barcelona Pl. dels Àngels, El Raval; ⓂUniversitat. Designer aprons, espresso cups, T-shirts, posters, gifts and toys, plus art and design books.
Museu Barbier-Mueller c/de Montcada 14, La Ribera; ⓂJaume I. The pre-Columbian art museum shop has a wide range of ethnic artefacts, from wallhangings and jewellery to terracotta pots and figurines. Definitely the place to pick up your panama hat.
Museu Textil i d'Indumentaria c/de Montcada 12, La Ribera; ⓂJaume I. Funky jewellery, silk ties, candles, kitchen aprons, bags and other design-led gifts and trinkets.

Music

La Casa Pl. Sant Vincenç Martorell 4, El Raval; ⓂCatalunya. Barcelona's best for hip hop, acid jazz, house and techno.
Discos Castelló c/Tallers 3 & 7, El Raval; ⓂCatalunya. Large vinyl and CD selections with a separate store for classical (no. 3). A

Sports

Botiga del Barça Maremàgnum, Moll d'Espanya, Port Vell, ⓂDrassanes/Barceloneta; and at FC Barcelona, Camp Nou, Eixample, ⓂMaría Cristina. You can buy Barça shirts anywhere on the Ramblas, but for official merchandise the hugely well-stocked club stores have it all – including that all important lettering service for the back of the shirt that elevates you to the squad.
Decathlon Pl. Vila de Madrid, Barri Gòtic; ⓂCatalunya. They've got clothes and equipment for 63 sports in this megastore, so you're bound to find what you want. Also bike rental and repair.

Toys, magic, costume and party wear

La Bolsera, c/Xuclá 15, El Raval; ⓂLiceu. Masks, hats, streamers, balloons, party poppers and much more.
El Ingenio c/Rauric 6–8, Barri Gòtic; ⓂLiceu. Juggling, magic and street-performer shop with a *modernista* storefront.
Mariela Marabi c/Flassaders 30, La Ribera; ⓂJaume I. Hand-made finger dolls and teddy bears, which you can assemble yourself.
Palácio de Juguete c/Arcs 8, Barri Gòtic; ⓂJaume I. Good toyshop near the cathedral.
El Rey de la Magica c/Princesa 11, La Ribera; ⓂJaume I. Spain's oldest magic shop – all the tricks of the trade, from rubber chickens to Dracula capes.
Xalar Bxda. Llibreteria 4, Barri Gòtic; ⓂJaume I. Designer and hand-crafted toys – traditional games, dolls' houses, etc.

Children's Barcelona

Taking your children to Barcelona doesn't pose insurmountable travel problems, but it's as well to be aware of the potential difficulties before you go. Below, in "Travelling with children", we've pointed out some of the things you might find tricky, as well as providing a few pointers for a smooth stay. Once you're happily ensconced, and have cracked the transport system, you'll find that not only will your children be given a warm welcome almost everywhere you go, but in many ways the city appears as one huge playground, whether it's a day at the beach or a daredevil cable-car ride. There's plenty to do for children of all ages, much of it free or inexpensive, while if you coincide with one of Barcelona's festivals (see Chapter 13 for full details) you'll be able to join in with the local celebrations, from sweet-tossing and puppet shows to fireworks and human castles. "Children's attractions" rounds up the best of the options for keeping everybody happy; for sporting suggestions and outdoor activities, see Chapter 14.

Travelling with children

With very young children, the main problem is using **public transport**, especially the metro, which seems almost expressly designed to thwart access to pushchairs/strollers. Most stations are accessed by stairs or escalators, and there are steps and stairs within the system itself, making it difficult (if not impossible) for single travellers with young children to get around easily. Even with two adults, you often face a stiff climb out of stations with the pushchair. However, the stations on line 2 – including Passeig de Gràcia and Sagrada Família – are accessible by elevator from street level, and many FGC stations have elevators to the platforms too, including Catalunya, Espanya (for Montserrat trains) and Avdga. del Tibidabo (for Tibidabo). If travelling by bus, try to stick to disabled-accessible routes, on which the buses will have room to handle a stroller. Children under 4 **travel free** on public transport, while there are reduced prices for tickets on the sightseeing Bus Turístic and the cable cars.

Disposable **nappies** (diapers), **baby food, formula milk** and other standard needs are widely available in pharmacies and supermarkets, though not necessarily with the same range or brands that you will be used to at home. Organic baby food, for example, is hard to come by – you can sometimes find the odd jar in a health-food store – and most Spanish non-organic baby foods contain small amounts of sugar or salt. If you require anything specific for your baby or child, it's best to bring it with you or check with the manufacturer about equivalent brands. For relatively cheap, well-made **children's clothing**

Prénatal has an excellent range, and there are branches all over the city, listed under "tiendas" on their website ⓦwww.prenatal.es. Or go to El Corte Inglés for children's and babies' designer labels.

Most establishments are baby-friendly in the sense that you'll be made very welcome if you turn up with a child in tow. Many museum cloakrooms, for example, will be happy to look after your pushchair as you carry your child around the building, while restaurants will make a fuss of your little one. However, specific facilities are not as widespread as they are in the UK or USA. **Baby-changing areas** are relatively rare, except in department stores and shopping centres, and even where they do exist they are not always up to scratch. By far the best is at El Corte Inglés, while El Triangle and Maremàgnum have pull-down changing tables in their public toilets.

Local restaurants tend not to offer **children's menus** (though they will try to accommodate specific requests), highchairs are rarely provided, and restaurants open relatively late for lunch and dinner. In addition, **smoking** is widespread, though this isn't always a problem, as you can sit outside on the *terrassa* on many occasions. Despite best intentions, you might find yourself eating in one of the international franchise restaurants, which tend to be geared more towards families and open throughout the day.

Suitable **accommodation** is easy to find, and most hotels and pensions will be welcoming. However, bear in mind that much of the city's budget accommodation is located in buildings without elevators; while, if you're travelling out of season, it's worth noting that most pensions (as opposed to more expensive hotels) don't have heating systems – and it can get cold. If you want a cot provided, or baby-listening/sitting services, you'll have to pay the price of staying in one of the larger hotels – and, even then, never assume that these facilities are provided, so always check in advance. You'll pay from around €10–12 per hour for **babysitting**, either arranged through your hotel or direct with an agency. The Plaça de Catalunya tourist office can provide an up-to-date list of babysitting agencies.

Children's attractions

If you've spent too much time already in the showpiece museums, galleries and churches, any of the suggestions below should head off a children's revolt. Most have been covered in the text, so you can get more information by turning to the relevant page. Admission charges are almost always reduced for children, though the cut-off age varies from attraction to attraction.

Cinema, shows and theatre

Cinema. Children's films shown at the Filmoteca (see p.214), on Sundays at 5pm.
Font Màgica. The sound and light show in front of the Palau Nacional on Montjuïc (p.82) is always a hit, though it starts quite late.
Imax Port Vell. Three different screens showing giant format/3D documentaries on nature, space and the human body. See p.75.
Statues and street theatre. The Ramblas is one big outdoor show for children, with human statues (p.45) a speciality, not to mention buskers, pavement artists, magicians, and food, bird and flower markets.
Theatre. There are children's puppet shows, music, mime and clowns at the **Fundació Joan Miró (Avgda. Miramar 71–75, Montjuïc ☎934 439 471, ⓦwww.bcn.fjmiro.es; ⓂEspanya & bus #50)**, with performances on Sat at 5.30pm, and Sun at 11.30am and 1pm. **Jove Teatre Regina (c/Sèneca 22, Gràcia ☎932 181 512, ⓦwww.jtregina.com; ⓂDiagonal)** puts on music and comedy productions for children every Sat and Sun at 6pm. And there are more children's puppet

shows and theatrical performances every Sat at 6pm and Sun at noon at **Teatre Nou Tantarantana** (c/les Flors 22, El Raval ☎ 934 417 022; ⓂParal·lel).

Museums and other attractions

L'Aquàrium. Adults might find the Aquarium a bit of a disappointment, but there's no denying its popularity with children. Under-4s get in free, and there are discounts for 4- to 12-year-olds. See p.74.

Museums. Museums with a special interest for children include the **Museu del Football Club Barcelona** (FC Barcelona Museum; p.116); **Museu d'Història de la Ciutat** (City History Museum; p.56); **Museu de Cera** (Wax Museum; p.48); **Museu de la Ciència** (Science Museum; p.121); **Museu de Zoología** (Zoology Museum; p.69); **Museu de la Xocolata** (Chocolate Museum; p.64); **Museu Textil i Indumentaria** (Textile and Industry Museum; p.67); and **Museu Marítim** (Maritime Museum; p.73).

Poble Espanyol. Open-air "museum" of Spanish buildings, craft demonstrations, gift shops, bars and restaurants. Family ticket available. See p.84.

Zoo de Barcelona. All the usual suspects, plus children's zoo and dolphin shows; free for under-3s, discounts for under-12s. See p.69.

Parks and gardens

Gardens. Top *Rough Guide* choice is the **Parc del Laberint** in Horta (p.115), where the hillside gardens, maze and playground provide a great day out.

Parks. In the city, the **Parc de la Ciutadella** (p.68) has the best range of attractions, from a boating lake to a zoo. Older children will love the bizarre gardens and buildings of Gaudí's **Parc Güell** (p.112), while the **Parc de Collserola** (p.121) is a good target for a walk in the hills and a picnic. At **Parc del Castell de l'Oreneta** (daily 10am–dusk), behind Pedralbes monastery, there are miniature train rides and pony rides on Sundays; it's at the end of c/Montevideo (take bus #66 from Pl. Catalunya or #64 from Pl. Universitat to the end of the line and walk up Avgda. d'Espasa).

Playgrounds. Most city kids use the squares as playgrounds, under parental supervision. In **Gràcia**, Plaça de la Virreina

and Plaça de Rius i Taulet are handsome traffic-free spaces with good bars with *terrassas* attached. Wherever your children play, however, you need to keep an eagle eye out for dog dirt. In the old town, the nicest dog- and traffic-free playground is in **Plaça de Vicenç Martorell**, in El Raval, where there are some fenced-off swings in front of a great café, *Kasparo* (see p.175).

Rides and views

Cable cars. The two best rides in the city are the cross-harbour cable car (p.78) from Barceloneta to Montjuïc, and the Telefèric de Montjuïc (p.83), which then lifts you up to the castle at the top of Montjuïc. Neither is for the faint-hearted child or sickly infant.

Las Golondrinas. Sightseeing boat rides around the port and local coast. See p.29.

Mirador de Colón. See the city from the top of the Columbus statue at the bottom of the Ramblas. See p.73.

Torre de Collserola. Stunning views from the telecommunications tower near Tibidabo. Under-3s go free. See p.120.

Tren Turístic de Montjuïc. The little trolley-train rumbles around the Montjuïc hillside, connecting all the attractions. See p.29.

Theme parks

Catalunya en Miniatura Torrelles de Llobregat, 17km southwest (A2 highway, exit 5) ☎ 936 890 960, ⓦ www.catalunyaen-miniatura.com. A theme park with 170 Catalan monuments in miniature, plus train rides, children's shows and playground. Open daily 10am–6pm, later opening April–Sept, closed Mon Nov–March. Adults €9.50, 4–11 years €6.50, under-4s free.

Illa Fantasia Vilassar de Dalt, 25km north of Barcelona, just short of Mataró (exit 9 on the main highway) ☎ 937 514 553, ⓦ www.illafantasia.com. Supposedly the largest water park in Europe, with slides, splash pools, swimming pools, water games and picnic areas. Buy a combined ticket (*billete combinado*) at Barcelona Sants station and you can travel free on the train to Premià de Mar, and then take the free connecting bus to the park. Open mid-May to mid-Sept daily 10am–7pm. Adults €11, 2–10 years €8.

Port Aventura 1hr south of Barcelona, near

Salou/La Pineda (exit 35 on A7) ☎977 779 090, ✆www.portaventura.es. Universal Studios' massive theme park based on five different cultures – Mexico, the Wild West, Polynesia, China and the Mediterranean – plus the Costa Caribe water adventure park. Shops, restaurants and shows, as well as fairground rides (including the biggest roller-coaster in Europe). Trains from Passeig de Gràcia/Barcelona Sants run directly to Port Aventura's own station (1hr 15min; info from RENFE on ☎902 240 202). Open March–Oct daily 10am–8pm, until midnight July & Aug; Nov & Dec Sat & Sun only; Christmas/New Year period open daily. Port Aventura, adults €34, 5–12 years €27 (under-5s free), two-day ticket €49/39; Costa Caribe €17/13.50; or combination three-day, two-park ticket €59/47.

Tibidabo. Dubbed "La Muntanya Magica", the rides and shows in the mountain-top amusement park (see p.119) are unbeatable as far as location goes, though tame compared to those at Port Aventura.

Directory

Absolutely anything about the city – addresses and telephone numbers, festivals dates or council office locations – can be gleaned from the Ajuntament's enormously useful website, @www.bcn.es, which has an English-language version. Or you can call ☎010 (some English-speaking operators available), again with virtually any request for information.

AirlinesAir Europa ☎934 784 713; Air France ☎901 112 666; Alitalia ☎902 1003 23; British Airways ☎902 111 333; EasyJet ☎902 299 992; Iberia ☎902 400 550; KLM ☎902 222 747; Lufthansa ☎902 220 101; Spanair ☎902 131 415; Swissair ☎901 116 706; TAP ☎901 116 718.

AirportEl Prat de Llobregat ☎932 983 838 for general information, ☎902 400 550 for flight information, @www.aena.es/aeropuertos/barcelona. Trains to the airport depart every 30min from Barcelona Sants (5.43am–10.13pm; €2.25) or Pl. de Catalunya (6.08am–10.08pm); Aérobus runs every 12min from Pl. de Catalunya, Pg. de Gràcia or Pl. d'Espanya (Mon–Fri 6am–midnight, Sat & Sun 6.30am–midnight; €3.45).

American Express Offices at Ramblas 74, Barri Gòtic, ⓂLiceu ☎933 011 166 (Mon–Fri 9am–8.30pm, Sat 10am–7pm) and Pg. de Gràcia 101, Eixample, ⓂDiagonal ☎934 852 371 (Mon–Fri 9.30am–6pm, Sat 10am–noon).

Banks and exchange Main bank branches are in Pl. de Catalunya and along Pg. de Gràcia, and there are ATMs all over the city, including on arrival at the airport, Barcelona Sants train station, Estació del Nord bus station and Pl. de Catalunya tourist office. Exchange offices include: airport (daily 7.30am–10.45pm); Barcelona Sants (daily 8am–10pm); El Corte Inglés, Pl. de Catalunya (Mon–Sat 10am–9.30pm); Postal Transfer, Pl. Urquinaona at c/Roger de Lluria (Mon–Fri 10am–11pm, Sat 11am–midnight, Sun noon–11pm); tourist office, Pl. de Catalunya 17 (Mon–Sat 9am–9pm, Sun 9am–2pm).

Bike rental Half-day rental costs around €10–15, full-day €25, with the following companies: Biciclot, c/Sant Joan de Malta 1, Eixample, ⓂClot ☎933 077 475, and Pg. Marítim 33–35, Port Olímpic, ⓂCiutadella-Vila Olímpica ☎932 219 778, @www.biciclot.net; Bicitram, Avgda. Marquès de l'Argentera 15, La Ribera, ⓂBarceloneta ☎607 226 069 or 636 401 997 (weekends & hols only); Decathlon, Pl. Villa de Madrid 1–3, Barri Gòtic, ⓂCatalunya ☎933 426 161; Scenic, c/Marina 22, Port Olímpic, ⓂCiutadella-Vila Olímpica ☎932 211 666; Un Coxte Menys, c/Esparteria 3, La Ribera ⓂBarceloneta ☎932 682 105, @www.bicicletabarcelona.com. For bike tours of the city, see p.28.

BusesThe main bus station is the Estació del Nord, c/de Ali-Bei, ⓂArc de Triomf ☎932 656 508, three blocks north of Parc de la Ciutadella – the information office is open daily 7am–9pm. Companies represented here include: Alsa-Enatcar ☎902 422 242, @www.alsa.es (to many regional Spanish destinations); Bacoma ☎932 313 801 (Andalucia); Eurolines ☎902 405 040, @www.eurolines.es (European destinations); Sarfa ☎902 302 025 (Costa Brava); Teisa ☎933 181 086 (La Garrotxa region); Hispania ☎932 312 756 (Tarragona); and

Alsina Graells ☎932 656 866 (Lleida, Andorra). It's a good idea to reserve a ticket in advance on long-distance routes – a day before is usually fine. You can also buy Sarfa tickets to the Costa Brava from the Pl. de Catalunya tourist office.

Car rental The major chains have outlets at the airport and at, or near, Barcelona Sants station. For local outfits and city locations, call the companies direct or check their websites. Atesa ☎933 230 266, ⓦwww.atesa.es; Avis ☎932 375 680; BCN Rent A Car ☎934 901 930; Docar ☎933 229 008, ⓦwww.docar.com; EasyCar no phone, Internet reservations only ⓦwww.easycar.com; Europcar ☎934 398 403, ⓦwww.europcar.com; Hertz ☎932 173 248, ⓦwww.hertz.com; Laser ☎933 229 012, ⓦwww.laserrentacar.com; Servi-Car ☎934 053 315; Vanguard ☎934 393 880, ⓦwww.vanguardrent.com.

Consulates Most foreign consulates in Barcelona are open to the public for enquiries Mon–Fri only, usually 9am–1pm and 3–5pm, though the morning shift is the most reliable. Australia, Gran Via Carles III 98, Les Corts, ⓜMaria Cristina/Les Corts ☎934 909 013, ⓦwww.embaustralia.es; Britain, Avgda. Diagonal 477, Eixample, ⓜHospital Clinic ☎933 666 200, ⓦwww.ukinspain.com; Canada, c/Elisenda de Pinós 10, Sàrria, FGC Reina Elisenda ☎932 042 700, ⓦwww.canada-es.org; Republic of Ireland, Gran Via Carles III 94, Les Corts, ⓜMaria Cristina/Les Corts ☎934 915 021; New Zealand, Trav. de Gràcia 64, Gràcia, FGC Gràcia ☎932 090 399; USA, Pg. de la Reina Elisenda 23, Sàrria, FGC Reina Elisenda ☎932 802 227, ⓦwww.embusa.es.

Cultural institutes The British Council, c/Amigó 83, Sant Gervasi, FGC Muntaner ☎932 419 700, ⓦwww.britishcouncil.es, has an English-language library, an arts and events programme, lists of language schools and a good noticeboard advertising lessons and accommodation. The North American Institute, Via Augusta 123, Sant Gervasi, FGC Plaça Molina ☎932 405 110, has newspapers, magazines and a reference library. At the Goethe Institut, c/Manso 24–28, Eixample, ⓜSant Antoni ☎932 926 006, there's a German-language library, films and events.

Dentists Dentists are all private, so it's wise to have travel insurance. For an English-speaking dentist, call ☎010 or contact the Pl. de Catalunya tourist office, or look in the local Yellow Pages (*Paginas Amarillas*) under "Clinicas dentales" or "Dentistes".

Doctors Any local health-care centre (Centre d'Atenció Primària, CAP) can provide non-emergency assistance. In the old town, there's one at c/del Rec Comtal 24, Sant Pere, ⓜArc de Triomf ☎933 101 421 (Mon–Fri 9am–2pm & 3–7pm, Sat 9am–5pm). Or call ☎010 or consult ⓦwww.bcn.es for a full list. In an emergency call ☎061 or go to one of the hospitals listed below.

Emergency services ☎112 for ambulance, police and fire services; ☎061 for ambulance.

Ferries Departures to the Balearics are from the Estació Marítima, Moll de Barcelona, Port Vell, ⓜDrassanes ☎933 068 800. Services are on regular ferries or the quicker, and more expensive, high-speed ferries or catamarans. Buy tickets inside the terminal from Trasmediterranea (☎902 45 46 45, ⓦwww.trasmediterranea.com) to Palma de Mallorca, Mahón and Ibiza; Iscomar Ferry (☎902 119 128, ⓦwww.iscomar.com) to Palma de Mallorca; or Umifasa (☎902 454 645, ⓦwww.umi-fasa.com) to Ibiza. Navi Grandi Veloci (☎934 439 898, ⓦwww1.gnv.it) has a year-round service to Genoa, Italy.

Hospitals For emergency hospital treatment go to one of the following central hospitals, which have 24hr accident and emergency services: Centre Perecamps, Avgda. Drassanes 13-15, El Raval, ⓜDrassanes ☎934 410 600; Hospital Clinic i Provincial, c/Villaroel 170, Eixample, ⓜHospital Clinic ☎932 275 400; Hospital del Mar, Pg. Maritím 25–29, Vila Olímpica, ⓜCiutadella-Vila Olímpica ☎932 489 011; Hospital de la Santa Creu i Sant Pau, c/Sant Antoni Maria Claret, Eixample, ⓜHospital de Sant Pau ☎932 919 000.

Internet access There are Internet places and cybercafés all over Barcelona, and competition has driven prices down to around €1 an hour – sometimes a bit more, sometimes a bit less. A stroll down the Ramblas, or through the Barri Gòtic, La Ribera, El Raval and Grácia will reveal a host of possibilities, but major centres include: Ciberopcion, Gran Via de les Corts Catalanes 602, Eixample, ⓜUniversitat (Mon–Sat 9am–1am, Sun 11am–1am);

Cibermundo Bergara, c/Bergara 3, Eixample, Ⓜ️Universitat (daily 9am–1am); Cibermundo Balmes, c/Balmes 8, Eixample, Ⓜ️Universitat (Mon–Fri 10am–11pm, Sat noon–11pm, Sun 1–11pm); Easy Internet, Ronda Universitat, Eixample, Ⓜ️Universitat 35 (daily 8am–1am), and Ramblas 31, Ⓜ️Liceu (daily 24hr); and Insòlit, Maremagnum, Port Vell, Ⓜ️Drassanes (daily 12.30pm–midnight).

Language schools The cheapest Spanish or Catalan classes in Barcelona are at the Escola Oficial d'Idiomes, Avgda. Drassanes s/n, El Raval, Ⓜ️Drassanes ☎933 292 458, Ⓦwww.eoibd.es – expect big queues when you sign on. Or try International House, c/Trafalgar 14, Eixample, Ⓜ️Urquinaona ☎932 684 511, Ⓦwww.ihes.com/bcn. The Generalitat offers low-cost Catalan classes through the Centre per a la Normalització Linguística; call ☎010 for information. Language courses are also offered at most Spanish universities; contact Barcelona University at Gran Via de les Corts Catalanes 585, Eixample, Ⓜ️Universitat ☎934 035 519, Ⓦwww.ub.es. The Pl. de Catalunya tourist office has a list of all other language schools in Barcelona. For a more informal experience, the Travel Bar (c/de la Boqueria 27, Barri Gòtic; Ⓜ️Liceu) hosts a "language exchange" every Tues at 9.30pm, where you can meet locals and foreign visitors and "practice without paying".

Laundries Lavomatic, a self-service laundry, has two old-town branches, both open Mon–Sat 9am–9pm: at Pl. Joaquim Xirau 1, Barri Gòtic, Ⓜ️Drassanes ☎933 425 119; and at c/Consolat del Mar 43–45, Pl. del Palau, La Ribera, Ⓜ️Barceloneta ☎932 684 768. It costs €3.75 per 7kg of laundry plus €0.75 per 5min for drying. Other self-service laundries include: Bugaderia Roca, c/Joaquín Costa 16, El Raval, Ⓜ️Universitat ☎934 425 982 (Mon–Fri 8.30am–7.30pm, Sat 8am–2pm); Wash N' Dry, c/Nou de la Rambla 19, El Raval, Ⓜ️Liceu ☎934 121 953 (daily 7am–11pm); LavaExpress, c/Ferlandina, El Raval, Ⓜ️Universitat no phone (daily 8am–11pm); and Aribau, c/Aribau 29, Eixample Ⓜ️Universitat ☎934 538 933 (Mon–Fri 9am–1.30pm & 4–8pm, Sat 9am–1.30pm). There are inexpensive laundry services in most of the youth hostels and some budget pensions; hotels will

charge considerably more. A law, much ignored in the old town, forbids you from leaving laundry hanging out of windows over a street, and some places can get shirty if you're found doing excessive washing in your bedroom sink. A dry-cleaner is a *tintorería*.

Left-luggage At Barcelona Sants the *consigna* is open daily 7am–11pm and costs €3–4.50 a day. There are lockers at Estació de França, Passeig de Gràcia station and Estació del Nord (all 6am–11.30pm; €3–4.50).

Libraries Biblioteca de Catalunya, c/de l'Hospital 56, El Raval, Ⓜ️Liceu ☎932 702 300, Ⓦwww.gencat.net/bc (Mon–Fri 9am–8pm, Sat 9am–2pm) – you will only be able to use this with a letter of academic reference, though there is the Biblioteca Popular Sant Pau (a public library) in the same building (Tues, Thurs & Sat 10am–2pm, Mon–Fri 3.30am–8pm). The Biblioteca de l'Universitat de Barcelona, Gran Via de Corts Catalanes 585, Eixample, Ⓜ️Universitat ☎934 035 315, Ⓦwww.ub.es (Mon–Fri 8am–8.30pm; Oct–June also Sat 9am–2pm) is open to the public. The British Council (see above) has the only English-language lending library in Barcelona; access is free, though you have to join (€55 a year) to use the loan and Internet services.

Lost property Best bet is the main lost property office (*objectes perduts*), around the corner from the Ajuntament at c/de la Ciutat 9, Barri Gòtic, Ⓜ️Jaume I (Mon–Fri 9.30am–1.30pm; ☎934 023 161). You could also try the transport office at Universitat metro station, or call the Institut Metropolità del Taxi ☎932 235 151, which hangs on to anything left in a taxi.

Newspapers and magazines You can buy foreign newspapers at the stalls down the Ramblas, on Pg. de Gràcia, on Rambla de Catalunya, around Pl. de Catalunya and at Barcelona Sants, as well as at major bookstores and in larger hotels. The same stalls also sell an impressive array of international magazines and trade papers. If you can't find what you're looking for there, try Llibreria Mallorca, Rambla de Catalunya 86, Eixample, Ⓜ️Passeig de Gràcia, which stocks a big selection of British and American newspapers and magazines.

Office services Workcenter, Pl. Urquinaona at c/Ausias Marc, Eixample, Ⓜ️Urquinaona

☎902 115 011, ⊛www.workcenter.es, is open 24hr for photocopying, scanning, printing (black-and-white and colour), 1hr photo development, Internet, fax and DHL courier service.

Pharmacies For minor health complaints look for the green cross of a *farmàcia*, where highly trained staff can give advice (often in English), and are able to dispense many drugs available only on prescription in other countries. Usual hours are 9am–1pm & 4–8pm. At least one in each neighbourhood is open 24hr (and marked as such), or phone ☎010 for information on those open out of hours. A list of out-of-hours pharmacies can also be found in the window of each pharmacy store.

Police The easiest place to report a crime is at the Guàrdia Urbana (city police) station at Ramblas 43, opposite Pl. Reial, ⓂLiceu ☎933 441 300 (open 24hr; English spoken). If you've had something stolen, you need to go to the Policía Nacional office at c/Nou de la Rambla 80, El Raval, ⓂParal.lel (you must go in person to get the report for your insurance claim; take your passport, provided that wasn't stolen, of course). Otherwise, contact the police on the following numbers: Policía Nacional ☎091, Guàrdia Urbana ☎092.

Post offices The main post office (*Correus*) in Barcelona is on Pl. d'Antoni López, at the eastern end of Pg. de Colom, Barri Gòtic, ⓂBarceloneta/Jaume I ☎902 197 197, ⊛www.correos.es (Mon–Sat 8.30am–9.30pm, Sun 8.30am–2.30pm; entrance from Via Laietana on Sun). There's a poste restante/general delivery service here (*llista de correus*), plus express post, fax service and phonecard sales. Postal Transfer, Pl. Urquinaona at c/Roger de Lluria, Eixample, ⓂUrquinaonoa (Mon–Fri 10am–11pm, Sat 11am–midnight, Sun noon–11pm), offers after-hours postal services, plus money exchange, fax/photocopying, phonecard sales, etc. Other central post office branches are at Ronda Universitat 23 and c/Aragó 282, both in Eixample (both Mon–Fri 8.30am–8.30pm, Sat 9.30am–1am). Each city neighbourhood also has a post office, though these have far less comprehensive opening hours and services.

Residence permits In Barcelona, residence permits where required – for EU and non-EU nationals – are issued by the Oficina d'Estrangers at Avgda. Marqués de l'Argentera 4, La Ribera, ⓂBarceloneta ☎934 820 544 or 934 820 530 (Mon–Fri 9am–2pm).

Taxis Barna Taxis ☎933 577 755; Fono-Taxi ☎933 001 100; Radio Taxi Barcelona ☎932 250 000; Radio Taxi 033 ☎933 033 033; Servi-Taxi ☎933 300 300; Taxi Amic ☎934 208 088.

Time Barcelona is 1hr ahead of the UK, 6hr ahead of New York and Toronto, 9hr ahead Los Angeles, 9hr behind Sydney and 11hr behind Auckland. This applies except for brief periods during the changeovers to and from daylight saving (in Spain the clocks go forward in the last week in March, back again in the last week of Oct).

Toilets Public ones are few and far between, and averagely clean, but sometimes don't have any paper (best to carry your own). Bars and restaurants are more likely to have proper (and cleaner) toilets, though you can't guarantee it – even in the poshest of places. Ask for *toaleta* or *serveis* (*lavabo* or *servicios* in Spanish). *Dones/Damas* (Ladies) and *Homes/Caballeros* (Gentlemen) are the usual signs.

Trains For national rail enquiries, sales and reservations, contact RENFE (☎902 240 202, ⊛www.renfe.es). Barcelona Sants (Pl. dels Paisos Catalans, Sants; ⓂSants-Estació) is the main terminal for domestic and international trains – there's a train information office (daily 6.30am–10.30pm), advance ticket booking counters and other services. Some Spanish intercity services and international trains use Estació de França, Avgda. Marquès de l'Argentera, La Ribera, ⓂBarceloneta (ticket office 7am–10pm). Regional and local commuter services are operated by FGC (☎932 051 515, ⊛www.fgc.es), with services from Pl. de Catalunya or Pl. de Espanya.

Travel agencies General travel agencies are found on the Gran Vía de les Corts Catalanes, Pg. de Gràcia, Vía Laietana and the Ramblas. For city tours, Catalunya holidays and local trips, contact Julia Tours, Ronda Universitat 5, Eixample, ⓂUniversitat ☎933 176 454 or 933 176 209. For youth/student travel there are: Asatej, Ramblas 140, 5th floor ☎934 126 338; and Abando, Ramblas 88–94 ☎933 182 593. The American Express office, Pg.

de Gràcia 101, Eixample, Ⓜ Diagonal ☎ 932 550 000, also has a travel agency.

Women's Barcelona The most useful contact address in the city is Ca la Dona, c/de Casp 38, Eixample, Ⓜ Urquinaona ☎ 934 127 161, ⓦ www.caladona.pangea.org, a women's centre used for meetings of over twenty feminist and lesbian organizations; information available to callers. The Ajuntament's official women's resource centre, the Centre Municipal d'Informació i Recursos per a les Dones (CIRD), Avgda. Diagnal 233, 5th floor, Eixample, Ⓜ Monumental/Glòries ☎ 934 132 722, ⓦ www.cird.bcn.es (Mon–Fri noon–2pm, plus Wed & Thurs 4–7pm), publishes a monthly calendar of events and news (available on its website). Llibreria Pròleg, c/Dagueria 13, Barri Gòtic, Ⓜ Jaume I ☎ 933 192 425, is a bookshop specializing in women's issues.

Work Without a particular skill or pre-arranged job, the only real chance of long-term work in Barcelona is in language schools. There's much less work about than there used to be and you'll need a TEFL (Teaching English as a Foreign Language) or ESL (English as a Second Language) certificate to stand any kind of chance. One other possibility, so long as you speak good Spanish, is translation work, most of which will be business correspondence – look in the Yellow Pages under "Traductores". Unless you're a citizen of a European Union country, obtaining a work visa for Spain is nearly impossible.

Contexts

Contexts

A history of Barcelona and Catalunya

Catalunya is more than a part of Spain: the Catalan people have a deeply felt individual identity, rooted in a rich and – at times – glorious past. Perhaps its most conspicuous manifestation these days is in the resurgence of the language, which takes precedence over Castilian Spanish on street names and signs, and has staged a dramatic comeback after being banned from public use during the Franco dictatorship. However, linguistics is only one element in Catalan regionalism.

Catalan cultural identity can be traced back as far as the ninth century. From the quilt of independent counties of the eastern Pyrenees, a powerful dynastic entity, dominated by Barcelona, and commonly known as the Crown of Aragón, developed over the next six hundred years. Its merger with Castile-Leon in the late 1400s led to eventual inclusion in the new Spanish Empire of the sixteenth century – and marked the decline of Catalan independence and its eventual subjugation to Madrid. It has rarely been a willing subject, which goes some way to explaining how ingrained are the Catalan notions of social and cultural divorce from the rest of the country.

Early civilizations and invasions

In the very earliest times the area which is now Catalunya saw much the same population movements and invasions as the rest of the Iberian peninsula. During the **Upper Paleolithic** period (35,000–10,000 BC) cave-dwelling hunter-gatherers lived in parts of the Pyrenees, and **dolmens**, or stone burial chambers, from around 5000 BC still survive. No habitations from this period have been discovered but it can be conjectured that huts of some sort were erected, and farming had certainly begun. By the start of the **Bronze Age** (around 2000 BC), the Pyrenean people had begun to move into fortified villages in the coastal lowlands.

The first of a succession of **invasions** of the region began sometime after 1000 BC, when the Celtic "urnfield people" crossed the Pyrenees into the region, settling in the river valleys. These people lived side by side with indigenous Iberians, and the two groups are commonly, if erroneously, referred to as **Celtiberians**.

Meanwhile, on the coast, the **Greeks** had established trading posts at Roses and Empúries by around 550 BC. Two centuries later, though, the coast (and the rest of the peninsula) had been conquered by the North African **Carthaginians**, who founded Barcino (later Barcelona) in around 230 BC, on a low hill where the cathedral now stands. The Carthaginians' famous commander, Hannibal, went on to cross the Pyrenees in 214 BC and attempted to invade Italy. But the result of the Second Punic War (218–201 BC) – much of which was fought in Catalunya – was to expel the Carthaginians from the Iberian peninsula in favour of the Romans, who made their new base at the former Carthaginian stronghold of Tarragona.

Roman Catalunya

The **Roman colonization** of the Iberian peninsula was far more intense than anything previously experienced and met with great resistance from the Celtic and Iberian tribes. It was almost two centuries before the conquest was complete, by which time Spain had become the most important centre of the Roman Empire after Italy. Tarragona (known as Tarraco) was made a provincial capital; fine monuments were built, the remains of which can still be seen in and around the city, and an infrastructure of roads, bridges and aqueducts came into being – much of which was used well into recent times. Barcelona was of less importance, although in 15 BC the emperor Augustus granted it the lengthy name of Colonia Julia Augusta Faventia Pia.

In the first two centuries AD, the Spanish mines and the granaries of Andalucia brought unprecedented wealth, and **Roman Spain** enjoyed a period of stable prosperity in which the region of Catalunya played an influential part. In Tarraco and the other Roman towns, the inhabitants were granted full Roman citizenship; the former Greek settlements on the Costa Brava had accepted Roman rule without difficulty and consequently experienced little interference in their day-to-day life.

Towards the third century AD, however, the Roman political framework began to show signs of decadence and corruption. Although at a municipal level the structure did not disappear completely until the Muslim invasions of the eighth century, it became increasingly vulnerable to **barbarian invasions** from northern Europe. The Franks and the Suevi swept across the Pyrenees, sacking Tarraco in 262 and destroying Barcelona. It was subsequently retaken by the Romans and rather belatedly defended by a circuit of walls and towers, part of which can still be seen. Within two centuries, however, Roman rule had ended, forced on the defensive by new waves of Suevi, Alans and Vandals and finally superseded by the **Visigoths** from Gaul, former allies of Rome and already Romanized to some degree.

The Visigoths established their first Spanish capital at Barcelona in 531 (before eventually basing themselves further south at Toledo), and built a kingdom encompassing most of modern Spain and the southwest of modern France. Their triumph, however, was relatively short-lived. Ruling initially as a caste apart from the local people, with a distinct status and laws, the Visigoths lived largely as a warrior elite, and were further separated from the local people by their adherence to Arian Christianity, which was considered heretical by the Catholic Church. Under their domination, the economy and the quality of life in the Roman towns declined, while within their ranks a series of plots and rivalries – exacerbated by their system of elective monarchy – pitted members of the ruling elite against each other. In 589 King Reccared converted to Catholicism, but religious strife only multiplied, resistance on the part of Arian Christians led to reaction, one of the casualties of which was the sizable Jewish population of the peninsula, who were enslaved en masse in the seventh century.

The Moors and the Spanish Marches

Divisions within the Visigothic kingdom coincided with the Islamic expansion in North Africa, which reached the shores of the Atlantic in the late seventh century. In 711 (or 714, no one is sure) Tariq ibn Ziyad, governor of Tangier, led a force of several thousand largely Berber troops across the Straits of Gibraltar (the name of which is a corruption of the Arabic, *jebl at-Tariq*, "Tariq's mountain") and routed the Visigothic nobility near Jerez de la Frontera. With no one to resist, the stage for the **Moorish conquest of Spain** was set. Within ten years, the Muslim Moors had advanced to control most of modern Catalunya – they destroyed Tarragona and forced Barcelona to surrender – although the more inaccessible parts of the Pyrenees retained their independence. It was not simply a military conquest. The Moors had little manpower, and so granted a limited autonomy to the local population in exchange for payment of tribute. They did not force the indigenous people to convert to Islam, and Jews and Christians lived securely as second-class citizens. In areas of the peninsula that remained under Muslim power through the ninth century, a new ethnic group emerged: the "Mozarabs", Christians who lived under Muslim rule, and adopted Arabic language, dress and social customs.

In the power vacuum of southern France, Moorish raiding parties continued beyond the Pyrenees and reached as far north as Poitiers in 732, where Charles Martel, the de facto ruler of Merovingian France, dealt them a minor defeat which convinced them to withdraw. Martel's son Pepin, and his famous grandson **Charlemagne** (768–814), both strove to restore order in the south and push back the invaders, with Charlemagne's empire including the southern slopes of the Pyrenees and much of Catalunya. After being ambushed and defeated by the Basques at Roncesvalles in 778, Charlemagne switched his attention to the Mediterranean side of the Pyrenees, attempting to defend his empire against the Muslims. He took Girona in 785 and his son Louis directed the successful siege of Barcelona in 801. Continued Frankish military success meant that Muslim influence in Catalunya had waned long before the Battle of Las Navas de Tolosa in 1212 (see p.252) – the turning point for the reconquest of the peninsula as a whole.

With the capture of Barcelona, the **Frankish counties** of Catalunya became a sort of buffer zone, known as the **Spanish Marches**. Separate territories, each ruled by a count and theoretically owing allegiance to the Frankish king (or emperor), were primitive proto-feudal entities, almost exclusively agrarian, and ruled by a small hereditary military elite. It was the building of local fortifications to protect and control the population, reaching its greatest pitch between 1000 and 1200, which led to the term *catlá* (or "lord of the castle") being used to refer to the people of the area – the root of today's "**Catalan**" (Castilian has an analogous root). Also, and as happened across much of the former Roman Empire, spoken Latin had taken on geographical particularities, and the "Romance" languages, including Catalan, had begun to develop. A document from 839 recording the consecration of the cathedral at La Seu d'Urgell is seen as the first Catalan-language historical document.

From Wilfred the Hairy to Ramon Berenguer IV

As the Frankish empire of Charlemagne disintegrated in the decades following his death, the counties of the Marches began to enjoy greater independence, which was formalized in 878 by Guifré el Pelós – known in English as **Wilfred the Hairy**. Wilfred was count of Urgell and the Cerdagne and, after adding Barcelona to his holdings, named himself its first count, founding a dynastic line that was to rule until the 1400s. He also made important territorial gains, inheriting Girona and Besalú, and regaining control of Montserrat (the first monastery there was founded around this time). In the wake of the Muslim withdrawal from the area, **Christian outposts** had been established throughout Catalunya, and Wilfred continued the process, founding Benedictine monasteries at Ripoll (about 880) and Sant Joan de les Abadesses (888), where his daughter was the first abbess.

Wilfred died in 898 on an expedition against Muslim enemies and was followed by a succession of rulers who attempted to consolidate his gains. Early counts, like **Ramon Berenguer I** (1035–76), concentrated on establishing their superiority over the other local counts, which was bitterly resisted.

Ramon Berenguer III (1144–66) added considerable territory to the his realms with his marriage in 1113 to a Provençal heiress, and made alliances and commercial treaties with Muslim and Christian powers around the western Mediterranean.

The most important stage in Catalunya's development as a significant power, however, came in 1137 with the marriage of **Ramon Berenguer IV** to Petronella, the 2-year-old daughter of King Ramiro II of Aragón. This led to the **dynastic union of Catalunya and Aragón**. Although this remained a loose and tenuous federation – the regions retained their own parliaments and customs – it provided the platform for rapid expansion over the next three centuries. As importantly, Ramon managed to tame almost all of the other counts, forcing them to recognize his superior status and in the course of this he promulgated the **Usatges de Barcelona**, a code of laws and customs defining feudal duties, rights and authorities – sneakily putting Ramon I's name on them to make them appear older than they were. He also captured Muslim Tortosa and Lleida in 1148–49, which mark the limits of the modern region of Catalunya, but now the region began to look east for its future, across the Mediterranean.

The Kingdom of Catalunya and Aragón

Ramon Berenguer IV was no more than a count, but his son **Alfons I** (who succeeded to the throne in 1162) also inherited the title of King of Aragón (where he was Alfonso II), and became the first count-king of what historians later came to call the **Crown of Aragón**. To his territories he added Roussillon and much of southern France, becoming known as "Emperor of the Pyrenees"; he also made some small gains against the Berber Almohads who now dominated Muslim Iberia, and allied with and intrigued against neighbouring Christian kingdoms of Navarre and Castile.

Under the rule of Alfons's son, Pere (Peter) the Catholic, the kingdom suffered both successes and reverses. Pere gained glory as one of the military leaders in the decisive defeat of Muslim forces at the **Battle of Las Navas de Tolosa** in 1212, but, swept up into the Albigensian Wars through his ties of lordship to the Counts of Toulouse, he was killed by Catholic forces at Muret a year later. In the years of uncertainty that followed the succession of his 5-year-old son, **Jaume I** (1213–76), later known as "the Conqueror", his rivals took advantage of the power vacuum and stripped the count-kings of Provence. Although they would retain Roussillon and acquire Montpellier, for all intents and purposes this signalled the **end of Catalan aspirations north of the Pyrenees**.

The golden age

In spite of these setbacks, Catalunya's age of glory was about to begin in earnest, with the 63-year reign of the extraordinary Jaume. Shrugging off the tutelage of his Templar masters at the age of 13, he then personally took to the field to tame his rebellious nobility. This accomplished, he embarked on a series of campaigns of conquest, which brought him Muslim Mallorca in 1229, Menorca in 1231 and Ibiza in 1235 (which explains why the Balearics share a common language with the region). Next he turned south and conquered the city of Valencia in 1238, establishing a new kingdom of which he was also ruler. Valencia, however, was no easy territory to govern, and the region's Muslim inhabitants rose up in a series of revolts which outlasted the king's reign.

Recognizing that **Mediterranean expansion** was where Catalunya's future lay, Jaume signed the **Treaty of Corbeil** in 1258, renouncing his rights in France (except for Montpellier, the Cerdagne and Roussillon), in return for the French King Louis's renunciation of claims in Catalunya. In this period Catalunya's **economic development** was rapid, fuelled by the exploits of Barcelona's mercantile class, who were quick to see the possibilities of Mediterranean commerce. Maritime customs were codified in the so-called *Llibre del Consolat de Mar*, trade relations were established with North Africa and the Middle East, and consulates opened in foreign ports to protect Catalan interests.

Equally important during Jaume's reign was the establishment of the **Corts**, Catalunya's first parliament – one of the earliest such bodies in Europe, and demonstrative of the confidence developing within the region. In 1249, the first governors of Barcelona were elected, nominating councillors to help them who became known as the Consell de Cent.

On Jaume's death, his kingdom was divided between his sons, one of whom, **Pere II** ("the Great"), took Catalunya, Aragón and Valencia. Connected through marriage to the Sicilian Crown, Pere used the 1282 "Sicilian Vespers" rising against Charles of Anjou to press his claim to that island. In August that year, Pere was crowned at Palermo, and Sicily became the base for Catalan exploits throughout the Mediterranean. Athens and Neopatras were taken (1302–11) by Catalan mercenaries, the *almogávares*, and famous sea-leaders-cum-pirates such as Roger de Flor and Roger de Llúria fought in the name of the Catalan-Aragonese crown. Malta (1283), Corsica (1323), Sardinia (1324) and Naples (1423) all fell under the influence of successive count-kings.

With the territorial gains came new developments with a wider significance. Catalan became used as a trading language throughout the Mediterranean, and 1289 saw the first recorded meeting of a body which became known as the **Generalitat**, a sort of committee of the Corts. Within it were represented each of the three traditional estates – commons, nobility and clergy – and it gradually became responsible for administering public order and justice, and maintaining an arsenal and fleet for the defence of the kingdom.

Social and economic developments

By the mid-fourteenth century Catalunya was at its economic peak. Barcelona had become an important city with impressive new buildings, both religious and secular, to match its status as a regional superpower – the cathedral, church of Santa Maria del Mar, the Generalitat building, the Ajuntament (with its Consell de Cent meeting room) and the Drassanes shipyards all testify to Barcelona's wealth in this period. Catalan became established as a **literary language**, and is recognized as the precursor of much of the great medieval European literature: the Mallorcan Ramon Llull's *Book of Contemplation* appeared in 1272, and his romance *Blanquerna* was written a century before Chaucer's *Canterbury Tales*. **Architecture** progressed from Romanesque to Gothic styles, churches displaying features which have become known as Catalan-Gothic – spacious naves, hexagonal belfries and a lack of flying buttresses.

Even while this great maritime wealth and power were being celebrated in such fashion, however, the seeds of decline were being sown. The **Black Death** made its first appearance in the Balearics in 1348 and visited Catalunya several times over the next forty years, and by the end of the century half the population had succumbed to the disease. As a result, there was increasing pressure on the peasantry by the landowners, who were determined not to let their profits fall.

The rise of Castile

The last of Wilfred the Hairy's dynasty of Catalan count-kings, Martin the Humane (Martí el Humà), died in 1410 without an heir. After nearly five hundred years of continuity, there were six claimants to the throne, and in 1412 nine specially appointed counsellors elevated Ferdinand (Ferran) de Antequera, son of a Catalan princess, to the vacant throne.

Ferran ruled for only four years, but his reign and that of his son, Alfons, and grandson, John (Joan) II, spelled the end for Catalunya's influence in the Mediterranean. The Castilian rulers were soon in dispute with the Consell de Cent; illegal taxes were imposed, funds belonging to the Generalitat were appropriated, and most damagingly non-Catalans started to be appointed to key positions in the Church, state offices and the armed forces. In 1469 John's son, Prince Ferdinand (Ferran), who was born in Aragón, married Isabel of Castile, a union that would eventually finish off Catalan independence.

Both came into their inheritances quickly, Isabel taking Castile in 1474 and the Catalan-Aragónese crown coming to Ferdinand in 1479. The two largest kingdoms in Spain were thus united, the ruling pair becoming known as "**Los Reyes Católicos**" ("Els Reis Catòlics" in Catalan), the Catholic monarchs. Their energies were devoted to the reconquest and unification of Spain: they finally took back Granada from the Moors in 1492, and initiated a wave of Christian fervour at whose heart was the **Inquisition**. Ferdinand and Isabel shared in the religious bigotry of their contemporaries, although Isabel, under the influence of her personal confessor and advisors, was the more reactionary of the two. In Catalunya, the Inquisition was established in 1487, and aimed to purify the Catholic faith by rooting out heresy. It was directed mainly at the secret **Jews**, most of whom had been converted by force (after the pogrom of 1391) to Christianity. It was suspected that their descendants, known as **New Christians**, continued to practice their old faith in secrecy, and in 1492, an edict forced some seventy thousand Jews to flee the country. The Jewish population in Barcelona was completely eradicated in this way, while those communities elsewhere – principally in Girona, Tarragona and Lleida – were massively reduced, and those who remained were forced to convert to Christianity.

Also in 1492, the final shift in Catalunya's outlook occurred with the triumphal return of **Christopher Columbus** from the New World, to be received in Barcelona by Ferdinand and Isabel. As trade routes shifted away from the Mediterranean, this was no longer such a profitable market. Castile, like Portugal, looked to the Americas, for trade and conquest, and the exploration and exploitation of the New World was spearheaded by the Andalucían city of Seville. Meanwhile, Ferdinand gave the Supreme Council of Aragón control over Catalan affairs in 1494. The Aragónese nobility, who had always resented the success of the Catalan maritime adventures, now saw the chance to complete their control of Catalunya by taking over its ecclesiastical institutions – with Catalan monks being thrown out of the great monasteries of Poblet and Montserrat.

Habsburg and Bourbon rule

Charles I, a **Habsburg**, came to the throne in 1516 as a beneficiary of the marriage alliances made by the Catholic monarchs. Five years later he was elected emperor of the **Holy Roman Empire** (as Charles V), inheriting not only Castile, Aragón and Catalunya, but also Flanders, the Netherlands, Artois, the Franche-Comté and all the American colonies. With such responsibilities, it became inevitable that attention would be diverted from Spain, whose chief function became to sustain the Holy Roman Empire with gold and silver from the Americas. It was in this era that Madrid was established as capital city of the Spanish Empire, and the long rivalry began between Madrid and Barcelona.

Throughout the **sixteenth century**, Catalunya continued to suffer under the Inquisition, and – deprived of trading opportunities in the Americas – became an impoverished region. Habsburg wars wasted the lives of Catalan soldiers, banditry in the region increased as the economic situation worsened, and emigration from certain areas followed. By the middle of the **seventeenth century**, Spain's rulers were losing credibility as the disparity between the wealth surrounding Crown and Court and the poverty of the mass of the population produced a source of perpetual tension.

With Spain and France at war in 1635, the Catalans took advantage of the situation and revolted, declaring themselves an **independent republic** under the protection of the French King Louis XIII. This, the "War of the Reapers" – after the marching song *Els Segadors* (The Reapers), later the Catalan national anthem – ended in 1652 with the surrender of Barcelona to the Spanish army. The **Treaty of the Pyrenees** in 1659 finally split the historical lands of Catalunya as the Spanish lost control of Roussillon and part of the Cerdagne to France.

In 1700, when the Habsburg king Charles II died heirless, France's Louis XIV saw an opportunity to fulfil his longtime ambition of putting a Bourbon on the Spanish throne. He managed to secure the succession of his grandson, Philippe d'Anjou, under condition that the latter renounced his rights to the throne of France. This deal put a Bourbon on the throne of Spain, but led to war with the other claimant, Archduke Charles of Austria: the resulting **War of the Spanish Succession** lasted thirteen years from 1701, with Catalunya (along with England) lining up on the Austrian side in an attempt to regain its ancient rights and in the hope that victory would give it a share of the American trade dominated by the Castilians since the late fifteenth century.

However, the **Treaty of Utrecht** in 1714 gave the throne to the **Bourbon** ("Borbón" in Castilian, "Borbó" in Catalan) Philippe, now Philip V of Spain, and initiated a fresh period of repression from which the Catalans took a century to recover. Barcelona lay under siege for over a year, and with its eventual capitulation a fortress was built at Ciutadella to subdue the city's inhabitants – the final defeat, on September 11, is still commemorated every year as a Catalan holiday, La Diada. The universities at Barcelona and Lleida were closed, the Catalan language banned, the Consell de Cent and Generalitat abolished – in short, Catalunya was finished as even a partially autonomous region.

Throughout the **eighteenth century**, Catalunya's interests were subsumed within those of Bourbon Spain, and successive monarchs were determined to Castilianize the region. When neighbouring France became aggressively expansionist following the Revolution of 1789, Spain was a natural target, first for the Revolutionary armies and later for the machinations of Napoleon. In 1805, during the **Napoleonic Wars**, the French fleet (along with the Spanish who had been forced into an alliance) was defeated at Trafalgar. Shortly thereafter, Charles IV was forced to abdicate with Napoleon installing his brother Joseph on the throne three years later. Attempting to broaden his appeal among Spain's subjects, the French emperor proclaimed a separate government of Catalunya – independent of Joseph's rule – with Catalan as its official language. The region's response was an indication of how far Catalunya had become integrated into Spain during the Bourbon period – despite their history the Catalans supported the Bourbon cause solidly during the ensuing **Peninsular**

War (1808–14), ignoring Napoleon's blandishments. Girona was defended heroically from the French in a seven-month siege, while Napoleon did his cause no good at all by attacking and sacking the holy shrine and monastery at Montserrat. Fierce local resistance was eventually backed by the muscle of a British army, and the French were at last driven out.

The slow Catalan revival

Despite the political emasculation of Catalunya, there were signs of **economic revival** from the end of the seventeenth century onwards. During the 1700s there was a gradual growth in agricultural output, partly caused by a doubling of the population: more land was put under cultivation, and productivity improved with the introduction of easy-to-cultivate maize from the Indies. Barcelona also saw a steady increase in trade, since from 1778 Catalunya was allowed to trade with the Americas for the first time; in this way, the shipping industry received a boost and Catalunya was able to export its textiles to a wider market. The other great export was wine, whose widespread production in the region also dates from this period. A chamber of commerce was founded in Barcelona in 1758, and other economic societies followed as commercial interests increased.

After the Napoleonic Wars, industry in Catalunya developed apace – significantly for the future, it was an **industrialization** that appeared nowhere else in Spain. In the mid-nineteenth century, the country's first **railway** was built from Barcelona to Mataró, and later extended south to Tarragona, and north to Girona and the French border. **Manufacturing** industries appeared as the financial surpluses from the land were invested, encouraging a shift in population from the land to the towns; olive oil production in Lleida and Tarragona helped supply the whole country; and previously local industries flourished on a wider scale – in the wine-growing districts, for example, *cava* (champagne-like wine) production was introduced in the late nineteenth century, supported closely by the age-old cork industry of the Catalan forests. From 1890, hydroelectric power was harnessed from the Pyrenees, and by the end of the century **Barcelona** was the fastest-growing city in Spain – it was one of only six with more than 100,000 inhabitants.

Equally important was the first stirring of what became known as the **Renaixença** (Renaissance), in the mid-nineteenth century. Despite being banned in official use and public life, the Catalan **language** had never died out. Books began to appear again in Catalan – a dictionary in 1803 and a grammar in 1814 – and the language was revived among the bourgeoisie and intellectuals in the cities as a means of making subtle nationalist and political points. Catalan **poetry** became popular, and the late medieval **Jocs Florals** (Floral Games), a sort of literary competition, were revived in 1859 in Barcelona: one winner was the great Catalan poet, Jacint Verdaguer (1845–1902). Catalan **drama** developed (although even in the late nineteenth century there were still restrictions on performing wholly Catalan plays), led mainly by the dramatist, Pitarra. The only discipline that didn't show any great advance was prose literature – partly because the Catalan language had been so debased with Castilian over the centuries that writers found it difficult to express themselves in a way that would appeal to the population.

Prosperity led to the rapid **expansion of Barcelona**, notably the mid-nineteenth century addition to the city of the planned Eixample district. Encouraged by wealthy patrons and merchants, architects like Puig i Cadafalch, Domènech i Montaner and Antoni Gaudí were in the vanguard of the **modernista** movement which changed the face of the city (for more, see p.96).

Culture and business came together with the **International Exhibition** of 1888, based around the *modernista* buildings of the Parc de la Ciutadella, and the **International Fair** on Montjuïc in 1929, which boasted creations in the style of *modernisme*'s successor, *noucentisme*.

The seeds of civil war

In 1814, the repressive Ferdinand VII had been restored to the Spanish throne, and, despite the Catalan contribution to the defeat of the French, he stamped out the least hint of liberalism in the region, abolishing virtually all Catalunya's remaining privileges. On his death, the Crown was claimed both by his daughter Isabel II (with liberal support) and by his brother Charles (backed by the Church and the conservatives). The ensuing **First Carlist War** (1833–39) ended in victory for Isabel, who came of age in 1843. Her reign was a long record of scandal, political crisis and constitutional compromise, until liberal army generals under the leadership of General Prim eventually effected a coup in 1868, forcing Isabel to abdicate. However, the experimental **First Republic** (1873–75) failed, and following the **Second Carlist War** the throne went to Isabel's son, Alfonso XII.

Against this unstable background, local dissatisfaction increased and the years preceding World War I saw a growth in working-class **political movements**. Barcelona's textile workers organized a branch affiliated to the First International, and the region's wine growers also banded together to seek greater security. Tension was further heightened by the **loss of Cuba** in 1898, which only added to local economic problems, with the return of soldiers seeking employment in the cities where there was none.

A call-up for army reserves to fight in Morocco in 1909 provoked a general strike and the so-called **Tragic Week** (Setmana Tràgica) of rioting in Barcelona, and then throughout Catalunya, in which over one hundred people died. Catalans objected violently to the suggestion that they should go to fight abroad for a state that did little for them at home, and the city's streets saw burning churches, barricades and popular committees, though there was little direction to the protest. What the Tragic Week did prove to Catalan workers was the need to be better organized for the future. A direct result was the establishment of the Confederación Nacional del Trabajo – the **CNT** – in 1911, which included many of the Catalan working-class organizations.

During **World War I** Spain was neutral, though inwardly turbulent since soaring inflation and the cessation of exports following the German blockade of the North Atlantic hit the country hard. As rumblings grew among the workers and political organizations, the army moved decisively, crushing a general strike of 1917. The Russian Revolution had scared the conservative businessmen of the region, who offered cooperation with the army in return for political representation in the country's government. However, things didn't improve. Violent strikes and assassinations plagued Barcelona, while the CNT and the union of the Socialists, the CGT, both saw huge increases in their membership. In 1923, **General Primo de Rivera**, the captain-general of Catalunya, overthrew the national government in a military coup that had the full backing of the Catalan middle class, establishing a dictatorship which enjoyed initial economic success. There was no real stability in the dictatorship, however, and new political factions were taking shape throughout the country. The general resigned in 1930, dying a few months later, but the hopes of some for the restoration of the monarchy's political powers were short-lived. The success of the anti-monarchist parties in the municipal elections of 1931 led to the abdication of the king and the foundation of the Second Republic.

The Second Republic

In 1931, Catalunya, under Francesc Macià, leader of the Republican Left, declared itself to be an **independent republic**, and the Republican flag was raised over the Ajuntament in Barcelona. Madrid refused to accept the declaration, though a statute of limited autonomy was granted in 1932. Despite the initial hope that things would improve, the government was soon failing to satisfy even the least of expectations which it had raised. In addition, all the various strands of political ideology that had been fermenting in Spain over the previous century were ready to explode. **Anarchism** in particular was gaining strength among the frustrated middle classes as well as among workers and peasantry. The **Communist Party** and the left-wing **socialists**, driven into alliance by their mutual distrust of the "moderate" socialists in government, were also forming a growing bloc. There was little real unity of purpose on either Left or Right, but their fear of each other and their own exaggerated boasts made each seem an imminent threat. On the right, the **Falangists** (founded in 1923 by José Antonio Primo de Rivera, son of the dictator) made uneasy bedfellows with conservative traditionalists and dissident elements in the army upset by modernizing reforms.

In an atmosphere of growing confusion, the left-wing **Popular Front** alliance, including the Catalan Republican Left, won the general election of January 1936 by a narrow margin, and an all-Republican government was formed. In Catalunya, Lluís Companys became president of the Generalitat. Normal life, though, became increasingly impossible: the economy was crippled by strikes, peasants took agrarian reform into their own hands, and the government singularly failed to exert its authority over anyone. Finally, on July 17, 1936, the military garrison in Morocco rebelled under **General Francisco Franco**'s leadership, to be followed by uprisings at military garrisons throughout the country. It was the culmination of years of scheming in the army, but in the event it was far from the overnight success its leaders almost certainly expected. Much of the south and west quickly fell into the hands of the Nationalists, but Madrid and the industrialized northeast remained loyal to the Republican government. In Barcelona, although the military garrison supported Franco, it was soon subdued by local Civil Guards and the workers, while local leaders set up militias in preparation for the coming fight.

In October 1936 Franco was declared military commander and head of state; fascist Germany and Italy recognized his regime as the legitimate government of Spain in November. The Civil War was on.

Civil War

The **Spanish Civil War** (1936–39) was one of the most bitter and bloody the world has seen. Violent reprisals were visited on their enemies by both sides – the Republicans shooting priests and local landowners wholesale, and burning churches and cathedrals; the Nationalists carrying out mass slaughter of the population of almost every town they took. It was also to be the first modern war – Franco's German allies demonstrated their ability to inflict terror on civilian populations with their bombing raids on Gernika and Durango, while radio became an important propaganda weapon, with Nationalists offering starving Republicans the "white bread of Franco".

Catalunya was devoutly Republican from the outset, many of the rural areas particularly attracted by anarchism, an ideology that embodied their traditional values of equality and personal liberty. However, the Republicans were hard-pressed from the start. Despite sporadic help from Russia and the 35,000 volunteers of the **International Brigades**, the Republic could never compete with the professional armies and the massive assistance from fascist Italy and Nazi Germany that the Nationalists enjoyed. Foreign volunteers arriving in Barcelona were sent to the front with companies that were ill-equipped; lines of communication were poor; and, in addition, the Left was torn by internal divisions which at times led almost to civil war within its own ranks. George Orwell's account of this period in his *Homage to Catalonia* is instructive; fighting in an anarchist militia, he was eventually forced to flee the country when the infighting became intolerable, though many others like him were not so fortunate and ended up in prison or executed.

Eventually, the nonintervention of the other European governments effectively handed victory to the Nationalists. The Republican government fled Madrid first for Valencia, and then moved on to base itself at Barcelona in 1937. The **Battle of the Ebro** around Tortosa saw massive casualties on both sides; Nationalist troops advanced on Valencia in 1938, and from the west were also approaching Catalunya from their bases in Navarre. When Bilbao was taken by the Nationalists, the Republicans' fight on the **Aragón front** was lost. The final Republican hope – that war in Europe over Czechoslovakia would draw the Allies into a war against Fascism and deprive Franco of his foreign aid – failed in September 1938, with the British Prime Minister Chamberlain's capitulation to Hitler at Munich, and Franco was able to call on new arms and other supplies from Germany for a final offensive against Catalunya. The **fall of Barcelona** came on January 25, 1939 – the Republican parliament held its last meeting at Figueres a few days later. Republican soldiers, cut off in the valleys of the Pyrenees, made their way across the high passes into France, joined by women and children fearful of a Fascist victory. Among the refugees and escapees was **Lluís Companys**, president of the Generalitat, who was later captured in France by the Germans, returned to Spain and ordered by Franco to be shot at the castle prison on Montjuïc in 1940.

Catalunya in Franco's Spain

Although the Civil War left more than half a million dead, destroyed a quarter of a million homes and sent a third of a million people (including 100,000 Catalans) into exile, Franco was in no mood for reconciliation. With his government recognized by Allied powers, including Britain and France, he set up **war tribunals** which ordered executions and provided concentration camps in which upwards of two million people were held until "order" had been established by authoritarian means. Until as late as the mid-1960s, isolated partisans in Catalunya (and elsewhere in Spain) continued to resist fascist rule.

The Catalan language was banned again, in schools, churches, the press and in public life; only one party was permitted and censorship was rigorously enforced. The economy was in ruins, and Franco did everything possible to further the cause of Madrid against Catalunya, starving the region of investment and new industry. Pyrenean villagers began to drift down into the towns and cities in a fruitless search for work, accelerating the depopulation of the mountains.

After **World War II** (during which the country was too weak to be anything but neutral), Spain was economically and politically isolated. There were serious strikes in 1951 in Barcelona and in 1956 across the whole of Catalunya.

What saved Franco was the acceptance of **American aid**, offered by General Eisenhower in 1953 on the condition that Franco provide land for US air bases – a condition he was more than willing to accept. Prosperity did increase after this, fuelled in the 1960s and 1970s by a growing tourist industry, but

Catalunya (along with the Basque country, another thorn in Franco's side) was still economically backward, with investment per head lower than anywhere else in the country; absentee landlords took much of the local revenue, a situation exacerbated by Franco's policy of encouraging emigration to Catalunya from other parts of Spain (and granting the immigrants land) in an attempt to dilute regional differences.

Despite the **cultural and political repression**, the distinct Catalan identity was never really obliterated: the Catalan Church retained a feisty independence, while Barcelona emerged as the most important publishing centre in Spain. Clandestine language and history classes were conducted, and artists and writers continued to produce work in defiance of the authorities. Nationalism in Catalunya, however, did not take the same course as the Basque **separatist movement**, which engendered the terrorist organization ETA (Euzkadi ta Azkatasuna; "Basque Homeland and Freedom"). There was little violence against the state in Catalunya and no serious counterpart to ETA. The Catalan approach was subtler: an audience at the Palau de la Música sang the unofficial Catalan anthem when Franco visited in 1960; a massive petition against language restrictions was raised in 1963; and a sit-in by Catalan intellectuals at Montserrat was organized in protest against repression in the Basque country.

As Spain became comparatively more wealthy, so the political bankruptcy of Franco's regime and its inability to cope with popular demands became clearer. Higher incomes, the need for better education and a creeping invasion of Western culture made the anachronism of Franco ever clearer. His only reaction was to attempt to withdraw what few signs of increased liberalism had crept through, and his last years mirrored the repression of the postwar period.

Franco's death and the new democracy

When Franco died in 1975, **King Juan Carlos** was officially designated to succeed as head of state – groomed for the succession by Franco himself. The king's initial moves were cautious in the extreme, appointing a government dominated by loyal Franquistas, who had little sympathy for the growing opposition demands for "democracy without adjectives". In the summer of 1976 demonstrations, particularly in Madrid, ended in violence, with the police upholding the old authoritarian ways.

To his credit, Juan Carlos recognized that some real break with the past was urgent and inevitable, and, accepting the resignation of his prime minister, set in motion the process of **democratization**. His newly appointed prime minister, Adolfo Suárez, steered through a Political Reform Act, which allowed for a two-chamber parliament and a referendum in favour of democracy; he also legitimized the Socialist Party (the PSOE) and the Communists, and called elections for the following year, the first since 1936.

In the elections of 1977, the **Pacte Democratico per Catalunya** – an alliance of pro-Catalan parties – gained ten seats in the lower house of the Spanish parliament (Basque nationalists won a similar number) dominated by Suárez's own centre-right UCD party but also with a strong Socialist presence. In a spirit of consensus and amnesty, it was announced that Catalunya was to be granted a degree of autonomy, and a million people turned out on the streets of Barcelona to witness the re-establishment of the Generalitat and to welcome home its president-in-exile, **Josep Tarradellas**. A new Spanish constitution of 1978 allowed for a sort of devolution within a unitary state, and the **Statute of Autonomy** for Catalunya was approved on December 18, 1979, with the first regional elections taking place in March 1980. Although the Socialists had won the mayoral election of 1978, it was the conservative **Jordi**

Pujol i Soley and his coalition party **Convergència i Unió** (CiU) who gained regional power – and who proceeded to dominate the Catalan parliament for the next quarter of a century. In a way, the pro-conservative vote made it easy for the central government to deal with Catalunya, since the demands for autonomy here did not have the extreme political dimension they had in the Basque country.

After the failure of an attempted **military coup** in February 1981, led by Civil Guard Colonel Tejero, the **elections of 1982** saw Felipe González's PSOE elected with a massive swing to the Left in a country that had been firmly in the hands of the Right for 43 years. The **1986** general election gave González a renewed mandate, during which time Spain entered the **European Community**, decided by referendum to stay in NATO, and boasted one of the fastest-growing economies in Western Europe. However, high unemployment, wage controls and a lack of social security measures led to diminishing support and the PSOE began losing much of its credibility. Narrow victories in two more elections kept the Socialists in power but after the 1993 results were counted it was clear that they had failed to win an overall majority and were forced to rely on the support of the Catalan nationalist coalition, CiU, to retain power. This state of affairs well suited Jordi Pujol, who was now in a position to pursue some of the Catalan nationalists' more long-cherished aims, in particular the right to retain part of the region's own income-tax revenue.

Contemporary politics

Following allegations of sleaze and the disclosure of the existence of a secret "dirty war" against the Basque terrorists, the calling of a **general election in 1996** came as no surprise and neither did the overall result. In power for almost fourteen years, the PSOE finally succumbed to the greater appeal of the conservative Partido Popular (PP), under **José Maria Aznar** – the first conservative government in Spain since the return of democracy. However, the PP came in well short of an outright majority and Aznar was left with the same problem as González before him – relying on the Catalan nationalists and other smaller regionalist parties to maintain his party in power.

In the **general election of 2000**, a resounding victory in the national parliament, whilst Catalunya was left under CiU control. For the first time, the PP was no longer dependent on other parties to pass legislation and was high on confidence, though within two years Aznar's government had begun to lose its way. A one-day general strike (June 2002) against labour reforms, and criticism of the handling of the sinking of the *Prestige* oil tanker (November 2002) off the Galician coast, contributed to the government's growing unpopularity, while Aznar's fervent support of US and British **military action in Iraq** led to further discontent in 2003. Polls showed that ninety percent of Spaniards opposed the conflict – manifested in Barcelona by a cacophonous nightly anti-war banging of pots and pans from the city's balconies.

However, in the local elections of 2003, Aznar and the PP defied the polls, holding off the PSOE in many major cities (Barcelona excepted). With the PSOE beset by corruption scandals and affected by the strong separatist showing in regional elections, it seemed that the best PSOE leader **José Luis Rodriguez Zapatero** could hope for was to deny the PP an absolute majority in the **2004 general election**. That was before the dramatic events of March 11, 2004, when terrorists struck at the heart of **Madrid**, killing 200 people in co-ordinated train bombings. Spain went to the polls in shock a few days later, and voted in PSOE against all expectations. With millions on the streets in the days after the attacks, it seemed the PP had been punished both for supporting the war in Iraq, and – prematurely to many – blaming the bombings on the Basque separatists, ETA. At the time of writing, it looked very much as if al-Qaeda had struck for the first time in Europe – if not influencing, then certainly affecting the politics of a scarred nation..

City and state – Barcelona and Catalunya today

The province's official title is the **Comunitat Autonoma de Catalunya**. The Catalan government, based in Barcelona – the **Generalitat** – enjoys a very high profile, employing eighty thousand people, controlling education, health and social services, urban planning, culture, regional transport, industry, trade, tourism, fisheries and agriculture. However, as long as the budget is based on tax collected by central government and then returned proportionately, the scope for real independence is limited, as the Generalitat has no tangible resources of its own and is forced to share jurisdiction on many strategic matters with the Spanish state.

Still, steps are being taken to create the illusion of independence, and two of the most visible symbols of the Spanish state, the Guardia Civil and the Policía Nacional, are gradually being scaled down, with urban **policing** and rural and highway duties being taken over by the Mossos d'Esquadra, Catalunya's autonomous police force. Culturally, emphasis has been on the promotion of the **Catalan language** – a key part of the nationalists' plan since autonomy. It's currently one of the fastest-growing languages in the world, and the Generalitat has succeeded in having all of Catalunya's children taught primarily in Catalan.

Parliament and local politics

The **Parlament de Catalunya** (Parliament of Catalunya) comprises a single chamber of 135 members, with elections held every four years. It sits in the old Ciutadella arsenal building in Parc de la Ciutadella, in parliamentary sessions that run from September to December and February to June, though extraordinary sessions can be called outside these months. As well as legislating for Catalunya within the strictures of the Statute of Autonomy, parliament also appoints the senators who represent the Generalitat in the Spanish Senate and has the right to initiate legislation in the Spanish Congress.

From 1980 (when autonomy was granted) until 2003, **Catalunya** consistently elected right-wing governments, led by the conservative Convergència i Unió (CiU) president of the Generalitat, **Jordi Pujol i Soley**. The Catalan predilection for the Right may come as a surprise in view of the past, but Catalunya is nothing if not pragmatic, and such administrations are seen as better able to protect Catalan business interests. The main opposition was provided by the **Partit Socialista de Catalunya** (PSC), while other Catalan parties, like the pro-independence **Esquerra Republicana de Catalana** (ERC) and the **Catalunya Verds** (Greens), have usually attracted minority support.

However, by way of contrast to conservative Catalunya, **Barcelona** itself remains by and large a socialist stronghold. Part of this is due to the city's industrial heritage, but it's also in good measure the result of the large immigrant population from elsewhere in Spain, who are little attracted to the CiU's brand of Catalan nationalism. Between 1982 and 1997, the **Ajuntament** (city council) was led by an incredibly popular and charismatic socialist mayor, **Pasqual Maragall i Mira**, who took much of the credit for the hosting of the 1992 Olympic Games and consequent reshaping of the city. However, much to the consternation of locals, he stepped down from his post as mayor in 1997, leaving his deputy, the little-known **Joan Clos**, to fill his shoes. Despite initial worries, Clos has done enough to convince the city that he can take Barcelona in the same pioneering direction as his predecessor – Clos was elected to a full four-year term in 1999 (with an increased majority) and re-elected in 2003.

Maragall, meanwhile, moved on to take charge of the PSC in Catalunya, but lost out to Jordi Pujol in the 1999 Catalan elections despite taking more votes than the nationalists. With Pujol's announcement that he wouldn't stand again for the presidency, the **2003 parliamentary elections** were ostensibly a straight fight between the CiU, under Pujol's former deputy Artur Mas, and Maragall's PSC. On one level, that was indeed the case, as the two parties finished neck and neck, the PSC again polling slightly more votes but winning slightly fewer seats than the CiU. However, the surprise was the performance of the **pro-independence** ERC, under the leadership of Josep-Lluís Carod-Rovira, which effectively doubled its vote from 1999 to hold the balance of power. After a short period of haggling, a coalition of the Left, led by the PSC and under the presidency of Pasqual Maragall, replaced the nationalists in power. It's not the easy alliance that it appears on paper, since the separatist ERC favours full Catalan independence, not something the PSC (or the national PSOE) supports. But with a left-wing Catalan government for the first time since autonomy, there's a strong incentive to make the coalition work.

Devolution, development and the economy

Despite their seeming differences, both political strands within Catalunya are convinced of the merits of **devolution**. Catalans see themselves as more economically advanced than the rest of Spain and demand the right to raise more of their own taxes and spend them on self-regulation. Although causing consternation in Madrid, regional fiscal autonomy is increasing and the current Spanish government has already agreed that Catalunya (and other regions) can collect and administer almost a third of the income tax raised locally, manage its own ports and take charge of regional programmes like employment training. Recent calls by the nationalist CiU have gone even further, demanding a revision of the Statue of Autonomy to allow for "shared sovereignty" and control over the whole of the region's finances.

Perhaps the most exciting development as far as the Catalans are concerned – and one which indicates clearly their future thinking – is the agreement that all Spain's regional governments should now have a representative at the **European Union**, working on committees alongside the Spanish delegates. In addition, the Spanish government is now committed to consulting the regions on any European issues that affect them directly.

Whatever the grumbles about the lack of progress in the devolution of real political power from the centre to the Spanish provinces, Catalunya's best argument may be its solid **economy**, which makes it, along with the Basque country and Madrid, one of the most prosperous regions of the country. Around half of all new firms starting business in Spain do so in Catalunya, and Barcelona is the third-richest city in the country; it boasts nearly a fifth of Spain's GDP, relatively low unemployment, and Europe's largest savings bank, La Caixa. Tourism is an important factor, accounting for almost fourteen percent of Catalunya's GDP, with up to twenty million visitors a year now coming to the region. Other major employers are telecommunications, metal products and chemical and pharmaceutical industries.

The **1992 Olympics** (p.78) are still regarded as a turning point in the city's recent history. They were an important boost, involving radical restoration of the old-town and port areas and prompting massive new developments – at a pace which the city has endeavoured to maintain ever since. In recent years, among countless ambitious projects, this has meant the complete renovation of the **Port Vell** neighbourhood (p.74), a cleanup of **El Raval** (p.69) and the current regeneration of **Poble Nou** (p.79) as part of the so-called **Project 22@**, breathing life into a formerly run-down urban area. The **2004 Universal Forum of Cultures** – a sort of culture and sustainability Expo – is at the heart of the project, providing a similar focus for regeneration to that provided by the Olympics. Other development schemes include the imminent completion of the soaring cigar-shaped **Torre Agbar** at Glóries (the third-highest building in the city after the Port Olímpic towers), the further expansion of the city's airport and metro system, the building of a high-velocity train (AVE) link with Madrid and France, the transformation of the Arenes bullring into a leisure centre, and even the mooted completion of the Sagrada Família.

Social matters

Economic success has led to familiar urban social problems. More than half of Catalunya's six million inhabitants now live in the city and its metropolitan region, with many complaining that the high-profile regeneration projects do little for their needs. Property prices, in particular, have boomed, depriving the young, the old and the poor of affordable **housing** and other amenities. That said, both the Olympic and Project 22@ schemes have incorporated social housing, leisure facilities and green spaces, while the public transport system in particular is something of a European model of excellence.

As elsewhere in Europe, **immigration** is another point of contemporary debate. While immigrants from elsewhere in Spain have long settled in Barcelona (indeed, were encouraged to do so by Franco to dilute Catalan nationalism), those bearing the brunt of racism are the newcomers from North Africa, the Indian subcontinent and South America. Popular wisdom has come to equate North Africans ("*moros*") with petty crime, whereas Romanies ("*gitanos*") are treated largely as pariahs. It's a dangerous nonsense with at least some of its roots in a Catalan nationalism that prides itself on a certain cultural superiority, but such bigoted views aren't simply confined to the Right – senior figures on the Left, too, have warned of the "dangers" of allowing too many "foreigners" into Catalunya. The facts, of course, tell a different story. Just two to three percent of the Catalan population at large has its origin outside Spain, though as most of these people live or work in the capital it's easy to construct a prejudice from their higher profile in the city. In contrast, almost a third of the Catalan population comes from other parts of Spain, while the fastest-growing immigrant population is actually that of other Europeans, free to settle in Catalunya with the relaxation of EU residency rules.

Catalan cookery

M any people judge the food of Catalunya to be the best in Spain. The region certainly has one of the oldest culinary traditions: its inns were celebrated by travellers in medieval times, while the first Spanish cookery book was published in Barcelona in 1477. Historically, Catalunya shares some of its dishes and methods with the region of Valencia to the south and parts of France (like Roussillon) to the north, but nonetheless it's possible to identify within its borders a distinct cuisine. Fish and rice have always played a major part in Catalan cookery, but there's also an emphasis on mixed flavours which you won't find anywhere else in Spain – some common traditional examples are rabbit cooked with snails, chicken with shellfish, meat or poultry with fruit, and vegetables with raisins and nuts. Meanwhile, contemporary Catalan chefs (see feature on p.186) have rewritten the rule book regarding taste and texture, and their deconstructivist menus – featuring intensely flavoured foams, reductions and concentrates – are currently at the forefront of cutting-edge European cuisine.

We've stuck to traditional **recipes** below, the sort of dishes you're likely to eat on a day-to-day basis in Barcelona and Catalunya. You don't need much in the way of special **equipment**, though a *paella* (the dish is named after the wide, flat metal pan it's cooked in) and a *cassola* (earthenware casserole dish) are both useful. They're widely available these days from specialist cookery stores. Other than that, you only need to be insistent on the best and freshest **ingredients** – the finest tomatoes you can buy, proper salted Catalan anchovies, authentic rice and, above all, good olive oil. All the recipes below are for four people unless otherwise stated.

Pa amb tomàquet

The "bread with tomato" combination is a classic taste of Catalunya, eaten for breakfast, or as a snack or appetizer. In traditional grill-restaurants and taverns you'll often be brought the wherewithal to do-it-yourself before your meal arrives – a basket of toasted bread, a handful of garlic cloves and an over-ripe tomato or two. The basic method is given below, but, for more of a meal, pile on shavings of ham or cheese, grilled vegetables or anchovy fillets.

Ingredients

Good continental bread
Vine-ripened tomatoes
Peeled garlic cloves

Olive oil
Salt

Method

Cut large slices from a loaf of good continental bread, preferably the dense, heavy variety, and grill them (a ribbed cast-iron grill-pan is ideal for this). Cut the garlic cloves in two and drag the cut sides over the toast. Cut the tomatoes in two and squeeze and rub well over the garlic-impregnated toast. Dribble generous amounts of olive oil over the slice and add salt to taste.

Amanida Catalana

Salad (*amanida*) is usually served as a first course in Catalunya and can be very filling.

Ingredients

3 large tomatoes, thickly sliced
2 hard-boiled eggs, quartered
24 green olives
1 large Spanish onion, very thinly sliced
1 large roasted red pepper/capsicum

(see Escalivada, below), cut into strips
Crunchy lettuce, as much as you require
200g tinned/preserved tuna
8 plump anchovy fillets

Method

This is one of the most common of restaurant salads, and with it you can improvise to your heart's content, but don't toss the ingredients all together – it's a composed salad, laid out on a plate, rather a bowl of mixed salad. For a more elaborate dish you can add shredded carrot or pickled vegetables, sliced cheese or thinly cut dry-cured ham or pork, salami or spiced sausage. Dress salad with salt and olive oil.

Escalivada

This fantastic mix of grilled peppers/capsicums, onions and aubergine/eggplant is a restaurant and domestic staple. It's usually available as a starter or an accompaniment to grills and roasts, or you can buy it ready-made on deli counters in Catalan markets. It's also very easy to make.

Ingredients

2 large aubergines/eggplants
4 red peppers/capsicums
4 small onions
Olive oil

1 clove garlic, chopped very finely (optional)
Salt

Method

Grill the vegetables whole on a barbecue, or under a grill, turning them until the skins are blackened all over. Or simply place them on separate trays and roast them in the oven on a high heat for the same effect – you'll still need to turn them periodically. When they are done, put the blackened vegetables in a shallow casserole dish or on a tray and cover them with a cloth or lid for ten minutes (some people place them in a paper bag). This process allows them to steam while they cool down, making it easier to remove the blackened skins. When they are cool enough to handle, peel the skins. Slice the soft internal pulp of the aubergine/eggplant into strips; seed the peppers/capsicums and cut into thin strips; remove the tough outer skin of the onions and separate out the soft inner leaves. Spread out the vegetables on a serving dish, dribble with oil, scatter with minced garlic if you like, and season with salt.

Espinacs a la Catalana

"Catalan spinach" can either be served as a starter or as an accompaniment to a main dish. You can use greens instead of fresh spinach, but you should remove the hard stems before cooking.

Ingredients

500g fresh spinach
3 tablespoons raisins, soaked in hot water, then drained
3 tablespoons pine nuts

2 tablespoons olive oil
2 cloves garlic, finely chopped
1 small onion, finely chopped

Method

Put the spinach in boiling water, cook for three minutes until tender and then drain, squeezing out excess water. Put to one side. Heat the oil in the pan, add the garlic and onion and cook gently until soft, taking care not to burn the garlic. Add the spinach, drained raisins and pine nuts, and toss together while heating through. Add salt and pepper to taste.

Sarsuela

This wonderful fish casserole is served in most coastal towns, using whatever fish and shellfish is available. You'll have to buy what you can, though you should be aiming for large prawns/shrimp in their shells, different kinds of white fish (cod and hake are fine), squid, mussels or clams. In Catalunya, cray-fish or lobster are often added, too. The point is to go for a variety of fish: the word *sarsuela* refers to a comic musical variety show.

Ingredients

3–4 tablespoons olive oil
2 cloves garlic, chopped finely
2 large tomatoes, skinned, seeded and chopped finely
2 onions, sliced
1 tablespoon Spanish brandy
1 teaspoon paprika
1 bay leaf
1 cup/quarter-pint dry white wine

2 tablespoons chopped parsley
2 lemons, cut into wedges
Assorted white fish, enough for a couple of fair-sized chunks each
8 large prawns/shrimp in their shells
4 small squid
16 mussels/32 clams
Ground black pepper
Salt

Method

Clean the fish and cut into chunks; slice the squid into rings; leave the large prawns/shrimp as they are. Scrub and clean the mussels or clams. Boil the fishy leftovers (skin and heads, etc; if you've bought fillets, use a couple of chunks and a few small prawns/shrimp) in a pot of water, adding salt and pepper, some fresh herbs and a sliced onion, to give a fish stock – which, when reduced a lit-tle, should be strained and put aside.

Heat the oil in a large pot or casserole, add the garlic, onion and chopped tomatoes and cook slowly for ten minutes – this is the *sofregit* (see feature p.268). Turn up the heat, add the brandy and flame, then turn it back down and add the paprika, fish stock, white wine and bay leaf. Stir the mixture, put in the chunks of white fish and simmer for five minutes. Stir, add the squid and whole prawns/shrimp and simmer for another five minutes; then add the mussels/clams, cover and cook for another five minutes or so, until the fish is ready and the mussels or clams have opened. Take care not to break up the fish by stirring too often. Add salt and pepper to taste, and garnish with fresh pars-ley and lemon wedges before serving.

The sauce is the source of good food, as a Catalan might say. Everything starts with a **sofregit**, basically sliced onion, chopped tomato and garlic that has been sautéed down to a soft, almost jam-like consistency. This underpins the construction of countless classic Catalan dishes, which might then be thickened before serving with the addition of a **picada** – a smooth paste (made in a mortar and pestle) of garlic, almonds, hazelnuts, fried bread, saffron, olive oil and parsley. The southern Catalan **romesco** sauce, made with chilli peppers, is a spicier version of *picada*, used as a dip (for grilled spring onions or fish) rather than as an ingredient. **All i oli** (garlic and oil) is a fiery Catalan mayonnaise, made without eggs, served with grilled meat (traditionally rabbit), fish and shellfish or stirred into *fideuà*. And there's also **samfaina**, a ratatouille-like stew of garlic, onion, tomato, aubergine/eggplant and pepper/capsicum. Again, this can be served as an accompaniment (for roast chicken, say, or salt cod), but it's also made into a sauce by cooking a lot longer until sticky and then puréeing.

Grilled fish with romesco sauce

There are many different varieties of *romesco* sauce, which originates from Tarragona province, and you can experiment with the quantities of the ingredients below until you find the taste that suits you. Made with small chilli peppers, fresh or dried, it can be a very hot sauce, though you can substitute cayenne pepper or even paprika for these, if you want to control the heat.

Ingredients

4 fish steaks, marinaded in olive oil, chopped garlic and lemon juice
2 lemons, quartered
2 tablespoons olive oil
1 small onion, finely chopped
3 tomatoes, skinned, seeded and chopped
3 cloves garlic, finely chopped

10–15 almonds (toasted under the grill/broiler)
2 tablespoons dry white wine
Chilli peppers/cayenne pepper/paprika to taste
1 tablespoon red wine vinegar
Salt

Method

Fry the onion and the garlic in the olive oil until soft, add the tomatoes, white wine and chilli peppers and cook over a low heat for twenty minutes. Crush or grind the almonds and add to the mixture, adding enough extra olive oil to achieve the consistency of a purée. Add the vinegar and a pinch of salt. Either put the whole lot through a blender or food processor, or pass through a sieve – you're aiming for a smooth, rather thick sauce. Leave to cool at room temperature. Take the fish out of the marinade, grill/broil, and serve with lemon wedges. Serve the sauce separately, to be dipped in or spooned over.

Pollastre amb gambes

The combination of chicken (*pollastre*) and prawns (*gambes*) is typically Catalan, otherwise known as *mar i muntanya* (sea and mountain).

Ingredients

8 chicken pieces
12–16 medium prawns/shrimp in their shells, washed and cleaned

3 tablespoons olive oil
1 onion, finely chopped
2 cloves garlic, finely chopped

2 tomatoes, skinned, seeded and chopped
1 carrot, peeled and finely chopped
Quarter-cup Spanish brandy
Half-cup dry white wine

Quarter-cup beef stock (you can use a stock cube)
2 tablespoons chopped parsley
Ground pepper
Salt

Method

Salt and pepper the chicken pieces, heat the oil in a large pan, and then add the chicken pieces and prawns/shrimp. Take the prawns/shrimp out after a minute or so, put to one side, and cook the chicken until golden-brown on all sides. Add the onion, garlic, tomatoes and carrot, and cook until soft (about 15min). Turn up the heat, add the brandy and flame (stand well back), then – when the flames have died down – turn the heat back down and add the wine, stock, half of the parsley, salt and pepper. Cover and cook for another twenty minutes, then add the prawns/shrimp and cook for another ten minutes. Take out the chicken and prawns/shrimp, put them on a warm serving dish and strain the sauce over them, sprinkling with the rest of the parsley.

Crema Catalana

The one dessert you'll be offered everywhere in Catalunya is *Crema Catalana*. It rounds off a meal impressively if you make it at home; the only tricky part is caramelizing the sugar topping.

Ingredients

2 cups milk
Peel of half a lemon
1 cinnamon stick

4 egg yolks
7 tablespoons sugar
1 tablespoon cornflour/cornstarch

Method

Simmer the milk with the lemon peel and cinnamon stick for a few minutes, then take out the lemon and cinnamon from the pot. Beat the egg yolks and half the sugar together, beat in the cornflour/cornstarch, too, then add the beaten egg mixture slowly into the milk and continue to simmer. Stir constantly until thick and smooth, taking care not to let the mixture boil, and then pour into a wide, shallow serving dish. Let the mixture cool and then put in the fridge.

When you want to serve it, sprinkle the rest of the sugar evenly over the custard so that it forms a thick layer on the top. To caramelize the sugar topping, you can use a kitchen blowtorch – or simply heat a wide knife or metal spatula and press down on the sugar until it goes brown and crunchy. Repeat this over the whole top of the dessert, wiping the knife/spatula clean and reheating it every time.

Books

The selection of books reviewed below provides useful background on the city. Its history, people and institutions are particularly well served by a variety of widely available general accounts, though if your interest is medieval Catalan agriculture or architectural monographs, plenty of specialist, technical works also offer themselves. Despite a long pedigree, Catalan literature is hard to find in translation, though novels by (mostly foreign) authors set in Barcelona provide an easy route into the feel of the city, past and present. A good first stop for all books is the online bookseller **Amazon** (ⓦ www.amazon.co.uk, www.amazon.com), which carries all of the books listed below as well as other hard-to-find and specialist titles. Another excellent source is **Books on Spain** (call for free catalogue, UK ☎ 0208/898 7789, ⓦ www.books-on-spain.com) for all aspects of Spanish history and culture. In Barcelona, most of the major **bookshops** (see p.232) carry English-language guides and titles about the city, or look in the **museum bookshops** (particularly in MNAC, MACBA, Caixa Forum, Museu Picasso and Fundació Joan Miró) for books on art, design and architecture.

History

Barcelona

⭐ **Jimmy Burns** *Barça: A People's Passion* (Bloomsbury, UK). On one level simply an informative history of the city's famous football team, alma mater of Cruyff, Lineker, Maradona, Ronaldo, Figo et al. But, like the club itself, the book is so much more than that, as Burns examines Catalan pride and nationalism through the prism of sport.

Felipe Fernandez-Armesto *Barcelona: A Thousand Years of the City's Past* (OUP, UK). An expertly written appraisal of what the author sees as the formative years of the city's history, from the tenth to the early twentieth centuries.

Robert Hughes *Barcelona* (Harvill Press, UK). The renowned art critic casts his accomplished eye over two thousand years of Barcelona's history and culture, with special emphasis on the nineteenth and early twentieth centuries – explaining, in his own

words, "the zeitgeist of the place and the connective tissue between the cultural icons".

⭐ **Matthew Stewart** *Monturiol's Dream* (Profile Books, UK). Witty and engaging account of the life and work of Narcís Monturiol, nineteenth-century Catalan utopian visionary, revolutionary and inventor of the world's first true submarine. Stewart places Monturiol firmly at the centre of Barcelona's contemporary social and political turmoil – printing seditious magazines, manning the barricades in the 1850s, fleeing into exile and returning to pursue his pioneering invention.

Colm Tóibín *Homage to Barcelona* (Picador, UK). Echoing Orwell, the Irish writer pays his own homage to the city, tracing Barcelona's history through its artists, architects, personalities, organizations and rulers.

Spain

Raymond Carr *Modern Spain 1875–1980* (OUP, UK & US) and *The Spanish Tragedy: the Civil War in*

Perspective (Weidenfeld & Nicolson, UK). Two of the best books available on twentieth-century Spanish histo-

ry – both are well-told narratives.
John Hooper *The New Spaniards*
(Penguin, UK/US). Excellent portrait of post-Franco Spain and the
new generation. It's a bit dated now
(last revised in 1995), but even so, if
you buy just one book for general
background on the rest of the country, this should be it.
Hugh Thomas *Rivers of Gold: The
Rise of the Spanish Empire*

(Weidenfeld & Nicolson, UK).
Thomas' scholarly but eminently
accessible history provides a fascinating historical snapshot of Spain's
most glorious period – its meteoric
imperial rise in the late fifteenth and
early sixteenth centuries, when characters like Ferdinand and Isabella,
and Columbus and Magellan, shaped
the country's outlook for the next
300 years.

Civil War

Gerald Brenan *The Spanish
Labyrinth* (Cambridge UP, UK &
US). First published in 1943, Brenan's
account of the background to the
Civil War is tinged by personal expe-
rience, yet still impressively rounded.

★ **George Orwell** *Homage to
Catalonia* (Penguin, UK & US).
Stirring account of the Civil War
fight on the Aragón front and
Orwell's participation in the early
exhilaration of revolution in
Barcelona. A forthright, honest and
entertaining tale, covering Orwell's
injury and subsequent flight from

the factional infighting in
Republican Spain.
Paul Preston *A Concise History of the
Spanish Civil War* and *Franco* (both
Fontana, UK). The leading historian
of twentieth-century Spain offers
Civil War, an easily accessible introduction to the subject, and *Franco*, a
penetrating and monumental biography of Franco and his regime.
Hugh Thomas *The Spanish Civil
War* (Penguin, UK & US). Exhaustive
political study of the period that's still
the best single telling of the convoluted story of the Civil War.

Art, architecture and style

★ **Gijs van Hensbergen** *Gaudí:
The Biography* (HarperCollins,
UK). At last, a worthy biography of
"arguably the world's most famous
architect". Van Hensbergen puts substantial flesh on the man while plac-
ing his work firmly in context, as
Spain lost its empire and Catalunya
slowly flexed her nationalist muscles.
John Richardson *A Life of Picasso*
(Pimlico, UK). The definitive biography, currently in two volumes, with
more to come. Volume 1, covering
the period 1881–1906, is an
extremely readable account of the
artist's early years, covering the
whole of his time in Barcelona.
Phyllis Richardson *Style City:
Barcelona* (Thames & Hudson, UK).
Part guide, part celebration of everything that's considered cool about
contemporary Barcelona. The book

covers the sharpest restaurant
interiors to the latest galleries,
artisans' studios to Art Nouveau bars,
accompanied by 350 colour photographs that show Barcelona in its
most flattering light.

★ **Philippe Thiébaut** *Gaudí:
Builder of Visions* (Thames &
Hudson, UK). Read van
Hensbergen for the life, but pick up
this pocket-sized volume for its
excellent photographic coverage –
not just Gaudí buildings and interiors, but sketches, historical photographs and architectural insights that
add up to a useful gateway to his
work in the city and surroundings.
Christopher Woodward *The
Buildings of Europe: Barcelona*
(Manchester UP, UK & US). This
instructive little guide was written in
1992, so stops well short of the latest

round of city reconstruction, but its thumbnail sketches and short essays about buildings, streets, squares and parks are handy reference points.

Food and wine

★ **Colman Andrews** *Catalan Cuisine* (Grub Street, UK/Harvard Common Press, US). The best available – possibly the *only* available – English-language book dealing with Spain's most adventurous regional cuisine. Full of historical and anecdotal detail, it's a pleasure to read, let alone cook from (no pictures, though).
Penelope Casas *The Foods and Wines of Spain* (Penguin Cookery Library, UK). Casas roams across every region

Particularly good on the period 1800–1910 (industrialization to *modernisme*), and the neglected Franco era of architecture.

of Spain in this classic Spanish cookery book, including the best dishes that Catalunya has to offer. Her *Paella* (Henry Holt, US) and *Tapas: The Little Dishes of Spain* (Knopf, US) cover the rest of the bases.
Jan Read *Wines of Spain* (Mitchell Beazley, UK). All you need to know to sort out your Penedès from your Priorat – an explanation of regions and producers, plus tasting notes and tips for wine travellers.

Catalan literature

Catalan was established as a literary language as early as the thirteenth century, and a **golden age** of medieval Catalan literature followed, lasting until the mid-sixteenth century, with another cultural and literary flowering in the nineteenth century known as the **Renaixença** (Renaissance). However, this long pedigree has suffered two major interruptions: first, the rise of Castile and later Bourbon rule, which saw the Catalan language eclipsed and then suppressed; and a similar suppression under Franco, when there was a ban on Catalan books and publications. In the post-Civil War period there was some relaxation of the ban, but it's only been since the return of democracy to Spain that Catalan literature has once again been allowed to flourish.

Catalan and Spanish speakers and readers are best served by the literature, since there's little still in translation – the Amazon websites are a good first stop for the translated authors mentioned below. The vernacular works of mystic and philosopher **Ramon Llull** (1233–1316) mark the onset of a true Catalan literature - his *Blanquerna* was one of the first books to be written in any Romance language, while the later chivalric epic *The White Tyrant (Tirant lo Blanc)* by **Joanot Martorell** (1413–68) represents a high point of the golden age. None of the works of the leading lights of the nineteenth-century Renaixença are readily available in translation, and it's to *Solitude (Solitud)* by **Victor Català** (1869–1966) that you have to look for the most important pre-Civil War Catalan novel. This tragic tale of a woman's life and sexual passions in a Catalan mountain village was first published in 1905, pseudonymously by Caterina Albert i Paradís, who lived most of her life in rural northern Catalunya.

During and after the Civil War, many authors found themselves under forcible or self-imposed exile, including **Mercè Rodoreda i Gurgui** (1909–83), whose *Camellia Street (El carrer de les Camèlies)* and *My Cristina and Other Tales (La meva Cristina i altres contes)* are relatively easily found in translation. For something lighter, you might track down the works of **Maria Antònia Oliver i Cabrer** (b.1946), novelist, children's author and short-story writer born in Mallorca, whose early novels were influenced by her birthplace, but whose *Study in Lilac (Estudi en Lila)* and *Antipodes* introduce Barcelona private eye Lonia Guiu. However, it's **Manuel Vasquez Montalban** (1939–2003) who ranks as the Catalan crime writer *par excellence* – and novelist, poet, journalist, political commentator and committed communist to boot. His Pepe Carvalho books (see "Novels set in Barcelona" opposite) do nothing less than expose the shortcomings of the new Spanish democracy as it plays out in fast-changing Barcelona.

Novels set in Barcelona

Bernado Atxaga *The Lone Man* (Harvill Press, UK). The Basque novelist sets a well-received psychological thriller during the 1982 World Cup, when two ETA gunmen hole up in a Barcelona hotel.

John Bryson *To the Death, Amic* (Hamish Hamilton, UK). Barcelona, under siege during the Civil War, is the backdrop for a coming-of-age novel recounting the adventures of 10-year-old twins Enric and Josep.

★ **Eduardo Mendoza** *City of Marvels, The Truth About the Savolta Case, The Year of the Flood* (all Harvill Press, UK). Mendoza's first and best novel, *City of Marvels* is set in the expanding Barcelona of 1880–1920, full of rich underworld characters and riddled with anarchic and comic turns. It's a milieu repeated with flair in *The Truth About the Savolta Case*, while *The Year of the Flood* adds a light touch to an unusual amorous entanglement in Fifties Barcelona.

★ **Manuel Vasquez Montalban** *Murder in the Central Committee, Southern Seas, The Angst-Ridden Executive, An Olympic Death, Offside* (Serpent's Tail, UK & US). Montalban's greatest creation, the fast-living gourmand-detective Pepe

Carvalho, ex-Communist and CIA agent, first appeared in print in 1972, investigating foul deeds in the city in a series of wry and racy Chandleresque thrillers. Only a handful have been translated into English, with *Murder in the Central Committee* a good place to start, as Carvalho confronts his Communist past. *Southern Seas* won the Planeta, Spain's biggest literary prize, while the city's institutions and events come under typical scrutiny in *An Olympic Death* and *Offside*. Also look for Montalban's *Barcelonas* (Verso Books, UK), part guidebook, part discursive analysis of everything from sex to soccer in Barcelona.

Raul Nuñez *The Lonely Hearts Club* (Serpent's Tail, UK & US). A parade of grotesques and hard-bitten characters haunt the city in this oddball but likable romantic comedy.

Colm Tóibín *The South* (Picador, UK). Tóibín's first novel uses the Barcelona he knows well as background for his tale of an Irish woman looking for a new life.

Barbara Ellen Wilson *Gaudí Afternoon* (Seal Press, UK). Pacy feminist thriller making good use of Gaudí's architecture as a backdrop for deception and skulduggery.

Language

Language

Language

In Barcelona, and in most of Catalunya, Catalan (Català) has more or less taken over from Castilian (Castellano) Spanish as the language on street signs and maps. On paper it looks like a cross between French and Spanish and is generally easy to read if you know those two. Spoken Catalan is harder to come to grips with, as the language itself is not phonetic, and accents vary from region to region. Few visitors realize how important Catalan is to those who speak it: never commit the error of calling it a dialect! However, despite the preponderance of the Catalan language, you'll get by perfectly well in Spanish, as long as you're aware of the use of Catalan in timetables, on menus, and so on. You'll find some basic pronunciation rules below, for both Spanish and Catalan, and a selection of words and phrases in both languages. Spanish is certainly easier to pronounce, but don't be afraid to try Catalan, especially in the more out-of-the-way places – you'll generally get a good reception if you at least try communicating in the local language.

Numerous **Spanish phrasebooks** are available, not least the *Spanish Rough Guide Phrasebook*, laid out dictionary-style for instant access. Note that many of the phrasebooks available in North America are geared to New World, Latin American usage rather than "European" Spanish. In Barcelona, *Parla Català* (Pia) is the only readily available English–Catalan phrasebook, though there are more extensive (and expensive) Catalan–English dictionaries and teach-yourself Catalan guides available (consult ®www.amazon.co.uk, www.amazon.com).

Pronunciation

Castilian/Spanish

Unless there's an accent, words ending in d, l, r or z are **stressed** on the last syllable, all others on the second last. All **vowels** are pure and short; combinations have predictable results.

A somewhere between the "A" sound of back and that of father.

E as in get.

I as in police.

O as in hot.

U as in rule.

C is lisped before E and I, hard otherwise: *cerca* is pronounced "thairka".

G works the same way, a guttural "H" sound (like the ch in loch) before E or I, a hard G elsewhere – *gigante* becomes "higante".

H is always silent.

J the same sound as a guttural G: *jamón* is pronounced "hamon".

LL sounds like an English Y: *tortilla* is pronounced "torteeya".

N is as in English unless it has a tilde (accent) over it, when it becomes NY: *mañana* sounds like "man-yarna".

QU is pronounced like an English K.

R is rolled, RR doubly so.

V sounds more like B, *vino* becoming "beano".

X has an S sound before consonants, normal X before vowels.

Z is the same as a soft C, so *cerveza* becomes "thairbaitha".

Catalan

With Catalan, don't be tempted to use the few rules of Spanish pronunciation you may know – in particular the soft Spanish Z and C don't apply, so unlike in the rest of Spain the city is not Barthelona but Barcelona, as in English.

A as in hat if stressed, as in alone when unstressed.

E varies, but usually as in get.

I as in police.

IG sounds like the "tch" in the English scratch; *lleig* (ugly) is pronounced "yeah-tch".

O a round full sound, when stressed, otherwise like a soft U sound.

U somewhere between the U of put and rule.

Ç sounds like an English S; *plaça* is pronounced "plassa".

C followed by an E or I is soft; otherwise hard.

G followed by E or I is like the "zh" in Zhivago; otherwise hard.

H is always silent.

J as in the French "Jean".

L.L is best pronounced (for foreigners) as a single L sound; but for Catalan speakers it has two distinct L sounds.

LL sounds like an English Y or LY, like the "yuh" sound in million.

N as in English, though before F or V it sometimes sounds like an M.

NY corresponds to the Castilian Ñ.

QU before E or I sounds like K, unless the U has an umlaut (Ü), in which case, and before A or O, as in "quit".

R is rolled, but only at the start of a word; at the end it's often silent.

T is pronounced as in English, though sometimes it sounds like a D; as in *viatge* or *dotze*.

V at the start of a word sounds like B; in all other positions it's a soft "F" sound.

W is pronounced like a B/V.

X is like SH or CH in most words, though in some, like exit, it sounds like an X.

Z is like the English Z in zoo.

Useful words and phrases

Words and phrases below are given in the following order: **English** - Spanish - *Catalan*.

Basics

English	Spanish	Catalan
Yes, No, OK	Sí, No, Vale	*Si, No, Val*
Please, Thank you	Por favor, Gracias	*Si us plau, Gràcies*
Where? When?	Dónde? Cuando?	*On? Quan?*
What? How much?	Qué? Cuánto?	*Què? Quant?*
Here, There	Aquí, Allí/Allá	*Aquí, Allí/Allá*
This, That	Esto, Eso	*Això, Allò*
Now, Later	Ahora, Más tarde	*Ara, Mès tard*
Open, Closed	Abierto/a, Cerrado/a	*Obert, Tancat*
With, Without	Con, Sin	*Amb, Sense*

Good, Bad	Bueno/a, Malo/a	*Bo(na), Dolent(a)*
Big, Small	Gran(de), Pequeño/a	*Gran, Petit(a)*
Cheap, Expensive	Barato, Caro	*Barat(a), Car(a)*
Hot, Cold	Caliente, Frío	*Calent(a), Fred(a)*
More, Less	Más, Menos	*Mes, Menys*
I want	Quiero	*Vull* (pronounced "vwee")
I'd like	Quisiera	*Voldria*
Do you know?	¿Sabe?	*Vostès saben?*
I don't know	No sé	*No sé*
There is (is there?)	(¿)Hay(?)	*Hi ha(?)*
What's that?	¿Qué es eso?	*Què és això?*
Give me (one like that)	Deme (uno así)	*Doneu-me* (a bit brusque)
Do you have?	¿Tiene?	*Té...?*
The time	La hora	*L'hora*
Today, Tomorrow	Hoy, Mañana	*Avui, Demà*
Yesterday	Ayer	*Ahir*
Day before yesterday	Ante ayer	*Abans-d'ahir*
Next week	La semana que viene	*La setmana que ve*
Next month	El mes que viene	*El mes que ve*

Greetings and responses

Hello, Goodbye	Hola, Adiós	*Hola, Adéu*
Good morning	Buenos días	*Bon dia*
Good afternoon/night	Buenas tardes/noches	*Bona tarde/nit*
See you later	Hasta luego	*Fins després*
Sorry	Lo siento/Disculpéme	*Ho sento*
Excuse me	Con permiso/Perdón	*Perdoni*
How are you?	¿Cómo está (usted)?	*Com va?*
I (don't) understand	(No) Entiendo	*(No) Ho entenc*
Not at all/You're welcome	De nada	*De res*
Do you speak English?	¿Habla (usted) inglés?	*Parleu anglès?*
I (don't) speak Spanish/ Catalan	(No) Hablo español	*(No) Parlo Català*
My name is...	Me llamo...	*Em dic...*
What's your name?	¿Como se llama usted?	*Com es diu?*
I am English/	Soy inglés(a)/	*Sóc anglès(a)/*
Scottish/	escocés(a)/	*escocès(a)/*
Australian/	australiano(a)/	*australian(a)/*
Canadian/	canadiense(a)/	*canadenc(a)/*
American/	americano(a)/	*americà (a)/*
Irish	irlandes(a)	*irlandès (a)*

Finding accommodation

Do you have a room?	¿Tiene una habitación?	*Té alguna habitació?*
...with two beds/double bed	...con dos camas/cama matrimonial	*...amb dos llits/llit per dues persones*

…with shower/bath	…con ducha/baño	…amb dutxa/bany
It's for one person (two people)	Es para una persona (dos personas)	Per a una persona (dues persones)
For one night (one week)	Para una noche (una semana)	Per una nit (una setmana)
It's fine, how much is it?	¿Está bien, cuánto es?	Esta bé, quant és?
It's too expensive	Es demasiado caro	És massa car
Don't you have anything cheaper?	¿No tiene algo más barato?	En té de més bon preu?
Can one…?	¿Se puede…?	Es pot…?
…camp (near) here	…acampar aqui (cerca)	…acampar a la vora
Is there a hostel nearby?	¿Hay un hostal aquí cerca?	Hi ha un hostal a la vora?

Directions and transport

How do I get to…?	¿Por donde se va a…?	Per anar a…?
Left, Right, Straight on	Izquierda, Derecha, Todo recto	A la dreta, A l'esquerra, Tot recte
Where is…?	¿Dónde está…?	On és…?
…the bus station	…la estación de autobuses	…l'estació de autobuses
…the train station	…la estación de ferrocarril	…l'estació
…the nearest bank	…el banco más cercano	…el banc més a prop
…the post office	…el correos/la oficina de correos	…l'oficina de correus
…the toilet	…el baño/aseo/servicio	…la toaleta
It's not very far	No es muy lejos	No és gaire lluny
Where does the bus to …leave from?	¿De dónde sale el autobús para…?	De on surt l'autobús a…?
Is this the train for Barcelona?	¿Es este el tren para Barcelona?	Aquest tren va a Barcelona?
I'd like a (return) ticket to…	Quisiera un billete (de ida y vuelta) para…	Voldria un bitlet (d'anar i tornar) a…
What time does it leave (arrive in)?	¿A qué hora sale (llega a)?	A quina hora surt (arriba a)?

Numbers

one	un/uno/una	un(a)
two	dos	dos (dues)
three	tres	tres
four	cuatro	quatre
five	cinco	cinc
six	seis	sis
seven	siete	set
eight	ocho	vuit
nine	nueve	nou
ten	diez	deu
eleven	once	onze

twelve	doce	*dotze*
thirteen	trece	*tretze*
fourteen	catorce	*catorze*
fifteen	quince	*quinze*
sixteen	dieciseis	*setze*
seventeen	diecisiete	*disset*
eighteen	dieciocho	*divuit*
nineteen	diecinueve	*dinou*
twenty	veinte	*vint*
twenty-one	veintiuno	*vint-i-un*
thirty	treinta	*trenta*
forty	cuarenta	*quaranta*
fifty	cincuenta	*cinquanta*
sixty	sesenta	*seixanta*
seventy	setenta	*setanta*
eighty	ochenta	*vuitanta*
ninety	noventa	*novanta*
one hundred	cien(to)	*cent*
one hundred and one	ciento uno	*cent un*
one hundred and two	ciento dos	*cent dos (dues)*
two hundred	doscientos	*dos-cents (dues-centes)*
five hundred	quinientos	*cinc-cents*
one thousand	mil	*mil*
two thousand	dos mil	*dos mil*

Days and months

Monday	lunes	*dilluns*
Tuesday	martes	*dimarts*
Wednesday	miércoles	*dimecres*
Thursday	jueves	*dijous*
Friday	viernes	*divendres*
Saturday	sábado	*dissabte*
Sunday	domingo	*diumenge*
January	enero	*gener*
February	febrero	*febrer*
March	marzo	*març*
April	abril	*abril*
May	mayo	*maig*
June	junio	*juny*
July	julio	*juliol*
August	agosto	*agost*
September	septiembre	*setembre*
October	octubre	*octobre*
November	noviembre	*novembre*
December	diciembre	*desembre*

Food and drink

Words and phrases below are given in the following order: **English** – Spanish – *Catalan*.

Some basic words

English	Spanish	Catalan
To have breakfast	Desayunar	*Esmorzar*
To have lunch	Comer	*Dinar*
To have dinner	Cenar	*Sopar*
Knife	Cuchillo	*Ganivet*
Fork	Tenedor	*Forquilla*
Spoon	Cuchara	*Cullera*
Table	Mesa	*Taula*
Bottle	Botella	*Ampolla*
Glass	Vaso	*Got*
Menu	Carta	*Carta*
Soup	Sopa	*Sopa*
Salad	Ensalada	*Amanida*
Hors d'oeuvres	Entremeses	*Entremesos*
Omelette	Tortilla	*Truita*
Sandwich	Bocadillo	*Entrepà*
Toast	Tostadas	*Torrades*
Tapas	Tapes	*Tapes*
Butter	Mantequilla	*Mantega*
Eggs	Huevos	*Ous*
Bread	Pan	*Pa*
Olives	Aceitunas	*Olives*
Oil	Aceite	*Oli*
Vinegar	Vinagre	*Vinagre*
Salt	Sal	*Sal*
Pepper	Pimienta	*Pebre*
Sugar	Azucar	*Sucre*
The bill	La cuenta	*El compte*
I'm a vegetarian	Soy vegetariano/a	*Sóc vegetarià/vegetariana*

Cooking terms

English	Spanish	Catalan
Assorted	surtido/variado	*assortit*
Baked	al horno	*al forn*
Char-grilled	a la brasa	*a la brasa*
Fresh	fresco	*fresc*
Fried	frito	*fregit*
Fried in batter	a la romana	*a la romana*
Garlic mayonnaise	alioli	*all i oli*
Grilled	a la plancha	*a la plantxa*
Pickled	en escabeche	*en escabetx*
Roast	asado	*rostit*

Sauce	salsa	*salsa*
Sautéed	salteado	*saltat*
Scrambled	revuelto	*remenat*
Seasonal	del tiempo	*del temps*
Smoked	ahumado	*fumat*
Spit-roasted	al ast	*a l'ast*
Stewed	guisado	*guisat*
Steamed	al vapor	*al vapor*
Stuffed	relleno	*farcit*

Fish and seafood/Pescado y mariscos/peix i marisc

Anchovies	Anchoas/Boquerones	*Anxoves/Seitons*
Baby squid	Chipirones	*Calamarsets*
Bream	Dorada	*Orada*
Clams	Almejas	*Cloïses*
Crab	Cangrejo	*Cranc*
Cuttlefish	Sepia	*Sipia*
Eels	Anguilas	*Anguiles*
Hake	Merluza	*Lluç*
Langoustines	Langostinos	*Llagostins*
Lobster	Langosta	*Llagosta*
Monkfish	Rape	*Rap*
Mussels	Mejillones	*Musclos*
Octopus	Pulpo	*Pop*
Oysters	Ostras	*Ostres*
Perch	Mero	*Mero*
Prawns	Gambas	*Gambes*
Razor clams	Navajas	*Navalles*
Red mullet	Salmonete	*Moll*
Salmon	Salmón	*Salmó*
Salt cod	Bacalao	*Bacallà*
Sardines	Sardinas	*Sardines*
Scallops	Vieiras	*Vieires*
Sea bass	Lubina	*LLobarro*
Sole	Lenguado	*Llenguado*
Squid	Calamares	*Calamars*
Swordfish	Pez espada	*Peix espasa*
Trout	Trucha	*Truita (de riu)*
Tuna	Atún	*Tonyina*
Whitebait	Chanquete	*Xanguet*

Meat and poultry/Carne y aves/Carn i aviram

Beef	Buey	*Bou*
Boar	Jabalí	*Senglar*
Charcuterie	Embutidos	*Embotits*

Chicken	Pollo	*Pollastre*
Chorizo sausage	Chorizo	*Xoriço*
Cured ham	Jamón serrano	*Pernil serrà*
Cured pork sausage	Longaniza	*Llonganissa*
Cutlets/Chops	Chuletas	*Costelles*
Duck	Pato	*Ànec*
Ham	Jamón York	*Pernil dolç*
Hare	Liebre	*Llebre*
Kid/goat	Cabrito	*Cabrit*
Kidneys	Riñones	*Ronyons*
Lamb	Cordero	*Xai/Be*
Liver	Hígado	*Fetge*
Loin of pork	Lomo	*Llom*
Meatballs	Albóndigas	*Mandonguilles*
Partridge	Perdiz	*Perdiu*
Pigs' trotters	Pies de cerdo	*Peus de porc*
Pork	Cerdo	*Porc*
Rabbit	Conejo	*Conill*
Sausages	Salchichas	*Salsitxes*
Snails	Caracoles	*Cargols*
Steak	Bistec	*Bistec*
Tongue	Lengua	*Llengua*
Veal	Ternera	*Vedella*

Vegetables/Verduras y legumbres/Verdures i llegums

Artichokes	Alcachofas	*Carxofes*
Asparagus	Esparragos	*Esparrecs*
Aubergine/eggplant	Berenjena	*Albergínia*
Avocado	Aguacate	*Alvocat*
Broad/lima beans	Habes	*Faves*
Cabbage	Col	*Col*
Carrots	Zanahorias	*Pastanagues*
Cauliflower	Coliflor	*Col-i-flor*
Chickpeas	Garbanzos	*Cigrons*
Courgette/zucchini	Calabacín	*Carbassó*
Cucumber	Pepino	*Concombre*
Garlic	Ajo	*All*
Haricot beans	Judías blancas	*Mongetes*
Herbs	Hierbas	*Herbes*
Lentils	Lentejas	*Llenties*
Leeks	Puerros	*Porros*
Mushrooms	Champiñones	*Xampinyons*
Onion	Cebolla	*Ceba*
Peas	Guisantes	*Pèsols*
Peppers/capsicums	Pimientos	*Pebrots*

Potatoes	Patatas	*Patates*
Spinach	Espinacas	*Espinacs*
Tomatoes	Tomates	*Tomàquets*
Turnips	Nabos	*Naps*
Wild mushrooms	Setas	*Bolets*

Fruit/Fruta/Fruita

Apple	Manzana	*Poma*
Apricot	Albaricoque	*Albercoc*
Banana	Plátano	*Plàtan*
Cherries	Cerezas	*Cireres*
Figs	Higos	*Figues*
Grapes	Uvas	*Raïm*
Melon	Melón	*Meló*
Orange	Naranja	*Taronja*
Peach	Melocotón	*Pressec*
Pear	Pera	*Pera*
Pineapple	Piña	*Pinya*
Strawberries	Fresas	*Maduixes*

Desserts/Postres/Postres

Cake	Pastel	*Pastís*
Cheese	Queso	*Formatge*
Fruit salad	Macedonia	*Macedonia*
Crème caramel	Flan	*Flam*
Ice cream	Helado	*Gelat*
Rice pudding	Arroz con leche	*Arròs amb llet*
Tart	Tarta	*Tarta*
Yoghurt	Yogur	*Yogur*

Catalan specialities

Amanida Catalana Salad served with sliced meats (sometimes cheese)

Ànec amb peres Duck with pears

Arròs a banda Rice with seafood, the rice served separately

Arròs a la Cubana Rice with fried egg and home-made tomato sauce

Arròs a la marinera Paella: rice with seafood and saffron

Arròs negre "Black rice", cooked in squid ink

Bacallà a la llauna Salt cod baked with garlic, tomato and paprika

Bacallà amb mongetes Salt cod with stewed haricot beans

Botifarra (amb mongetes) Grilled Catalan pork sausage (with stewed haricot beans)

Bunyols Fritters, which can be sweet (like little doughnuts, with sugar) or savoury (salt-cod or wild mushroom)

Calçots Large char-grilled spring onions, eaten with *romesco* sauce (see below), available February/March

Canelons Cannelloni, baked pasta with ground meat and bechemal sauce

Conill all i oli Rabbit with garlic mayonnaise

Conill amb cargols Rabbit with snails

Crema Catalana Creme caramel, with caramelized sugar topping

Entremesos Hors d'oeuvres of mixed meat and cheese

Escalivada Grilled aubergine/eggplant, pepper/capsicum and onion

Escudella i carn d'olla A winter dish of stewed mixed meat and vegetables, served broth first, meat and veg second

Espinacs a la Catalana Spinach cooked with raisins and pine nuts

Esqueixada Salad of salt cod with peppers/capsicums, tomatoes, onions and olives, a summer dish

Estofat de vedella Veal stew

Faves a la Catalana Stewed broad beans, with bacon and botifarra, a regional classic

Fideuà Short, thin noodles (the width of vermicelli) served with seafood, accompanied by all i olli

Fideus a la cassola Short, thin noodles baked with meat

Fricandó (amb bolets) Braised veal (with wild mushrooms)

Fuet Catalan salami

Llagosta amb pollastre Lobster with chicken in a rich sauce

Llenties guisades Stewed lentils

Mel i mató Curd cheese and honey, a typical dessert

Oca amb naps Goose with turnips

Pa amb tomàquet Bread (often grilled), rubbed with tomato, garlic and olive oil

Panellets Marzipan cakes, served for All Saints' Day

Perdiu a la vinagreta Partridge in vinegar gravy

Perdiu amb col Partridge with cabbage dumplings

Pollastre al cava Chicken with cava (champagne) sauce

Pollastre amb gambes Chicken with prawns

Postres de músic Cake of dried fruit and nuts

Rap amb all cremat Monkfish with creamed garlic sauce

Salsa Romesco Spicy sauce (with chillis, nuts, tomato and wine), often served with grilled fish

Samfaina Ratatouille-like stew (onions, peppers/capsicum, aubergine/eggplant, tomato), served with salt cod or chicken

Sarsuela Fish and shellfish stew

Sípia amb mandonguilles Cuttlefish with meatballs

Sopa d'all Garlic soup, often with egg and bread

Suquet de peix Fish and potato casserole

Xató Mixed salad of olives, salt cod, preserved tuna, anchovies and onions

Drinks

Beer	Cerveza	*Cervesa*
Wine	Vino	*Vi*
Champagne	Champan	*Xampan/Cava*
Sherry	Jerez	*Xerès*
Coffee	Café	*Cafè*
Espresso	Café solo	*Cafè sol*
Large black coffee	Café Americano	*Cafè Americà*
Large white coffee	Café con leche	*Cafè amb llet*
Small white coffee	Café cortado	*Cafè tallat*
Decaff	Descafeinado	*Descafeinat*
Tea	Té	*Te*
Drinking chocolate	Chocolate	*Xocolata*
Juice	Zumo	*Suc*
Crushed ice drink	Granizado	*Granissat*
Milk	Leche	*Llet*
Tiger nut drink	Horchata	*Orxata*
Water	Agua	*Aigua*
Mineral water	Agua mineral	*Aigua mineral*
…(sparkling)	…(con gas)	*…(amb gas)*
…(still)	…(sin gas)	*…(sense gas)*

A glossary of Catalan

Ajuntament Town hall
Avinguda Avenue
Barri Suburb or quarter
Bodega Cellar, wine bar or warehouse
Call Jewish quarter
Camí Path
Carrer Street
Casa House
Castell Castle
Comarca County
Correus Post office
Església Church
Estació Station
Estany Lake
Festa Festival
Font Waterfall
Forn Bakery
Generalitat Catalan government
Gòtic Gothic (eg Barri Gòtic, Gothic quarter)

Granja Milk bar/café
Llotja Stock exchange building
Mercat Market
Monestir Monastery or convent
Museu Museum
Palau Aristocratic mansion
Passeig Promenade/boulevard; also the evening stroll thereon
Pati Inner courtyard
Patisseria Cake/pastry shop
Plaça Square
Platja Beach
Pont Bridge
Porta Gateway
Rambla Boulevard
Ríu River
Sant/a Saint
Sardana Catalunya's national folk dance
Serra Mountain range
Seu Cathedral

Rough
Guides
advertiser

ROUGH GUIDES ADVERTISER

ROUGH GUIDES ADVERTISER

293

295

Index

and small print

A Rough Guide to Rough Guides

In the summer of 1981, Mark Ellingham, a recent graduate from Bristol University, was travelling round Greece and couldn't find a guidebook that really met his needs. On the one hand there were the student guides, insistent on saving every last cent, and on the other the heavyweight cultural tomes whose authors seemed to have spent more time in a research library than lounging away the afternoon at a taverna or on the beach.

In a bid to avoid getting a job, Mark and a small group of writers set about creating their own guidebook. It was a guide to Greece that aimed to combine a journalistic approach to description with a thoroughly practical approach to travellers' needs – a guide that would incorporate culture, history and contemporary insights with a critical edge, together with up-to-date, value-for-money listings. Back in London, Mark and the team finished their Rough Guide, as they called it, and talked Routledge into publishing the book.

That first *Rough Guide to Greece*, published in 1982, was a student scheme that became a publishing phenomenon. The immediate success of the book – with numerous reprints and a Thomas Cook prize shortlisting – spawned a series that rapidly covered dozens of destinations. Rough Guides had a ready market among low-budget backpackers, but soon also acquired a much broader and older readership that relished Rough Guides' wit and inquisitiveness as much as their enthusiastic, critical approach. Everyone wants value for money, but not at any price.

Rough Guides soon began supplementing the "rougher" information about hostels and low-budget listings with the kind of detail on restaurants and quality hotels that independent-minded visitors on any budget might expect, whether on business in New York or trekking in Thailand.

These days the guides – distributed worldwide by the Penguin group – offer recommendations from shoestring to luxury and cover more than 200 destinations around the globe, including almost every country in the Americas and Europe, more than half of Africa and most of Asia and Australasia. Our ever-growing team of authors and photographers is spread all over the world, particularly in Europe, the USA and Australia.

In 1994, we published the *Rough Guide to World Music* and *Rough Guide to Classical Music*; and a year later the *Rough Guide to the Internet*. All three books have become benchmark titles in their fields – which encouraged us to expand into other areas of publishing, mainly around popular culture. Rough Guides now publish:

- Travel guides to more than 200 worldwide destinations
- Dictionary phrasebooks to 22 major languages
- History guides ranging from Ireland to Islam
- Maps printed on rip-proof and waterproof Polyart™ paper
- Music guides running the gamut from Opera to Elvis
- Restaurant guides to London, New York and San Francisco
- Reference books on topics as diverse as the Weather and Shakespeare
- Sports guides from Formula 1 to Man Utd
- Pop culture books from *Lord of the Rings* to Cult TV
- World Music CDs in association with World Music Network

Visit **www.roughguides.com** to see our latest publications.

Rough Guide Credits

Text editor: Olivia Swift
Layout: Link Hall
Cartography: Katie Lloyd-Jones, Stratigraphics
Picture research: Mark Thomas
Proofreader: Niki Twyman
....

Editorial: London Martin Dunford, Kate Berens, Helena Smith, Claire Saunders, Geoff Howard, Ruth Blackmore, Gavin Thomas, Polly Thomas, Richard Lim, Lucy Ratcliffe, Clifton Wilkinson, Alison Murchie, Fran Sandham, Sally Schafer, Alexander Mark Rogers, Karoline Densley, Andy Turner, Ella O'Donnell, Keith Drew, Andrew Lockett, Joe Staines, Duncan Clark, Peter Buckley, Matthew Milton; **New York** Andrew Rosenberg, Richard Koss, Yuki Takagaki, Hunter Slaton, Chris Barsanti, Thomas Kohnstamm, Steven Horak
Design & Layout: London Dan May, Diana Jarvis; **Delhi** Madhulita Mohapatra, Umesh Aggarwal, Ajay Verma

Production: Julia Bovis, John McKay, Sophie Hewat
Cartography: London Maxine Repath, Ed Wright, Katie Lloyd-Jones, Miles Irving; **Delhi** Manish Chandra, Rajesh Chhibber, Jai Prakesh Mishra, Ashutosh Bharti, Rajesh Mishra, Animesh Pathak
Cover art direction: Louise Boulton
Picture research: Mark Thomas, Jj Luck
Online: New York Jennifer Gold, Cree Lawson, Suzanne Welles, Benjamin Ross; **Delhi** Manik Chauhan, Amarjyoti Dutta, Narender Kumar
Marketing & Publicity: London Richard Trillo, Niki Smith, David Wearn, Chloë Roberts, Demelza Dallow, Kristina Pentland; **New York** Geoff Colquitt, David Wechsler, Megan Kennedy
Finance: Gary Singh
Manager India: Punita Singh
Series editor: Mark Ellingham
PA to Managing Director: Julie Sanderson
Managing Director: Kevin Fitzgerald

Publishing Information

This 6th edition published June 2004 by **Rough Guides Ltd,**
80 Strand, London WC2R 0RL.
345 Hudson St, 4th Floor,
New York, NY 10014, USA.
Distributed by the Penguin Group
Penguin Books Ltd,
80 Strand, London WC2R 0RL
Penguin Putnam, Inc.
375 Hudson Street, NY 10014, USA
Penguin Books Australia Ltd,
487 Maroondah Highway, PO Box 257,
Ringwood, Victoria 3134, Australia
Penguin Books Canada Ltd,
10 Alcorn Avenue, Toronto, Ontario,
Canada M4V 1E4
Penguin Books (NZ) Ltd,
182–190 Wairau Road, Auckland 10,
New Zealand
Typeset in Bembo and Helvetica to an original design by Henry Iles.

Printed in Italy by LegoPrint S.p.A

© Jules Brown

320pp includes index
A catalogue record for this book is available from the British Library

ISBN 1-8435-321-2

1   3   5   7   9   8   6   4   2

SMALL PRINT

Help us update

We've gone to a lot of effort to ensure that the 6th edition of **The Rough Guide to Barcelona** is accurate and up-to-date. However, things change – places get "discovered", opening hours are notoriously fickle, restaurants and rooms raise prices or lower standards. If you feel we've got it wrong or left something out, we'd like to know, and if you can remember the address, the price, the time, the phone number, so much the better.

We'll credit all contributions, and send a copy of the next edition (or any other Rough Guide if you prefer) for the best letters. Everyone who writes to us and isn't already a subscriber will receive a copy of our full-colour thrice-yearly newsletter. Please mark letters: **"Rough Guide Barcelona Update"** and send to: Rough Guides, 80 Strand, London WC2R 0RL, or Rough Guides, 4th Floor, 345 Hudson St, New York NY 10014. Or send an email to **mail@roughguides.com**

Have your questions answered and tell others about your trip at **www.roughguides.atinfopop.com**

Acknowledgements

Jules would like to thank Katrien and Caroline, who kindly shared their favourite things in the city and contributed greatly to the shopping and nightlife sections of the guide; Monica Worsley, Maria Fernanda Nevado and Rosa Bertran for their warm welcome and useful advice; Andy Mitten and Mark Ellingham, who cast an expert eye; and Olivia for her careful, insightful and patient editing. In Barcelona, Katie, Fox and Jules had a great time when people came to stay – so thanks to Granny, to Jayne and Mike, and to Ian, Linda and Fidel. And finally a big hola! to little Ripley Orwell.

The editor joins the author in thanking Link Hall for skilled setting, Nikki Twyman for careful proofreading, Katie Lloyd-Jones and Stratigraphics for expert maps, Mark Thomas for creative picture research, and the number of other people at Rough Guides who helped to get the book together, among them Daniel May, Diana Jarvis and Karoline Densley.

Readers' letters

Thanks to all the readers who have taken the time and trouble to write in with comments and suggestions. Listed below are those who were especially helpful: apologies for any errors, ommissions or misspellings.

Richard and Anne Baldwin, Janet A. Borch, Ian Bouncer, John Bowen, Andrew Brown, Maggie Chetty, Jill Clark, Sue Courchée, Nik Devlin, Kate Driver, Roger Hunter, Aysha Itani, Roger Kennington, Peter Marshall, Richard Oswald, Gerard Platt, Mary-Elizabeth Raw, Mark Schlemmer, Molly Sendall, Ursula Sharma, Geoff and Tracy Walker, and M. Welch.

Photo Credits

SMALL PRINT

Index

Where there's a map of a place listed, this is indicated by the name appearing in colour

A

B

C

O
INDEX

314

Map symbols

maps are listed in the full index using coloured text

- - - - -	International boundary	⛪	Monastery
- - -	Chapter boundary	⚲	Church (regional)
	Motorway	⊜	RENFE
═══	Major road	◆	Metro station
═══	Minor road	⑤	FF.CC. station
	Pedestrianised road	ⓘ	Tourist office
▭▭▭	Steps	⊠	Post office
━━━	Railway	⊞	Hospital
▪▪▪▪▪	Funicular railway		Building
•---•	Cable car	⊡	Church
───	Wall		Park
───	Waterway		Forest
✈	Airport		Beach
🏛	Abbey		Cemetery

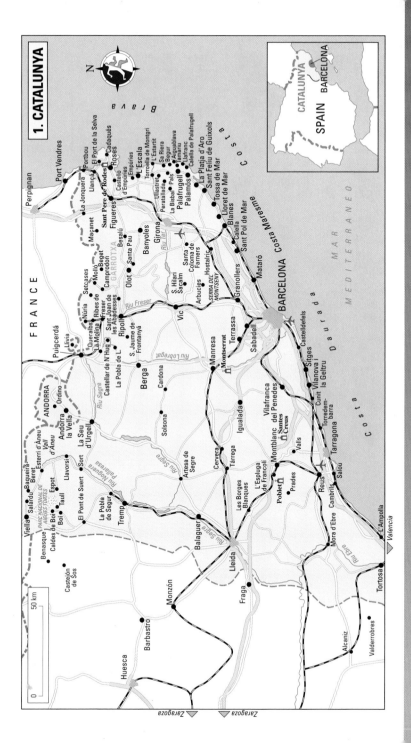

1. CATALUNYA

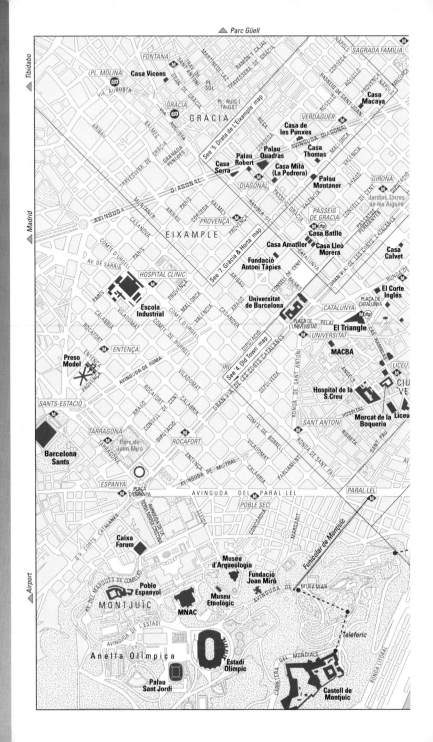

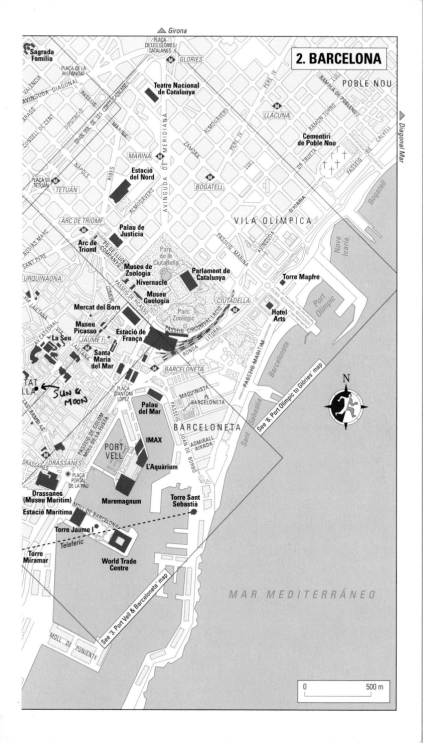

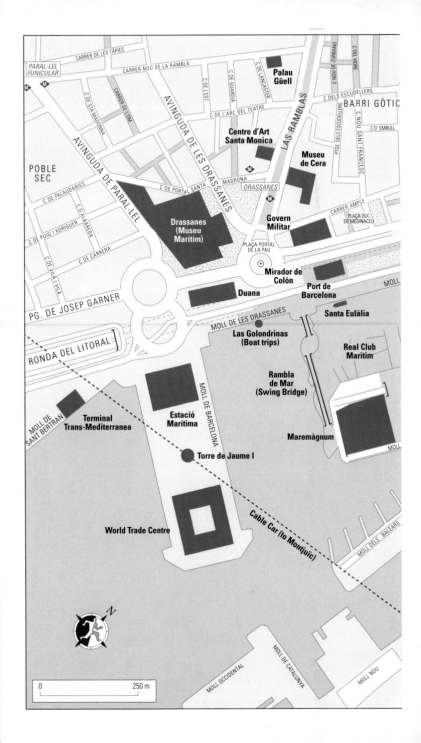

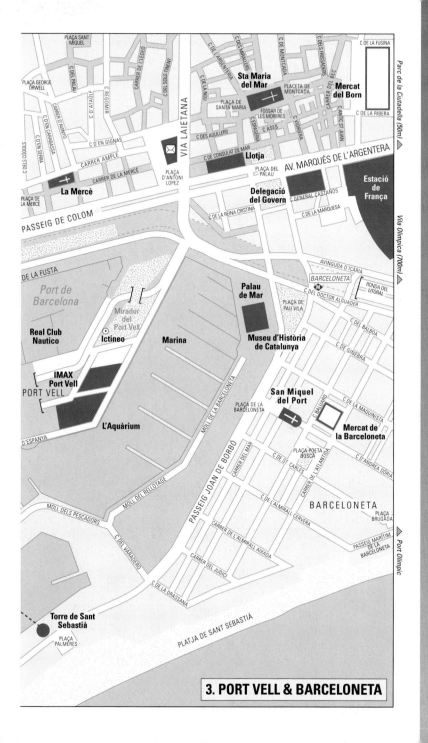

3. PORT VELL & BARCELONETA

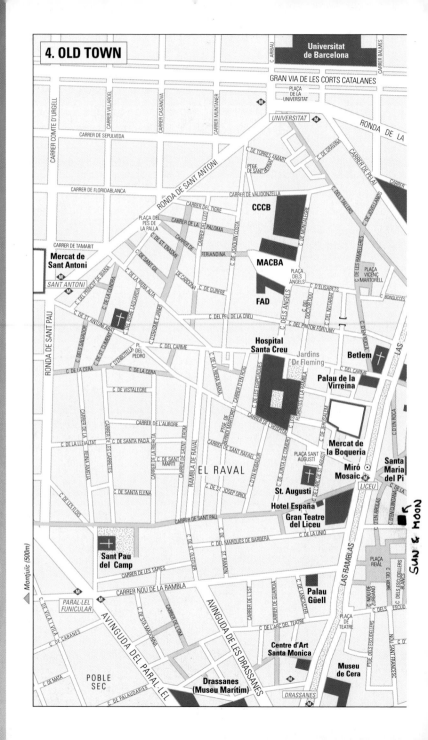

4. OLD TOWN

Universitat de Barcelona

GRAN VIA DE LES CORTS CATALANES

PLAÇA DE LA UNIVERSITAT

UNIVERSITAT

RONDA DE LA

CARRER COMTE D'URGELL
CARRER VILLAROEL
CARRER CASANOVA
CARRER MUNTANER
CARRER BALMES

CARRER DE SEPULVEDA

C. DE TORRES AMART
PTGE DE SANT BERN
C. DE GRAVINA
CARRER DE PELAI
CARRER

CARRER DE FLORIDABLANCA

RONDA DE SANT ANTONI

CARRER DE VALLDONZELLA

C. DES TALLERS
C. DE JOVELLANOS

CARRER DEL TIGRE
CARRER DE LA PALOMA
CCCB

PLAÇA DEL PES DE LA PALLA
CARRER DE LLEO
C. DE ST ERASME
C. DE

C. DE QUAQUIN COSTA
C. DE MONTALEGRE

CARRER DE TAMARIT

Mercat de Sant Antoni

SANT ANTONI

C. DEL PRINCEP DE BLANE
C. DE LA REINA AMALIA
C. DE SANT GIL
C. DE CARDONA
FERLANDINA
MACBA

PLAÇA DELS ANGELS
PLAÇA VICENÇ MARTORELL

C. DE GUIFRE
FAD
C. DES ANGELS
C. D'ELISABETS
C. DE NOTARIAT
BONSUCCES

RONDA DE SANT PAU

C. DE ST ANTONI ABAT
C. DE L'ISBEL LAGUARDIA
C. DE L'ERASSE I JANET
C. DE GÜIFRE
C. DEL PEU DE LA CREU
C. DE DOCTOR DOU
C. DEL PINTOR FORTUNY
C. D'EN XUCLA

C. DELS SALVADOR
C. DE ST CLIMBAU
C. D'ENSOTELLA
PL. DEL PEDRO
C. DEL CARME
Hospital Santa Creu
Jardins Dr Fleming
Betlem
C. DEL CARME

CARRER DE LA CERA
C. DE LA CERA
C. DE LA NEU REDO
Palau de la Virreina

C. DE VISTALEGRE
C. DE LES EGIPCIAQUES
C. D'EN ROIG
LAS

CARRER DE L'AURORE
PTGE DE BENEDI MARTORELL
CARRER DE L'HOSPITAL
FLORISTES DE LA RAMBLA
C. D'EN ROCA

CARRER DE LA
C. DE LA LLEIALTAT
C. DE SANTA PACIA
CARRER DE SANT JEROM
CARRER DE SANT RAFAEL
PLAÇA SANT AGUSTI
Mercat de la Boqueria

REINA AMELIA
C. DE SANT MARTI
RAMBLA DE RAVAL
EL RAVAL
C. DE JUNTA DE COMERÇ
Miró Mosaic
Santa Maria del Pi

C. DELS CARRETES
C. DE LES FLORS
C. DE SANTA ELENA
C. DE ST. JOSEP ORIOL
St. Augusti
LICEU
C. DE LA

Hotel España
Gran Teatre del Liceu
C. DE LA UNIÓ
C. D'EN AROLAS
C. D'EN QUINTANA

Montjuïc (500m)

Sant Pau del Camp

CARRER DE SANT PAU

C. DEL MARQUES DE BARBERA

CARRER DE LES TÀPIES

ST RAMON
PLAÇA REIAL
C. DELS ESCUDELLERS BLANCS

POBLE SEC

CARRER NOU DE LA RAMBLA
AVINGUDA DEL PARAL·LEL
C. DEL EST
CARRER DE GUARDIA
Palau Güell
C. NOU DE ZURBANO
C. DELS ESCUDELLERS

PARAL·LEL FUNICULAR
C. DE STA MADRONA
C. DE LOM
C. DE L'ARC DEL TEATRE
PLAÇA DE TEATRE

C. DE CABANES
AVINGUDA DE LES DRASSANES
Centre d'Art Santa Monica
NOU SANT FRANCESC

C. DE MATA
C. DE PALAUDÀRIES
Drassanes (Museu Marítim)
Museu de Cera

DRASSANES

SUN & MOON

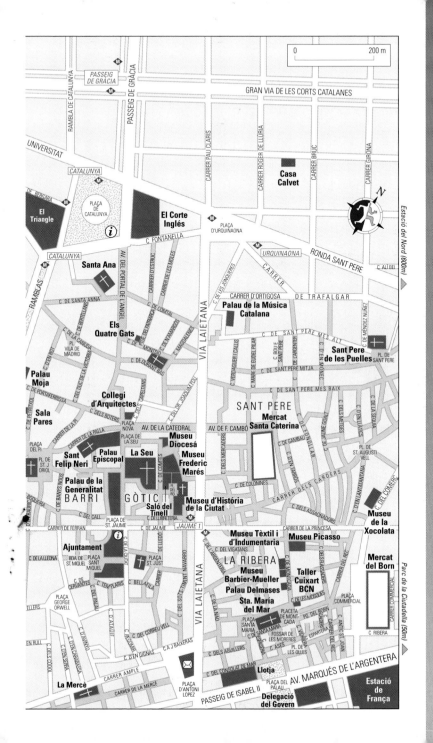

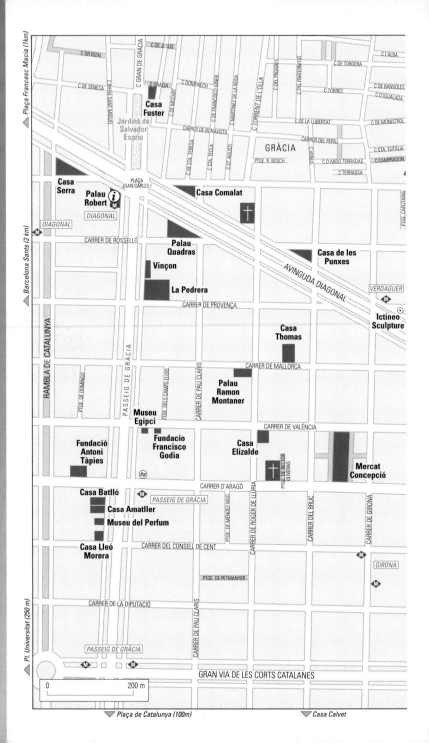

5. DRETA DE L'EIXAMPLE

N

CARRER DE SANT ANTONI MARIA CLARET

PTGE. LLAVALLOL

CARRER DE LA INDUSTRIA

PTGE. D'ALIÓ

CARRER DE LA BRASIL

C/SOLE SOLER

PTGE. DE LES TORRES

PASSEIG DE SANT JOAN

CARRER DE CÓRSEGA

PTGE. MARINER

CARRER DE SARDENYA

PTGE. CONRADI

CARRER DE ROSSELLÓ

CARRER DE NÁPOLS

CARRER DE SICÍLIA

PTGE. DE SIMÓ

SAGRADA FAMÍLIA Ⓜ

CARRER DE ROGER DE FLOR

CARRER DE PROVENÇA

Ⓜ VERDAGUER

PLAÇA DE LA SAGRADA FAMÍLIA

Casa Macaya

Sagrada Família

PLAÇA MOSSÈN JACINT VERDAGUER

CARRER DE MALLORCA

PTGE. GAIOLÀ

PTGE. MAIOL

PTGE. FONT

CARRER DE VALÉNCIA

AVINGUDA DIAGONAL

Casa Planells

PASSEIG DE SANT JOAN

CARRER D'ARAGÓ

CARRER DE NÁPOLS

CARRER DE BAILEN

CARRER DE ROGER DE FLOR

CARRER DEL CONSELL DE CENT

CARRER DE SICÍLIA

CARRER DE SARDENYA

PTGE. DE TASSO

CARRER DE LA DIPUTACIÓ

CARRER MARINA

Ⓜ TETUAN

PTGE. DE BOCABELLA

PTGE. DE PAGÈS

Ⓜ MONUMENTAL

PLAÇA DE TETUAN

GRAN VIA DE LES CORTS CATALANES

▽ Parc de la Ciutadella (900m)   ▽ Estació del Nord (500m)

▷ Hospital Santa Creu i Sant Pau

Teatre Nacional de Catalunya ▷

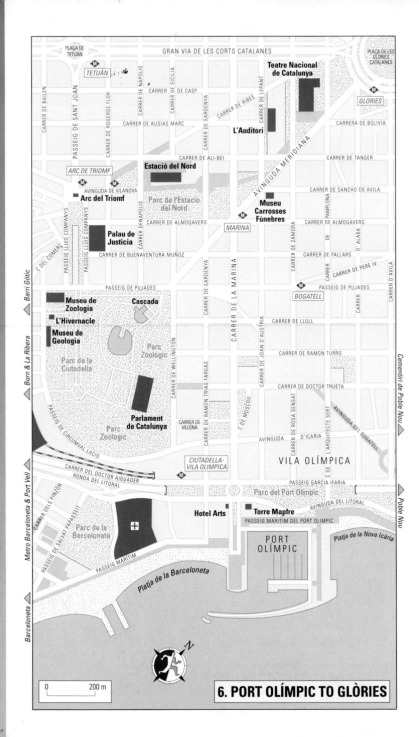

6. PORT OLÍMPIC TO GLÒRIES

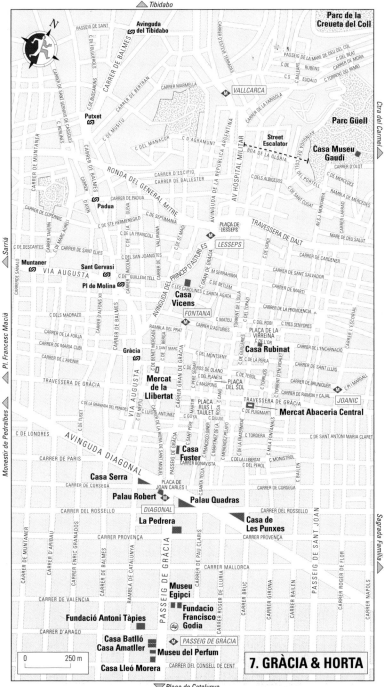

Tibidabo

Parc de la Creueta del Coll

PASSEIG DE SANT

Avinguda del Tibidabo

CARRER DE BALMES

PASSEIG DE LA MARE DE DEU DEL COL

C DEL BEAT

C DE BISCARROSSA

CARRER DE BERTRAN

CARRER MARMELLA

C DE BALLARS

RUBENS

CARRER DE MORA

C S EUDALD

C TORRENT DEL REMEI

C DE MISTRAL

Ⓜ VALLCARCA

Putxet

CARRER D'ORIENT SUSI

C DE BIOSCARRAS

Parc Güell

CARRER DE MUNTANER

C DE MUSTIU

C DEL MANACOR

C D'AGRAMUNT

CARRER DE LA FARIGOLA

AVINGUDA DE LA REPÚBLICA ARGENTINA

Street Escalator

BDA DE LA GLÒRIA

BDA DEL PORTELL

Casa Museu Gaudí

CARRER DE SANT GERVASI DE CASSOLES

C DE BERLINS

CARRER D'ESCIPIO

CARRER DE BALLESTER

AV HOSPITAL MILITAR

C DELS ALBIGESOS

C DE SANT CUGAT

CARRER D'OLOT

C DE MERCEDES

CARRER DE COPÈRNIC

CARRER DE PADUA

Padua

RONDA DEL GENERAL MITRE

C DE STE HERMENEGILD

C DE SEPTIMANIA

RAMBLA DE MERCEDES

MARE DE DEU SALUT

C DE DESCARTES

CARRER TAVERN

C DE MARC AURELI

C DE LA FRANCOLI

CARRER DE SANT ELIES

C DE LA FRANCOLI

PLAÇA DE LESSEPS

TRAVESSERA DE DALT

CARRER DE CARDENER

Muntaner Ⓜ

Sant Gervasi Ⓜ

VIA AUGUSTA

C DEL SAN JOANISTES

Ⓜ LESSEPS

CARRER DE SANT SALVADOR

Pl de Molina Ⓜ

AVINGUDA DEL PRINCEP D'ASTURIES

CARRER DEL PROGRES

C DE M SERRAHIMA

C DE GRAN DE GRACIA

CARRER DE SANT SALVADOR

CARRER DE MARTI

C DELS MADRAZO

C DE LES CAROLINES

C SANTA AGATA

Casa Vicens

CARRER DE LA PROVIDENCIA

C DE BALMES

Ⓜ FONTANA

C MATEU

C DEL ROBI

C TRES SENYORES

CARRER DE LA FORJA

CARRER DE MARIA CUBI

RAMBLA DEL PRAT

CARRER D'ASTURIES

TORRENT DE L'OLLA

C DEL TOPAZI

CARRER DE L'ENCARNACIÓ

CARRER DE L'AVENIR

Gràcia Ⓜ

RAMBLA DEL PRAT

C SANT MARC

C DEL MONTSENY

C DE LA PERLA

PLAÇA DE LA VIRREINA

C DE L'OR

Casa Rubinat

CARRER DE SANT LLUIS

C.P.I MARGALL

TRAVESSERA DE GRÀCIA

VIA AUGUSTA

C DE BENET MERCADE

C DE PERES DE OLANO

C DE LA PERLA

CARRER DE BRUNIQUER

Mercat de la Llibertat

CARRER GRAN DE GRÀCIA

C DE PLANETA

C DE TEROL

TORRENT D'EN VIDALET

PLAÇA DEL SOL

C DE MASPONS

PLAÇA DEL SOL

C DE TORRIJOS

CARRER DE RAMON Y CAJAL

Ⓜ JOANIC

C DE LA GRANADA DEL PENEDES

PLAÇA RUIS I TAULET

C MARTIR

C GOYA

C DE RODA

C CANO

C DE PUIGMARTI

TRAVESSERA DE GRÀCIA

Mercat Abaceria Central

C DE TUSET

C DE LUIS

ANTUNEZ

C SANT PERE

C DILUVI

C FRANCISCO GINER

CARRER DE SANT ANTONI MARIA CLARET

AVINGUDA DIAGONAL

C MARTINEZ DE LA ROSA

C TORDERA

C MIA FONTANALS

C DE LONDRES

CARRER DE PARIS

PASSEIG DE SANT JOAN DE MALTA

C DE LA FRATERNITAT

C DE LA LLIBERTAT

C MONISTROL

C BAILEN

Casa Serra

CARRER DE CORSEGA

PLAÇA DE JOAN CARLES I

Casa Fuster

CARRER BONAVISTA

C DEL PEROL

CARRER DE CORSEGA

Palau Robert Ⓜ

Palau Quadras

Ⓜ DIAGONAL

CARRER DEL ROSSELLO

CARRER DEL ROSSELLO

La Pedrera

Casa de Les Punxes

CARRER DE MUNTANER

CARRER D'ARIBAU

CARRER ENRIC GRANADOS

CARRER DE BALMES

CARRER PROVENÇA

RAMBLA DE CATALUNYA

PASSEIG DE GRÀCIA

CARRER DE PAU CLARIS

CARRER DE LLURIA

CARRER PROVENÇA

CARRER BRUC

CARRER GIRONA

CARRER BAILEN

PASSEIG DE SANT JOAN

CARRER ROGER DE FLOR

CARRER ROGER DE LLURIA

CARRER MALLORCA

CARRER ROGER DE FLOR

CARRER NAPOLS

CARRER DE VALENCIA

Museu Egipci

Fundació Antoni Tàpies

Fundacio Francisco Godia

CARRER D'ARAGO

Casa Batlló
Casa Amatller

Ⓜ PASSEIG DE GRÀCIA

Museu del Perfum

Casa Lleó Morera

CARRER DEL CONSELL DE CENT

| 0 | 250 m |

7. GRÀCIA & HORTA

Plaça de Catalunya

Cra del Carmel

Sarrià

Pl. Francesc Macià

Monestir de Pedralbes

Sagrada Família

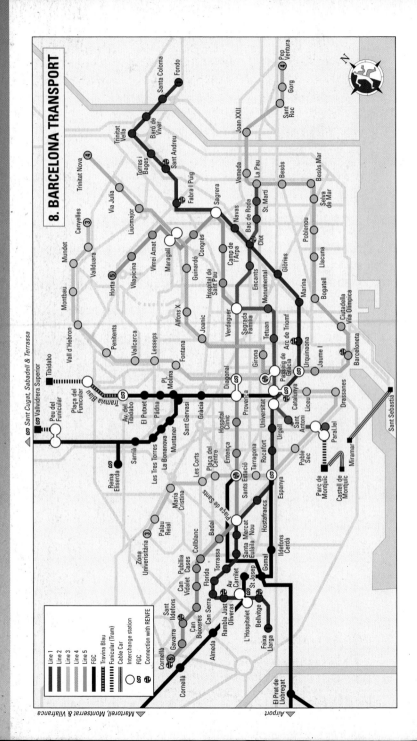

8. BARCELONA TRANSPORT